Swindon
The Complete Works

To all those Swindon people
who tried to fool me into thinking
that they were 'nothing special'

Swindon

The Complete Works

A detailed history of the Great Western Railway's centre of manufacturing during its heyday in the 1930s, '40s and '50s

Peter Timms

crecy.co.uk

First published 2021

© Peter Timms 2021

ISBN 978 191080 9860

Printed in Turkey by Pelikan Print

Crécy Publishing Ltd
1a Ringway Trading Estate, Shadowmoss Rd, Manchester M22 5LH
www.crecy.co.uk

Front cover: BR diesel mechanical 0-6-0 shunter (later TOPS class 03) D2194 at Swindon paired with its distinctive GWR style shunter's truck. The building of these locomotives was shared between Swindon and Doncaster. *Harry Luff/Online Transport Archive*
Ex-GWR Castle class 4-6-0 No 5062 Earl of Shaftesbury sparkles in the sunshine at Swindon works where it had just been overhauled. Built at Swindon in June 1937, the locomotive was withdrawn in August 1962.
Harry Luff/Online Transport Archive

Back cover main: A large locomotive boiler and firebox being lifted off the gap riveting plant after attention in the AV Shop. *BRWR*

Back cover inset from top:
A fitting end to the independent spirit. 'Western' class diesel No. D1010 brand new and as yet un-named at Swindon. *KR Collection*
The first of the last. The first of what would be the final shunting engine produced at Swindon. This is an 0-6-0 diesel hydraulic, No D9500 built at Swindon in 1964 destined to have but a brief life with British Railways before being withdrawn in 1969. These engines may have been the modern successor to the ubiquitous steam pannier-tank but by this stage there was little work left for them; shunting turns having been considerably reduced and the branch lines and yards in which they might have expected to have operated, decimated by line closures and general rationalisation of facilities.
KR Collection

Contents

Introduction

The Railway Town

For a long time after the coming of the railway, Swindon was almost unique. It was an industrial town in southern England: away from the coalfields and iron-making works of the Midlands and the north. In the heyday its Railway Works, and houses for the workers, covered a combined area of just over 6,000 acres or 9.4 square miles. It stood on a plain next to the otherwise sleepy market town on the hill, 150ft above. At least 'sleepy' was how it was in 1930. By 1960, although still more or less intact, the railway industry locally was feeling the effects of society's changing demands.

Most people living in this country up until the 1960s associated Swindon, or to be precise New Swindon, with just one thing: the Railway Works. Those living in or around the area described it as a 'railway town' because they knew it was home to hundreds of local railway workers besides those at the Works.

The railways of this country were so much a part of everyday life. They represented reliability and stability in almost every community, no matter how rural. From London to the north-west and down to the south-west it seemed everyone knew where those fine-looking locomotives that sped them to favourite seaside resorts were built. Swindon men on war service often said that mention of their home town abroad got a favourable reaction from foreign engineers.

Some observers had noted that this railway town was orderly and self-sufficient, with low unemployment: its inhabitants educated, law abiding and hard working. When the first public library opened in the town in 1943, there were often queues to come in and use it. After eight months it was recorded that 30% of the townspeople had registered with the library: 12% above the national average at that time.

On the other hand, writers including J.B. Priestley and John Betjeman had an aversion to industrial towns, especially Swindon, with its proximity to rich countryside and ancient villages. In 1950 Mr Betjeman wrote; 'Swindon has too much building and not enough architecture.' But he goes on to admit that: 'there are no flats and no slums in the full northern industrial sense of that word.' In some weather conditions low-lying smog hung over the town and John Partridge remembers that this was particularly noticeable from the top of Liddington Hill. A writer in *Wiltshire Life* magazine, in 1946 said:

> To most Wiltshiremen Swindon is, I am afraid, a name which merely brings to mind a blurred and rather depressing memory of drab streets and industrial gloom – a town not to be visited unless necessity demands it. They think of it as a region where men and women, mainly employees of the Great Western Railway, reside only because their livelihood demands it.

The Company and the Department

Because its trains were on show to the travelling public, the GWR's mechanical engineering ability was widely admired and press reports fuelled its reputation. The company's organisational capacity to move vast numbers of people and goods about the country was also highly regarded. The GWR prospered, thanks mainly to tourism and coal, even during the worst of the depression. They managed to pay their shareholders a dividend when the LM&S and L&NE railways could not, despite the restrictions placed upon all British railway companies.

The government imposed a 'common carrier' status on British railways, requiring them to carry everything offered at a rate set by a parliamentary tribunal. No such obligation was imposed on the road haulage industry. They were free to undercut the railways: a situation that was to last until the mid-1950s. By an Act of Parliament, a large proportion of profits the GWR raised from revenue

LOCOMOTIVE SHOPS.

A	ERECTORS, BOILERMAKERS & MACHINE SHOPS.
B	TENDER SHOP.
D	CARPENTERS & MASONS YARD.
E	ELECTRICIANS.
F	SMITHS.
G	MILLWRIGHTS. G2. CRANE REPAIR SHOP.
H	PATTERNMAKERS.
J	IRON FOUNDRY.
K	COPPERSMITHS & SHEET METAL WORKERS.
L2	TANK SHOP.
N	BOLT SHOP.
O	TOOL ROOM.
P1	BOILER MOUNTING & TESTING.
Q	SMITHS.
R	FITTERS & MACHINE SHOP.
SP	SPRINGSMITHS.
T	BRASS FINISHERS.
U	BRASS FOUNDRY.
V	BOILERMAKERS.
W	CYLINDER & FRAME SHOP.
X	PERMANENT WAY POINTS & CROSSINGS.

CARRIAGE AND WAGON SHOPS.

2	SAW MILL.	14	SMITHS.
3	FITTERS & MACHINE SHOP.	15	FITTERS, PLUMBERS, ETC. & MACHINE SHOP.
4	CARRIAGE BODY BUILDERS.	16	WHEEL SHOP.
5	ELECTRIC, TRAIN LIGHTING.	17	ROAD VEHICLE BUILDING & REPAIRS.
7	CARRIAGE FINISHING.	18	STAMPING SHOP.
8	CARRIAGE PAINTING.	19	CARRIAGE LIFTING & REPAIRS, HORSE BOX & CARR. TRUCK REPAIRS.
9	CARRIAGE TRIMMING.	21	WAGONS & CONTAINERS.
10	LAUNDRY.	22	OIL & GREASE WORKS.
12	CARPENTERS.	23	PLATELAYERS YARD.
13	CARR. & WAGON FRAMES.	24	CARRIAGE REPAIRS.

SWINDON WORKS

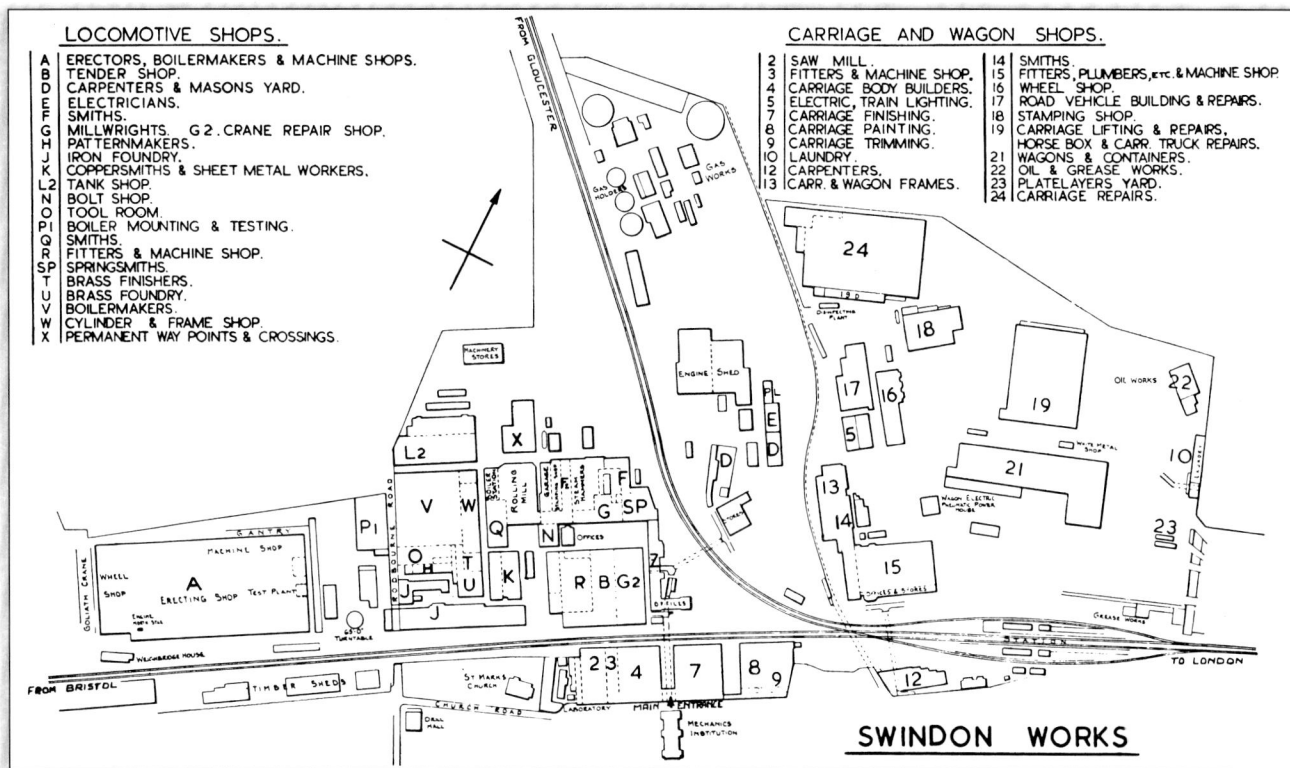

A plan showing the layout of the Works' buildings and the two railway routes running between them. This was produced for the visitors in the mid-1950s. The obvious omissions are the sidings and access roads that covered virtually all the areas between the workshops. There was also no need to show the huge Timber Stacking Ground and Concentration Yard at the far west of the site. *BRWR*

were to be used to keep user charges down once the shareholders had been paid. This was also designed to keep their accumulation of assets in check.

The public face of 'the Western', the equipment they used and the services provided, reached a peak as early as the 1930s. Further increases in the lengths and speeds of its trains would have meant extensive reconstruction of the tracks and stations. Therefore management and design engineers concentrated on making the railway services more economical, flexible and reliable. There was no mention of improving the pay and conditions of the staff in the company's publicity. Perhaps, during the depression, there was little need to invest in loyalty and morale but that was not the reason. The rates of pay for railway professions had been set by national agreements and working conditions were, in theory, covered by elaborate 'machinery' with which to negotiate grievances.

The 1930s may have become known as the 'heyday' of the GWR but behind the publicity, internal and external matters conspired against them. The company survived the economic depression remarkably well and history has been kind about their achievements during the Second World War, but this should not detract from the scale of difficulties they faced.

The west end of the Locomotive Works in winter. *R. Grainger*

It wasn't until well after nationalisation that the Western Region of British Railways, along with the other regions, started to run at a loss. Goods' traffic was always more profitable than passengers but it slowly began to decline from the end of the Great War with the development of reliable heavy road vehicles. It was only the latter that could truly claim to provide a 'door-to-door' service. Due to several extraordinary factors, there was a temporary recovery for the railways during the Second World War. The government-controlled railway companies worked well during this period and the backlog of maintenance and shortages of materials and coal was certainly not due to inefficiency.

From 1940 onwards there were restrictions on capital investment for transport. The post-war redevelopment plans for the CME Department had to be scaled back at a time when expenditure was badly needed for what the Accounts

A gang assigned to the finishing off of the royal engine No. 4082 *Windsor Castle* prior to the funeral of King George V. The royal coat of arms is about to be fitted to the locomotive running plate. An identical one was also fitted to the opposite side. 'A' Shop: January 1936.
Author's collection

Department termed: 'renewals and repairs'. The situation got worse after the war with the shortages of most raw materials and, in 1949, the devaluation of the pound. Even modified capital investment programmes could not be met by the start of the 1950s because now there was a shortage of steel as well.

The railway workshops could not replace 'old for new' plant and machinery on anything like the scale that was required. Replacing locomotives was down by 50% in 1952; new wagon building was down by 65% and no new coaches were to be built at all that year. As prices and wages continued to rise, it became more expensive for the railways to achieve the same amount of work. Despite all adversity, the products 'built at Swindon' continued to inspire a loyalty and pride not seen elsewhere.

A Centre for Manufacturing

Swindon was not the birthplace, nor was it the headquarters, of the Great Western Railway. It is, however, usually the first place that comes to mind when people think of the old GWR. The sheer size of the area that the Works and the surrounding railway yards once covered was such that even aerial photographs could not encompass it all. According to the Works' own publicity, in its heyday: 'Swindon Works comprise one of the largest

railway establishments for the construction and repair of locomotives, carriages and wagons in the world.' This statement doesn't actually tell us much, and indeed, of the four British companies formed in the 1920s, the Great Western was the smallest but one.

Most of the 12,000 men and women who worked 'inside', were involved in manufacturing, repairs and administration of the Chief Mechanical Engineers' (CME) Department. The numbers of people employed at any one time were always given as approximate for publicity purposes. Of course, accurate totals were kept but for different grades and departments such as workshop and stores personnel or office clerks, none of whom were exclusive to Swindon or to the CME Dept.

The Railway Act of 1921 required that all British railway companies be grouped together to form what became known as the 'big four' after the Great War. The GWR did not amalgamate with any other large company and this was said to have been the main reason why, they alone, managed to keep their independence and their name. Another consequence of that situation was that the GWR did not absorb any other large works, unlike the other three railway companies.

The GWR's Carriage & Wagon Works had long been established alongside the Loco Works. This might seem an obvious 'marriage' but there was no operational reason for this and, on most other pre-grouping railways, the two had evolved on separate sites. What were also on the Swindon site, alongside the mechanical engineering facilities, were the company's Gas Works, Laundry, Stores Department and Motive Power Depot.

Some small works were absorbed at 'the grouping', such as Caerphilly, which now became the factory for repair and overhaul of tank locomotives working in South Wales. Similarly Wolverhampton Works, taken into GW ownership many years earlier, dealt with the smaller engines in the company's northern division. Both these satellite factories had had their carriage and wagon facilities moved away. Cardiff Cathays Works took all the carriage and wagon repair work from Caerphilly, but in 1938/39 the carriage work was moved to Swindon. Cathays took on extra wagon work in its place. At Swindon, overhead cranes with twin crabs, on carriage lifting beams, were installed in 19C Shop. These would speed up repairs, and offset the additional workload.

Myths

There are certain misleading beliefs that many supporters of Swindon history like to inform us of, such as: 'Every male of working age, in the town, worked "inside".' With nine out of ten households dependent on wages from the railway company, it is easy to see how this idea has come to be accepted. But of course, a significant proportion of men and working women made a living by serving the railway community. Shopkeepers, bus drivers, school teachers, council and church people, were needed as they would be in any town. A local census dated 1951 showed that 12,671 Swindon men worked on the railway somewhere. That was more than half the men of working age in the town. This did not include many more who came in from outside the borough, or all the female railway workers.

Swindon was not a one-industry town before the war. Throughout the depressed 1930s, Garrard Engineering and W.D. & H.O. Wills employed about 1,000 local people apiece; J. Compton Sons & Webb employed 600; The Cellular Clothing Co. Ltd and Nicholson's Raincoat Co. Ltd employed large numbers of females. During the war, The Plessey Company, Marine Mountings, Vickers-Armstrongs and Armstrong Whitworth relocated here from more dangerous places. They all took in large numbers of Swindon people, including some skilled labour from the Railway Works.

Locals sometimes lament: 'I could walk up Regent Street and recognise everyone I passed.' In their enthusiasm to get their point across they exaggerate a little, because even as long ago as 1930 what we think of as a railway community had been well integrated with the market town 'up the hill'. So, even without taking the Regent Street story too literally, the sentiment is not disputed: New Swindon was at least a close-knit community.

Most writers and ex-railway staff sum up the old days as 'hard but fair'; health and safety, to use a modern term was, they say, non-existent. 'Swindon locomotives and rolling stock were the best in the world' is another impressive statement all too readily accepted. Even if this were true, they were comparatively costly and slow to produce. It wasn't until the Second World War that British manufacturing was shown to be inefficient in many ways, compared to the American system of mass production. However, this criticism can only be partly levelled at these Works, as 90% of its activity involved repairs. As Mr Stanier pointed out in 1929, lines of production cannot be readily applied to that type of work.

Terms and Phrases

With such a close-knit community, certain phrases were bound to be used that were not immediately recognisable to outsiders (anyone beyond walking distance of the Works). R.J. Blackmore worked in 'the factory' and regularly wrote an eloquent piece for the staff magazine or the *Swindon Railway News*. Referring to the influx of Londoners, in the 1950s, he said: 'Terms like "backsies", "trip"! and "inside" fall on new ears with arresting effect.'

An elderly Swindon lady told me about the time a new vicar in the district came to their school, Ferndale Road Girls: 'It was during the war and he asked us whether our fathers were away fighting for our country. It wasn't 'til later that I realised why he looked so disappointed: he thought most of them were in prison.' Saying your father was 'inside' in north Wiltshire had a meaning all of its own.

The various trades 'inside' the Works had labelled each other with unflattering terms. The loco side fitters called their carriage colleagues 'five-eighths fitters' because the

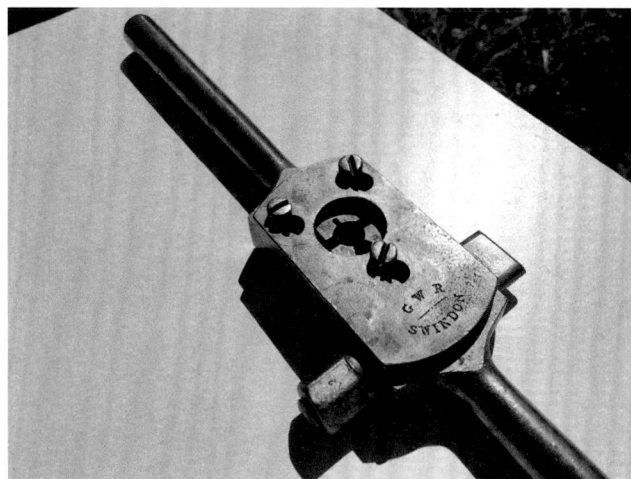

'Everything made at Swindon was of the highest quality' is a statement that is widely accepted, but not necessarily true. This die wrench, for instance, must have been made in the Works. The underside is similarly marked but the finish is very poor. No outside manufacturers' inspectors would have passed it and no Works' buyers would have accepted it.

work they undertook was comparatively light and therefore, according to them, easier. Carpenters were known by some as 'wood butchers', moulders were 'sand rats' and a 'wagon basher' riveted up wagon underframes. The boilermaker, whose work was particularly heavy and noisy, was a 'fitter with his brains knocked out'.

'New workers learned very quickly that nothing was more likely to subject them to ridicule than using the wrong terminology,' said Stan Leach. 'On the carriage and wagon side, the use of the word "truck" instead of "wagon" tripped up some people. They picked that word up when playing with clockwork train sets as children.' Talking to dozens of ex-workers over the years, I came to realise that there was no compromise when it came to using the right terms: wagons were 'built' while coaches were 'constructed', and anyone that thought otherwise was not from round these parts.

An old Wiltshire saying for a job well done was 'that's near enough'. Peter Reade records, in his book, an anecdote that the Works' smiths would recount. It concerned the foreman who had come to see how a new job was progressing: 'I hope you've made a good job of that Jack.' Jack replied: 'Well it's near enough, I reckon.' The foreman then said: 'Near enough is not good enough, it has to be just right.' 'Oh well,' said Jack, 'it's just right then,' said the foreman, walking away, adding, 'that's near enough then.'

Swindonians also adopted various terms to describe the almighty employer including: 'the company', 'the Western', 'the Great Western', 'the factory', 'inside', 'the GWR' and 'the railway' (pronounced 'row-way', of course). Their random use hereafter serves to emphasise how equally well used these terms were. I hesitate to use the name 'God's Wonderful Railway' as it is debatable whether it was in general use in the heyday.

1
The Economic Depression

Effects on the Works

On Saturday, 12 April 1930 the Works was open to the public with the admission fee going to the Railway Benevolent Institution. Examples of the latest locomotives, including 6000 *King George V*, were on show. New rolling stock too, was shown off: a complete set of thirteen coaches for the *Cornish Riviera Express*, which had been outshopped in time for the summer service the year before, received a lot of attention. Other attractions included a display by the Works' Fire Brigade under the direction of chief fire officer C.T. Cuss. The townspeople and visitors from further afield could be forgiven for thinking that the dire economic situation was all but over.

The GWR published its full traffic and operating statistics at the end of each year in the company magazine (the only British railway to do so). Of the figures for the year 1930, the 'general manager', Mr Milne, said: 'we have a world-wide depression in industry, particularly in the coal, iron and steel trades from which the GWR derives about 80% of its total freight tonnage.' The GM also noted that increased road competition was still very much a threat. It was ironic that, at that time, British railway companies were the largest contributors to the cost of road construction and maintenance. This was because they owned more road vehicles and therefore paid more towards the costs than anyone else.

Mr K.J. Cook said in his book *Swindon Steam 1921– 1951*: 'Railway accountancy is very strictly controlled by Acts of Parliament with the object of safeguarding the interests of rail users against monopolies.' The controls included wage levels that had been set after the First World War when the men's negotiating powers were still ineffective. In the 1930s the British economy was in no condition to introduce a minimum wage, as the Americans had done for their industrial workers and others in 1938.

The Wagon Works went on to 'short time' in 1929 as the company reduced wagon maintenance and manufacture.

Work on secondary and branch line carriage stock had also been cut to a minimum. Short-time working was extended to workshops on both sides of the Works in 1930. First the Saturday morning shift went then, in September, Tuesday became the start of the working week. By now the workforce would have realised that the country was going into a long drawn out recession, with all the implications for their job prospects. Only a year before the company had recorded the highest locomotive mileage ever, and the Loco and Carriage Works had been working at full capacity.

The GWR was able to absorb some of the loss of revenue by running fewer train services, which would then mean less maintenance work at Swindon. However, the ongoing programme to replace main-line locomotives, carriages and wagons was almost as ambitious as ever. Of particular note were a set of eight 'super saloon cars' that the directors authorised in 1931, to rival the luxury carriages of the Pullman Car Co. They were to provide 'luxurious travelling' for ocean liner passengers disembarking at Plymouth Millbay docks and continuing their journey on up to Paddington. The first two vehicle interiors were designed and fitted out by the specialist firm of Trollope & Sons, London, SW1, to 'reflect tasteful high quality without being over-elaborate'. Swindon would then complete the order.

This revived some of the morale and optimism in the carriage shops. This work was the talk of the town at a time when men were in fear of their jobs. Some people thought that they had got it wrong and the fortunes of the department had turned: perhaps more orders would follow.

Plans for extending and rebuilding Works' facilities did include financial assistance from the government as part of the scheme to relieve unemployment. During this period: a plant for disinfecting coaches was built; a 70-ton replacement weighbridge was installed in the Carriage Works; the Locomotive Weigh House was fitted with replacement balancing pans and instruments and the

The luxurious standard of the interior furnishings of this 1931 carriage contrasts starkly with the meagre and uncertain existence of the craftsmen who built it. This was one of the 'Super Saloons', which were built for the clientele disembarking from ocean liners anchored in Plymouth Sound and travelling by the GWR up to Paddington. *GWR Magazine supplement*

building extended; a springsmith shop was built; the chair foundry was extended; and a huge new carriage repair shop was completed on land recently acquired from the council.

Thousands of tons of ash and soil had to be brought in by the CME Dept to extend the built up land at the west end of the site and, by the early 1930s, this large area was brought into use. It included a concentration yard for scrapping redundant stock and machinery and a large timber-stacking yard with workshops and sidings. Later they stored spare boilers there too.

In 1935 a national newspaper carried a story saying that Swindon Works had announced their biggest building programme for some years. Starting in the new year, 225 new locomotives including twenty-five more 'Castle' class engines, were to be built to replace ageing stock. Orders for 302 new passenger coaches and 3,500 freight wagons were also to be placed, said the report. The rebuilding of 'constituent' engines to take GW boilers, and other standard fittings, was stepped up as conditions started showing signs of improvements.

The department's budget had been cut each year due to falling receipts. From a business point of view the railway accident at Shrivenham in 1936, could not have come at a worse time. The costs of recovering the wreckage and having an extra 'King' class engine out of service would be substantial. After assessing the damage to 6007 back in the Works, the CME decided to exploit a loophole in the way the accounts were set up to fund the remedial work. The condition of the main frames and boiler was good enough to form the basis of a rebuild, as if it was a routine overhaul, and this in practice is what happened.

However, the engine and tender were condemned and lot numbers were issued for replacements. A new engine history card and mileage record was made out too. This reclassification meant that the costs would now initially come from capital instead of their own depleted revenue account. The money would then be repaid in instalments over the anticipated life of the asset.

Locomotive Rebuilds

In at least one way the economic situation directly created some extra activity in the Loco Works. Because of the decrease in the Welsh coal traffic, the GWR found itself with a surplus of 2-8-0 tank engines. They had been designed primarily for working in South Wales, hauling coal trains short distances between the collieries and ports. Ships were gradually changing to oil fuel and stockpiling coal was suddenly stopped. A batch of new 2-8-0Ts, still being built, would not now be needed and were to be stored in the newly closed carriage shops at Caerphilly Works.

Here the frames are being laid out for the 1930 batch of 'King' class locomotives. The *GWR Magazine* justified the expense at a time when the company was starting to cut jobs by saying that 'the building of more express locomotives has effected considerable economies by: 1 the haulage of longer and heavier trains and presumably less of them and 2 by reducing the number of banking engines needed.' *Author's collection*

There was however, a need for engines that could work medium- and long-distance coal trains. At the time they were worked by the double-framed 'Aberdares', which were becoming due for replacement. With the weight of the water tanks and coal bunkers on the driving wheels, tank engines had better pulling power than tender engines due to increased adhesion. Swindon therefore rebuilt batches of the '5205' class 2-8-0Ts, and made them into 2-8-2Ts: renumbering them as the '7200' class. They then weighed a massive 92 tons, making them the heaviest steam locos that would be lifted by the overhead cranes in the A Erecting Shop. (Interestingly the 2-8-0Ts had starting life on the drawing board as 2-8-2Ts, but the wheel arrangement was thought to be unsuitable for the Welsh valley lines and they were altered before reaching the shop floor. Now the original drawings could be used as a basis for the modifications.)

Mr Churchward's 2-6-0 tender engines, the '4300' class, were very versatile but in the 1930s there was not enough suitable work for 342 of them. The earliest 100 engines were, therefore, withdrawn and their wheels and motion used for two new classes of 4-6-0s. These were the '6800' and lighter '7800' classes: outshopped from 1936 and 1938 respectively. What the new designs lacked in route availability they more than made up for in power and adhesion due to larger boilers. Both types were paired with 3,500 gallon tenders.

Effects on the Workforce

Generally, job security on the railways was very good but in the workshops, especially for the last in, it was not necessarily a job for life before the war. New production methods nearly always meant less labour, so sometimes

the men affected were moved to other work and the balance was corrected with natural wastage. It was when the 'dividend was down' that the company had a policy of discharging labour. Word would spread through the town like wildfire when jobs were 'under threat' due to manufacturing orders being cut.

The steam locomotive was particularly labour intensive. Indeed, it was one of the factors that would later hasten its demise. However, it did provide work for a lot of men in all communities, none more so than Swindon. This helped to stimulate the ailing economy to a great extent. Against this came the opening of the new Stafford Road Works in Wolverhampton in 1932. They were now able to take a larger share of the company's engine repair work than before.

The majority of the men discharged to save money had to come from the shop floor. The company came to realise that it was those who produced the work who could be replaced or recalled in greater numbers when business improved. Consequently the pay and prospects of secure employment for the tradesmen and the semi-skilled was not so good. It was also a reason for the resentment felt towards 'them upstairs'. The 'last in' were at greatest risk but, as it was not known how many would be 'let go', this did not allay the fears of many. Some men thought that it was management's chance to 'get their own back' for the General Strike.

Some labourers 'inside' were instructed to go and work in the open air or face dismissal. This must have seemed better than having to face destitution, but few could stick it for long. Once autumn had set in, the weather became ever more severe. Older men, probably inadequately clothed, soon went 'on the sick' and I have heard of cases locally where such working conditions almost certainly shortened a man's life.

As many apprenticeships as ever were being awarded at the Works and elsewhere in the town. This gave credence to the belief that trainees 'inside', were cheap labour. It was probably true because most of the costs were for administration and most of that was done by the College (Technical Institution). New engineering workshops for various trades were opened behind the College in the early 1930s.

Cyril Mountford lived in Jolliffe Street and was apprenticed to a trade in the C&W Works from 1929. He was hoping to become a carriage bodymaker like his father and grandfather. At the end of his third year, Cyril had passed the City and Guild examinations with sufficient credits to be offered a 'day studentship'. This meant that the company were prepared to pay his wages while he sat in the classroom. This he did, one day a week, for six months of the year at the College, as well as his usual evening classes. If he successfully completed the four-year course he would be qualified to degree level. The select few, like Cyril, were no longer such 'cheap labour'.

The years 1929 to 1934 were the worst nationally, with unemployment rising to 3.5 million or 15.6% of the labour force. The situation took a while to affect the Swindon workers. According to the GWR Magazine, there were 13,531 employed in the Swindon factory in 1931. A year later another source said the figure was just over 11,000, the lowest of the whole period. The short-sighted way in which workshop labour at Swindon was handled is noticeable in an Evening Advertiser report in 1932: 'In August, while 820 were discharged on the "carriage side", many "loco side" tradesmen were being taken on.' Although only one in three CME workers were based at Swindon, the majority of job losses came from within the town, which had by then more than 3,000 people registered as workless.

The concessions that the employees and their families came to rely on were, no doubt, the reason why there was little outward animosity shown towards the capitalist railway owners. Consequently, there was little communist propaganda spread about locally. That is not to say that there wasn't a strong undercurrent of socialist thinking, fuelled by those with influence. Mr Dick Pearce, a prominent member of the Amalgamated Engineering Union in Swindon, received a personal invitation from the railway workers of the Soviet Union. He duly left and attended their May Day Festival and Demonstration in 1933, 'after being waved off at the station by Reuben George and other socialists', said the local evening paper.

Lower wages paid for the additional welfare benefits but the Swindon 'factory' worker was at least as well off as his parents and grandparents had been at his age. One reason for this was people were having smaller families. Industrial workers generally were less militant than they had been in the past, no doubt due to the depressed economy. The threat of being without work certainly preoccupied the Swindon 'factory' men during the years 1928 to 1938. On the one hand the men wanted to work fast and earn their piecework money, but on the other hand there was a real fear that once orders were completed there would be little or no work in the foreseeable future.

Certainly, the average working man remained God-fearing but by the 1930s things were not what they used to be. Fred Uzzell of Kingshill Road wrote his life story when he retired from the Loco Stores in 1936. He was a strong critic of the bad language used by a minority of Works' men: 'The swearing done there is awful, though I don't suppose it is worse than other large factories for wickedness, but at Swindon there are many who never use a bad word and yet never go to a place of worship.'

In 1938 the company continued to make a slow recovery from the recession and there was work available for the skilled and semi-skilled in engineering generally. It was therefore a shock when about twenty-four men on the loco side were under notice to go, and some short-time working was introduced in March for wagon workers. Then there were threats of further cuts in the labour force. In May it was announced that well over 1,000 were to go in July on the carriage & wagon side. This was due to building programmes being completed and no further orders placed. However, the company would soon have to completely rethink its short- and medium-term plans as war became ever more likely.

Despite all the hardships of the 1930s, the railway factory workers' prospects were better than those who worked in rural areas and Swindon suffered far less of the changing fortunes characteristic of other towns dominated by one employer.

Employment Benefits

The men had secured a few hard-fought concessions by the start of the 1930s: partly because the government did not wish to see a repeat of the General Strike. One union demand that was agreed to was a 'last in, first out' policy, which was of little comfort to some but did cut down the partiality and favouritism shown by some foremen when they decided who would be kept on and who would have to go. The Great Western Railway ran a successful business and could not have done so by being more benevolent towards its servants, given the conditions of the times. This makes the early Swindon idea all the more fantastic: that if you allow for the medical, recreational, educational and spiritual welfare of the workers and their families, they might just serve you better.

Unlike single women, men had little or no hope of alternative employment locally; a situation that allowed management a long period of industrial harmony. The men received eight days' holiday annually, plus six bank holidays, which were all unpaid until 1938, adding to their predicament. Between 1930 and 1933 the Mechanics' Institute lost a third of its paying members. In May 1933, following an appeal by the Swindon Unemployed Association and the local MP, the GWR agreed to allow men who they had 'let go' and their families membership of the Medical Fund, subject to certain conditions.

Men discharged over the previous twelve months were also allowed access to the facilities of the Mechanics' Institute. This meant they could apply for the free passes for the annual holiday trains, and again this concession extended to wives and children. No doubt this proved popular for those eligible as it was almost no cheaper to stay at home on 'Trip Day'.

Although Beryl Wynn's father, Albert Odey, was never discharged due to the depression, he didn't enjoy 'Trip'. This was because the labour discharges were always announced a few weeks later if the company was doing badly and he worried about being chosen to go. With the railwaymen's strikes in the early years of the twentieth century, the company were forced to realise that they could now be held to ransom by an unhappy workforce. They allowed employees certain concessions over and above what was required by law and a lot of Swindon families came to rely on them. The cynical might say that this was a subtle way of buying loyalty.

The GWR employee, if he or she was the main provider for the family, could take advantage of cheap coal (minimum two bags or 2 cwt). According to a notice dated 1932, the Stores Dept had 'secured contracts at very favourable prices', no doubt due to the depressed market. To even out the demand on supplies of this 'domestic coal', which the company also delivered, they offered to pass on the reduced price if staff bought it during the summer months.

In Swindon 'scrap' and 'refuse timber' was also available from the GWR for a small handling fee. At this time hundredweight wood tickets cost you a shilling: a little more if you required delivery to one of the surrounding villages. What the company chose to call 'refuse' could be reused around the home, although there wasn't much of this until after the war. 'Scrap' wood was used as fuel or as firelighters and could be collected from a wood wharf by Whitehouse Bridges, thus saving the small hauliers' fee. A surviving notice, dated 1931, in the Steam Museum, told workers not to take wood home on workmen's trains.

Other useful scrap could be purchased, such as flue tubes from old locomotive boilers. Jack Fleetwood remembers that they were a shilling each in the 1940s, so they would have been about half that during the height of the depression. Two or three of these tubes slotted together made a sturdy washing line, although when it was available, signal rodding was preferred as it didn't rust so quickly. Jack said that sometimes, after paying, you could discreetly swap the old flue tubes and take out new ones on the same docket.

CLOSING OF SHOPS

THE CARRIAGE AND WAGON WORKS AND SAW MILLS WILL BE CLOSED FROM 12-30 PM ON THURSDAY, JULY 13TH UNTIL 8-0 AM MONDAY JULY 24TH.

THE WAGES FOR WEEK ENDING JULY 8TH. WILL BE PAID ON THURSDAY JULY 13TH. AND FOR WEEK ENDING JULY 15TH. ON JULY 21ST. AND 24TH.

BY ORDER. 1933.

A poster produced in the Print Room, where engineering drawings were copied. It is endorsed with the C&W Manager's Office No. 4 stamp, which made it official and discouraged the men from pasting unauthorised notices of their own. Before the war the factory closed down production for one week in July. At the time of this instruction, 1933, there was no holiday pay for wages grades. Because the workforce worked a week 'in hand' they did get paid on their return on Monday, the 24th. That money would be 'short' because the annual holiday commenced on Thursday afternoon and not at the end of the working week, which was Saturday. This reduced pay had to last until Friday week. *Author's collection*

Communal alleyways ran behind all terraced houses in the town and were known locally as 'backs' or 'backsies'. This picture shows one of the six backs serving opposing terraces of cottages, all occupied by railway families, in the GWR estate. *Swindon Society courtesy of Bob Townsend*

A familiar sight around the town was allotment fences made out of old enamel railway signs. When railway equipment was surplus to requirements, the Stores Dept dealt with its disposal. If the men wanted to buy redundant 'scrap' items they were charged a nominal sum. Enamel station signs and, later, steel coach panels made durable fences and kept rabbits away from the vegetables.

'Getting By'

The wages' grades in the CME Dept did little more than 'get by' in the 1930s, and despite a steady fall of prices in the shops, workers without a trade lived below the poverty line. Junior salaried staff would see their pay increase over time, sufficient for them to provide for a wife and family. The manual workers had little or no scope to improve their living standards, unless they were young enough to work on into the following two decades. The lean times of their parents' and grandparents' generations were back, if they had ever really gone away. 'Waste not, want not' and 'make do and mend' were sayings well

known to Swindon people before the war, the period normally associated with these phrases.

Beryl Wynn (nee Odey), whose father was a French polisher in the Carriage Works throughout the 1930s, told me that: 'although our dad always had full employment, mother had to get all the groceries "on tick" every short week and pay up every balance week' (piecework balance money was paid fortnightly). So it is difficult to imagine how railway families managed when the working week was cut to four and even three days. They could not fall back on assistance from relatives or from the government. It was not until 1946 that mothers could claim family allowance for each child, excluding the first.

For the poor souls whose 'services were no longer required', the dole queue was almost certainly the only other alternative. The dole pay-out was subject to a means test, which meant an official would come to the house and make an assessment; the family piano, the mantle clock and other non-essentials would have to be sold before any money could be claimed. Casual work would have to be sort as well to supplement the meagre

A gang of men installing a new wagon weightable in the Loco Yard Sidings. The table would be used to weigh wagon loads of scrap metal. This had been put through the shears in a building behind F Shop, an area known as Scrap Yard. The weighbridge house where the balancing table gauges would be read was a converted signal box. The date is about 1929 or 1930, a time when men were starting to fear for their jobs. All of this gang, except 'Nobby' Newbery on the right, a Works' labourer, were employees of Henry Pooley & Sons Ltd, the weighing machine company. *S.A.S. Smith courtesy of Ray Eggleton*

dole allowance. If it was suspected that poverty was causing a deterioration of health, a person or family might receive handouts organised by the church or civic groups. The mayor elected in 1932, Mr William Robins, was a clerk in the factory (later he worked in the stores order office and was organising secretary of the Railway Clerks' Association). He said one of the most beneficial schemes during his term was the borough council allocating allotment land to the unemployed.

The weeks following 'Trip' holiday were bound to be difficult for the manual worker if he and his family spent the whole week away. Some never went away: preferring instead to make a point and remind everyone that it was an annual 'lock-out', enjoyed only by the bosses. Adams,

the pawn broker in Fleet Street, always did brisk trade at this time of year.

Two local artists (a Will Thomas was one) had a series of farcical sketches of 'Trip' published as postcards earlier in the century. The theme was usually the financial predicament that the holiday had caused. One showed the 'annual wash' on the eve, another, the 'annual rush' to board the trains and then the 'annual hush' afterwards depicting the wife and kids hiding behind the door when the rent collector or money lender came to call. These pathetic situations appeared comical because there was more than a little that railway families could identify with.

Rabbits could be bought from a man known as 'Artful Dodger', who came round selling them from a pony and

Enlarging some of the 2-8-0 tank locomotives into 2-8-2s provided much-needed work for some men in the Loco Works during the depressed 1930s. No. 5217 was built in 1924 when some official locomotive portraits were photographed in light grey to highlight the detail. It was not one of those rebuilt. The lower picture shows the first of the fifty-four engines as converted. *GWR*

cart. They were a bit cheaper than those in the shops, at around a shilling each. The skin could be sold on to 'Cockle Jack' the rag and bone man, for 3 (old) pence. He lived near Jack Fleetwood, in Regent Place, and Jack said he would repair shoes too, for a few coppers. Cheap meat such as offal, kidneys, heart, liver and chitterlings would be purchased from the local butcher's shop daily, especially in the summer, as people had no means of keeping it cold. Late on Saturday was the best time to get bargains from the butchers. Horse meat was available as an alternative during wartime, if not before, and some people ate pigeon meat too.

It was the men in the workshops who viewed impending retirement with anxiety and hoped they could find some sort of paying work elsewhere when they reached sixty-five years old. If they were unwilling or unable to pay into something such as the Sick Fund Society, where a superannuation allowance was paid upon retirement, they would, assuming they lived that long, come to wish they had. Only the lowest paid would qualify for state pension payments but not until they reached seventy. Some locals said their fathers and uncles suffered hardship in retirement even after the war, although by then, subject to a medical check, some men could continue in their work after reaching sixty-five.

Community Co-operation

Councillor J. Nash arranged a meeting between the committee of the Swindon GWR Chargemen's Association, of which he was chairman, and local business and political people with influence. The idea was to try to encourage them to help improve business for the railway company. They also appealed to the local MP, to the Chamber of Commerce, to co-op societies, to traders and to the town's people via the press. The idea was to try to get back goods' traffic that had been lost to road hauliers.

The railway companies and their staff had become alarmed at the amount of public money being spent on the roads (although £60 million per annum came in to the Exchequer from petrol duty, £40 million was being drawn from ratepayers for new roads and maintenance). The chargemen suggested to buyers and businesses that only goods that had been brought in by rail should be purchased as everyone in the town was more or less dependent on the GWR for their livelihoods. They also reminded the assembly that the less the railway workers received in wages, the less they were able to put back into the local economy.

While it remained a town that was dominated by one industry, Swindon was a close-knit community and its people had strong compassion for their own. A good example of this was the establishment of an organisation called the Swindon Council of Social Service. It was formed in 1933 with the object of promoting and supporting all or any purposes deemed by law to be charitable. In particular, they supported the advancement of education, health and relief of poverty, distress and sickness. Funds were made up of donations from businesses and individuals including groups of workers within the GWR Works. No doubt many were motivated to give by the thought that they themselves could be in dire straits at any time with the fragile economic situation prevailing.

The SCSS was made up of committees of professional people from local organisations such as Swindon Trades' Council, the Chamber of Commerce, the YMCA, the St John Ambulance Brigade, the Red Cross Society and many more. Applications from or on behalf of 'the distressed and destitute' could be made at their office at No. 1 Faringdon Road. Following investigation, all genuine cases of severe hardship would be assisted. The various committees would dispense clothes and footwear, give financial aid, arrange washing facilities and medical treatment, and help with an allotment and so on. Professional people were available to assist with situations that they were qualified or trained for. For instance, people having suicidal tendencies could be counselled and if legal advice was needed to help a workless man or his family being threatened with court over a debt, that was given free of charge.

Between the wars an annual day out to the seaside was laid on for the children of the poor. The Swindon daily paper *The Evening Advertiser* paid for the special train to take them and some supervising adults to Weymouth. In 1930 it was reported that more than a 1,000 children were looking forward to it. Youngsters from the district whose fathers had fallen in the Great War or were unemployed were sought and offered the day out. There was some stigma attached to this charitable offering and for this reason some mothers refused to let their children go.

2

In the Locomotive Works

Range of Output

It is often said of Swindon Works in its heyday, that basic and raw materials (timber, iron and steel, oil, leather, fabrics, water and power) went in, and locomotives, carriages and wagons came out. Some people even take the idea a stage further and proudly boast that 'Swindon Works made everything themselves' and that 'they were totally self-sufficient'. As regards the second part of that legend, nothing could be further from the truth.

It is true that the diversity of manufacturing processes and skills practised in this one works was impressive. Some might say excessive and outdated because it was not always cost-effective to make every component within their capability. It was the job of the CME's 'principal assistant' to investigate, with the help of the Accounts' Department, the cost of manufacture against the cost to 'buy in'. Mr H.W. Gardner, when he was assistant chief accountant to the CME, said that his

department covered work being done for other departments, private firms and other railway companies, and this is at odds with another myth: that Swindon looked after itself alone. Foundryman Jack Fleetwood said: 'We did do some work for the GWR Signal Works at Reading and their people did tend to be very particular about the standard of workmanship they required of us.'

The manufacturing capabilities of this railway factory were only realised outside when they started to deliver completed orders for the Ministry of (War) Production, particularly during the years 1941 to 1944. Much of the work for the war effort was very different to the type of mechanical and timber work with which they were familiar,

One of the few components made in the Works suitable to be overhauled on a line of roller conveyors were loco axleboxes. This was because of the large numbers dealt with and the amount of separate operations involved. This plant was laid out in the AM Shop and worked very well. First the boxes were boshed (cleaned) before going on to have parts such as keeps, crown bearings, bronze liners and white metalling bosses removed. They were then planed as a set

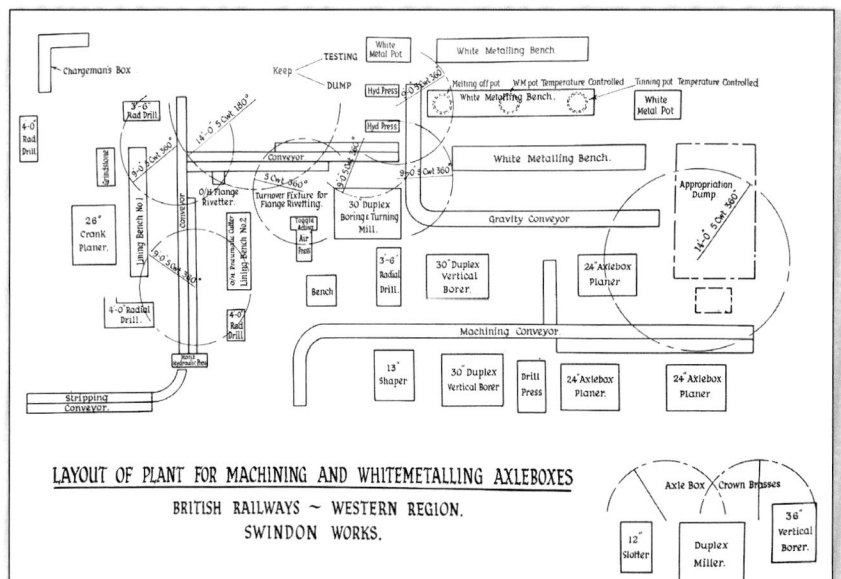

LAYOUT OF PLANT FOR MACHINING AND WHITEMETALLING AXLEBOXES
BRITISH RAILWAYS ~ WESTERN REGION.
SWINDON WORKS.

according to axle diameter sizes received from the AW Shop. Next the bevels were milled before going on to have the journals bored to suit the measurements received. Further operations were carried out on a shaper and a drilling machine. Finally the boxes were passed by conveyor to be refitted with refurbished or replacement parts. If passed by the inspector, the complete assemblies were then sent on to the erecting shop. *BRWR*

and tested their capability, organisational efficiency and resourcefulness. It was made known at the war's end that the Works satisfactorily completed all that was asked of them. They had taken on work that could not be done elsewhere and usually delivered ahead of time. The loco works' manager during the war, K.J. Cook, was awarded an OBE in 1946 for organising the war work undertaken during his term of office.

As well as supplying motive power for the Traffic Department, the Locomotive Works produced and repaired an impressive range of other mechanical equipment for the GWR. This included: pumping and hydraulic machinery, sheet metal fabrications, patterns, ticket issuing machines, merchandise containers, different types of road vehicle bodies and electric motors for overhead crane mechanisms.

Other sundry items that were produced and repaired in the Loco Works included signal and train lamps, chains, nuts, bolts, rivets, steel wire and hemp rope. Even some machine tools had been manufactured in the factory, many years before, and two cylinder borers of 1865 and 1881 were still going strong. Their electric motors later replaced the old belt drives and they worked on until the 1960s.

Dozens of types of chains and lifting tackle were made here and so were the stores' catalogues that went with them. Some constructional work at Swindon, and throughout the department, was done by CME men or contractors with the approval of the chief (civil) engineer. The company's engineering handbook stipulated that iron and steel brought in for such construction had to conform to British Standard Specification No. 153: dictating that a high minimum quality of steel was required and, where practical, all materials should be of British manufacture.

Iron, Brass and Chair Foundries

According to the company's figures, in the 1930s the Iron Foundry or J Shop, produced between 9,000 and 10,000 tons of castings annually. Another 1,700 tons, approximately, of non-ferrous castings (mostly brass but also white metal and gun metal or bronze) came out of the Brass Foundry (U Shop). Jack Fleetwood was a 'sand rat' (moulder), in the Works' Foundries all his working life, and he told me:

> In the Iron Foundry, scrap castings were recycled, with or without additional pig iron and coke. When the fire in the furnace had burnt up, the blast was gradually increased to raise the temperature sufficient to melt the metal. In the Brass Foundry redundant ferrous metal and alloy castings were also returned to the furnaces, including any we had to scrap, which were known as 'shitters'. Samples from the ingots were analysed in the laboratory then, if necessary, returned to the furnace with additional metals to produce the required composition. So, to some extent, we were self-sufficient.

Once melted, the metal in the cupola or blast furnace had to be used within a short time. If it cooled beyond a certain point its properties changed and the casting would be inferior. The dross was skimmed back as the metal was poured into a hollow shape or mould. When it cooled a solidified form equal to the space of the mould was left. Again, random samples were sent to the laboratory to check the composition. Moving molten metals to the moulds manually was potentially dangerous. Jack said he could never understand why the heaviest jobs in the Brass Foundry, where there were no lifting aids, had to be moved the furthest from the furnace. In the Iron Foundry North Bay, where all their larger work was undertaken, they had cranes up to 20-ton capacity, in constant use.

Wood or metal patterns had to be brought in from the Pattern Store for the work 'in hand'. They were painted in various colours and some were made up of two or more parts that slotted together. The colour denoted the type of metal that would be used in the mould produced. Mahogany was used to make patterns but imported pine was more usual: those in frequent use, for such parts as brake blocks or axleboxes, were made of metal. The company claimed to have approximately 75,000 different types of casting patterns on site.

The moulder's job was to produce the hollow and the usual way to do this was by 'closed box moulding'. For this a loose pattern was pressed halfway into one half of the box, filled with packed sand. It was the shape of the proposed finished piece but slightly oversized to allow for shrinkage. The other half of the box, also filled with sand, was pressed down hard on top until the two could be clamped together. The pattern was then removed carefully by separating the box. It was vital that the sand, together with the additives, gave the right consistency to bond together. Jack told me:

> The type of sand we used varied, depending on the work. It would often need further grinding and sifting if it came straight from the quarries. Until after the war, sand additives were mixed in on site too. Red, green and sea sand had such things as oil, coal dust, clay, plumbago powder or treacle added. The right balance had to be made between binding the sand and leaving it permeable enough to disperse hot gases and stop 'scabbing' or lumps left on the cast surfaces. Horse manure too, was used. It wasn't until about 1950 that shunting wagons with draught horses was completely phased out in the Works: then they had to buy in manure. Sand mixing was done in an apple mill or, if large amounts were required, by hand, by using a good polished shovel. Most was used only once or reused as packing sand. In the Brass Foundry 'petrobond' was 'bought in' after the war. This was fine sand which produced a smoother surface finish.
>
> A wagon load of red sand regularly arrived outside the Brass Foundry, from Kidderminster. Labourers were then normally paid two hours

overtime to shovel the sand out of the 12-ton wagon and move it into the shop. Because of the terrible weather conditions in the winter of 1947, the steel doors on the sand wagon were frozen solid. The men made a fire underneath using the contents of the furnaces that were emptied that evening, so they could start unloading in the morning. What they didn't realise was that the floor of the vehicle was made of wood and it burned through and collapsed. The contents remained inaccessible but now the line was blocked too. After much head scratching, it was realised that nothing could be done with the 'crippled' wagon and its load until the weather improved: which turned out to be weeks later.

If the casting was to be hollow or have any cavities, cores would be added by the coremaker. Channels would also have to be incorporated to allow the molten metal to be poured in and the hot gases to escape. To suspend the cores within the mould, copper studs known as 'chaplets' were used. Locomotive combined cylinder and saddle blocks were probably the most exacting work undertaken in the Works' foundries and required the best-quality cast iron. Up to twenty-six separate cores could be used but I never saw a 'scrapper'. By contrast, assorted [plain] scrap was used for loco and carriage brake blocks, which were known as 'slippers'.

During what was probably my first winter in the Foundry I thought I was going to die of cold. The older hands said: 'Just go and ask Foreman Webb for some extra heating,' so I did. His reply was: 'Work a little harder, that will warm you up.' When I came out of the office, the men were laughing their heads off; they had caught another naïve newcomer.

Another method was 'bedding in moulding', where the mould was packed into sand in the foundry floor then covered by a top-part moulding box. This avoided the need for expensive bottom-part moulds, particularly when making bulky irregular castings. If no top box was needed the process was known as 'open sand moulding'. All the moulds had to be ready by early afternoon as this was when the furnaces, which were lit first thing in the morning, would be ready. Large castings, weighing several tons, took more than two weeks to complete because of all the preparation and afterwards the cooling, fettling and cleaning. Fettling involved grinding off any ridges left from where the two halves of the mould met.

It was not uncommon for railway companies to keep successful methods of production to themselves. For instance, Swindon never recorded the process they used for making their 'yellow brass', which is still admired today on surviving locomotives and rolling stock. Arthur Lawrence worked in the Brass Foundry in the 1920s and '30s. More than once he had to attend a court of law as the company's brass was the subject of a legal dispute over ownership or liability. Arthur or others from the foundry and the laboratory would have to swear under oath that the material in question had been tested and found to be Works' brass. The source of this information is Arthur's daughter but unfortunately she couldn't give me any more details.

After leaving the foundry the usual sequence was for castings to have one surface milled flat. This was used as a datum from which other measurements were taken, on a marking off table. Smaller work was marked off for machining using a surface plate and a scriber. Various operations then followed before partial assembly then, if they were locomotive parts, on to the erecting shops. As well as moulders, there were Foundry workers who were known as dressers, furnacemen, knockers-out, cupola men and ladle runners.

Of other work undertaken in the Works' foundries, Jack said:

> We cast bells out of silver bell metal: an alloy of copper [80 parts], tin, zinc and lead, which was expensive to produce. They were used by the company's shipping and were fitted to dock shunting engines and to traversing tables as warning signals. Other, smaller bells were used with signalling equipment and in ATC boxes in loco cabs. If it was a matter of replacing a part that could be cast, we did it. If a large steam hammer or press developed a crack in its frame, a pattern was made of the part and a new piece, sometimes weighing several tons, was cast. If a roll needed replacing in the rolling mills we would cast a replacement. We also made some of our own moulding boxes as well.

Not all of the company's castings were produced here though: the Engineering Dept made the lineside signs and nameboards displayed around the system. The official policy was that Swindon only cast larger batches of such things, otherwise they couldn't compete on costs.

Behind the Iron Foundry was the Chair Foundry or J2 Shop where semi-skilled men produced track chairs and other castings for the permanent way. The primary function of these chairs was to support the rails. They were also designed to resist the oscillating traffic loads without fracturing or allowing the rails to splay apart. The chargeman chair-moulder in the 1950s, Harry Johnson, said his forty-three men were the best paid of their grade in the factory due to their piecework earnings. Jack said of the Chair Foundry: 'The work was hard and tedious, and the conditions were dirty and cramped.'

Train Headboards

One Foundry job that aroused particular interest was the casting of new titled train headboards in the period 1956 to 1958. Swindon was to cast them for certain principal Western Region passenger trains. Their rakes of coaches were to be turned out in brown and cream too, very similar to the old Great Western colours. The new headboards

The 1.30pm train from Paddington to Penzance was given the name the Royal Duchy in 1955. It is seen here at Exeter in 1957 with a Swindon headboard. *Ken Ellis*

were to be more decorative than the earlier ones made at Doncaster. Tom Stanton in the Drawing Office carried out the research on the coat of arms and heraldic devices that would be incorporated in their designs.

The final designs were passed on to the Pattern Shop. An extract from the *Swindon Railway News* described the next stage of production: 'After studying the drawings, the pattern maker (Viv Rogers) marks out a full-size layout of the job on a drawing board. In doing this he has to increase all dimensions quoted to allow for shrinkage which occurs when molten metal cools within its sand mould.' Jack Fleetwood remembers Viv as a very competent pattern maker. When, as in this case, only a few castings were to be made of each pattern, soft wood was used.

The finished patterns, together with a single attachment bracket, were then passed to the Brass Foundry. Jack was one of the senior moulders here, who used his skill to get an exact impression of the pattern using 'green' sand 'rammed up' into two halves of an iron moulding box and clamped together. The pattern was then removed and the two halves were clamped back together. Molten aluminium at 750 degrees celsius was poured through the channel previously let into the mould, while skimming back the dross. Thirty minutes later the casting could be knocked out. There were to be at least two of each of the fourteen new types of headboards (some trains would require engine changes en route so more were made). The piecework price to the moulder was 23 shillings each if he completed one

every three hours. Jack took particular pride in this work:

Some other designs were produced using hard resin but a man from the General Manager's Office at Paddington came down and said he didn't like them. So they were to be of LM6 aluminium, this specification gave them some flexibility and less brittleness than the Doncaster ones. [In service the enginemen handling them were not always very careful and although they stood up well to vibration on the locomotives they could, and did occasionally break if dropped.] Strangely enough, breathing in the molten aluminium fumes would cure a headache, even a hangover.

Locomotive Boilers

Locomotive boiler barrel construction involved cutting heavy steel plate and feeding it through bending rolls to form cylinders, the tapered sections requiring great skill to get right. Dozens of fire (flue) tubes to carry hot gases from the firebox through the boiler were held by tubeplates at either end of the barrel. The tubeplates and firebox throat plate were sheared to shape and flanges formed under a press so as to allow fixing by riveted seams, to adjacent structures. The inner copper and outer steel firebox wrappers were formed under hydraulic presses from single sheets cut out with a template that reduced the number of

	Page	BOILER CLASS	OUTSIDE LENGTH FIREBOX	FRONT BRICKS L4	R4	K	M	N	O	P	S	T	U	V	X	KEY BRICKS	5"×4" SPLITS
A	3	STANDARD Nº 1	9'- 0"	"	1		5	3	6	5	2						
B	4	" " 2	7'- 0"	"	1		6	3	4	2							
D	5	" " 4	7'- 0"	"	1		4	1	5	3	2						
E	6	" " 5	5'-10"	"	1		5	3	1								
G	7	" " 7	10'-0"	"	2		2	3	4	9	4	4					
H	8	" " 8	10'-0"	"	"		5	2	6	6	5	3					
J	9	" " 9	6'- 6"	"	2		4	1	7								
K	10	" " 10	6'- 0"	"	"		6	3	3								
F	11	" " 21	5'- 6"	"	2		5	7									
W	12	" " 12	11'-6"	"	"	1	4	3	2	8	4	4	1	1			
Z	13	" " 14	7'- 6	LS	R5 1		5	2	6	5	1						
O	14	" " 15	9'- 3	"	1		10	5	5	4	1						
M	15	R.O.D.	8'- 6"	L4	R4 1		1	16	2								
V	16	1393 & 1366.	3'-11"	"	"		4	4									
S	17	4800.	4'- 6"	"	"		4	4									
U	18	2021.	5'- 0"	"	"		5	5									
T	18	METROPOLITAN.	5'- 1"	"	"		5	5									
Q	19	SIR DANIEL	5'- 4"	"	"		6	6									
P	20	2301 & Stº GOODS Stᴬᵀ	5'- 4"	"	"		6	6									
N	21	113ᵀᴴ Lot. & 3200	5'-10"	"	"		6	6									
-	22	Stᴰ STATIONARY.	5'- 6"	"	"		5	5						6	6		
-	23	110ᵀᴴ Lot "	6'- 4"	"	"		12							6	6		
-	24	116ᵀᴴ " "	7'- 0"	"	"		2		3	2	2	1					
-	25	L.M.S. Own Bricks.	9'3"	SEE DRG Nº D41.16306.													
-	26	" G.W. Bricks.			L4 R4 1		6	4	4	9	4						

— INDEX —

KEY BRICKS column annotated: "Nºs 9 -16 AS REQUIRED" / "AS REQUIRED"

BOILER PREFIX LETTERS STAMPED ON BOILER BACKPLATE AND BORDER OF ENGINE NUMBER PLATE THUS:-"AH" THE FIRST LETTER INDICATING BOILER CLASS.

Details of standard locomotive boilers in use on the GWR in 1945 taken from an internal publication about firebox brick arches.

joints, which were the weak points. Hundreds of steel and copper staybolts would hold the two together. The cab sides and roof were also riveted and fitted up by boilermakers, using jigs; the former were rarely removed during overhaul.

Safer acetylene generators were developed and in early 1932 they were installed in the coppersmith's shop along with other welding plant purchased from Quasi-Arc Co. Ltd of London. Now the work of fabricating locomotive firebox plates and the subsequent maintenance of copper fireboxes would be considerably reduced by using welded seams in place of riveted lap joints.

Welding copper fireboxes by oxyacetylene torch was, however, very uncomfortable and slow for the gangs of men trained to do it. Because copper is a very good conductor of heat, the insides of the fireboxes being worked on became very hot. Two men worked simultaneously for a short period and were then replaced by another two. At the same time, the copper plate around the seam had to be hammered to counteract the effects of shrinkage.

As a child in the mid-1940s, Mick Ponting noticed that his neighbour Mr Heath, who lived opposite him in Whitby Grove, arrived home early each day from the factory. He asked his father, a boilermaker, why this was and was told: 'Old Charlie' (Heath) welds copper fireboxes and through the Works' Committee it was agreed that these men should work shorter shifts.'

Doug Webb's father was a chargeman wire rope splicer and his older brother became an apprentice boilermaker. The rule was that the company would only pay to train the eldest son, so Doug was consigned to labouring work 'inside'. He started in the Boiler Shop alongside Rodbourne Road, like his brother, in 1936. The head boiler foreman at that time was Mr Eburne. Doug said: 'I started as a "water boy"; as the men worked on fireboxes and boiler barrels I poured water over the cutting tools to keep them cool.' Some of this was done from the inside, so Doug often had to work with a candle and a box of matches signed out from the stores.

Until the early 1930s, drilling out staybolts on boilers in for overhaul was slow and costly. Drill bits would go blunt and break regularly until French Wageor electric drills were brought in. They were very powerful and had a forward thrust driven by compressed air. Like similar equipment used for drilling and reaming holes once the stays were out, the new drills hung in suspension from above and could be operated by one man.

Working on steam boilers was very noisy. This was not only due to the hydraulic riveting guns used against the heavy plate barrel and box fabrications, but also because of the manual hammering of rivets that were inaccessible to the machine. 'Caulking' helped to make the joints watertight by burring the edges of the end plates: this was done with a hammer, meaning more noise. Any subsequent seepage would be quickly plugged by mineral build-up from hot water. Working on boiler shells relied on co-operation between men and they communicated by hand signals. The noise was such that it soon caused hearing problems, and it is well known locally that a Swindonian with indistinct speech and a hearing aid was likely to have been a boilerman, or a tinsmith, 'inside'.

As well as V Shop (boilermakers), Doug spent time in P1 Shop, where the completed boilers weighing anything up to 24 tons were taken to have their fittings attached. They were then tested with steam from a master boiler, thus avoiding the need to fire them up at this stage. A 2in to 3in layer of asbestos that had been soaked to form a paste was then added by the 'plasterers' while the boiler was still hot. This ensured it dried out thoroughly and quickly.

A lift powered by hydraulic water took the boilers on trolleys down to a tunnel under Rodbourne Road. They were then winched through to a second lift and brought up into P1 Shop. 'The irregular bursts of high-pressure steam soon played havoc with your nerves,' said Doug. The men could apply for other types of work in the vicinity and vacancies were displayed on the noticeboard. When Doug did manage to move he was based in the nearby 'Tube House' with chargeman Ernie Fisher and his assistant Jesse Pettifer. Here the fire tube ends were machined to fit the tube plates: one end was stretched and the other narrowed. 'I still found myself in the boiler shop a lot of the time but the balance (piecework bonus) was better here. Another thing I remember about the "Tube House" was the dust coming down when the rats ran along the pipes overhead: this made the woman that were here in the war feel uneasy until they got used to it.'

Doug saw one poor fellow, a 'hooker on', crushed by a boiler when the slings suspending it gave way: 'I can't think of his name but I remember he lived in Princes Street.

A large locomotive boiler and firebox being lifted off the gap riveting plant after attention in the AV Shop. *BRWR*

The mood in the shop was very subdued for the rest of the day.' I did some research and am fairly sure that Doug was referring to Charles Wheeler, aged fifty, who was due to marry an Eva Humphries in a few weeks. The date of the accident was given as 1 March 1940. After witnessing this and seeing a friend suffer a nasty injury when some scrap iron fell on his arm in the Rolling Mills, Doug decided he had had enough and, with his father's blessing, left the Works shortly afterwards.

Steam Hammers, Stamps and Spring Smiths

The heaviest forging work was carried out in the Steam Hammer Shop on the loco side with hammers from 30 cwt. up to 5 ton capacity. Heavy steel blooms weighing up to 4 tons were heated in coal-fired furnaces each equipped with waste-heat boilers. They were lifted in and out by hydraulic cranes to be forged down into such things as locomotive coupling rods, connecting rods and extension frames. When he thought they were getting near to size for machining, the smith would have them checked with calipers.

Smaller forgings were produced with steam hammers of between 10 and 20 cwt. These were sited in an area adjacent to the Steam Hammer Shop, known as F2 Shop. The range of work done here included fashioning large numbers of hand and machine tools. Both were commonly forged from 18% speed tungsten steels by the toolsmiths. Chainsmiths were employed on repairs and renewal of chains and slings and the fitting of special links, rings, hooks etc., to other lifting tackle. By the 1940s, some smithing operations were being done by acetylene and electric arc welding in this shop.

The 6-ton Brett steam-powered drop hammer in the centre of the Stamping Shop. This was the largest of five here in the 1940s. It had been used extensively in the manufacture of armour plating during the war. The ground shook when the hammer block, weighing several tons, fell on to the white-hot steel bloom. Even though the Stamp Shop was in the middle of the Locomotive Works, people living near Redcliffe Street corner knew when the 'big hammer' was working. *S.A.S. Smith courtesy of Ray Eggleton*

Forging large components was labour intensive, as can be seen here in one of the two Steam Hammer Shops. Peter Reade told me that: 'Large overhead pipes supplied each hammer with steam by way of a large cylinder. Inside the cylinder a piston was attached directly to the hammer block. The amount of steam entering the cylinder, and moving the piston up and down, was controlled by a lever on the side of the hammer frame. Another lever at the back of the machine was used to deliver very heavy blows or hold the hammer down on the work, under pressure.' *GWR*

In the Stamp Shop five steam-operated drop stamps of 30 cwt upwards were installed. The largest was the Brett 6-ton capacity drop hammer for stamping out the larger locomotive components. Drop hammers were like steam hammers except that their huge steel blocks, weighing several tons, were lifted up to a predetermined height and dropped on to white hot blooms. For lighter blows, the block height was reduced. The intricate shapes of the dies used for the stampings were produced on the die machine section using a Keller automatic die-sinking machine.

Locomotive parts that required stamping operations included crossheads, reversing, brake and rocking shafts, trailing horn blocks and eccentric rods. In the past, this work would have been forged, which by comparison was slow and less accurate.

On the east side of the smiths' group of shops, alongside the Gloucester line, was the SP (spring) Shop. This shop was completely remodelled in the early 1930s. All of the company's laminated, coil and volute springs were made here. The approximate annual output was 15,000 engine and tender laminated springs, 30,000 carriage and wagon laminated springs and 93,000 coil springs. The steel used was heated in gas-fired furnaces, which were all automatically temperature controlled by Electroflo pyrometers. It was then cut, shaped and heat treated by quenching in water or oil.

Rolling Mills

Another 'hot shop' was the Rolling Mills. Machinery within this large workshop at the north end of the Locomotive Works included a 10in and a 14in mill, each driven by a stationary steam engine built in the Works in the nineteenth century. A third mill had a set of 24in blooming rolls. Rolled sections of steel or iron were heated and repeatedly squeezed through the rolls until reduced to the desired cross section.

By the 1930s the production of wrought iron rail for which this shop was originally intended had been phased out. The railways of this country now used British 'standard' rail sections that came direct from the steel works. A lot of other work that could have been cast, drop forged, extruded and planed in this shop was also being done elsewhere. The workshop therefore was now only partially utilised and other trades working around the factory were using parts of it as a base.

Doug Webb worked in the Rolling Mills as a 'puller up' in the 1930s when Billy Davis was the foreman. Doug said that 'it was hell in there: very hot and, until you got used to it, very dangerous. I had no choice; as a labourer I could be moved from one type of work to another.' Puddling furnaces reduced wrought iron including scrap to a molten state to produce billets and blooms, and the 'puller up' moved it all into and out of the furnaces. Steel used in the Rolling Mill was either in the form of purchased billets or it was scrap axles from rolling stock that had been melted with pig iron in a blast furnace and

Part of the machine loading board displayed in the T Shop Foreman's Office. Besides showing at a glance all the work in hand, this information helped to ensure continuity of production and eliminate idle time between jobs. T Shop machined brass and copper parts, much of which had been cast in the non-ferrous foundry. *GWR*

recast. Large pieces of white hot metal were slid along on rollers and across the floor, which was lined with iron plates. For this reason, no outsider dared walk through the shop. The iron used was 'grade C', which was made from assorted scrap, and 'A' and 'B' iron, which came from selected scrap.

One or two 'shinglers' used large pairs of forceps to turn white-hot iron under a 70 cwt steam hammer. By the 1930s this was believed to be the only place in the country still using this method. Shinglers wore face guards, white smocks, leather aprons and iron boots while 'handling' the mass between hammer blows. A third man controlled the rate of the blows with a lever at the side. After the metal was compressed sufficiently it was slid across the floor by a 'rougher' or taken elsewhere on a truck by a 'coacher'. The former was then passed quickly through roughing rolls and back through finishing rolls, which squeezed it into a long bar. Setting the rolls and seeing that the drawn metal became the correct profile was the job of the 'roller', and he was the chargeman. The finished rolled iron or steel was either taken to the benches to be straightened or it was cut into sections, causing a spectacular show of flying sparks. All this had to be done before it cooled too much and hardened.

Here reconditioned pressure gauges are being tested against masters on Dewrance testing apparatus. This took place on the fitting section in T Shop. Vacuum, steam and water gauges could be checked for leaks and calibrated up to their working pressures. *BRWR*

Tool Room

Engineering tool rooms would normally make their own jigs, and perhaps gauges, but not usually drills, taps, dies, milling cutters and reamers. Their manufacture was more specialised, but the Swindon Works toolroom, otherwise known as 'O' Shop, proved they could make the lot by grinding the cutting surfaces of hardened blanks. This started during the war when the usual suppliers could not meet the demand and such things became difficult to buy in. The tool room was the showpiece of any engineering works. At Swindon there were 100 machine tools for such things as thread grinding, jig boring, gear cutting (or hobbing) and tool tipping, and 140 skilled tool and gauge makers.

For a visit of the Mechanical, Electrical and Carriage & Wagon Engineers in May 1953, some of the more impressive work carried out, was noted in the tour guidebook:

A 50-ton capacity overhead crane in what became known as the 'A Shop bosh bay'. It was built into the original part of the building just after 1900. These cranes travelled above the pit roads powered by Swindon-built electric motors. The hydraulic hoists, seen here, were also made at the Works. A Harold Smith was chargeman of the cranemen, the traversing table men and associated labourers in the 1950s. *BRWR*

A close-up view showing the cylindrical planing of the boiler side of a fabricated smokebox saddle in W Shop. *BRWR*

A high standard of workmanship with close tolerances for engine parts depends on accurate tools and gauges coupled with constant checking [calibration]. In 1929 a Lindner thread grinding machine of German origin, the first on any British railway, was installed mainly for the production of boiler stay bolts. The results were impressive and the cost of manufacture of the stay taps was less than half the price asked by the trade. Consequently the output of new and repaired boilers was considerably improved by their use. In 1930 a second similar machine was installed and all taps were then produced by this method. A fixture was developed in the shop to enable all types of dies and chasers with flat threads to be ground on the machine. A suitable hardening and tempering procedure was developed and special measuring instruments installed in the inspection section which included the following: 1) An optical machine called a Hilger projector, which could magnify profiles of threads, gauges etc., by fifty times, enabling an accurate check on the shape, to be made. 2) A horizontal OMT Omtimeter with which it was possible to measure accurately to 1/20th of a 'thou' [thousandth of an inch] on external and internal measurements. 3) A Sigma screw diameter and radius measuring machine which could measure diameters of threads to an accuracy of 1/10th of a 'thou' up to a diameter of 4in. 4) An Edgwick optical dividing head that could measure angles to an accuracy of three seconds of a degree, was used for checking jigs, gauges etc. 5) An Edgwick diamond hardness tester, used for checking the hardness of various items manufactured in the Tool Room.

6) A Spekker steeloscope [also made by Adam Hilger Ltd] was installed during the war to enable rapid checks of the special alloy steels which were used extensively in the manufacture of war work, and by its use it was possible to identify the alloys of steel used and to give approximately the percentage content of the alloying metals.

Early in the war, the Ministry of Supply arranged for the transfer of a Lindner jig boring machine to be installed in the Tool Room in a special enclosure. Later, two more thread grinding machines were brought in from the makers, the Coventry Gauge and Tool Company Ltd. One was a universal thread grinding machine for internal and external work with a capacity up to 8in diameter × 18in in length. The second was a Matrix machine to take similar diameter work up to 40in in length.

The mechanical clocks used in the Works were made by well-known makers but were repaired on site in a workshop next to Foreman Bill Holland's office, above 'O' Shop: the Works code name for its Tool Room. As was often the case, this shop's offices were above its tool store. Dave Ellis worked in O Shop in the 1950s and remembers Fred Gabb was 'chargeman clock repairs' and George Reason was the other senior person on that section.

R Shop Including 'The Scraggery'

R (fitting and machine) Shop came into use in 1864 and today it houses the Steam Museum. In the north-east corner of this shop was an area known to all as 'the scraggery'. Automatic machine tools in this area, particularly combination turret lathes, were often the apprentices' and other novices' first experience of machine work. The 'scraggery' also contained a number of 'hot press nut making machines' made by Etchells & Sons Ltd. The gangs of machines here continued to be belt driven until the 1950s.

Jack Fleetwood started 'inside' on 16 July 1937, when he reached fifteen years of age. As with all new starters, he presented himself at the office just inside the Bristol Street tunnel entrance and was taken to the office in the workshop where he would be working by another recently appointed junior. Until Jack could start his apprenticeship at around the time of his next birthday he spent the year in the R Shop 'scraggery'.

Here there were about thirty juniors working basic lathes under two chargemen. The automatic machinery was set up by turners acting as tool setters but the production was done by the youngsters, who also fed the lengths of bar into the lathes. The work undertaken included facing (scragging), chamfering and threading blank nuts on horizontal and vertical spindle machines. Making bolts by turning down the bar, selecting a slower speed and putting a thread on using a die head, was another job. Jack said:

Swindon [Works] got through a lot of bolts. It had been policy never to reuse them if they had come off locomotives and had been drilled to take splitpins. But assuming they were in good condition, they did start re-using them after the war. Nuts and bolts could be 'bought in' cheaply enough and that's what most engineering firms did. Not us though, because while the low paid were producing them, we could make them just as cheap.

Heavier work was also done in the R Shop proper, on milling, boring and slotting machines; there were planing machines with tables of 9 and 11ft lengths too. For instance, fabricated piston crossheads came to R Shop for a series of operations on machine tools such as a Butler's planer, a heavy-duty puncher slotter, a vertical boring machine and a Lang lathe with a 28in swing. Special jigs were used in conjunction with some of these operations to hold the work and guide the cutting tool acting upon it.

The operators would have to put on canvas gloves and pull all the swarf from the bottom of the machine and put it into bins. The labourers would take it all away and sweep up what went on to the floor. No machinist tool repairs were supposed to be done by the operators. The chargehand would call the maintenance gang and get the paperwork ready for them. The idea was that as little time as possible was lost so the piecework was not unduly disrupted. Mr (Arthur) Evans was the R Shop foreman in the 1930s and early '40s. Mr B.J. Hale, Mr (Ted) Gooderson and Mr (Syd) Nash were the chief machine shops' foremen during that time.

X (Points and Crossings) Shop

(See also Chapter 20)
The appropriately named X Shop, and the Chair Foundry that supplied it with track chairs, were two of the only workshops in the Works not involved in producing anything for the CME Dept. In the early days, rail had been drawn from blooms in the nearby Rolling Mills but was now brought in. George Hobbs was X Shop Foreman from the early 1920s until the mid-1940s.

As Impressive in Performance as in Appearance

BUTLER

PLANING FOUR MOTION BARS SIMULTANEOUSLY AT SWINDON WORKS, WESTERN REGION, BRITISH RAILWAYS

The BUTLER MACHINE TOOL Cº LTD
HALIFAX   Telephone: 61641   ENGLAND

This was an advertisement in the engineering press. It shows a Butler spiral-electric planer at Swindon. Four locomotive motion bars are held in locating jigs while the table moves past the cutting tools in a horizontal plane. *BRW*

It was not simply a case of building the layout to suit the existing trackwork. There were four standard types of GWR points and crossings' trackwork and each came in a range of sizes. For instance a 'turnout' could be left or right hand and the 'lead' line, which branched away from the main, could require any one of twenty-five different degrees of curvature. These were defined by the length of the radius, in chains. Similarly, 'cross-over' variations were determined by the measurements between the opposing forks or points where the lines diverged. All assemblies would be made to one of these specifications. Most of the workshop floor space was used, not for plant and equipment, but to lay out and check the assemblies before being disassembled for dispatch.

The company's rails came from various steelworks and by the 1930s they were using British 'standard' steel rail produced by the Bessemer or open hearth processes. X Shop received blank sections, which were machined into a bullhead profile. Both point and splice rails were machined on a 'Hulse' planer with a tilting table. From about 1950 flat-bottomed rail was used for new work. They machined it, shaped it and bolted it to tieplates and track chairs, which were themselves bolted to sleepers to form complete assemblies. Mr Hobbs gave a lecture to the Swindon Engineering Society about the work he oversaw in X Shop. For the purpose of explaining the manufacture and assembly of a typical layout, he chose a pair of 14ft switches with a crossing of 1 in 8 as an example. This, he said, would take six men about five days to produce.

Publicity from the late-1940s stated that: 'Considerable calculation and unusual precision were involved in work of this nature which provided some 3,500 new switches and crossings annually.' All drawings were sent down from the Chief Engineer's Department at Paddington and they were invoiced for the costs of the work.

Assembling the trackwork off site to make sure it would dovetail with the existing layout halved the time that the line was 'occupied' by permanent way gangs and disrupting train services. Although they worked from drawings, the assemblies were built to suit the measurements supplied for the existing layout. Cranes lifted the partially disassembled trackwork into general utility vans (GUVs) or bogie wagons code-named 'Gane A' at the Milk Bank loading dock next to the station. The choice of carrier depended on whether it was to be attached to the rear of a goods or passenger train. Some small cargoes were sent out by road transport if they were urgent.

X Shop also held a range of associated materials and fittings such as fish-plates and bolts, V points and switch tongues, and wing, guard and stock rails, any of which could be sent out to the permanent way maintenance gangs upon request. Special rails were also cut and machined in X Shop, for engine pit roads, sand drags and turntable races.

The new heavier flat-bottomed rail, which was taking over, required different materials to fix to the sleepers. New plant and equipment to cope with the changes being introduced in the 1950s necessitated a new shop. This was opened on the Works' site in 1958 but, for this purpose, it lasted only four years.

One of the heavy duty multi-head planing machines used in X Shop to machine two, three or four rail sections simultaneously. The table was supported by a pivot and could be tilted to give the desired angle for cutting the webs in the rail sides. *GWR*

3
Loco Side Workers

The Rank and File

More often than not, sons followed their fathers into these Works. They were maintaining an unbroken line of ancestors who were railway workers going back well before 1900. In 1954 the *BRW Magazine* reported the case of Chargeman (Jack) Steward, an erector in A Shop, whose grandfather came to Swindon in 1852, like so many at that time, from the industrial north of England. Grandfather's son worked 'inside' all his life and his grandson (Steward), along with his two sons, also in A Shop, would put in many more years yet.

Bert Harber's father, William, had come down from Wolverhampton to be apprenticed in the Locomotive Works in the days when the time served was seven years. When Bert started, his father was in AM Shop, his three brothers and three uncles were also employed in different parts of A Shop and a fourth uncle, Ralph Morkott, was boilermaking. Only Bert's father-in-law did not work 'inside', having left some years before.

The local historian Frederick Fuller said of the Works after the Great War: 'The old master-servant relationship had gone forever.' By then the men had organised themselves to an extent that the company, or the government, could no longer disregard. The men were joining trades' unions for two reasons: to show allegiance to the class struggle and/or to ensure some assistance should they find themselves before a court, on strike or 'on the sick'.

Labourers and newcomers to the workshops could join the National Union of Railwaymen, the Transport and General Workers' Union or the Amalgamated Engineering Union. Before the war, and after a period in post, tradesmen were eligible to join a union representing their craft, and that's what some shopmen chose to do. There were about thirty-two different types of crafts represented at railway shopmen's negotiations. Patternmakers, plumbers, foundrymen, coppersmiths, braziers, metalworkers and electricians all had their own societies within the federation of engineering and shipbuilding trades.

According to the Swindon and District directories of the 1930s, there were ten local branches of the AEU. Mr W. Hobson was the district secretary. Even during the height of the depression, they had an average of 3,000 members between them: the vast majority of whom must have worked 'inside' at the time. Each branch met regularly and most hired a room at a specific public house, licensed hotel or workingman's club. One branch met at the main Mechanics' Institute and another at the Labour Exchange.

On the loco side, fitters stripped and assembled components and made sure moving parts interacted correctly with each other. Turners operated lathe machines whereby the work rotates on its axis at the optimum cutting speed of the particular material, while the cutting tool moves in a horizontal plane only. They bored out the centre, cut internal and external threads and face-finished the surfaces of work pieces, which were usually cylindrical. The gangs of men who assembled the component parts of a steam locomotive were the fitter/erectors in the main. Other trades who worked in the erecting shops included machinists, bench fitters, welders, electricians, blacksmiths and boilermen.

Workers were divided up into gangs usually consisting of men of the same grade, such as labourers, skilled or semi-skilled. Sometimes they had assistants (apprentices) temporarily attached to the gang. Individual gangs were known to each other by the surname of their chargeman. I have heard it said that some chargemen were not very agreeable towards those of lower station, such as apprentices and labourers in their charge. Alan Lambourn said that some chargemen had been known to clip an apprentice round the ear. A good worker was sometimes overlooked when promotion was being considered because the foreman didn't want to lose a good man's output. Another unfair practice was that of promoting a union agitator in the certain knowledge that this would temper his militant ways.

Dinner break in R Shop in 1924. Although this was a machine shop, some fitters worked at benches. They would assemble machined parts, using hand tools where necessary. *R. Hatherall, courtesy of R. Clarke*

A transportable Swindon-made moulding machine for brake block moulds. The centre drum held Kidderminster facing sand. *BRWR*

Carriage men were moved across to the loco side during the war and were not always treated fairly by their hosts. Ted Randell didn't like it in A Shop, he told me:

> I was started on Chargeman Berry's 'light repairs' and soon found that many of the loco erectors would not pass on the little tips that made the job easier. For instance, when climbing into the side tanks to check that the [water level] float wasn't sticking, you had to put a block of wood in first. This was to stand on when hauling oneself out of the small hole. Newcomers were left to look foolish when they had to call out for assistance. The erecting shops' foreman Pat O'keefe had a 'downer' on the 'carriage men' too, and was always finding fault. Sometimes Chief Foreman Millard had to get involved but, despite his reputation, he was more sympathetic towards us. When we went back to the carriage side in about 1949, Mr Millard said he would like to have kept some of us and sent some of his own men instead.
>
> Mind you the engine erectors could be merciless to their own too. Ted Bathe, known as 'Sacko', kept an umbrella for anyone who had was found to have made a mistake in the course of their work. To cheers from onlookers, he would open it over the head of the victim. This ritual was inspired by the Chief of Nigeria's visit to the Works in 1937. One of his entourage held a large gold umbrella over the Chief at all times to ward off evil spirits. A common mistake worthy of the umbrella was letting a wheelset roll out onto the traverser road while a locomotive was being 'wheeled'. Foreman Millard did not discourage this type of larking about: perhaps because it deterred slack working practice.

The carriage & wagon and the locomotive sides of the Works were both working for the same industry and were on the same site (with most other companies they were separate). In almost all other aspects, they were independent of each other. The sense of belonging and camaraderie seems to have been lacking towards those on the other side of the tracks. Carpenters, electricians and one or two other trades had workshops on both sides but they were not encouraged to apply for vacancies on the opposite side. Not only was this division acknowledged and accepted 'inside' but, before the war in particular, the two communities existed apart outside too.

Ivor Wilkins arrived in E Shop (electrical maintenance) in late 1954 after a showdown with Mr Proudler in the loco staff office. He had requested a transfer from 5 Shop (electric train lighting) on the carriage side. Ivor was not the first to tell me that the people in the staff offices were unhelpful and obstructive. Presumably they resented spending time filling one vacancy and creating another. However, being short-staffed in the 1950s, the authorities could not afford to call the bluff of men who threatened to leave and this is what Ivor and others did.

Apprentices

Many boys in the town wanted to become engine drivers and their fathers would point out that they would not like the shift work. There were only limited opportunities to work on the footplate in any case. Most of those young men would then settle for the idea of working in the factory, hoping that they would be eligible for what they thought was the more glamorous loco side. In the 1950s some boys were more interested in aircraft than trains and would apply first to Vickers-Armstrongs, where there was an apprentice training school.

The majority of the men in the shops were what was known as journeymen: they had successfully completed a recognised apprenticeship in one of the engineering or building trades. Journeymen (of French origin meaning skilled men paid by the day) or tradesmen who built locomotives could be boilersmiths, coppersmiths, blacksmiths and tinsmiths, among others. In the Locomotive Works most were, however, trained in what was called

Apprentice Mike Farrell is producing firebox crown staybolts in the 1940s. He is using a Ward No. 7 combination turret lathe in R Shop. *BRWR*

'fitting, turning and locomotive erecting'. When these young men were asked what trade they were learning 'inside' the accent was on the 'erecting', as that set them apart from the less glamorous carriage fitter and turner.

Fitting, turning and erecting, still sometimes called 'engine fitting and turning' in the 1930s, was a primary trade on the loco side along with patternmaking, just as coach building and finishing was on the carriage side. The pay scales for these primary trades were, however, no better than some other trades such as bricklayers, boilersmiths, carpenters and tinsmiths.

In the College prospectus for 1945 it states that there were 160 Works' apprenticeships of various kinds given at the Works, all spanning a full five years. Until national training schemes were set up in the late 1920s and '30s, the time 'served' would be six or seven years depending on the trade. I have heard it said that when a boy was born his name could be registered at the Works for an apprenticeship place when the time came. I can't see how this would have benefitted the company and therefore I suspect it is a myth. Another myth is that apprenticeships always started on the sixteenth birthday. Surviving documents show that of the thirty-four applicants taken on to learn the craft of the coppersmith between April 1934 and the start of the war, only fourteen commenced the day they reached sixteen years.

First sons of men employed 'inside' often got 'free passage', meaning no training costs were sought by the employer. However, the company did not intend to be 'out of pocket' over it, first son or not. Many ex-apprentices have told me that they did get their money's worth out of the trainees. Alan Lambourn said: 'Despite the expectation of being there to learn, we were nevertheless expected to produce. This, together with the low wages, made us cheap labour.' The memorandum of regulations under which apprentices were employed made sober reading. The regulation 'Notice to leave the Company's service will be given on completion of apprenticeship,' was more likely to be enforced for locomotive than for carriage apprentices coming out of their time.

Jack Fleetwood's father was classed as semi-skilled and therefore could only manage to secure a semi-skilled position for his boy. He could not afford to pay for a premium apprenticeship, even though the repayments, totalling £110, were spread over the whole term. Nor could he afford to keep him while Jack repaid the costs of learning a trade. Because of working 'inside' himself, on internal transport, Mr Fleetwood senior was given a choice of trade for Jack when he reached sixteen years of age. He could choose from rough painting of wagons and buildings, moulding or machining:

Father enquired as to which work paid the most and was told that the moulder got an extra shilling a week on the rate. Therefore I started my apprenticeship in the Foundry as a moulder. I was allocated to Georgie White's gang doing simple repetition work. George was the coremakers' chargeman in the Iron Foundry at this time [1938].

Foremen

Photographs of the workers coming and going from the Works were more popular before the 1930s, a time when the Works' foremen wore bowler hats. That is, therefore, how they are remembered nowadays. But by the 1940s, the younger foremen especially were more likely to be seen in the more fashionable trilby. Either was sufficient to distinguish them from the men under them in their flat caps.

At Swindon, foremen were in charge of a workshop or of one type of trade as set out below. Promoted staff had usually been chosen from within the shop: the usual route was to chargeman, then piecework inspector, then foreman. Peter Chalk got the impression that belonging to organisations such as the Plymouth Brethren or the Freemasons was an advantage when being considered for promotion. Workshop foreman at Swindon would be responsible for anywhere between twenty and 100 men, occasionally more, and in areas with higher concentrations of men there would be more than one foreman. The more men under his control the higher a foreman's status was considered to be.

Swindon's massive A Shop was really four shops under one roof. Here there were four chief foremen on the payroll: one for each of the main sections: erecting, machines, boilers and wheels. All these areas overlapped with similar work being done in other locomotive workshops, so each foreman's jurisdiction was not confined to this one building. It sounds a bit 'top heavy' but it should be remembered that between them these men supervised around 1,500 men who were working with the company's most valuable assets.

Furthermore, to co-ordinate each of the Erecting Shops' main sections there was an assistant chief and a chief foreman in overall charge. Stan Millard succeeded Mr Plaister as 'chief A and B Erecting Shops' foreman' in 1934 when he was only in his thirties. He remained in that post until he died, in office, in 1954. His funeral service was held at the Wesleyan chapel in Fleet Street, possibly the last time this building was used for this purpose.

Mr (Ernie) Simpkins, from G Shop, succeeded Mr (Stan) Millard and Mr (Jim) Owen, another long-serving A Shop foreman, remained as assistant chief foreman. Mr Owen had been, at some time, president of the Foreman's Association and retired in the early 1960s. Section foremen in the AE Shop in the mid- to late-1950s were Mr (Dennis) Cole, Mr G Gardiner, Mr (Arthur) Graham, Mr (Pat) Keefe and Mr (Sid) Maslin. The last two mentioned worked a fortnight 'about' on nights, said Jim Lowe.

On the carriage side there were chief foremen for bodymakers, finishers, fitters, painters, trimmers, wagon builders and for the saw mill workers. The most senior foremen had, in earlier times, been referred to as superintendents but by the 1930s this title was used more for the senior divisional and outdoor engineers. When the term 'chief' was used by the men, they were likely to be referring to the chief mechanical engineer.

When he was works' manager, Mr Collett brought a fitter in as chief foreman to take charge of the boiler shops. Normally, of course, someone from within their own ranks would be promoted, so this was a controversial decision. The reason for this change of policy was said to

Drilling, tapping, spot facing and milling cylinders and smokebox saddles were all carried out on a purpose-built machine tool supplied by Kendall & Gent Ltd of Gorton. *BRWR*

Riveting the side flanges on a loco axlebox, which is loaded into a turnover fixture. AM Shop, 1951. *BRWR*

The GWR standard locomotive headlamp, which until 1937 was painted red. One or two of these lamps were carried on the front of every engine in various positions. This indicated the headcode applicable to the type of train that was being worked. The exception was the royal train, which carried a lamp in all four positions. 'The style of these and other train lamps, which were made in the sheet metal workers' shop, was simplified over the years to make them cheaper to produce. Outside firms started to undercut the Works on cost. We managed to stay competitive but were constantly being told we may lose the order,' said Colin Bown. The restricted supply of raw materials and labour in wartime prompted an appeal in the *GWR Magazine*. The company asked for more care to be taken with the handling of engine tools and lamps. They said: 'Damaged lamps are now received in Swindon Works at the rate of 200 per week, of which a number are scrapped as being beyond repair.' *Author*

be 'to bring precision into boilermaking'. In 1914 or thereabouts when this situation came about, the resentment felt by the men towards their new boss was of little concern to management. When the foreman in question retired in 1937, Mr Collett was still in a position to decide who would replace him. Perhaps he sensed that attitudes had changed in the intervening period. Certainly a more even-handed approach was taken over grievances and work practices. The possibility too, that morale might affect production would no longer be ignored. The replacement this time was a boiler man by trade.

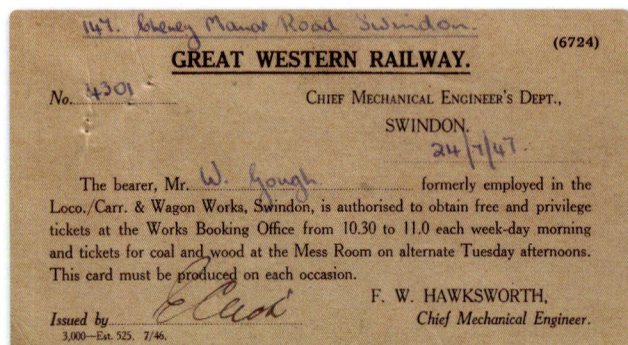

Tinsmiths outside their workshop during their dinner break, about 1950. From left to right, back row: Desmond Iles, Bob Turner, Alan Titcombe, Les King, Alan Gunter, Les Osbourne and Colin Bown. Front row: Gordon Staples, Bert Kewell, Roy Selwood and Vic Spackman. *C. Bown*

Before the war the fear of being unemployed was usually enough to keep the men in check. For occasional lapses, the foreman's word could get a worker dismissed. Not all foremen ruled by fear, but on the other hand, if they became too familiar with their men they risked being considered a 'soft touch' and could lose the respect that came with authority. Knowing the power he had over his men, a bit of restraint on the part of the foreman would work just as well. Peter Reade told me of an incident that happened to him soon after he started 'inside' in 1939:

It was a crime to be caught sitting down and it could get you instant dismissal. I recall one occasion when I was leaning against the side of a [steam] hammer and I felt a tap on my shoulder. I turned round, and Mr Parker was stood there: 'Are you tired sonny?' he asked. 'No Mr Parker,' I replied; 'Are you ill sonny?' 'No Mr Parker.' 'Well just stand up straight when I walk through the shop,' he said, and then left. The blacksmith told me I was lucky not to have been sent home for a couple of days. I kept my eyes peeled after that I can tell you.

Herbert Parker lived in Springfield Road. He retired shortly after the incident above, having been a foreman for thirty-two years.

Retired staff enjoyed some privileges in the 1930s and '40s. This was when the wages grade workers did not have to pay in to a Works' pension. Whether such concessions were negotiated nationally or locally, I do not know. William Gough had been a chargeman vertical retort stoker in the Great Western Gas Works and presumably retired just before the date shown. Despite years of heavy and dirty work, Mr Gough was able to use this card for many years to come. The company records would have Mr Gough listed by name, former occupation and check number, and these are written on the reverse of the card. *Author's collection*

147. Okus Manor Road Swindon.

GREAT WESTERN RAILWAY. (6724)

No. 4301

CHIEF MECHANICAL ENGINEER'S DEPT.,
SWINDON.
24/7/47.

The bearer, Mr. W. Gough formerly employed in the Loco./Carr. & Wagon Works, Swindon, is authorised to obtain free and privilege tickets at the Works Booking Office from 10.30 to 11.0 each week-day morning and tickets for coal and wood at the Mess Room on alternate Tuesday afternoons. This card must be produced on each occasion.

Issued by..........

3,000—Est. 525. 7/46.

F. W. HAWKSWORTH,
Chief Mechanical Engineer.

Foremen, like inspectors and chargemen, all had their own associations. The Inspectors' Association held their meetings at the Staff Association Club in Bridge St. Mr G. Ellison was their secretary and, in 1949, Mr W.J. Comley took over. Committee members would address their meetings and often members or guests were invited to talk on industrial and related topics. AOB (any other business) might well spark debate about inter-shop relations or perhaps their role within the workshop staff structure. An annual Christmas dinner and summer outing was a tradition among these various groups of railwaymen.

Working Conditions

Despite the state of the economy in the 1930s and the uncertainty of secure employment, improvements for the men were successfully negotiated. The previous fifty-four-hour, six-day week was brought down to forty-seven or forty-eight hours by starting at 8am instead of 6am. It was then worked over no more than six turns. There were no proper (tea) breaks when Jack Fleetwood first started 'inside', although this meant that, for those who could get away with it, no time was deducted while consuming some refreshment. Like many others, Jack took in a tea can, some sugar and a tin of condensed milk, and took his chances. He told me:

> Some foremen were sympathetic: if Taffy Thomas, the foreman in the Iron Foundry, came across anyone having a drink or a crafty draw, he usually said 'that's alright lads', as he lit his own pipe. Then you had the situation of the foundry foreman nervously looking out for the loco works' manager while the rest of us still had to watch our backs for the junior foreman Charlie Webb. Mr Webb was a 'works man' and did not negotiate over the rules.
>
> Even if you were working and you sensed someone approaching, you kept your head down. If Taffy's shiny shoes came into view, you often found a sweet on the bench after he had gone. Only if people from Paddington were being escorted around did the CME himself appear. Labourers were given some overtime to get the shop tidy for VIPs. I occasionally spotted Mr Hawksworth when he was in charge but I never saw the reclusive Mr Collett. Mr Cook, the loco works' manager, came through sometimes and always spoke: he was more down to earth.

Before the war the older men in the workshops, doing skilled work, had become classed as semi-skilled. This was because when they were young there was no formal training. However, if their work was particularly heavy, noisy or hot, they might be still paid skilled men's rates. This avoided the situation whereby younger, less experienced men, received more money than the older hands, working alongside them. The main reason for the concession though was to try to retain men to work in the harsh conditions.

A 'grade 1' workshop man would expect to reach the top of his pay scale. In industrial towns such as Swindon that meant he was getting 46 shillings a week in the 1930s. The equivalent rate was slightly lower in smaller towns and rural areas, and slightly higher in London. On top of this he got the war wage bonus or cost-of-living allowance. This was introduced in 1915 to offset the effects of inflation on lower-paid railway workers. It was funded by the government, who reviewed it twice yearly and adjusted it if necessary. In the mid- to late-1930s, the war wage amounted to 16 shillings and 6 pence a week. All workshop grades received the same except apprentices: they received a fractional amount as they were not yet breadwinners.

Then there was the fortnightly piecework bonus, which was a percentage of the flat rate. The amount received depended on the productivity, averaged out over the week, between all the gangs on a section within the workshop. A good average weekly balance, for a 'factory' man, was around 35%. Piecework payments went up during the war and were raised further in the 1950s when unions gained more power.

Nights at Swindon were worked on a rota. There was a small group of workshops that had a permanent night shift: others never had more work than could be done by their day shift. Of course, in some shops the scale and urgency of the work fluctuated. A few men preferred nights, in which case they could take on extra from those who disliked them. When Jack became junior foreman in the Brass Foundry, he continued to give away his nights and was told his enhanced pay included a night allowance, so he had to do his share. He told me:

> During the war, when you went in at night there was often a freight train stopped in the 'up loop' at Rodbourne Lane: usually with a '2800' class locomotive simmering at the front. When you came out in the morning it was often still there! Even with the odd spell of nights, the factory men did not envy the shifts worked by the men at the running sheds and on the footplate. The first thing you did when you arrived at night was to put your sandwiches in a tin box to stop the rats getting them. Because of the reduced light in wartime, we would sprinkle white powder onto newly cast surfaces to identify rough spots, and until an alternative was found, we used household flour to which the rodents were attracted.

War changed everything and the rigid observance of the rules by foremen were generally relaxed during the 1940s. Walter Gleed ran a bakers' business in Lydiard Millicent: a village 5 miles distant. Every Friday morning he was allowed to bring his green van into the Fire Station Yard in Bristol Street and supply the workers with his renowned lardy cake. This arrangement was probably a concession due to the works' own lack of facilities and the longer working days.

Permanent hand washing facilities like these were installed in the larger workshops as required by Factory and Workshop Acts. Access to clean and dry towels could not, in practice, be guaranteed, and some men brought in their own. This photo is believed to have been taken inside the Patternmakers' Shop. *Swindon Society collection*

Ray Eggleton in the Coppersmiths' Shop remembers being able to order the cake for the first dinnertime after being paid. 'This started sometime in the 1940s, probably just after the war,' he said. A labourer was sent over to pay for the order and return with a box full on a sacktruck. No doubt the service was available to other shops and departments but, with the shortage of ingredients, demand may well have outstripped supply.

One of the early concessions gained through the Joint Works' Committee was that men in the 'hot shops' (areas where iron and steel was worked when hot) could have access to cold drinks. The dehydration from sweating caused fatigue, they argued, and affected production. A solution was made from oatmeal, which was thought to reduce sweating. Jack said: 'It seemed to be beyond the wit of man to stop the oatmeal being spilt and attracting rodents, so this idea was short-lived.'

With some types of welding work the fumes made men feel ill and fatigued. Mick Ponting, who started 'inside' in 1948 (apprentice coppersmith), remembers that at that time men who welded galvanised iron, such as the ends of carriage body frames, were entitled to a pint of milk each day. Mick never actually saw anyone have the milk, which was thought to stop the nausea caused by the fumes before proper facemasks were available.

GWR land and premises came within the Rats and Mice Act of 1919, and if infested, the company was required to take all necessary steps to exterminate the pests. Swindon men have told me that the only steps taken were a reliance on cats, before poison was used in the 1950s. There were, for many years, two cats in the Iron Foundry but they had always refused to stay in the Brass Foundry, so Jack and his mates caught rats in humane traps. They then tried to gas them but this was a slow process as they seemed to like coal gas and would push their noses up the pipe. The company handbook offered no suggestion as to methods of eradication, only that 'if necessary the CME Dept should seek the assistance of the divisional engineer.'

A preparation marketed as Rozalex was made available to men and women in the workshops. They applied it at the start of the shift to protect against skin irritation and rashes caused by oil, grease, sand, detergent, glue and turpentine etc. To obtain hot water for washing hands and face, some men said they had to drop a piece of hot metal into a bucket of water. The hard soap that was issued monthly from the shop stores gave some men rashes that they could never get rid of. It was made in the Oil Works from China clay and cheap detergent, said 'sparky' Ivor Wilkins.

Taking snuff or chewing tobacco was very popular in the workshops. The old boys who took snuff turned their white moustaches brown. Until the end of 1939, smoking was

This photo gives a sense of the working conditions in the Rolling Mills. The description written on the back of the print states 'rough rolling a gothic section from a 70lb steel billet in a three-high 14in mill at 1,000 degrees centigrade'. *BRWR*

strictly prohibited as a fire precaution. As the war progressed this rule was relaxed in stages in most parts of the Works.

I asked Vic Tucker what the AM Shop was like to work in during the war. His first thoughts were: 'The blackout was in place day and night, so it was not only half dark during the day, it could get hot too. If somebody had been allowed time to go round and open the windows and roof lights and close them at night it would have solved the problem. It wasn't until towards the end of the war that the blackout precautions were removed.'

During the war workers received extra clothing coupons if their work was particularly dirty. The office boys who visited the various carriage repair shops thought they should get the same consideration, as they were required to wear smart cloths that soon got dirty. They elected Harry Bartlett, one of their own, to go and put their case to Mr Richens, the staff assistant to the C&W Works' manager. He listened to what Harry had to say and then told him to get out. Walter Sheppard, a clerk in 18 Shop Office, heard about what was taken to be a

rejection and took up the case. Walter was secretary of the local branch of the Railway Clerks' Association. From 1944 the office boys got extra clothing coupons, and this lasted until the end of rationing.

You were not supposed to wander away from where you worked even in the dinner break. Jack Fleetwood remembered being questioned as to his business outside his workshop when he was an apprentice: 'It was the carriage & wagon works' manager, Mr Evans, who stopped me: what was he doing over "the loco side anyway?"' said Jack indignantly. After the war, a lot of rules that had been strictly enforced for years were starting to be disregarded.

I never heard the word 'morale' mentioned by workers reminiscing about the one-industry town. Although some 'factory' men did say they daydreamed about working in more pleasant surroundings. Ron Culling said one of his mates in R Shop was fond of saying that his next job was going to be a 'railtapper's harker' whenever work was getting him down.

The Factory Acts

The Factory and Workshop Act of 1901 was a parliamentary enactment designed to ensure that manufacturing could be achieved without risk to health and without the exploitation of women and young persons under the age of eighteen. A factory was defined, for the purposes of the Act, as 'any workshop where power other than just manual labour was in use'. A workshop was defined as 'a place where only manual labour was exercised by way of trade or for other purposes of gain': the latter applied more to the sheds and warehouses of the Chief Goods Managers' Dept. The whole of the company's workshops, whether they belonged to the (Civil) Engineers', the Signal Dept or the CME Dept, were thus classified as factories or workshops, even if only one person was employed in them.

Works' managers and divisional superintendents in overall charge of workshop personnel were responsible for seeing that measures were taken to prevent personal injury to their workers. A current rule book and general appendix giving clear safety instructions was issued to each employee, and an abstract of the Factory and Workshop Act, The Workman's Compensation Act and the Notice of Accident Act 1906 were displayed in each premises. District factory inspectors had, on behalf of the Home Office, full powers to examine places of work that came under the Act at any time and see that safety and health provisions were being implemented.

Company officials were also required to make regular inspections to ensure machinery and appliances were maintained in a safe condition and used only for their intended purpose. Men suffering from a disability were not to be employed in positions they could not cope with because of the potential for accidents or strain injuries. Ambulance (first aid) cabinets were supplied to all depots and workshops and they were to be inspected regularly and stocked by a competent person. All of the workforce were encouraged to learn first aid and were supplied with basic instruction booklets (see Chapter 11).

The Act required that a supply of clean water for drinking and washing was laid on where twenty-five or more men were employed. In reality, many men in the shops spoke of limited access to fresh water during the shift, particularly before the war, unless they were working with furnaces and forges. Peter Reade remembers being given a drink designed to stop sweating when he first went into the smiths' shop in 1939, but soon after, he said: 'That was stopped. Yes we had access to drinking water but as a hammer driver I only felt the need of it in hot weather.'

Every factory floor on the Great Western that employed young persons under the age of sixteen had to obtain a certificate of fitness. The 'loco' and 'carriage works' managers' would hire a certifying surgeon who would inspect the site and, if acceptable, issue the certificate. For this, certain standards regarding temperature, ventilation, sanitation and illumination had to be met. Since 1939 a programme of changing from gas to electric lighting had been undertaken to comply with the Factory and Workshop Act. All the company's electric lighting installation and maintenance had been the responsibility of the CME since 1924.

The conditions at the Works, in many cases, appear to have fallen short of the requirements of the Act, as many production areas were off limits to boys under sixteen years of age. They did work in some of the carriage shops: the large 15 (fitting and machine) Shop was one. Conditions to keep the men healthy and safe were not so clearly defined, concentrating more on the procedures once accidents had occurred. For instance, every accident that resulted in an absence from work of three days or more was to be recorded in the general register and notice sent to the district inspector of factories.

The department would have to provide records of regular treatment to seal walls, floors and ceilings and of lime washing. For 3d (3 old pence) the men could take a brush and a bucket of whitewash from the medical centre and treat walls at home: 'It made the dark corners lighter if nothing else', said Jack Fleetwood. 'At work the ventilators in our shop were, for the majority of the war, covered with blackout sheets, making conditions very unpleasant at times. This was not picked up by any factory inspector.'

4

Overhauling Steam Locomotives

Taking a locomotive out of traffic and through the Works was very expensive, even though the stock numbers took account of a realistic percentage being 'out of traffic' at any one time. It was Paddington, as opposed to Swindon 'control', who also decided which engines would be overhauled, permanently withdrawn or stored. They took into account regional requirements, the age of the engine and the mechanical state upon inspection prior to overhaul. The GWR locomotive stock was comparatively efficient and well managed but, by the 1950s, they were relying on many elderly passenger locomotives for their express services. Consequently, the amount of time they spent in the Works or 'stopped' at depots increased and availability decreased.

Shopping Proposals

'Control' at Paddington managed the locomotive 'tickler card' system, with information sent in from the operating divisions. These cards ensured that each loco came forward in turn, for shopping, in accordance with its 'tentative date'. It was the business of the engine history clerks at divisional offices, to know the tentative date of each locomotive in their division. This was the date at which it could no longer be reliably maintained by periodical examinations and running repairs at its home depot. Beyond it, the loco was considered to be due for factory attention. Other factors considered were its age, type and time/mileage

since last visit. A report on the mechanical condition, known as a 'shopping proposal' was now carried out by the running shed inspector. This was submitted to shopping control. They informed the Chief Mechanical Engineer's Office, Swindon, who decided whether proposals could be accommodated at the current rate.

Reception and Factory Preparation

The following is an account of the way steam locomotives passed through the AE Shop in the 1950s. It is based on information from several former locomotive erectors who worked there, Jim Lowe in particular.

Locomotives coming into this Works for attention would arrive at the east or London end of the Loco Works. This was recorded as entering the factory pool on the engine history. They usually arrived at Swindon overnight and, if necessary were turned while in steam to face London before being parked on the reception sidings near the CME offices.

The layout of A Shop and associated buildings as it was, prior to the reorganisation for building the first main-line diesels.

No. 4901 *Adderley Hall* in the Reception Shed apparently being prepared for the Erecting Shop. This engine is recorded as having been withdrawn two months before this picture was taken, in September 1960. These dates were known to be inaccurate in some cases, as seems to be the case here. Jim Lowe told me that these early withdrawals sometimes made it into the Works before a decision was made as to their future. *R. Grainger*

The locomotives left here would then be moved about by Works pilot engines. There was no need to remove the con rods at this stage, or disconnect the valve spindles, as for towing 'dead' engines on the main line. The reversing gear would have to be placed in mid-gear before it was moved though. All the engine preparation in and out of the Works came under the control of foreman Stan Morris: when he retired in about 1958, his replacement was a Mr Tucker from the progress/work study section.

The purpose-built Reception Shed, sited between A Shop and the main line, came into use in 1944. It was known by the men as 'the BSE' as these were its code letters. The two through roads had pits so that incoming locomotives could have their smokeboxes cleared, fires and brick arches dropped and water drained from their boilers and tanks or tenders. The latter were now detached, to be dealt with separately in B Shed. The coal was taken out and ash was put into hoppers and dropped into wagons: a 2-ton overhead crane being provided for this and for the handling of coal. The Running Department encouraged depots to send locomotives in with a minimum of coal. That's how they would be returned as coal was expensive.

Until 1956 some smaller engines as well as tenders were dealt with in the original erecting shop known as B Shed.

They would be parked on one of the two roads east of the Telephone Exchange until taken inside. Travelling cranes were also repaired in B Shop and they were parked on the curve of the Gloucester branch. All other locomotives for planned overhaul were taken into the AE Shop. From 1956 when the rail car diesel repair section was set up, B Shop had to stop taking steam locomotives to make room.

The names of the repair classifications were changed after nationalisation. The three types of overhauls were now called 'general', 'heavy' and 'intermediate'. Erecting Shop foreman Sid Abrams would chalk the type of classified repair or overhaul to be undertaken on the side of each locomotive while it was in the Reception Shed. It was claimed that an average of ten engines per week were overhauled at Swindon in the late 1940s. The annual figure for 1956 recorded that 368 engines had 'heavy' or 'general' overhauls, 255 had 'intermediate' repairs and twenty-six had 'casual' repairs. These figures were significantly lower than those of 1936. This was due to strictly applying the policy of carrying out all 'light' or 'running' repairs at the principal running shed in each division, while Swindon, or another works, did all the major repairs.

Works' Pilots: The Factory Link

Engines and stock could not be shunted around the Works, without buffers in place. Therefore 'dead' tender engines had to be coupled to pilot engines, at the rear or cab end, and propelled for all movements eastward. Moving locomotives and tenders in and out of the Erecting Shops required three pilot turns and three sets of enginemen.

One pilot turn involved hauling locomotives from the reception sidings to the reception shed. Another dealt with small 0-6-0 tender engines, tank engines and all tender movements in and out of B Shed. A third pilot was required to move engines that had been shunted through BSE Shed on to the erecting shops' traversers and to take ex-Works' engines away. The B Shop pilot had other duties too: during quiet periods it took wagons of sand and supplies to and from the nearby foundries. It also took track chairs from the Chair Foundry and turnings from R Shop via the short traversing table between the Iron Foundry and B Shed.

Four or five withdrawn but not yet condemned tank engines were kept for Works' pilot duties until their boiler certificate ran out. Even the odd rebuilt 'Dean' 0-6-0 tank engine was used until the early 1950s. The V Shop boiler inspector, Brian Carter, checked the continued worthiness of these engines after boiler washouts. They could be seen stabled on the turntable roads with their shunters' trucks when not required, as they and their crews were allocated to the Works and not the Running Shed. The accompanying shunters' truck carried tools such as shunting poles, brake sticks, jacks, packing and a long rerailing tool: all would have been made 'inside'. With continual engine movement in and out of A and B Shops, the occasional derailments had to be dealt with immediately.

According to *Railway Magazine* for December 1951, a visitor to Swindon Works noted ex Barry Rly 0-6-2 tank Nos 258, 269, 272 and 0-6-0 No. 1709 still working more than a year after withdrawal. Supplementing the Works' pilot engine stock with tanks acquired from the absorbed railways of South Wales had been the policy for some years. The last of these engines came to Swindon after withdrawal and they were used around the Works until 1957. After that the Western Region used GWR shunting engines displaced by new diesel equivalents.

No. 5988 *Bostock Hall* awaiting the stripping gang in the early 1960s. *R. Grainger*

The footplatemen had a large corrugated shed by the turntable, which they shared with others who worked at the Reception Shed. Only if one of them were off sick did the Running Shed supply a driver or fireman. Pay was, however, collected with their colleagues round at the shed. Some A and B Shop pilot drivers were men who had been demoted for a misdemeanour elsewhere on the GWR. Their hours would now be just Monday to Friday or Saturday morning. Unlike all other footplate work, there were no nights or Sunday work here to make their earnings up to a living wage, hence the reason it was used as a punishment and a deterrent to others. Other drivers may have been taken off main-line work for health reasons, usually deteriorating eyesight (green card men). The firemen were usually new starters as the factory link was the lowest of the enginemen's links.

Light Repairs

Chargeman Harold Rayer's gang dealt with 'casual' or 'light' repairs. The use of the word 'light', in this case was a bit misleading. If the work required could not be carried out at the engine's home depot or at the principal depot of its operating division, then it was unlikely to be 'light'. The need for unscheduled Works' attention might be due to collision, working parts failing (including a hot axlebox) or occasionally misuse.

Two Wolverhampton-based 'Kings' came into Rayer's section in 1956 with damaged fireboxes. They had both been fitted with Alfloc water treatment equipment, which should by this date not have been causing problems. Perhaps the wrong concentration was used or the boilers were filled with soft water at another running shed. Washing out their boilers, it was claimed, had not been neglected (the water treatment reduced the need for this to about once a month). Nevertheless, it was found that in each case a large patch of sludge had caused the inner fireboxes to bulge. Jim Lowe said:

The stays would have to come out and the affected plates, flattened. It is likely that these defects were below the footplating so the boilers would have to come out. This would explain why they came to the Swindon. These situations usually led to a heated discussion between head office [Paddington] and the shedmaster at the home depot.

Two 'Manor' class engines, 7809 and 7815, have been stripped down leaving only the frames, the cabsides and the combined cylinder block and smokebox saddles. 23 April 1963. *R. Grainger*

There were two sections for the light repairs (see diagram): the one at the back of A Shop was for work where the boiler or wheels needed to come out. Regardless of whether the boiler needed attention, the opportunity was taken by the Boiler Shop inspector to check it. Engines for light repairs outside the overhaul circuit were cleaned (with white spirit and oil) only after the work was completed so it could be dirty work. These engines would still require a trial run afterwards.

Engine Progress

After alterations to the layout of the AE shop extension and BE Shop, a 'sectionalised flow system' of overhaul was begun in 1934. It became better known as the 'repair circuit'. The work of stripping and rebuilding during major overhauls was now divided up into four stages with gangs of men permanently employed on one stage.

There was always a tendency to be pessimistic about potential changes to working practices on the shop floor. Hugh Freebury, who worked there in the run up to the changeover, said that there was strong opposition to the repair circuit. Loco erectors thought that they, or their workmates, would be 'let go' if time was saved. However, the possibility of higher piecework payments tempered the men's resistance somewhat. I haven't seen any information about how much less time locomotives then spent under repair but at Caerphilly, where a similar system was introduced, the saving was significant.

By now the GWR fleet was made up of a smaller range of locomotive types with many interchangeable parts. These parts were now being machined quicker using automatic machine tools, jigs and fixtures, although engines brought in for repair still had to have their worn working parts machined and replaced to suit. By the mid-1930s the CME Department was keeping pace with the ever-increasing demands of the Traffic Department.

The massive A Shop was divided up into AW wheel section, AM machines, AV boilers and AE erecting bays. At the eastern end of the building was the engine test plant. When this was being used, the wooden-bodied No. 4 dynamometer car would usually be positioned alongside to provide additional recording apparatus. After the extensions to A Shop in 1921 to take the larger locomotives, there were enough extra-capacity engine pits, electric traversers and overhead cranes to deal with 400 larger-type engines annually.

Unlike the manufacturing shops, the erecting shops relied solely on incoming finished parts and those parts arriving ahead of schedule. Rebuilding a locomotive had to be done in a set order; if parts were unavailable all subsequent work was held up. Production meetings took place every morning to discuss the availability of reconditioned or new parts, gauges and specialist tools to complete the next stages of each engine being worked on.

The Engine Progress Office would act to minimise problems aired at the meeting by either instructing the 'progress chaser' involved with the delivery of parts from other workshops or enquiring as to stores availability. The movement of all components through the shops was scheduled in the Progress Office. All progress staff had been chosen from among the tradesmen so they would understand production workshop routines and priorities. The head of the A Shop progress office was Reg Thatcher and his 'chaser' was Frank Soper in the 1950s.

The progress of engines passing through or being built in the AE Shop could be seen at a glance using a board upstairs in the chief foreman's office. As completed work slips were received from the shop floor and endorsed by the inspector, so the engine's progress card moved across the board towards completion. The day shift didn't see the night shift workers until the morning, so any communication about the work in hand was passed on in various ways: either via the progress board, by notes left by the chargemen or by shorthand messages chalked on to the locomotive concerned.

All the wages grades in the shop were on piecework in the 1950s. There were three p/w chargemen: Jim remembers Gilbert King on the A1 bay and Alfie Bown on A2. They calculated the fortnightly figures that were forwarded to the wages office via the group office. Maurice Smith was the senior p/w inspector.

Stripping, Cleaning and Distributing Parts

The locomotive was taken into the Erecting Shop facing east by a traversing table. When adjacent to the chosen stripping pit road it was winched across by capstan and cable and dismantled in a set order. The sixty pits in the A2 bays were served by 100-ton overhead cranes that could lift the largest steam locomotives complete and move them anywhere along the bay. The eighty pit roads in the A1 bays were used for erecting the smaller classes up to the capacity of the 50-ton overhead cranes. The AV Shop (boiler repairs) was situated between the A1 and A2 bays.

A short-travel crane was installed high up in the raised roof of the boiler bay and this was used primarily to suspend upended boiler barrels while their firebox and smokebox was 'riveted up'. The bays in A2 were used for the larger engines and each road was long enough to take a smaller engine too, something up to the length of a '4200' class 2-8-0T. There were two or three stripping pits in A1 and four in A2.

Overhaul required that the engine be stripped down to leave just the frames and cylinder blocks. These were then cleaned by hand using scrapers. All detachable parts were taken to 'the bosh' for cleaning. Stripping the engine down often required a hammer and cold chisel to shift nuts. Even with the nut off, heavy hammer blows were usually needed to knock out the bolts. Larger seized and rounded nuts would require the services of 'Ernie the burner': he would cut through them with oxyacetylene torch equipment. The procedures for stripping and rebuilding locomotives at Swindon had changed little since the 1930s, and in many aspects since before the 1914–18 war.

The chief erecting shops' foreman Mr Millard, at his desk. The control board behind shows the progress of locomotives being stripped and re-erected in the A Shop circuit. It was updated following the meeting held every morning when the AE Shop foremen reported the progress and delays in their areas. *BRWR*

First the connecting rods, coupling rods and horn ties were removed, then the rest of the valve gear. It was all put on to a bosh trolley that had been placed at the end of the pit nearest to the traverser. The loco was then lifted sufficiently for the wheels to be run out. Any work in the pits underneath would require electric lamps for illumination; electric and compressed air points had been installed in the pits and this did away with the need for dangerous flare lamps. Some men kept candles to use as it saved time getting lamps from the stores.

An assembled boiler and firebox being lowered into its designated frames in the course of rebuilding. *BRWR*

The operations to overhaul driving wheels in the AW Shop were lengthy and this work had to be started as soon as possible. Although the loco was rebuilt using wheels and other parts from stock, those removed had to be made serviceable within a strict period of time to maintain the pool of serviceable spares. Used wheels were dealt with as a set and, depending on their state, they were either skimmed back to true on a Niles heavy-duty wheel lathe or new tyres were fitted then skimmed. Driving wheel tyres that had been out on the road would develop hard spots due to braking. Machining them required a powerful lathe like the Niles, which had its own 50hp electric motor.

Steel tyres were heated in a Selas gas-fired tyre furnace in the shop floor of the wheel section. The wheel centre was lowered into the hot tyre, which had expanded. As it cooled the tyre shrank on to it. To make sure it held fast, a Gibson ring was driven into a recess around the inside between the two. The lip of the tyre was then rolled over it by a machine to hold it in place. Used tyres were taken off by heating and reversing the process.

A lot of locomotive wheels were received into the A Wheel Shop from the home depots. One reason might be damaged crank pins due to violent slipping, in which case the rods would also be damaged. They would both receive prompt attention because they left an otherwise serviceable engine standing idle. If they didn't need replacing, the crank pin-bearing surfaces were usually lightly machined. Replacing a pin was a fairly major undertaking as it meant taking the wheelset apart. If that was done, the opportunity was taken to check the axle for cracks. Using the electromagnetic flaw detection method for this only became standard practice in the 1950s. It had been tried in the 1930s but not installed because the loco works manager', Mr Hannington, said that cracks due to wear and tear were likely to occur at the wheel seats. He thought separating the two for that reason alone was too costly. Only finished wheels and axles without counterbalance weights would go on to a balancing machine before being checked by the inspector.

With the frames lowered on to baulks of timber or jacks, the coppersmiths removed all steam and water pipework; the cylinder casings were only removed (by tinsmiths) if the K Shop inspector agreed. The cab roof, spectacle plates and kneeboards were taken off by boilermakers. This allowed the boiler to be unfastened, lifted out and craned to the end of the bay. It was then lowered on to a trolley to be towed outside to the 'Barn'. After inspection, the flue tubes were removed. As much sludge and scale was raked out as possible before it continued on to the Boiler Shop. The Barn gang were the only men to get as dirty as the stripping gangs. Nobody envied the men on either type of work but, like tradesmen generally, they didn't want to move once they got used to it. The bogies and pony trucks were sent to Fred Dingley's section in the A1 Bay to be stripped and rebuilt. In the late-1950s, this section assembled the D800 bogies.

The bosh trolley ran on the rails and was fitted with upright posts (stanchions) to contain the long motion parts.

They could then be taken to the bosh for cleaning via the traversing tables. Here they were immersed in a tank of boiling caustic soda solution to remove dirt and oil (which could be recovered) before being inspected and sent on to various shops for repair or scrap. The 'boshing plant' was renewed in 1939/40 and moved closer to the stripping pits. It was then served by a Wharton 6-ton overhead crane capable of 'dipping' a bogie truck or the largest pairs of driving wheels complete. Labourers Bill Harper, Roy Gibbs and Len White worked here in the 1950s.

After all the dismantled parts were cleaned (boshed) and rinsed, inspectors marked each part with a strip of paint: the colour depended on whether they were reusable, repairable or scrap. Those that were suitable were sent to various repair workshop gangs and put into a refurbishment cycle. Surfaces of piston valves and internal passages of cylinder blocks, among others, needed decarbonising, while boiler parts including fire tubes and superheater flues would need to go for descaling.

After boshing, all the bolts and nuts were checked by the 'green card' men of the reclamation gang. It was usually the large 'turned bolts', hydraulically pressed into hornblocks and used for securing cylinder castings to the frames, which were damaged and therefore thrown out. The smaller 'soft' or 'black' bolts for holding fittings other than motion parts were usually salvageable. Two days were allowed for stripping a locomotive down and dispersing the parts.

The frames with only the cab sides left in position were then taken by crane to the 'frame rectification section'. Chargeman Georgie Gardner's gang handled this stage of the rebuilding. When George became foreman, Ron Glass took over (Ron had several relatives in the shop including Reg Glass: chargeman of the connecting rod gang in AM Shop). The frames were inspected for fractures, loose bolts and rivets etc. and, if necessary, were welded and patched. Carbon deposits were removed from the steam passages and cylinder ports using long chisels.

Rebuilding

Erecting 'new builds' was done on special narrow pit roads in the north-west corner of A Shop, where the chargeman was Ernie Slade. This bay had its own circuit over two or three pits but used the one valve setting plant. Each pit had steel plate bases that were flat and level, providing a datum upon which the loco frame could be erected and then 'Zeissed' (optically aligned). Each pair of new main frame plates came separately from W Shop on specially adapted trailers hauled by a Fordson tractor. They had first passed through a heavy set of rolls in the boiler shop. Then they were taken to W (machine) Shop, where they were marked off from templates and flame cut on a double-headed oxygen/coal gas cutting machine.

In the erecting shop the pairs of longitudinal frame members were now jig drilled and reamed. They were then lifted upright by the overhead crane and stood on frame stands and jacks. The next job was to secure them together with cross stays and stiffeners and square them up using frame stretchers. 'Bolting up' the frames was a job left for the night shift. From now on the building of new locomotives followed almost the same sequence as for rebuilding after overhaul. The main difference was that 'new builds' did not usually receive reconditioned parts.

Depending on the locomotive type, such things as the bar form extension frames and angle irons, an overhauled cylinder block, cylinder and motion plate castings and a smokebox saddle, were refitted. The cylinder block and smokebox saddles had been back to W Shop for inspection and overhaul. Here was where they would have originally been machined using cylinder borers and a radical planning machine respectively. If necessary, new cylinder block(s) were cast in the Foundry before also being machined in this shop. All overhauled parts were received from the machine shops or from the Stores a little ahead of schedule. Steel parts from the Stores would have been undercoated, oiled or greased to prevent surface rust in storage. Each stage of the refitting had to be passed by the inspectors.

In service the bolts holding the cylinders invariably became distorted due to the forces of the motion against the rigid frame. So before refitting, the holes would be broached and oversized bolts, washers and nuts drawn from the shop stores. This was also a job traditionally done by the night shift. The next stage was to level the frames by adjusting the screw jacks at the back end, ready for the optical alignment survey. With the measurements obtained, the hornways and cylinders would be machined relative to each other to bring them 'back to true'. Two machines with grinding heads, operating simultaneously, skimmed the opposing hornways to ensure that the axle centre lines would be at absolute right angles to the cylinder centres.

A purpose-made machine powered by compressed air was now attached to the cylinders and slowly rebored them using tipped tools. The diameter measurements of the rebored cylinders were sent over to the machine section so that pistons and piston valves could be turned down and ground to suit. If the rebored cylinder had reached its limit, a cast iron liner could be made. This was cooled in a tank of refrigerant called Drikold and inserted. As the liner returned to normal temperature it expanded and held fast. (In general, where there was a choice, cooling had the advantage over heating in that it did not change the metal's properties so much.) With the frames 'lined up' there was no need to machine the axleboxes out of centre and out of square, to suit.

During the five days in the next section in the care of Frank Comley's gang, a previously overhauled boiler from the AV Shop, with some fittings attached, was put back into the frames and then the engine was 'wheeled'. The boiler was bolted to the saddle at the smokebox end. At the back end, long angle brackets with feet that slid slightly against the upper edges of the frame were used. They allowed for longitudinal expansion when the boiler was hot.

Outside Walschaerts' valve gear as used on the '1500' class and inside on GW four-cylinder locomotives.

John Brettell finished his apprenticeship in 1946 and started in A Shop on Georgie Gardner's gang, where he was the chargeman responsible for refitting boilers, valve gear and motion bars etc. 'Next to the work of building and stripping boilers, locomotive erecting was generally considered the most undesirable area to work in because it was heavy going. Another thing I remember was that with all the glass in the roof, A Shop could be uncomfortably hot in the middle of a summer's day as neither side of the locomotive was in the shade,' said John.

A new steel boiler with a copper firebox would have been constructed in the boiler shop by their boilermakers but repairs and overhauls were done in A and, before the war, B Shops. On its way back to the erecting shop, the boiler had safety valves, regulator valves and water gauges etc. fitted, so that the boiler steam test could be carried out: all this was done in P1 Shop. In the 1940s, a standard No. 15 boiler designed for the 'County' class was used to provide steam of sufficient pressure for a hydraulic test followed by a steam test, thus avoiding the need to 'fire up' each one individually. Whether it had replaced an earlier static boiler I do not know.

Before leaving P1, new boilers were moved to a fixture where they were plastered with a 2 to 3in layer of asbestos. The insulation was dried while the boiler was hot using mains' steam. Cleating with galvanised steel sheets then followed. They had been put through rollers to produce cylindrical and cone-shaped sheets to cover the boiler. This was a tinsmith's job.

Wheeling

Replacing coupled wheelsets required the co-operation of eight or nine men and is worth describing in a little more detail. Erectors working nearby were borrowed and the overhead crane was brought into position above the partly rebuilt locomotive. The crane hoists, each with two giant hooks, were attached at each end of the frames. Then, with hand signals from the 'slinger' on the ground, the crane driver slowly lifted the locomotive to just above head height and level.

Now the baulks and jacks that had supported the loco were moved away. The sets of driving wheels that had previously arrived at the end of the pit road could now be moved into roughly the right positions using pinch bars. Men positioned themselves in the pit underneath, one to each axlebox, ready to 'jump' (lever) their axlebox into the descending horn gap; the horn ties having been removed for this operation.

Everything was now ready to 'receive' the loco and the 'slinger' gestured to the driver to start to lower it down. Just before the frames reached the top of the axleboxes, a stop was made to reposition the wheels if necessary. As the slow descent continued, the chargeman watched to make sure the load stayed level once contact was made. He would blow a pea whistle as an emergency stop signal to the man in the crane cabin. This, and the shout of a fitter/erector whose axlebox had got caught, made doubly sure that damage wasn't done by continuing down. Everyone was relieved when all the axleboxes were safely 'home' in their horn ways.

The horn ties were now fitted. The engine was then lifted again so that the wheels could be turned, the cranks lined up and coupling rods fitted. Steel blooms for coupling rods, like the con rods, had been forged, machined, heat treated and cooled in oil to make them both hard and tough to resist wear and stress, then finished ground. The rods of the larger engines required three men to lift them into position. They would then require some force to get the bushes over the crank pins even with a coating of oil. Then the springs were 'put up' and slide bars fitted. The screw or lever reverse, the valve gear rockers, brake hanger brackets and cylinder drain cocks, were all then fitted in turn. Spectacle plates (window glasses) were now put back in the cab if they had been removed.

Finishing Off and Painting

The last four days that a loco was in the Erecting Shop were spent on Stan Lewington's 'finishing off' bay (when Stan retired his replacement was Jack Steward from B Shop). This bay was across the shop so the move required, not the crane, but the winch and traverser. The first job was to blow out the smokebox, steam chests and passages with a compressed air line and check they were clear of nuts and bolts etc. Small mirrors on rods were used to check the less accessible places. Carpenters from D Shop refitted the cab footplating: one was always Bill Hurst and the other was often Pete Pragnell. One electrician and his mate would then wire up the Automatic Train Control equipment. Howard Smith, whose father was the Works chief fire officer, did this for several years.

The valves and pistons were inserted, after which the con rods, crossheads and other motion parts were fitted.

Here locomotive *King George V* is on the traverser at the start its journey back into traffic. It may have had a 'heavy general' overhaul or perhaps just a 'sole and heel' intermediate repair. Richard Naylor gives the AE Shop a light and airy look for his watercolour painting. This is not artistic licence: the high roof incorporating a lot of glass allowed plenty of natural light.

The cock gear and injectors were 'put up' and the coppersmiths would follow on with fitting the associated pipework. Moving parts would be lubricated prior to fitting and a gang of about three men made sure wicks, corks and oil were placed correctly in the oilboxes. Fitters were responsible for fitting all oil-soaked pads during assembly. The bigger engines would, if applicable, now have the two nameplates refitted over the centre wheel splashers.

The painting and varnishing was done simultaneously with this final refitting work. Some locomotives just having 'light' or 'running' repairs were not repainted: if the general condition of the paint was thought sufficiently good to last until the next Works' visit it was cleaned down and one coat of varnish applied. Loco painter Terry Couling told me:

> We had a cabin halfway down A Shop: the cleaners used one end and we used the other. Our chargeman would be issued with a list of engines nearing completion, on the Monday morning, and allocate us accordingly. We would collect the paint and exterior varnish from the main stores in B Shed, on a sacktruck. We didn't strip the old paint off unless previous layers were coming away, in which case we scraped it with wood chisels. Care being taken not to score the metal underneath. It took about one gallon of black and a half gallon of green to cover the bigger engines, excluding the tender of course.

> The single coat of varnish took less time to apply as we missed some bits that couldn't be seen. I think the foreman was Ernie Hewlett in my early days [from 1956]. Freddie Porter, Bert Leighfield and Harry Welsh were painters and Art Cannon was our chargehand, he always gave Harry the lining on the 'Kings' for some reason. I marked off the numbers of engines I worked on in an Ian Allan ABC book. So for instance, I know I worked on all the 'King' class engines over time.

> All steel parts had been coated to stop surface rust and a gang of cleaners degreased the surfaces prior to starting. Two of us were allocated to a steam locomotive: a tradesman and me the apprentice. We would complete two engines a week or, if there was no lining to do, two and a half engines. The tenders

An overhauled '2800' class heavy freight locomotive parked on a turntable road just before or just after its trial run. The large corrugated cabin behind was used by the A and B Shop pilot enginemen as well as the gangs who worked in the Reception Shed. *Author's collection*

were done in B Shed, where they had their own painters. We started by filling holes and indentations with yellow stopping. The boiler was painted first so as to stay clear of the fitters who were still 'finishing off'. We had ladders that hooked over handrail for this stage. On unlined tank engines we also painted the brass including safety valve covers. As we didn't roughen the brass first the paint came off quite quickly in service. The inside motion and undersides were done last; these were difficult to get too and fiddly, especially the pipework at the back end. The standard classes were even worse.

We had already painted the underside of the boiler before it was lowered into the frames; the wheel centres too were painted by us before assembly. The cab roof and footplating were painted by labourers and, like everywhere else, they just got one coat of paint. The buffer beam alone often required two coats of red to cover it. The driver's side could be more difficult if there was a reversing rod, mechanical lubricator and/or vacuum pump etc., so on the next pit you would alternate with your mate. We used long-bristled brushes for the lining out of the passenger engines: this was where the skill came in. A compass was used for the corners, and a chalk line used for the long straight lengths, otherwise the lining was done freehand. The varnish would get rid of any chalk marks.

Valve Setting

The next stage in the locomotive's circuit involved lifting it along the bay to have its valves set. The piston valves allow steam in and out of the cylinders by sliding back and forward across ports. Out on the road the driver could alter the distance of valve travel to suit the running speed and conditions.

This plant had been built at Swindon to suit the requirements here in the A Erecting Shop. The locomotive was lowered on to adjustable rollers. Those in contact with the big end driving wheels were driven by a 15hp electric motor. The operator could start, stop, reverse and 'inch' the rollers round by push-button control. This moved the wheels and valve gear very precisely. A second man would check the position of the piston valves in relation to the cranks.

It was one or other of the two eccentric rods in each set of valve gear that was adjusted if necessary. Minor alterations up to 1/16th of an inch could be made by the setters. Anything more required the blacksmith to 'draw' (lengthen) or 'jump' (shorten) the rod. Jim remembers Bob Jarvis and his mate Hubert 'Hue' Keen were the valve setters in the 1950s. Apprentices said their skills and 'tricks' (methods not found in the textbook) were not readily passed on. Chargehand Tom Weaver and a mate were usually the smiths who altered the rods for the erectors if necessary.

The tank engine bays in A and B Shops had a simplified plant with rollers powered by compressed air. This did away with the laborious method of moving the loco with a pinch bar under the wheels along a section of track; steam cranes excepted. The wheels needed to be inched round so as to bring the cranks into certain positions while measuring the corresponding valve events (positions). Some running sheds adjusted the valves between overhauls and they had to do it the hard way.

Driving wheels from the AW Shop that were going back on to locomotives were put next to the valve setting plant. Nearby, eccentric sheaves and straps together with their white metal liners were stacked, having arrived from Colin Wood's section in the AM Shop. When he was not assisting the valve setter, Hue would fit the sheaves to the axles of the wheelsets and clamp them together with the two halves of the strap.

Back to Finishing

While the engine was having its valves set, the 'finishing off' gang who had been allocated to it would work on another engine, perhaps putting up brake gear. When the engine returned and before it was lowered for the last time, the fitter 'pulled on' (tightened up) the nuts on the spring hangers until they were slightly overtight: this was achieved by knowing the predetermined length and the number of threads showing on the bolt end. Then it was lowered and if a bogie or pony truck was to be fitted it was placed in position on the pit road. Inspectors Norman Jarvis or Jim Cole checked the finishing work and later when the engine was in steam one of them would also check its ability to create sufficient vacuum and retain it.

Locomotives normally spent seventeen or eighteen working days and nights being overhauled and the Works were expected to keep no more than 5% of the total stock out of service at any one time. Attempts were made to have no more than a further 6% stopped at the depots. In the 1950s there were an expanding number of services that required heavier and faster trains. At the same time, the majority of suitable locomotives, the four-cylinder 'Castles' and 'Kings', were of an age where maintenance and repairs at the depots was increasing and therefore availability was decreasing. For this reason these express passenger types were not held at the Works out of traffic any longer than absolutely necessary. They, in particular, would be worked on day and night.

The day foreman would leave instructions as to the work to be undertaken by the night shift and check with the stores that all parts and tool equipment would be available. Certain jobs were traditionally done at night, such as the stripping down. In the later stages, if the engine schedule allowed it, 'putting up' the inside motion or fitting the inside valves and pistons was work often left for a night gang, as was fitting the crosshead slide (or motion) bars. There were two upstairs mess rooms in the A Shop where some of the night workers spent their hour break playing cards or putting their feet up and having a doze.

Back Outside

After the new or overhauled locomotives arrived outside on the traverser, they were towed back to the Reception Shed. An allocated tender was brought up from B Shop if applicable: rarely ever was it the one it came in with. The pilot responsible for this also brought up the tank engines overhauled there. The tender or bunker was coaled and watered and the boiler was filled with water. Ray Gwillam says in his book *A Loco Fireman Looks Back* that measured amounts of coal were dropped back in, but Jim Lowe said no, there would be no reason for this. Mr Gwillam may have been getting mixed up with engines being prepared for controlled road tests. These were a different type of test running to that usually carried out on ex-Works engines.

Steaming the engine was not usually done until the day following its departure from the shop. A gang of men under chargeman Jack Rogers raised the steam: they were unskilled but the NUR had negotiated more than the labourers' rate for them. Jack had been a Swindon 82C driver. The fire in the firebox was started using oily rags and timber that was stacked on the footplate beforehand (Only the GWR used wood as firelighters: the other companies kept furnaces going for the purpose and shovelled hot coal from one to the other, which saved time). Scrap offcuts of wood for 'lighting up' came from the carriage side in wagons. At least two open goods wagons could usually be found on the turntable roads from which the firelighters barrowed the wood to the locomotives.

With sufficient steam pressure on the gauge, Jack Rogers' men were allowed to move engines along the reception shed as long as they did not go over any points. They then handed over to the trial crew, who continued to raise steam, oil round and top up the axlebox keeps and big end oilboxes. Enginemen were divided into various links. Light engine trials were part of the duties of men in No. 8 link: they were not the most experienced or the most junior. Their cabin was on the west side of the Works' weightable and was shared with the Con Yard and No. 1 Saw Mill pilot crews. The 'trial fitters' also had a cabin near the turntable and they dealt with any adjustments prior to the light engine trial.

Gradually, as the coal was added and the boiler pressure increased, the pressure gauge needle would start to move. The large injector was opened and closed to check that the vacuum that released the brakes was holding. A boiler inspector, often Brian Carter, was on hand to see that the boiler was functioning normally as steam was raised. George Petfield said Ernie Nutty, the senior technical assistant in the 1950s, was often 'on hand' as he could listen to an ex-Works locomotive move away and say what adjustments, if any, were needed to the valve settings.

The Weigh House

The locomotive was then moved to the Weigh House to have the springs adjusted to even out the load on each axle. Fred Drinkwater was the chargeman here, like his father before him. If Fred was not there, an experienced fitter would deputise for him. The Weigh House had new machinery installed in 1929/30 consisting of six balancing tables on 7ft lengths of track, each capable of measuring axle loads up to 13 tons. It was all purpose-made for the company by Henry Pooley & Sons Ltd of Birmingham. Because of the lack of activity during the annual holiday shutdown in July, the balancing pans could be cleaned and calibrated. Jim remembers: 'A firm called W&T Avery (who subsequently bought out Pooley) were contracted to complete this before the Works reopened.'

In the Weigh House the locomotive was driven on to the balancing pans (or tables) and the weight on each driving wheel was taken in turn. After recording the weights, the locomotive was moved over the pit and fitters' mates would slacken each laminated (or leaf) spring nut underneath, according to Mr Drinkwater's instructions.

The spring hanger nuts had been deliberately over-tightened in the erecting shop because it would now only be possible to 'pull off' or slacken them. This was because it was impossible to get enough torque to do it the other way round with the weight bearing down on the springs. The engine was then driven back over the tables and the weights rechecked. With the loco balanced, the adhesion would be improved and the wear on the bearing surfaces such as the big-end bushes would be minimised.

Outside the other end of the Weigh House was a rail joint with a drop of ¾in. The engine, and tender if applicable, was taken over this step and back again to 'unsettle' the springs, which were now carrying their working weight. If this road was occupied, large washers could be used instead. After checking the loading once more on the scales and topping the tender up with water, the engine was ready for its trial trip. Jim said that the method of adjusting the loading on BR Standards was by using shims of different thicknesses. The load on the spring could be taken off using a small hydraulic jack, which allowed shims to be added or taken away.

Engine Trials

On average, four engines were 'trialled' each weekday. Jack Leonard, who lived in Wootton Bassett, was the running inspector in the 1950s. He would give the driver any special instructions about the 'light engine' trial. The Running Dept was part of the CME's Dept but separate from the Works, therefore all local running inspectors came under the control of the divisional locomotive superintendent at Bristol.

On the footplate the fire was managed so that the safety valves lifted outside after weighing, at which point the inspector checked the reading showing on the pressure gauge. When he was happy, the fireman rang the signalman at Rodbourne Lane to ask to crossover to the down main line. The engine was usually taken down to Dauntsey on the original main line to Bristol, a distance of 10 miles.

All but the smallest classes went to Dauntsey unless the occupancy of the line was very high. Then all but the largest locos, those without speedometers, went to Little Somerford: 12½ miles out on the South Wales route.

Narrow gauge engine No. 9 *Prince of Wales* is seen outside the south-east corner of A Shop in March 1960. It had just been overhauled on a narrow gauge section of track laid on timber baulks, over a pit. The locomotive has recently been steamed to check that all connections were steam tight, but not road tested. This would be done back home between Aberystwyth and Devil's Bridge on the Vale of Rheidol railway. Now for the long ride back to west Wales chained to its trolley wagon. The Works had been maintaining this locomotive and her sisters since the 1920s. *Ken Ellis*

Another exception was special main-line trials, when the latter route was preferred. The outward journey was taken fairly leisurely in case there were any major problems. With so many working parts as well as joints and valves needing to be steam and watertight, it was inevitable that some adjustments would be necessary. Ronny Hinder and Colin Benfield were two regular A Shop fitters on the 'trials gang': both had fathers who were drivers. Whoever refitted the pipework in the cab before it left the shop usually went on the trial run as they knew whether the connections had left- or right-hand threads.

On the outward trip, one of the fitters sometimes rode on the front, or rather the back as the engine was running tender first. Ronnie was particularly fond of doing this: 'Presumably he could diagnose any problems with the motion by listening to it from there,' said Jim. Apprentices allocated to the 'trials gang' also went out, so it could get a bit crowded on the footplate. In the siding at Dauntsey Station the bearings and bushes were checked for overheating and oil penetration.

Some delay was normal waiting for a clear road back to Swindon on the return journey. The engine was worked up to 30mph at the first milepost and the inspector checked the speed with a stopwatch against the mileposts, which were ¼ mile apart. If there was a speedometer fitted, that would be checked at the same time and adjusted if necessary. At the top of Dauntsey Bank the engine should have been doing 60mph and, assuming Wootton Bassett distant signal was off, the driver would 'open her up' passing Tockenham signal box.

When it arrived back at the Works, the engine was parked on one of the table roads that radiated out around the turntable. The inspector would then hand the 'trial fitters' a snag list of things to check or attend to. They dealt with the mechanical faults but a boilermaker, tinsmith or coppersmith might be needed if other problems arose. For safety reasons, 'not to be moved' signs were placed on the lamp irons, front and back, if anyone was working on the locomotive. Major problems might require the engine to go back 'inside'. When the inspector was satisfied, he released the locomotive to 82C, the BR code for Swindon shed.

The 'factory trials' of smaller engines stripped and rebuilt in B Shed took place between the Weigh House and the junction with the Gloucester branch: a distance of ¾ mile. The engine made two or three passes up and down what was known as the 'engine line'. If there were no major problems the locomotive was, like the A Shop engines, taken to shed by the trials crew before they knocked off. Shed fitter Ellis Millard and a mate, who were actually A Shop personnel, would attend to any mechanical adjustments and repairs that arose while here. Each class of engine would then have to work so many miles while remaining under Works' control.

A view during the trial of 'Star' class 4-6-0 No. 4047 *Princess Louise*. Chargeman W. Hanks and other A Shop fitters are flanked by the two enginemen. They are probably at Dauntsey 'waiting for the road' to return to the Works. *R. Clarke*

5
Offices and Staff

Ask people who had ancestors in the Works' offices what they know about their working lives and about half will say 'nothing'. Employment records don't help much either, they just state either clerk, typist, secretary or telegraphist. The other half will tell you they were 'in accounts'. However, that is an umbrella term, as outlined in this chapter, and Swindon Works had dozens of sections to compile the Stores and CME Departments' expenditure and returns.

In the mid-1950s, publicity from the Western Region claimed that there were 600 clerks at Swindon, working on accounts and statistical duties, out of a total workforce of 10,000. Of them, it was said that only one in three dealt with 'factory' work. These staff figures were compiled before the electronic machine sections were fully utilised.

The Case for Accounts

There was a statutory requirement on the GWR to keep financial and statistical accounts under the Railway Companies' (Accounts and Returns) Act of 1911. They had to be made up, in prescribed form, to 31 December each year. By the early years of the twentieth century there was a growing realisation about the value of bookkeeping for all departmental business transactions. During the period covered in this book the margins between costs (or expenditure) and returns (or revenue) were much narrower than had been the case previously in manufacturing industries. Although the reduction in profits was offset somewhat by the increase in mass production, there began to be a growing realisation that costs could be minimised more effectively by the efficient management of accounts.

Thomas Minchin, an accounts' clerk at Swindon Works, presented a paper to the Swindon Engineering Society in 1921 entitled 'Cost Accounting'. In it, he said that an accurate determination of costs had a direct effect on manufacturing efficiency: an idea that, he implies, was far from universally accepted at that time. 'Only now was the company realising the value of complete accounting because without it inefficiencies cannot be properly identified', he said. In 1930 the assistant works' manager said of the extent of the Swindon accounts: 'One cannot argue against the necessity of such an elaborate accounts' system.'

It appears from studies such as that undertaken by Mr Minchin that Swindon was well ahead of its head office at Paddington. The latter compiled their cost accounts as overall sets of figures, which were worthless for evaluation. Presumably this situation had developed because the work undertaken was not sold outside and the company had not learned to be competitive. The general manager, Mr F.J.C. Pole, said in his memoirs that his chief accountant had insisted that the cost of producing divisional profit and loss accounts would be too enormous and too difficult, and so was not taken up in his time (up to 1929). However, by then it was realised that it was no longer enough for the company to know it was making a profit based on comparing monthly variations in traffic and docks receipts or maintaining a 'healthy' general balance sheet each year.

Like all shrewd business people, the GWR directors saw opportunities to be exploited during the most depressed years of the 1920s and '30s. At the annual general meeting, the chairman said that economies made would continue when trade revived. Swindon, with its superior methods of costing, had not waited until events forced economies upon them.

Qualifications for Employment

Even before the war there were two or three local factories taking on female labour. Most Swindon girls leaving school did not want to be 'stuck' on repetitive production work if they could avoid it. Even factory offices were frowned upon by them and their mothers. The Railway Works, however, was different, and a position in the CME Dept was THE place of choice. Many of the brightest girls from Commonweal, Euclid Street and later Headlands' grammar schools, went 'inside'.

During the 1930s the demand for positions at the Works exceeded vacancies and the requirements for acceptance were raised accordingly. A good report and qualifications from school were essential. Having a father working in 'accounts' also helped but there was still the entrance test and a medical before acceptance. (After the war the labour situation changed and taking the entrance exam was unnecessary if the applicant's schooling achievements came up to a certain standard.) For all CME Dept applications, these examinations were carried out at Park House on the corner of the GWR estate.

The Day Commercial Course at the College, was another option. The subjects taken by potential Works' staff were bookkeeping and typewriting. Day classes expanded for the 1933/34 session and it was advertised as a 'full-time two-year course for young men and woman wanting office situations'. It's hard to imagine how parents could afford to not only keep their sons and daughters for an extra two years but also pay the college fees during the recession.

In the 1940s there were more employers in the town competing for staff to work in their offices, particularly after the war. From about 1946 it was possible to become a junior clerk in the Works' offices, including CME accounts, by successfully completing the reintroduced Day Commercial Course at the College. The syllabus was now made up of the old school subjects including physical exercises, French, commerce, shorthand typing, craftwork and handwriting. Otherwise, a prospective employee would be required to hold the Higher School Certificate or, in the 1950s, five GCE passes including mathematics and English. Then they did not have to take the entrance test, which, by all accounts, was 'difficult'. By this time other less well-qualified girls were being taken on as machine operators only, previously known as class 2 clerks.

Junior Staff

Each office had an office junior, sometimes more than one. They were usually referred to as the 'girl' or 'boy'. These terms weren't meant to sound demeaning; they were given to those who were between school, or further education, and before becoming a junior clerk at eighteen years of age. Before the Great War young starters were called 'lad clerks', there being no junior females in the Works' offices then. Staff who had worked there then continued to use this term decades on. Becoming a junior clerk, in time, was still dependent on a good conduct report and passing the examination.

Because they were very young at the time, there are still some people about today who started work in the shop offices well before 1960. They were the young men who were placed in an office attached to a workshop to carry out the duties of the office 'boy' (office 'girls' were not allocated to workshop offices, and, until the 1960s, they rarely visited workshops in the course of their duties

This office view shows the earlier style of sloping desks. By the 1940s, nearly all these had been remade into flat desks by carpenters from D Shop. *GWR*

either). The experiences of former shop office 'boys' that I have met who were destined to learn a trade rather than becoming a clerk are recorded in other chapters.

Females worked on most clerical sections and their duties are recorded in the following chapter. The typists' sections and machine rooms in the CME building were staffed entirely by females. Their prospects for promotion, especially the machine operators, were better than anywhere else in accounts. The company acknowledged that female operators were faster and better when using accounting machinery than men.

CME Accounts' Section (Mid-1930s)

The locomotive and carriage & wagon accounts' sections were merged in the 1930s. After which the CME accounts' department was divided up into the following main sections:

WAGES: The compilation of wages, including piecework, war bonus and stoppages (paybill production), was carried out by two sections. Mr Cole was the clerk in charge.

MATERIAL COSTS: The charges for materials supplied through the Stores Dept were sent to the CME Dept via head office (the Chief Accountants Office, Paddington). Mr Richards and later Mr Couling were the clerks in charge.

INVOICES: All charges by other departments, private firms and companies including other railways, were received in the form of invoices. Mr Dadge was the clerk in charge.

ESTABLISHMENT CHARGES: This related to expenditure incurred in supervising, maintaining and running the establishment. As opposed to costs attributable to completed work and jobs carried out. Mr Furseland was the clerk in charge.

REPAIRS AND PARTIAL RENEWALS OF ROLLING STOCK. Mr Furseland was also clerk in charge here.

LOCOMOTIVE RUNNING EXPENSES. Senior clerk unknown.

A Powers-Samas machine section in one of the CME Offices in the 1930s. 'This electro-mechanical machinery was noisy and not very nice for staff trying to concentrate at their desks,' said Daphne Kibblewhite. Notice the double-glazed sash windows. *GWR*

The work of the clerk in accounts was to compile and record: 1) expenditure and receipts (financial accounts), and 2) work or assets exchanged (statistical returns). Mr Gardner, the assistant works accountant in the 1930s, summed up the work as: 'To tabulate in the most convenient form, the results of past working.'

The CME Dept accounts were based at Swindon Works and the three largest accounts offices were 21, 22 and 26. They would have up to fifty staff working in each at any one time. Each section had a telephone and outside lines were available via the exchange. By the 1950s every double desk had a phone and some people were able to dial straight out to the General Post Office networks. A shrewd clerk soon worked out who to ask for and who to avoid when telephoning or visiting other departments. The office furniture was all 'getting on a bit' by the 1950s. A Works' carpenter told his daughter-in-law, who was a clerk in the offices, that when he had to replace some of the oilskin pads built into desks there were small creepy-crawlies living underneath.

All offices held various reference books and books of conversion tables. Personnel could obtain 'rough books' from the stores, which had hardcovers and were impressed with the company initials. The blotter doubled as a home-made directory of names and extension numbers and a note was made of anyone who could help when there was a particular problem. Only clerks in shop offices worked nights if their workshop had a night shift, and even then it was not often. The company acknowledged that sitting at a desk when tired significantly reduced efficiency.

Some office wall clocks were connected to a 'master' clock in No. 8 office. It was 9ft high and its mechanical mechanism generated tiny electrical pulses that drove and regulated 'slave' clocks around the Works and at the junction station. There were still some mechanical clocks in use. They were checked and wound by a fellow who would go round the Works on a bike. He was known as 'clocky' and he also helped with any repairs, cleaning and adjustments.

Senior Accounts' Staff

The clerk in charge of the larger offices or sections was senior in status to colleagues responsible for fewer staff, and was graded as a 'special C'. Some offices had a raised area at one end where the clerk in charge and his assistant had their desks. Anyone of a 'lower station' who needed to speak to them did so by respectfully standing at the lower level. This had the effect of making those who were new and unsure of themselves feel even more self-conscious.

Mr Kelynack was the chief accountant to the CME in the 1930s: Frank Bailey and Harold Gardner were his assistants. In 1941 Mr Gardner took over as head of CME and Stores Accounts. The new 'chief' was a member of the town council and had been mayor of Swindon. He was an honorary auditor of the GW (Swindon) Amateur Theatrical Society throughout the 1930s as well as being the last honorary treasurer of the GWR Medical Fund, taking over from his former boss Mr Kelynack in 1946. Along with others from the factory, Mr Gardner lectured at the College

The front cover of a card for the retirement presentation of Richard Dening in 1931. The programme for the evening included entertainment provided by a small orchestra, the 15 Shop 'Glee Party' singers and solo musicians. The Great Western Hotel was, and still is, directly opposite Swindon Junction station.
B. Carter collection

some days and evenings. He had been on the staff at the College's Commercial and Literary Dept since the 1920s and many of his students were employed by the GWR.

Following nationalisation, direct control of the CME and Stores accounts and statistics were transferred to Paddington under the control of Mr Dashwood, who was 'chief accountant to the general manager'. Mr Gardner was then appointed assistant to the accountant (rolling stock and stores) Western Region, but remained the most senior clerk at Swindon; his assistant was Cliff Sanders. Although he was fifty-five years of age in 1955, Mr Gardner worked on for about another ten years. (I remember seeing him on his evening visits to the Cross Keys in Wood Street throughout the 1970s).

The Dening Family

Barbara Dening worked in CME, and later, Stores' accounts. Her family, like most in New Swindon, had several members that spent all their working lives in 'the railway'. Barbara's grandfather, Richard Dening, retired in 1931 as chief foreman of the carriage fitters in 15, 15A, 18 and 19D Shops, and as president of the Foreman's Association. Her father Henry became 'clerk in charge' of 22 Office and her two aunts, Freda and Irene, started in the Works' accounts in 1913 and 1915 respectively. It is thought that the first females came into the offices to operate new adding machines, which were introduced in 1913, but Barbara thought the Dening Sisters may have gone in to train as shorthand typists. (The next female recruitment drive was when 'girl' and 'lady clerks' were invited to replace men who had gone to war. Most of this intake started in, or after, April 1917. Their numbers gradually increased from then on).

Like their older brother Henry, Freda and Irene won the Brunel medal for shorthand and advanced bookkeeping respectively. Barbara thought they were the only females to get these awards, and the only time three Brunel medallists came from the same family. They were awarded in 1920, 1921 and 1922. The Works' phone directory shows that, in the mid-1930s, Freda was the only female listed as having a telephone at her desk. She was in overall charge of the loco side typists for many years and retired early, in 1952, aged fifty-five. She wanted more time to care for her ailing parents at the family home in Goddard Avenue. Irene Dening (born 1900) held a senior position in the Stores accounts from at least as early as 1932. She worked her full term and had been Personal Assistant to the Stores Superintendent for some time before she retired.

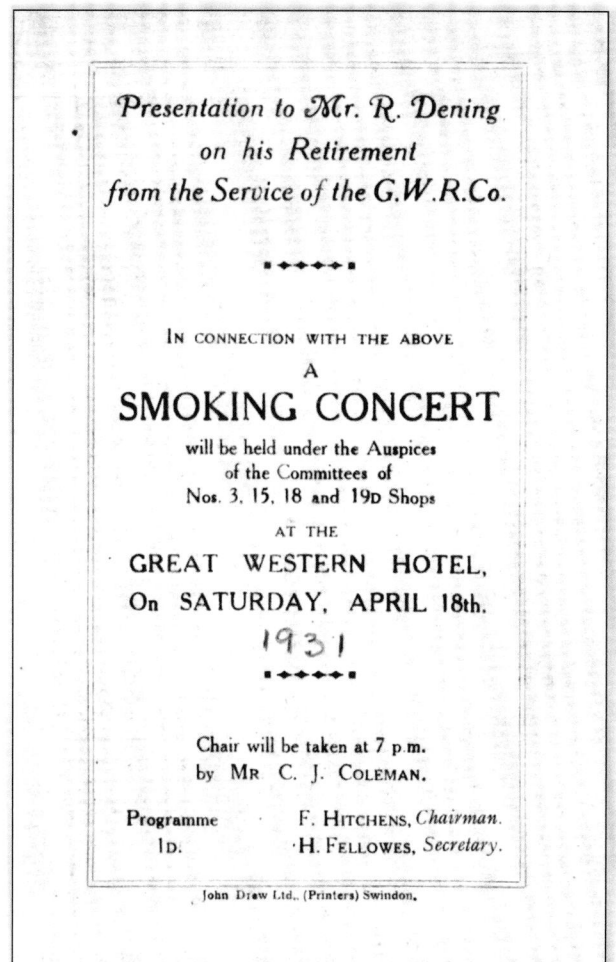

Presentation to Mr. R. Dening on his Retirement from the Service of the G.W.R.Co.

■ ◆ ◆ ◆ ◆ ■

IN CONNECTION WITH THE ABOVE

A

SMOKING CONCERT

will be held under the Auspices of the Committees of
Nos. 3, 15, 18 and 19D Shops

AT THE

GREAT WESTERN HOTEL,
On SATURDAY, APRIL 18th.
1931

■ ◆ ◆ ◆ ◆ ■

Chair will be taken at 7 p.m.
by MR C. J. COLEMAN.

Programme   F. HITCHENS, *Chairman*.
1D.   H. FELLOWES, *Secretary*.

John Drew Ltd., (Printers) Swindon.

The CME Office Building

Following the merger of the accounts sections in the early 1950s, most were now centralised in the CME's building. Its position was, and still is, situated in the 'angle': an area in the fork between the Paddington–Bristol main line and the Gloucester branch. The offices therein were centrally heated by large iron radiators, the fireplaces in the earlier parts of the building having been boarded over to stop draughts. Large windows and high ceilings had been incorporated to capture maximum natural light. Limited photographic evidence seems to suggest that the glass partitions between some offices had replaced earlier solid walls. Alterations of this kind were probably done when the CME offices were refurbished to accommodate staff who came in from the railway companies absorbed in the 1920s. The glass partitions, forming the central corridors, were part of the original design.

Each window frame held two sets of sash windows, not to keep the heat in but to minimise noise and fumes from the nearby workshops. This could also help to make the atmosphere inside rather stuffy as the majority of men smoked a pipe or cigarettes. Unlike the workshops, there had been no smoking ban in these offices prior to 1939. Barbara Carter (nee Dening) who started in 'CME accounts' in 1940 said:

A lot of women in the offices smoked as well. I didn't because my father suffered with asthma and I thought I might get it if I smoked. The double sets of windows were very effective at keeping out the noise and the fumes as long as they stayed closed. One of the girls in my office made herself very unpopular by keep opening them.

A second floor had been added to the original part of the office block to accommodate a combined drawing office in 1904. Further extensions were added to the building as more office space was required up until the 1920s, by which time the Works had reached its limit in terms of working space requirements. Despite the obvious differences of each new phase, the final result was an impressive three- and four-storey building towering over drab workshop buildings. Over the period covered by this book some offices moved as the work and methods changed; others were renamed, amalgamated or became obsolete. Most offices were classified by numbers but were better known by the type of work undertaken.

Statistics

Compiling engine and train mileages occupied more than 100 staff and came under the section known officially as 'statistics, addressograph and duplication machine service'. This was one of the larger sections in the CME building and occupied two adjacent offices on the third floor of the north range. The offices worked in different ways and the two sets of staff do not appear to have ever interchanged, as was usual. Recollections of working in these offices are covered in the following chapter.

The CME Dept needed to know the 'light engine' movements, train miles run and loads hauled by its locomotives. The Superintendent of the Line's (Traffic) Dept needed information relating to passengers and tonnages carried plus receipts and times of goods in transit. Therefore it made sense to compile the information sent in from each operating division all under one roof. The information was accumulated using comptometer machines, before being passed on to be processed by addressograph, duplicating and Powers-Samas machinery.

In the early and mid-1930s, it was Mr Bartlett who was responsible for applying the Powers-Samas punch card system to loco and train mileage statistics. He was the 'clerk in charge' of both offices and he reported direct to the CME. Messrs Westbury, Hunt and Glastonbury oversaw the female machine operators employed on freight statistics. Later the departments were reorganised and the 'clerks in charge' were Harold Lewis and Bert Fluck, who reported to the Chief Accountant.

The accumulated figures, now called statistics, of locomotives and trains, were interlinked. Some information involving the former was passed to and acted upon by the CME Running Dept. They used it to: 1) assess the cost-effectiveness of modifications, overhauls and repairs, 2) measure coal and oil consumption, 3) determine the footplatemen's mileages worked, for

paybill purposes. There was an average of 11,000 locomotive drivers and firemen in the GWR's CME Dept at any one time during the 1930s, '40s and '50s.

Guards came under the Traffic Dept and their statistics were compiled in the freight (mileage) sections. The traffic statistics were sent on to Paddington for analysis by their accounts staff. Four-weekly sets of figures were then published for comparison with the same period in previous years.

Further Education

The College, sometimes referred to in documents as the Secondary Technical School was, and still is, an imposing building near the bottom of Victoria Road. It was run by the Borough of Swindon Education Committee. Works' staff would attend either the Engineering and Science Dept or, in the case of office workers, the Commercial and Literary Dept. Before the war especially, because a good proportion of both students and lecturers were employed in the Works during the day, most of the technical departments' courses were evening classes (known unofficially as 'night school').

Clerks, secretaries and typists from the Works, usually in the early years of their careers, were known as 'senior students'. They could enrol and undertake further education in English, arithmetic, accounting, statistics, costing, business economics, shorthand, bookkeeping and business methods.

According to the annual report on the work of the College for the session of 1931–32, the decrease in enrolment of the junior evening institutes (courses) was due to a low birth rate during 1914–18: no mention is made of the severe economic depression that must have had an effect on people wishing to take up extended studies. Gradually the range of educational opportunities for employees at the Works was being expanded. The commercial department were offering 'advanced day commercial' courses at this time. The number of students participating was small and confined to those preparing for degrees in commerce and for membership of professional bodies.

Up to and including the 1930s, the most successful students had been able to go on and study at the London School of Economics. Each year in August, pamphlets containing particulars of LSE lectures and classes were sent out by the GWR Secretary's Office, Paddington, to the Office of the Chief Clerk at Swindon. Names of staff over the age of eighteen years wishing to attend the courses of the next session were required by return of post. The company secretary's clerk makes it clear in the accompanying letter, that 'no student will be admitted to these classes unless he has sufficient elementary knowledge of the advance stages of the subject (accounts)'.

Students would attend a department at the LSE exclusively for railway staff, one evening a week after work and a day for the annual examination. The most senior clerks at Swindon Works such as Messrs Dening,

The imposing façade of the College in Victoria Road. Many staff from the Works attended day and evening classes here. A good proportion of the teaching staff were employed at the Works. *Author's collection*

Minchin, Gardner and Sanders, among others, gained the Brunel medal earlier in their careers for consistently high marks each year. To qualify, the student had to obtain three first-class passes in the LSE-approved courses in no more than four years.

As with engineering students, there was also an annual GWR chairman's prize for the most outstanding clerical student. Another scheme, to encourage education in engineering and commerce, was the Churchward Testimonial Fund. From 1929 a number of book prizes were awarded each year to the best students in the CME Department. The trustees of the fund, Messrs Hawksworth, Auld and Kelynack, considered the progress made and marks obtained throughout the year. Most of the awards came to Swindon because they provided much of the departmental training. The money came from a fund set up at the suggestion of Mr Churchward himself. The great engineer made the first payment from money collected and presented to him upon his retirement at the end of 1921.

Carriage & Wagon Offices

The C&W office block formed the façade of the large fitting and machine (No. 15) shop just to the north-west of the station. This building was probably the most striking of any Works' buildings seen by the travelling public. As you looked at it, some of the general stores offices were on the right, with the CME stores' offices above; on the left were the managers' offices, the Time Office, the Drawing Office and the Registrars' Office. Above them were the Progress Office, Accounts' and Chief Clerks' Offices and, until 1952, the Wages Office. After the latter had moved out it became the Cost Office, where George Ruddle was in charge.

The C&W office block also had staff and record sections, a Correspondence Office, Special Loads Office, Drawing Stores, Estimating Office and, in 1930, the timber storekeeper and his staff moved into the building. Mr Evans was the carriage & wagon works manager until he retired in 1946. Upon nationalisation, Mr Johnson became C&WW manager and Mr Colton was his assistant; Mr Ford had been C&WW chief clerk from 1931 to 1948.

Cost Offices

The Cost Office, or No. 8 Office, on the 'locomotive side' was one of a group that were collectively known as the Locomotive Works Manager's Offices. They were on the ground floor of a detached building that was one of the original Works' buildings seen on the plan of 1846. The office was a comparatively large one with more than twenty staff. It was divided up into sections, each dealing with different types of railway mechanics, such as boilers, locomotives and plant machinery. From the First World War onwards there were an ever-increasing number of females in the offices of Swindon Works. The typists' pool was in this building and it was staffed exclusively by women. Freda

Dening was in charge here for many years. Elsewhere in the offices of the locomotive works manager, however, there were few, if any female clerks before the 1950s.

The work of the Cost Offices (loco and carriage & wagon) was to tabulate, by hand, all expenditure incurred in manufacturing on either side of the works. Costs were calculated from three elements: labour, materials and establishment charges. An average figure was then deducted from materials for scrap that was sold on. The information was then sent on to the machine room, where it was computed and turned into accumulated data. This could then be analysed and compared by drawing office and management staff to see which viable production methods showed the best value for money. It also showed how varying numbers of staff employed affected production.

Obtaining the best material prices was also a factor but that was the responsibility of the Stores Dept. Incidentally, the advanced Powers-Samas accounting machines were used at Swindon from 1929 and their first application was the costing of repairs to locomotives, boilers and tenders. They compiled figures sent in from the Loco Cost Office. Cost Office clerks would have to liaise regularly with the shop floor staff, in person or by telephone, in the course of their work.

Someone had the foresight to write the surnames on the back of surviving Loco Cost Office outing photos, taken in 1935 and later, and I think they are worth recording here too: J.W. Higgs (chief costing officer, whose counterpart on the carriage side was F. King); B.R. Howell (head of boiler, machinery and plant section); H.R. Plaister (head of engines and progress section); H.T. Osborn (head of building section). Others noted are: C.T. Kent, Bond, Earp, Manning, W.M. Dunscombe, Haggard, Tombs, Cole, Edward Lomas, Wakefield, Dibsdall, West, Gibbs, Bond, Beattie, Money and Gooding. Sometime after the Second World War, probably at the time of Nationalisation in 1948, this office had been renamed the (Loco) Estimating Office: Mr Higgs was still in charge at that time. Messrs Osborn, Kent, Gooding and Plaister were still there too, along with Ken Jones,

A snapshot taken by Miss Vera Prior, who later became assistant to the clerk in charge of the CME Power-Samas machine section. It shows her office decorated for the Coronation of 1937. Most, if not all staff who worked here, would be given the day off with ordinary rate pay as it was declared a public holiday.

A.D. Spackman, J. Thomas, Trevor Howard and R.G. Moses.

Of the aforementioned staff, Mr Plaister and Mr Osborn were probably the longest serving in this Cost Office as their names also appear alongside an outing photo dated 1912. Of the personnel in the carriage side cost office, I know only Harry Bartlett and Ivor Wilkins, who were transferred there from the shop floor in the late 1950s when Trevor Howard and Jim Higgs were in charge. This office, too, was renamed Estimating Office but, as usual, their staff continued to use the old name.

A diary or scrapbook consisting of a sparse collection of entries relating to the all-male staff of the Loco (side) Cost Office has surfaced recently. It consists of a random selection of snapshot photographs, doodles, thoughts and articles. This localised version of the GWR staff magazine was among the effects of Ken Jones, who worked in this office. Ken, who had been a prominent member of the GWR Staff Association, was ninety years old when he died in 2015. Therefore he probably began his working life in one of the CME offices during the First World War. It has not been established whether he had any part in putting the diary together.

The contents are, almost without exception, about the social activities of the office. There are staff photos, cuttings of retirement write-ups in the railway press and itineraries of annual outings. As was usual, there are caricature drawings of colleagues in humorous situations (most offices had someone who was famed for their cartoon ability). The humour would be apparent to those who knew the victims and their particular mannerisms.

What is not mentioned or depicted are methods of working: something of which the management would have taken a dim view. Before nationalisation they would not have wanted their methods to get into the hands of their competitors. However, I suspect that the main reason that the compilers omitted such detail was because they did not think it had entertainment value. Producing an ongoing newspaper of this type was common among office workers of the period, so I am told. I've seen very few Swindon Works examples, so I presume few have survived. Space permits only a couple of references to it here but it might help to give a sense of the lighter side of office life in Swindon Works:

A poem *Ode to the Tanks* dated 1941 seems to refer to a wartime contract that caused the office staff some headaches. Whatever the problem was exactly, it was significant enough to be the only entry throughout the Second World War. The anonymous writer obviously had a flair for satire in this form. My guess is that one section of the office has been given the job of estimating the costs of manufacturing parts and assembly of armoured fighting vehicles [tanks]. It sounds like the compiling of the accounts for this work was not as straightforward as they would have liked. Perhaps that's why the huge contract went to Horwich Locomotive Works.

Powers-Samas punchcard machines used at Swindon in the 1930s and '40s for the production of paybills, material charges and mileage statistics. Maintenance of these machines was provided by service mechanics and electricians. They were employed by the manufacturers but were permanently on site. *GWR Magazine*

Some of the loco side' typists section attending the wedding of a colleague at Christ Church. The only person identified in this 1930s photo is section head Freda Dening, sixth from the left. *B. Carter*

A piece from the year 1947 includes several sketches that suggest William 'Maurice' Dunscombe, one of the loco cost clerks, was an umpire for the company all-line tennis competition. No doubt the subtle additions that are pencilled in are intended to make harmless fun of the subject. As well as employing some very good sportsmen and women, there were also some very capable referees among the Works' staff. More than one reached the very highest level and refereed football cup finals, for instance. Two cartoon illustrations show Mr Dunscombe holidaying in Switzerland that year as well.

Retirement

By the late 1930s representations were being made on behalf of female staff with a view to setting up a pension scheme. Many of those who joined the company during the First World War were now realising that belonging to such as scheme would be advantageous. The directors agreed to this in 1938, for female clerks. At this time, the GWR as a whole employed 1,831 females who would be eligible.

The retirements' section of the staff magazines showed that many of the accounts' people in the department left with forty-five years of service: a few managed nearly fifty years, as they were allowed to work beyond the age of sixty. Because works and office staff

could be retained during the war, some 'clocked up' even more than that. A Mr J. Street managed fifty-seven years by the time he was released in 1946, nearly all in the East Time Office! There was no upper age limit at which senior officers had to retire and this applied to departmental heads as well. They would not, however, be able to hang on to office as long as their bosses in the 1930s: Mr Collett and Mr Auld. Mr Collett, the chief mechanical engineer, reluctantly retired at the age of seventy, not because of pressure he got from the board of directors, but because his assistant Mr Auld, also seventy, would not stay on any longer and support his cause.

The 'send-off' for long-serving and popular staff was a ritual that was undertaken regularly in the Works' offices. Ben Howell, mentioned in the last section, retired in November 1945. He was, for many years, a section head in the Loco Works' Manager's Offices. Just before his sixtieth birthday, a gathering took place in the Cost Office where Mr Howell was based. A concert and supper was also arranged in honour of Mr Howell's forthcoming retirement at the GWR Athletic Association pavilion. The locomotive works' manager, K.J. Cook, presided and opened proceedings by giving a breakdown of Mr Howell's working life. He had come up from the shop floor after learning the rudiments of fitting, turning and erecting. After time away working in shipyards on the Bristol Channel, Ben, as he was familiarly known, returned to the Works in 1910. 'The chief' (Mr Cook) then referred to his long association with the 'loco family' and wished him a long and happy retirement at his Shrivenham Road home. Ben Howell was then presented with a sum of treasury notes subscribed by his many friends.

6
Office Staff Recollections

Generally, office people had more opportunities to move around in the course of their work than the shop workers. Consequently they all seemed to know one another, at least by name. Everyone was expected to maintain a professional, courteous manner, but there was some bad feeling that persisted through the 1930s towards clerks who had remained loyal to the company during the General Strike of 1926.

Barbara Dening: CME and Stores Accounts

By the mid-1930s, with more applicants than positions available, it had become more difficult to secure employment as a clerk in the Works. Candidates had to pass a medical as well as an 'educational' examination. By obtaining the matriculation certificate at school, which was equivalent to the later 'O' level grade, prospective employees could bypass the company's written exam. In common with most school leavers, Barbara Dening took this examination before the end of her final term and passed with credit in the required subjects. This, together with a favourable final report from her school, The Elms at Faringdon, enabled her to 'get a start' in the offices of the CME Dept. Barbara began her working life in 40 Office in 1940. She said:

I decided to continue my studies at the College after work to advance my career. This was my choice, as the company did not insist on it. [Some other junior clerks, taken on at that time, did not arrive with such good credentials. They were expected to attend evening classes to study subjects appropriate to their work, such as shorthand, typewriting, commerce, bookkeeping and office appliances.] We worked twelve-hour shifts but I left work early on night school evenings so as to be there from 6pm to 9pm. It was a long day, often working in artificial light due to the blackout. To try to counteract the dingy lighting, the office was painted brilliant white and gained the nickname 'White City'. I did manage to get away early on Thursdays to attend the Wesleyan Guild, my weekly social evening out.

For the first six months Barbara was using an advanced Muldivo calculating machine to compile timber measurements and prices. There were eight ladies to a section including the section head. Her first net wage in 1940 was 5s 8d (5 shillings and 8 pence) and Barbara still has that first, very austere, payslip. Muldivo 'super-automatic' calculators were installed in the Works in the mid-1930s. They were a bit bigger than the basic typewriters of the day and were driven by A/C motors. The earlier versions of these machines were hand operated.

Barbara's friends and colleagues included Jean, the daughter of senior wages' clerk Fred Hook; Marjorie Parsons, whose mother conducted the Swindon Ladies Choir; and Doreen Pullen, who was an impersonator with a concert party entertaining the troops, in her spare time. Another girl, Ivy Davis, ran a sort of magazine club in the office. Of that, Barbara said:

Each of us bought a different women's magazine which, after we had read it, was passed on to Ivy, who redistributed them among the contributors. Another co-operative scheme enabled the participants to buy saving certificates which the government were promoting during the war. Twenty of us got together and all paid in a shilling a week; a certificate was purchased and every twenty weeks each person received one.

Reg Cook used to come and have his tea in 40 Office. He looked after the Storehouse where all the old documents were kept. Reg always looked scruffy, probably because the old papers he was handling had become very dusty. To supplement his low pay, Reg would get you scarce items on the black market.

No. 40 Office was really two long offices on the first floor of the CME building. It was in the northern aspect above the Cash Office 'money make-up' sections and the Wire Rope Shop. Half of the office was taken up with accounting machinery, the other half had girls working at long desks. Across the corridor was a Stores office laid out very similarly but with a more open view out across the Gloucester branch towards the General Stores and the Running Sheds.

Some older staff still called these machine sections by the old name of Addressograph Offices. The first addressograph mechanical appliances had been used at Swindon in the early 1900s for printing workmen's details on to paybills. Although these early models had gone, they did retain some machines that had seen years of wear and tear by the 1930s and '40s. This pioneering type was now just one among a whole range of accounting machinery.

Glass screens separated the desks from the machinery. Around the walls of the office were fitted cabinets containing the punchcards and, in common with all offices, cupboards of stationary and business ledger books. Percy Richards was office chief of the CME machine sections and Muriel Whale was section chief over the sorter and tabulator machine operators. I think it is likely that Mr Richards was also responsible for the Stores Machine Room too. Barbara said, of her boss:

> Mr Richards rode an upright bicycle down from Old Town every day. This inspired me to do the same in an effort to avoid being late so often. I lived in Eastcott Road, about a mile from the Works. Some evenings and weekends Mr Richards served as a major in the Home Guard and because I was the quickest typist in the office he would get me to do all the HG paperwork.

After being there a few years, Barbara was required to go and issue coal and slow combustion fuel tickets to retired workmen. Someone had to go down, every other Tuesday afternoon, to an office near the tunnel entrance. The job appears to have been given to clerks from any office that could be spared. Later, Barbara was moved across the corridor to the Stores Accounts Machine Room. Miss Foulds was the most senior person there and Barbara was the senior operator over the twelve or more females on key-punching machines. These girls typed the information from cost statements into the machine, which then converted it and stamped it into punchcards as combinations of holes. Because of the strict division of staff in the two departments, there was some resentment at the appointment of an 'outsider' as section head.

Harry Dening: CME Accounts

Henry (known at work as Harry) Dening was Barbara's father. He started his working life in a workshop office, probably on the loco side, about 1907. By the time Henry was twenty he had gained his advanced bookkeeping qualifications, which had taken him three years. Later, Barbara told him, jokingly, that she would beat that, which

This was No. 40 Office in the 1930s: the machinery section was behind the photographer. Two of the girls in the front are Nancy Verrinder, left, and Molly Adkins; behind them are Marjorie Gooding left and Ethel Fletcher, while in the next row back are Beryldene Hunt left and Enid Munden. *Central Library: local studies section*

she did, but then admitted the course was condensed due to the wartime conditions. Mr Dening, a Methodist, also taught at night school. Initially this was to help make ends meet, but he must have progressed quickly because Barbara remembers him telling her that his salary had reached £400 per annum. This is thought to have been in the early 1930s when even a grade 1 clerk with five years' experience received no more than £350.

Mr Dening took charge of 22 (Accounts) Office sometime in the 1930s. We get some idea of the conduct observed in his office by something he told his daughter: he said that he only had to look up from his desk and any talking stopped. She remembers the story because he went on to say 'wearing my spectacles for short sightedness, I couldn't actually see a thing when I looked up, but nobody seemed to have worked that out'. Just after the war, Mr Dening suddenly lost his voice and could only whisper

A young Henry Dening at the start of his career in an unknown workshop office. *B. Carter*

faintly. Because of this, he was given a single office, still on the first floor next to those of the chief clerk and his assistant. He communicated by writing notes, to which sometimes a reply would be written back, something he found very amusing.

Harry Dening died while at work in 1947, and after a period under the deputy, Mr (Tom) Minchin, Frank (or Francis) Dance took over as clerk in charge of 22 Office. (Mr Dance also looked after the finances of St Marks Church as parish treasurer.) It was during his time as acting clerk in charge that Mr Minchin had to ask Barbara if he could borrow her late father's notebooks so he could properly manage the office. 'He obviously felt uncomfortable about asking,' she said.

Daphne Kibblewhite: CME Accounts

Daphne lived in Cricklade Road and attended Euclid Street Grammar School until the age of sixteen. She had obtained a place at teacher training college in London but her father, a boilermaker in the GWR, did not want her to go. This was 1939 and with the possibility of another war he thought Daphne should stay put. Therefore she applied to become a clerk in the Railway Works and after a short while was invited to take the entrance exam at her former school. When a vacancy came up she was accepted subject to a medical. Once the war started, waiting for a vacancy became a thing of the past. Daphne also started her working life in No. 40 office, on Monday, 4 September 1939, the day after war with Germany was declared. Because it was such a big busy office with lots of staff, she only vaguely remembers Barbara Dening. What Daphne does remember is:

> My friend from school, Betty Crouch, started about the same time but she went into the Duplicating

Some of the staff of No. 40 Office at Christmas 1942 or 1943. Those identified are, left to right standing: Maurice Chequer office boy, Eunice ?, unknown, Joan Hazel, unknown, Betty Workman, unknown, unknown. In the front are: unknown, unknown, Norah Coole then Daphne Kibblewhite. Daphne suggested that some of the men here probably worked in other offices. *D. Kibblewhite*

Office where short-runs of internal booklets, circulars and posters were printed. Percy Richards was clerk in charge of mechanical accounting in 40 Office: his personal secretary was Nora Hunt. Mr [Frank or Francis] Dance was Mr Richards' assistant and Mr [Steve] Wheeler was next in line of seniority and not far off retirement. Mr Gregory and Mr Jones were there to start with as well but as the younger men got called up they were moved, possibly to No. 48 [Mileage] Office. Miss [Gladys] Hamblin and Miss [Elsie] Calladine were the senior clerks on our machine section.

Presumably because of a good report from school and because I was sixteen I was not given errands to run and tea to make: the normal duties of the newest office girl. I was put on an electric Muldivo machine. I can't remember how much training I got but soon I was calculating fortnightly piecework payments on my own. I totalled up the amount of work done [expressed as £.s.d.] according to the chargeman's certificates, this I then divided by the number of men in the gang or gangs. The clever part was converting the figures to suit the metric machines, then reverting back to a figure in sterling and doing it quickly. Later I was also calculating the cost to the company of producing sawn timber. My machine made light work of compounding dozens of different-sized batches. Sometimes I sorted coal tickets into street order by hand if another operator was using my machine. I was sent over to Milton Road post office on occasions to buy stamps to stick on enginemen's insurance cards.

Yvonne Hodey: CME Accounts

I could have gone into the departmental stores, Morse's or McIlroy's, or factories such as Wills's and Compton's but I applied at the Railway Works. I passed the medical exam in January 1953 and started work 'inside' the following month. As the office junior, I sat at a single desk at the back of 21 Accounts CME. The office seemed vast with about forty or fifty male and female staff. It was very daunting at first. I was positioned in a 'cubby hole' out of sight but within earshot of the clerk in charge, Mr Rendall, and his assistant, Mr Nash. I made the tea, ran messages and collected from, or delivered post to, Mr Chesterman in the Correspondence Office. This was in the days when you called your elders Mr or Miss … and never by their Christian name, unless invited to do so.

Once judged to be trustworthy, another regular job for the junior was to take money to the bank, sometimes quite large sums. I would collect a large canvas bag of money from the clerk in charge of Central Wages, Mr Roberts, or from the assistant chief accountant, Mr Sanders. This was money paid in for concessionary bus and rail tickets, at the

Works' Booking Office, which had been bagged up for transportation at the Cash Office. On one occasion I was stopped by a policeman, who told me I should not be out walking with all that money.

Making the tea was fun. It was a major operation, done in very little space under the staircase on the ground floor, with girls from different offices. Carrying large trays of teas for the whole office up and down the stairs was tricky to say the least. Then we had to wash up and do a repeat performance in the afternoon. The staff I remember in 21 Office during my time were Mr West, Mr Harris, Mr Youll, Don Curtis, Miss Wykeham-Martin, Winnie Stroud and Dorothy Wirdnam. Office girls who worked elsewhere included Cecilia Brown, Janet Knighton and Jennifer Allen, who was in 22 Office. Most people had close relatives 'inside' but since Grandfather Stevenson retired, before the war, I only had a cousin, Maureen Stokes. She worked in the Stores managers' office [see Chapter 10].

After nine months, Yvonne became a junior clerk and was moved to what she remembers as the 'Powers-Samas Dept'. This was the accounts' machinery section of 40 Office and in 1953 Mr 'Pop' Richards was in charge, as he had been for some years. This office was just down the corridor from 21 Office on the first floor. After a short training period, Yvonne operated punchcard machines. She was put on to a pay rate starting at 25 shillings net.

Jack Hartley: Mechanical & Electrical Engineer's Staff

Jack had started his training to become a clerk at Swindon Junction station and Transfer Goods Yard Office. Later he asked to move into the Works to get more experience. He told me:

I went into the Correspondence Office, on the first floor of the CME's building, in 1951 or '52. This was one of several sections manned by the mechanical & electrical engineer's personal staff. Mr [Harold] Coleman was chief clerk here at that time. Our office was amalgamated with the Carriage Correspondence Office shortly after I arrived. Mr [Sid] Brown became chief clerk in charge of the C&W side of it.

Correspondence clerks dealt with all the incoming letters and sent them on to the relevant department if necessary. Otherwise the appropriate 'technical' person wrote shorthand replies and the typists typed them ready for signing. The incoming letters were then stored in 5ft-high, floor-standing, wooden cupboards with sliding doors. They lined the main corridor outside our office. When matters were settled, the accompanying correspondence was removed to the Storehouse to make way for more. [A corridor ran down the middle of the first

floor of the east wing, where the offices of the M&EE were situated. Jack only had dealings with two: staff sections and records. The majority of the other offices here were for senior M&EE staff. Previously, these were the offices that had been occupied by the GWR CME's, Mr Collett then Mr Hawksworth, and their assistants.]

I worked for a time on the electrical section dealing with 'wayleaves'. This was concerned with annual rents and rates collected from firms running electrical cables and telephone lines across our land. Our outgoing correspondence was sent on to the 'electrical assistant to the M&EE', to be signed. There were two distinct groups of personal staff working for the M&EE at this time: clerks and technical staff. The latter were all 'time served' tradesmen. It seemed to be the clerks that did all the work while the 'techs' took the credit and were paid more! Consequently a growing resentment built up towards them.

A Mr B was a case in point: he had a technical position but was just a staff administrator and he looked down on us. We had a meeting and decided to write to the general manager at Paddington. This resulted in a 'works' study' investigation. The clerical side wanted to be regarded as equal and eventually we were. Clerks were now in charge of clerks and on the same pay rates as our counterparts with engineering backgrounds.

Promotion got me moved to the carriage & wagon section of the office and I had four females working for me. Mary Covey is the only name I can now recall (probably the prettiest). They filed all the internal and external letters away with others of similar subject matter. The Records' Office also handled correspondence and our work overlapped with them. About a dozen people worked there compiling crane, stationary boiler, machinery and publication records using a card system. The person in charge was a technical man whose name I can't now remember. A little later William [Maurice] Dunscombe, who had moved upstairs from the Works [shop floor] to become a cost clerk/estimator in the Loco Cost Office, became head of records. His assistant was Bob Johnson or Johnston.

Noreen Harris: Motive Power Office

The offices of the CME's outdoor section were centralised at Swindon until 1956. Otherwise known as the Running Department and later the Motive Power Dept, its responsibilities could be divided into three main parts: 1) the administration of footplate staff and inspectors; 2) running shed stores including mechanical parts, coal and oil; 3) locomotive history records. In the early 1950s the carriage, wagon and train working sections of this department were transferred to the offices of the carriage & wagon engineer.

The impression that girls leaving school and looking for office work got was that nowhere compared to the Works. It persisted even after more and more large firms became established in the town. From what Noreen and others have told me, it appears that generally, women with these other employers were put on repetitive work requiring little mental skill:

In the early 1950s I came to Swindon to find work as I had relatives in north Wiltshire. I took lodgings with a Mrs Kent in Plymouth Street because Plymouth was where I came from. First of all I worked at Plessey's, then Vickers-Armstrongs. I did six months at each, doing clerical work. It was boring and I was educated beyond what I was doing. I had heard good reports about the Railway Works, so I applied there. With the general school's certificate I was moved up the waiting list to go into the Motive Power Dept. When I did start, in 1952, Mr Pellow was the MP Superintendent.

The office I was in dealt with personal records and I was on the footplate section. We compiled information on firemen and engine cleaners' promotion and progress. There were six to a section and I remember Eric Lane, John Cavello, Vera Carter and Nancy Titcombe from those early days. Nancy had been a 'knocker-upper' during the war and Vera, who worked on the conciliation staff section, was a town councillor.

Junior females, not males, had to take turns at making the tea for the office. We did this in the Messengers Room, which was accessed via the 'posh entrance' at the front of the CME building. While in the MPD I had my twenty-first birthday and [as was a tradition] I received a large brass key, which was made in the workshops. A short hairstyle was all the fashion in those days, like Audrey Hepburn's. If we girls were going out that evening we would be able to wash our hair in the basins in the cloakroom, apply some gel and return to our desks without it being noticed.

Sometimes I was asked to go and issue coal sales tickets to staff at the tunnel entrance. Down there they had under-floor heating ducts and on more than one occasion a rat had got in and died and the smell was awful. I always walked through the middle of the tunnel because rats sometimes ran along the water channels either side.

Another clerk and I were sometimes asked if we wanted to go into town with a collection tin for the Widows and Orphans' Fund. Presumably this wasn't a very popular task because they offered us another day off in lieu, as an incentive, and of course we always said yes. The Saturday morning shift was stopped while I was in this department so I started working for Mr Bartlett, the landlord at the Glue Pot, where I was now lodging. He paid me 10 shillings a week for working in the bar some evenings or at weekends.

Jim Bond: Weightable Office

Jim or 'Jimmy' worked as a 'material checker' in the weightable office attached to the Iron Foundry. His job was to record the weights of wagon-loads of castings leaving the foundry. Jim was born in the 1890s, so was a little before the generation of railway workers that I met to record their stories. But for two reasons, he may well have been just another long-forgotten office worker among the thousands that passed through the Works over the years. Firstly, Alderman James Bond became town mayor in 1950 and secondly, that was the Jubilee year of the Borough of Swindon.

As part of the celebrations, HRH Princess Elizabeth visited the town and the Works. Thousands of Swindonians lined the route to see the royal guest and Mayor Bond accompanied her throughout the day. Then there were the press photos and a Pathé News film to ensure his place in history. Dave Ellis, a correspondence registrar in the Motive Power Dept, told me that he called in to Jimmy's office the following day, 16 November 1950, and discussed the royal visit with him. 'He was a bit of a celebrity for a while,' said Dave.

Mike Clarke: Various C&W Offices

Mike worked in several offices on the carriage & wagon side in the 1950s. He was born in Swindon and lived in Tiverton Road, Gorse Hill. As was usual, he came from a railway family and married into another: Father Fred 'Nobby' Clarke worked for the GWR and then the Western Region as a driver at the Transfer Goods Depot. Mike's father-in-law, Jim Hawkins, did unskilled work preparing engines for overhaul in the reception sidings. Of Mike's time in the offices, he told me:

I left Commonweal school and started in 15 Shop Office in 1951. Len Curtis was the other 'boy' not long out of school and two weeks later Graham Gibbs, from Wanborough, started too. I was to be trained as an office clerk but, at first, I got the duties of 'office boy' on account of not yet reaching sixteen years of age. With Graham, Len and myself, there were fifteen staff in our office plus the chief clerk: Fred Simpkins. His boss was W.G. Lloyd: the chief clerk for the Carriage & Wagon Works. Mr Simpkins' assistant was Harry Bennett and the other clerks I remember were Harold Wyniatt, Charlie Spalding, Reg Bennett, Albert Vockins, Harry Smith, Harry Matthews, Bill Taylor and Len Cole. Len dealt with general enquiries at the office window and also issued the pass-outs to shop floor staff.

To me, all the trained staff in our office seemed quite old, but most were probably no more than middle aged. Later, I began my clerical training in this office along with Ron Berry and Dave King. The 15 Shop Foreman was Ashley Walker, who lived in Drove Road. He always had a button hole flower and carried a rolled umbrella on his walk to work. The assistant foremen were Jack Gray, 'Nippy' James, Howard Smith and another whose name escapes me now.

My work for now would be classed as general clerical for someone of my age and experience. I was given a hand-drawn map of all the chargemen's desks in 15 Shop and I had to deliver their gang's time sheets. After they were submitted I had to record all the details on the sheets in a ledger. I can still remember most of the chargemen's names: Fred Farncombe, Ernie Buller, Ray Greening, Con Morse, Ernie Lucas, Percy Hall, Reg Shipway, Archie Menham, ? Williams, ? Moore, Sam Harris, who was chargeman of the vacuum brake cylinder gang, and Ernie Churchill, who was 'chargeman plumbers' in 15A Shop. I also had to visit Tom Chesterman, who was chargeman in the nearby grinding shop.

In those days there was still a gang of women 'rivet hotters' in my shop. [It is often said that the women in the engineering workshops were gradually replaced by men after the war but Mike remembers this gang stayed through the 1950s.] The two piecework inspectors in 15 Shop in 1952 were Reg Pithouse and Jack Money. At this time I also spent one day a week in the Drawing Stores with Arthur Marchment, who was a cantankerous individual. Here we issued out engineering drawings to the carriage side chargemen of the gangs who needed them in the course of their work. I remember that I also issued small packs of tea and sugar to the staff in 15 Shop Office. For some reason this was all kept in the Drawing Stores.

In about 1953 I moved to 16 (Special Loads) Office, where Charlie Coleman was my boss. This was one of the carriage & wagon main offices at the front of 15 Shop. The work here involved the planning of how and when heavy, long or 'out of gauge' loads could be moved by railway wagon: anything that could not be accommodated by the Western Region's standard types of goods' wagons. We had to find the best route with the fewest sharp curves and decide which train to attach each particular load to. The wagons were held in 23 Shop Yard over by Whitehouse Road.

I finished up in 14 Staff Office, where Bill Howell was in charge. Other members of staff here were Clem Smith, John Morkot, Don Hulbert, Jim Dean and Mabel Piff, a lovely lady nearing retirement. My first duty was to examine the paper rolls taken from time clocks around the Carriage & Wagon Works to make sure that the watchmen had clocked in to each point on their rounds. Any irregularities were reported to the chief C&W watchman. I think I may have taken over this duty from a Mr Scotford.

Other work I did here was issuing the free passes and privilege (known by all as 'priv') tickets for 'trip' holidays. The passes were green card tickets about

The Loco Wages Office sometime between 1952, when it was combined with the carriage wages' office, and 1956. Fred Boucher and Walter Sheppard are seen in the centre, facing the photographer. The section dealing with workshop stores wages was off to the left. *BRWR*

2in × 1in, very similar to Edmondson train tickets used by the public. I remember that on one occasion a man arrived to collect a pass he had ordered by phone. It should have been made out for Margate Harbour station but someone had written Market Harborough (we only had rubber stamps for the main destinations). He wasn't amused. When houses or flats in the railway village came up for let, it was the job of 14 Office to advertise the vacancy and I remember going round the factory putting up notices to that effect on the shop noticeboards.

Like a lot of the workforce, I gradually became worried about my employment prospects in the Works. There was a general air of despondency on the railways, so I left in 1957 and went to Vickers-Armstrongs at South Marston. There they were producing or maintaining components for the Valiant, Scimitar and Attacker aircraft. My pay doubled there but I preferred the family atmosphere of Swindon Works.

Brenda Berry: (Passenger) Mileage Office

Brenda lived in Hughes Street and in 1953 she left school and went into 'the railways' (the Works), aged sixteen. She came from a railway family: her brother Ron and Sister Kathleen were 'inside', as was her father and his father before him. Ron went into the carriage side offices in 1950: 'At least I assume that's where he was because he wasn't in the CME offices,' said Brenda (not necessarily the case). Older sister Kathleen was a comptometer operator

69

during the war; later when her husband's job took him to London, Kathleen got a job on the Western Region at Paddington. Brenda's father, Robert, was a riveter in the C&W Works, making it likely that his son Ron was in that side of the Works too, as she suspected. Brenda was put to work in the Mileage (passenger train) Office:

> Our working hours were 8.30am to 5.30pm and we regularly worked overtime to 7.30pm. My wages started at £2 9s 6d a week before stoppages and I gave my mother a pound a week. 'The mileage' was a mixed office at the top of the CME building [within a four-storey extension completed in the late 1920s]. We shared the floor with the Comptometer (Goods Mileage) Office, which was on the other side of the central corridor from us. At one end of our office was a small lift used to haul up work from the floors below. At the other end was a long coil of rope which, in the event of evacuation, would be used to abseil to safety. I never heard of it being necessary for anyone to try.
>
> The wooden desks we had were long and seated three people; along the inner wall of the office, glass-fronted cupboards were fitted. All the furniture and fittings looked very antiquated. There was an assortment of chairs of varying comfort and when a senior person left, their chair was inherited by the next in line. The bosses, Mr Lewis and Mr Fluck, worked in a partitioned area known as the Glass House with half a dozen general clerks. My first section head was Mr [Reg] Pickering and his deputy was Ernie Mafeking Smith, so named as he was born in 1900. Most of the unmarried females in the office were thought of as 'old maids'. Office staff worked closely together and we soon got to know each other's business, both professionally and socially.

Each section within this Mileage Office covered an operating division of the GWR, later the Western Region. Each member of staff was responsible for a different depot or several small depots. Brenda received the drivers' reports for engine diagrams worked from Worcester shed. Consignments of these 'returns' arrived daily, 'possibly in leather satchels' said Brenda. Another person on her section (there were five of them) dealt with Hereford Running Shed and so on. They used mileage charts but the main route distances were soon learned by heart. It was 120 miles from Worcester to Paddington, remembers Brenda, with an extra ¾ of a mile out and back to Ranelagh Road for servicing the locomotive before the return trip. There were six London turns a day from Worcester at that time.

As well as passenger train services, enginemen and guards recorded 'light engine' and empty coaching stock movements: the miles and man-hours of which all had to be totalled up. Engineering trains in particular were often out at night, bank holidays and weekends and the figures compiled by mileage staff were used to work out enhanced payments of up to time-and-three-quarters.

Every other Tuesday the rates for permanent way 'ballasting work' were calculated. All the tabulated information was passed on to the machine section to be converted on to standard Swindon forty-five-column punch cards. 'Finally we stacked each driver's records together and over a flat piece of wood we pierced the top left-hand corner with a screwdriver. Then we tied them together with string and sent them back, care of the relevant divisional superintendent.'

Brenda and former colleagues, Madeline Midwinter (nee Liles), Tony Averies and Brian Reynolds, kindly supplied me with the names of staff in the passenger mileage office in the mid-1950s. Some of those listed below had been here for many years before that too: Reg Pickering was section head of the London division; Gerald Rouse was departmental head; Ernie Smith was head of the section dealing with the Bristol division. Others remembered were: Maurice Slocombe, Win Tompkins, Kath Bury, Sheila Clarke (nee Gardiner), Miss Edwards, Reg Baker, Owen Clarke, Esme Haysom, Ken Critchley, Dick Stanton, Ella Bizley, Tony Groves, Cynthia Hyde (nee Axton) and John Summerhayes, who worked on Bristol section and dealt specifically with Bath Road Depot.

Margery Booker: (Freight) Mileage Office

No. 47 (Mileage) Office was where freight train statistics were received from all over the GWR, and later the Western Region, and compiled. Both Mileage Offices were comparatively large: approximately sixty people worked on passenger traffic statistics and about forty were involved with compiling the figures for freight train movements.

Margery Booker lived in Stafford Street, up the hill at the back of Old Town, in those days. She left Commonweal School in 1945 and had secured a job as a telephone operator for the GPO. Her father didn't work in the Railway Works but knew of its reputation. He persuaded Margery to apply to go 'inside' instead. Unusually, none of the Bookers were on the Works' payroll already:

> In the freight mileage office we sat at long desks, four in a row, using mechanical [comptometer] calculating machines [for some reason the company only wanted female machine operators]. Together with another four girls in the row in front, that was our section. We totalled up things like loads, numbers of wagons per train and distances between goods yards. From this we typed up weekly summaries and, as we weren't really typists, there was a lot of rubbing out. There were often arguments about whether windows should be opened as it could get warm and stuffy if they remained closed and noisy, from passing trains, if they were opened.
>
> We covered the Bristol division, which included

Swindon. There were another three sections, each one dealing with two or three operating divisions of the GWR. So, of the thirty-two clerks employed on this work at any one time, I can still recall quite a lot of the names but they did not all work there at the same time: Pam Clayton [nee Comley], Lily Pinchin, Joan Young [nee Dash], Dill Richens, Jean Veitch, Margaret Jones, Olive Redman, Joyce Livermore, Josie Byrne [nee Jackson], Sybil Little [nee Cooksey], Dorothy Newton, Mary Watts, Mavis Triggs [nee Carter], Nora Instone [nee Walters], Jean Strange, Dorothy Woodham, Joan Morris [nee Burroughs], Ellie McLean, Muriel Sheppard, Rosemary Groves [nee Watts], Audrey Marsh, May Ashley, Kathleen Medcalf, Mary Power, Mary Keene and Valda Bartlett.

Then there were the four section heads: Flora Morgan, Margaret Ackrill, Edna 'Eddie' Garrett and Lucy Ebourne, whose family had a greengrocer's shop near the market. They were all older and unmarried. During my time, Mr Fluck and Mr Lewis were in overall charge. They, and their personal clerks, worked in an office that was partitioned off with glass panels, within the passenger office. As we had fewer staff than the other Mileage Office, another section used the back of our office: they were unconnected to us. I got married in 1955 and left to start a family in 1960.

Mary Almond: CME Accounts

Mary 'Nutty' Almond worked in the Stores Ledger Office on clothing accounts from 1955. This office was on the second floor the CME building overlooking the main line. Like Brenda, Mary also remembered a rope fire escape:

The rope was elasticated and was anchored, at one end, to the radiator. If there had been a fire it could have been a disaster as there was so much wood and paper everywhere. The stairways at each end of the building [also partially made of wood] could barely cope at the best of times. When the gong [electric bell] went the stairways immediately became packed with staff and you got swept along with the flow.

Another thing I remember about the CME offices was the dirt and dust coming in from outside. To compensate, we were all issued with a towel and a bar of soap. Keeping the windows closed all the time helped but, of course, in the hot weather it was tempting to open them. One girl did and a pile of invoices was swept out and she had to go and try to retrieve them all. There was no such problems in winter, of course. Our office, along with some of the other smaller offices, still had an open fireplace, although it was no longer used.

Jack Hartley at work in 1959 or 1960 when he was in the CM&EE's administrative general section.
*Swindon Railway New*s

Jack Hartley: CM&EE Section

By 1960 Jack was working in the chief mechanical & electrical engineers' (the word 'chief' had been reinstated in the title) administrative (general) section. One of his jobs was processing applications for permits for visitors to the Works. A piece appeared in the *Swindon Railway News* in April 1960 that focused on the two key planners of Works' tours, Bert Stratford, the senior watchman and guide, and Jack Hartley. One passage read: 'At a time when theatres, cinemas and soccer clubs were playing to diminishing audiences, the drawing power of Swindon Works increases. 26,080 visitors arrived last year. Many came by rail and this means valuable revenue, estimated at £7,500 annually.'

The other part of Jack's work at this time was handling the clerical side of reports in connection with claims against the Western Region. These were often associated with damage to goods in transit: anything from farm machinery coming loose from their fastenings in open wagons to wooden packing crates breaking apart. The latter would require the Works' timber storekeeper to get involved. His timber inspectors would investigate to determine whether the packaging and type of wood used was sufficient to withstand the expected wear and tear of the journey.

The M&EE's personal staff included two general claims inspectors whose work involved assessment of damage by rail movement. One of them would be dispatched to wherever on the region the goods in question were being held, and write a report. In the late 1950s 'these inspectors were Charlie Eynon and a chap named House, possibly Bill' said Jack.

Janet Morgan: CME Accounts

Janet spent the majority of her working life as a teacher but thinks, looking back, that her first experience of working life was the best:

> I was sixteen in 1960 when I went into the Works and everyone used to make sure I was managing alright as the newcomer. There were about fifty staff working on mechanical accounts. I operated an automatic key punching machine which put holes into punchcards according to the data I typed in. By 1960, it was not only paybills, but much of the Works' other accounts, that were compiled and kept using data held on computer punch cards. I was converting information for material costs, rolling stock and stores accounts, invoices, as well as paybills. It was very noisy. In more recent times I have developed hearing problems that must have been caused during the four years I spent in the CME Machine Room. Miss Ackrill was my boss and Mr Young was the 'office chief'; we never called anyone by their first name.

> I lived in Drove Road and the bus took me 'door to door'. I would go out and meet my boyfriend in The Park at dinner times: the Works' hooter giving its five-minute warning always ensured I made it back just in time. Another thing that made it pleasant was that everyone 'looked out' for each other. When an ambulance came through the tunnel entrance we all stood against the walls and were respectfully quiet for a while afterwards, hoping that the casualty would be okay. When the last ever steam locomotive was named, all of the Works' people were invited to the ceremony and some of them were close to tears.

Janet's father George was a boilermaker and had been named 'apprentice of the year' sometime in the mid-1930s. Her older sister, Pam, worked in one of the wages' offices nearby: she also played in the Western Region hockey team. George was very pleased that his daughters worked 'inside': becoming the fourth generation of railway workers in his family.

Female Staff and Marriage

Offices with both male and female staff must have produced some lasting romances, but little of it is recorded in the staff magazines. One exception was Frederick Richens and Helen Bavin, who were both twenty-six years old and both worked on the same section in the CME's Offices. They married in July 1932 and shortly afterwards they left Swindon, almost certainly so that Fred could take up a promotion within the GWR.

Upon becoming married, female staff had to resign. This rule did not apply in wartime, and presumably thereafter as Barbara Dening left to be married in 1950 and it was her husband who wanted her to stay at home full time, not the company. She told me:

> When the 'intended' arrived at work in the morning, she usually found that her colleagues had come in early and decorated her desk. A poem and some words offering marital advice would be prominent among the embellishment. They were allowed to leave a few minutes early the evening before the 'big day', to a cacophony of banging noises. Staff in other offices heard the din, so as the victim passed their office they joined in.

Noreen Harris remembers being given a first-class travel pass to use when going on her honeymoon. When it was known that a person in the office or shop was to be married, it was usual to have a collection and presentation of a gift to wish them well. Margery Smith remembers that, in the Mileage Office, someone would bring in a set of hand bells. As the person getting married or celebrating their twenty-first birthday arrived and left the bells were rung by colleagues on the landing outside the office.

7
The Drawing Office

Overview

The Drawing Office was on the second floor of the CME office building. It was divided up into three main sections: 1) General: stationary boilers, buildings, surveying, pumps, cranes, machinery and electrical. 2) Locomotive, which until the early 'fifties' was made up of: boilers, frames, experimental, valve gear and motion. 3) Carriage & Wagon: bodies, running gear, bogies and special loads. (After about 1950, the amount of C&W work was reduced as Swindon was one of several drawing offices working on standard designs.) Within the combined DO there was also the chief draughtsman's office and an administration office.

The extension to the Print Room (or House) above B Shop, where drawings were copied and photographs were developed, was completed in 1951. The plan for this extension also shows another area next to it where draughtsmen that dealt with cranes, surveys and plant machinery were relocated too, although not until 1958 or 1959. The Print House and new DO annexe were reached by an overhead walkway from the main building. The Estimating Office, where costs could be calculated from engineering drawings, was at the far end of the locomotive section directly above the chief mechanical engineer's office. The Drawing Office Stores was a little way away on the other side of B Shed.

The L-shaped Drawing Office covered an area of 11,100sq ft. It had been added between 1904 and 1906 and was designed to be open plan to take maximum advantage of the natural side and overhead lighting. Sometime in the 1930s or '40s a centre section of desks was added to increase capacity. Newcomers were placed there, only moving out nearer the windows if and when seniority allowed. A case study document dated October 1957 gives the numbers of draughtsmen and technical staff (as opposed to the managerial, secretarial and clerical) as forty-two for both the locomotive and carriage & wagon offices and another fifty-two for the general, mechanical and electrical office.

At the Drawing Board

This was the place where ideas became tangible. There was a universal respect for the draughtsman whose job it was to interpret those ideas or show that they were unworkable.

The appropriate section leader allocated incoming work to the individual. That person might then need to visit the foreman or chargeman on site. He would make sketches, take measurements and look at drawings if any already existed. When working from an existing drawing, some novices were tempted to take a rule and simply increase or decrease the dimensions proportionately. It might save him going to the workshop or calculating measurements from the information given. Despite the often given advice about 'never scaling off a drawing' because they were not always drawn to scale, this tripped a lot of newcomers up at least once.

Sometimes the 'chief' (draughtsman) would allocate special jobs to someone he considered especially capable. The initial plan and any preliminary sketches were drawn using a pencil and cartridge paper before being traced on to tracing paper using Indian ink. Finally, the draughtsman put his initials to his work and, if acceptable, so did a senior colleague who checked it.

The size of the drawings varied, depending largely on what scale the draughtsman chose to use. Very small components would be drawn larger than actual size and large plans or general arrangements were 'laid out' or scaled down. Component parts shown in section were indicated by various cross hatching. Before the war, drawings had any subsequent alterations coloured in to highlight them. Rolling stock general arrangements were normally 1½in to 1ft. Until the use of copying machines and the dyeline process of reproduction were adopted in the 1950s, traced copies were printed in the Print Room.

In the Drawing Stores paper-backed linen copies were wound around a wooden pole with a brass numberplate on the end, for use in the shops. Rolled drawings could be laid out flat using paperweights in each corner.

CAUTION
__ To Be Shunted With Care __
BEFORE THIS CRANE IS ALLOWED TO TRAVEL ON THE MAIN LINE
THE SPRING STOPS MUST BE SCREWED UP. THE JIB LOWERED
ON TO THE MATCH TRUCK & SECURED BY THE JIB HEAD CHAINS
THE SPRING STOPS MUST BE SCREWED DOWN BEFORE LIFTING.
FOR MOVING SLOWLY WITH LOADS THIS CRANE IS REGISTERED
TO LIFT—   6 TONS AT 15 FEET RADIUS
            5 " " 20 "   "
            4 " " 25 "   "
            3 " " 30 "   "
WHEN STATIONARY WITH EXTENSION GIRDERS FULLY OUT
THIS CRANE IS REGISTERED TO LIFT—
            12 TONS AT 15 FEET RADIUS
            10 " " 20 "   "
            8   " " 25 "   "
            6   " " 30 "   "
THESE INSTRUCTIONS ARE FOR WORKING ON A LEVEL ROAD.
DOUBLE ROPE MUST BE USED FOR ALL LOADS OVER 6 TONS.

HEIGHT OF LIFT ABOVE RAIL LEVEL

	Down Rope	Bottom
36'-10"	15'-0"
35'-6"	20'-0"
33'-0"	25'-0"
29'-4"	30'-0"

TABLE OF WEIGHTS ON WHEELS

	A		B		C		D		TOTAL
	T	C.Q	T	C.Q	T	C.Q	T	C.Q	
1	19.12.2	19.6.1	9.2.2	4.16.3	53.3.0
2	11.10.1	11.8.0	10.17.2	10.17.0	44.12.3

1 JIB CARRIED ON DERRICKING ROPES
EXTENSION GIRDERS IN POSITION
TANK 3/4 FULL 4" OF WATER IN GAUGE GLASS
1 CWT OF COAL IN BUNKER 2 CWT OF COAL IN
FIREBOX. CRANE IN FULL WORKING ORDER

2 JIB RESTING ON MATCH TRUCK
EXTENSION GIRDERS IN POSITION
TANK 3/4 FULL 4" OF WATER IN GAUGE GLASS
1 CWT OF COAL IN BUNKER 2 CWT OF COAL IN
FIREBOX. CRANE IN FULL WORKING ORDER

_ C. W. R _
_ 12 TON STEAM TRAVELLING CRANE Nº 32 _
_ SHEWING WEIGHTS ON WHEELS _
_ SWINDON _ OCTOBER _ 1927 _
_ Nº 84314 _

G.W.R. SWINDON * 13 JAN 1933 * DRAWING OFFICE

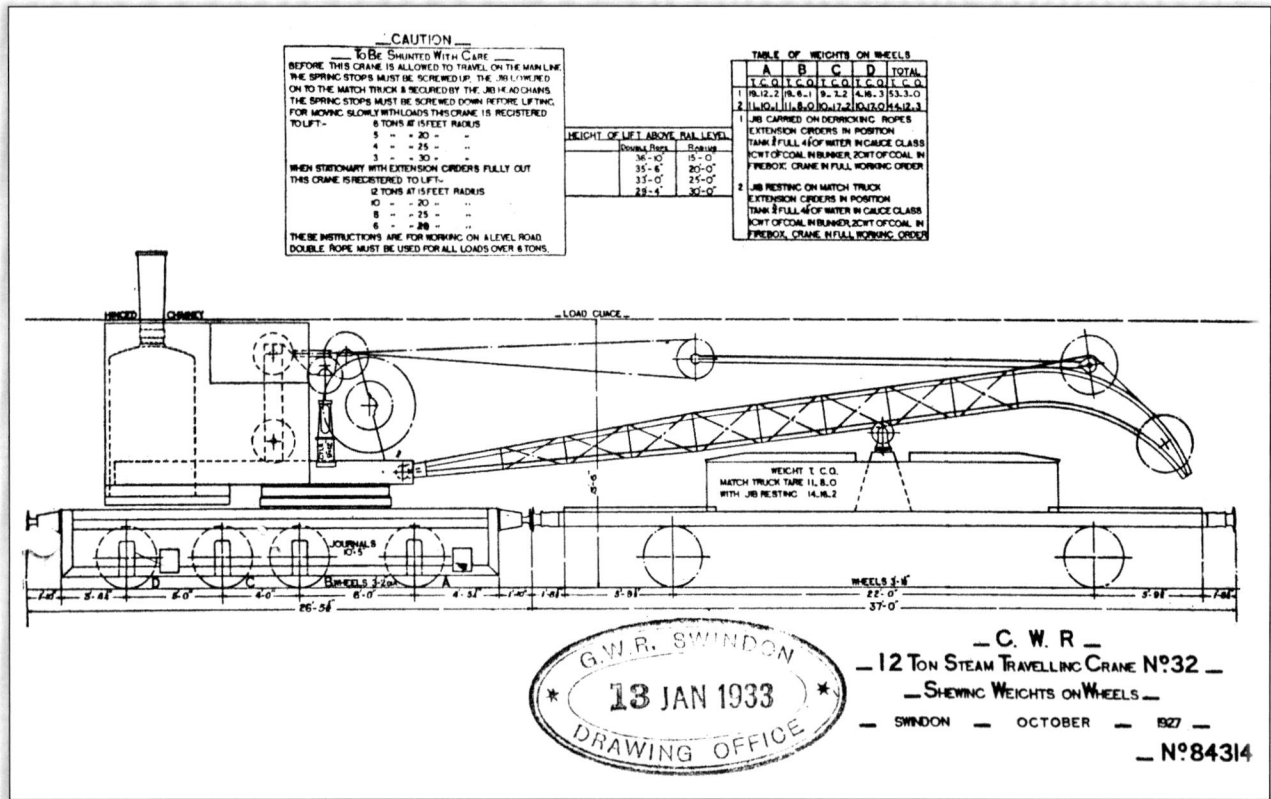

Colour washing to produce blue prints was also done in the Print Room, care being needed to achieve an even tone. As well as producing drawings with associated engineering detail, the draughtsmen would occasionally produce illustrated booklets to be kept for reference. Two that I have are Notes on Valve Setting as Applied to Steam Cranes and Travelling Crane Diagrams. The Works had been binding their own books since Mr Angle, a clerk, set up a section in the 1930s. Before that they sent this work out.

Orders for new work, as opposed to planned maintenance and repairs, came into the office, having been approved by the chief mechanical engineer. At the board meeting of October 1920 it was agreed he could authorise work not exceeding an estimated £100. This was increased to £250 in 1944. Anything above that figure had to go before the general manager's monthly meeting, which was attended by heads of all departments, and a representative of the board.

CME Dept work involving the Drawing Office was either classed as design or development. The latter was usually submitted via the works managers or the running department superintendent. Some work was also undertaken at Swindon for the (Civil) Engineers' and Signal Departments.

Virtually all draughtsmen worked at drawing boards resting at an angle of 10 degrees on benches 3ft high. The benches contained plan-chests with 4in and 5in deep drawers, all of which were considered old fashioned by the 1950s. A tee-square slid up and down the board from the left and this gave a horizontal datum from which a steel set square could be used for the verticals. 'You had to provide your own compasses, set squares, parallel rule and slide rule; pencils and rough books they supplied,' said Reg Willcocks. Pencil extenders too, were provided so pencils could not be exchanged until they were no more than an inch long. All office males were expected to wear a tie but jackets could be removed while working as they restricted the outstretched arms. However, if called in to see the boss, they were expected to be 'properly dressed'.

When they moved to a temporary drawing office at the junction station, George Connell and Reg worked at new Admel drawing boards. They were designed to be used in a more upright position, taking up less room than the old equipment. When they moved over to the main office the new boards went with them. An external investigation made in 1955/56 found that: 'an excessive amount of non-productive routine work of a semi-clerical nature was being done by senior technicians which diverted them away from their specialist work.' The inspectors also criticised the unnecessary amount of detail given on drawings, which meant that they had to be produced to a larger scale.

The Drawing Office and other offices were refurbished as a result of these investigations and another carried out by their own 'works' study officers' soon after. That's when the old desks/filing cabinets and boards were replaced. The new equipment was not appreciated by everyone at first and some men adjusted the angle of the boards and carried on as before. The swivel chairs, too, took some getting used to. Tracer Beryl Stanley said Eric Hill of the plant and machinery section was quite musical and could get a tune out of the counterbalance cords on either side of the new drawing boards.

This 1948 view shows the larger east wing of the Drawing Office where locomotive and carriage & wagon work was undertaken. In the late 1950s the C&W sections moved into the north wing, displacing the General DO, which was relocated to the annexe above B Shop. *Author's collection*

Tracers

The tracing stage in the production of drawings was taken away from the draughtsman in the early 1950s. This relieved them of some of their skill and continuity and was not popular. Females, often with no previous experience in engineering, were trained up to become tracers and it caused resentment, especially among the older staff. Beryl Hunt went into the DO as a lady tracer in 1955. She had written to the chief draughtsman while she worked temporarily in the Mechanics' Institute library:

> He came over personally to ask me to come and have an interview. Because I had stayed on at grammar school until I was eighteen, I did not have to take the entrance examination or start as an office girl. Mrs A. Maureen Downey was the first tracer in the Works: she came over from the Drawing Office at Marine Mountings in 1951. Mrs Downey had trained four girls and I was one of her second 'brood' so to speak. The other three were Pat Williams, Patsy Truman, Christine Fleming and myself: all based in the Loco DO. There were three rows of desks as you looked down the office; our section was in the centre nearest the entrance. Up on the wall, to inspire us, was the drawing board of Isambard Kingdom Brunel. Nearby some wag had hung a sign saying 'All hope abandon, ye who enter here'.

We were all younger than our years but Pat was particularly shy and always took everything seriously. For instance, Pat's pet guinea pig had a litter the same day that Billy Smart's Circus came to town and this information was quickly seized upon. She was called to the telephone because Billy Smart had heard the news and enquired 'could they act'. Pat explained they were not yet trained, which started everybody laughing and gave the game away. A.E. Durrant described Pat as 'pretty' in his book *Swindon Apprentice*, and said he was smitten with her. [It is not difficult to understand why management had long resisted men and women working together.]

It was our job to make copies of drawings on tracing linen ready for copying, using Indian ink. We 'pounced' the linen with French chalk to cover the greasy surface and used ruling pens that were adjustable, for lines of different thickness. In those days it was not the 'done thing' for women to visit workshops where men worked so any technical knowledge was picked up from the drawings. It took a long time to become competent in tracing and letterwork. We also coloured 'blue prints' for use as office copies and 'photo prints'. The latter were printed onto photographic paper and when necessary, taken to board meetings at Paddington.

Among the first intake of tracers was Ann Haig, a tall model of a girl. I remember when she was reprimanded for taking too long on a tracing, Ann drew herself up to her full height of 5ft 10in and said to the senior draughtsman, Mr Harland, 'Do you require quality or quantity because I can do either.' Poor Mr Harland [a rather short man] walked away embarrassed. The story went into the annals of the DO, to be retold whenever the opportunity arose. In the late 1950s the 'works' study' people recommended the tracing pool be split up and I went to the survey section. Soon after, we moved to an office built above B Shed, which was accessed by way of an overhead walkway and through the print room; previously this had been the experimental section.

Staff

Normal starting time was changed from 9am to 8.30am in the mid-1950s. This did away with the Saturday morning shift, at least for the foreseeable future. Each sub-office had a registrar who signed the staff in as they arrived. They would draw a red line in the register under the last person in as the bell went. Sam Trollope and Fred Spindler worked in the Loco DO as clerks/registrars. As well as timekeeping, they collected and returned the drawings to the store and arranged to have prints made. In the administration office, Gordon Thorpe and Secretary Gwen Ives looked after the clerical side of the loco office. Gordon was a football league referee in his spare time. Sam would also go out with one or two draughtsmen who manned recording instruments in the track testing car. This vehicle was still known better by the old name of the 'whitewash coach'.

Management knew Swindon would be getting its share of new work following the announcement of the Modernisation Plan in January 1955 and the Drawing Office would now have to increase its staff. It turned out that the additional design work involved diesel shunters, diesel multiple units and new main-line diesels, all to be built at Swindon. Overtime was reintroduced for those working on these sections and the draughtsmen concerned could, to some extent, choose whether to stay on in the evening or put in a few hours on Saturday.

Notices were posted in the Loco Works for 'time served' men to train as draughtsmen. Reg Willcocks applied and joined the salaried staff there in October 1956. He was a boilermaker who had moved to the L2 Shop and had become a chargeman plater at just twenty-seven years of age. In L2 Reg had worked on modifications to the first track-relaying machines, which had been built at Swindon (Draughtsman Ken Webb had worked out the original designs for them after the war).

To accommodate a larger workforce, a 1,600 sq ft room above the junction station became a temporary office for training new draughtsmen. Newcomers had traditionally started off in the general sections but now it

was locomotive draughtsmen that were required. Reg and Graham Norris, who had started the same day, found themselves on one of the only sections still dealing with steam engines. Reg remembers:

Ron Webb and John Ireland were among those I remember here, together with Ken Dadge, the section leader. There was a carriage & wagon section of about eight people in this 'overflow' office too, making twenty in all. We were given only minor jobs at first. My first task of any substance was to work out and draw an auto brake system for Doncaster built engines based on our own Automatic Train Control.

George Connell came up into the Loco DO from the workshops the following year, 1957. His training was usual for such a position, he had been apprenticed to fitting, turning and loco erecting and had gained his Ordinary National Certificate at the College. Reg was qualified in engineering to City and Guilds standard and was now being encouraged to go back to night school and study for the ONC, which he did.

George stayed in the station office for the first six months, drawing small modifications to diesel locomotives so they might be investigated for viability. The ideas had originated from the staff suggestion scheme. He would go and find the right type of locomotive in the factory and make rough sketches with dimensions of the parts involved: 'I remember I worked on cab controls at first, they were submitted together with my report to the suggestions committee via my section head,' said George.

Design work connected with steam locomotives was rare after the mid-1950s. However, when George returned to Ken Dadge's section he did spend a few weeks drawing a complete smokebox arrangement for the 'Standard' class 4 locomotives. Some of those built at Swindon ones were going to receive double blastpipe and chimneys to improve their draughting. George still has a copy of the drawing, which shows it was checked as complete in October 1958, although most of the work was done several months before.

In 1957 new gradings were introduced so that draughtsmen with a workshop background became technical assistants. Previously only the Research and Development staff had been classed as TAs. After their six-month probationary period Reg and George were made professional and technical grade As. Perhaps to standardise the pay scales, the tracers too became P&T As. An old tradition that was slowly changing, no doubt due to all the outside influence after nationalisation, was promotion. Draughtsmen and other salaried staff had traditionally moved up the seniority scale only after years of service. Many of the older staff resented the new P&T grading structure, which made the juniors equivalent to the old grades more quickly. P&T staff would now be judged on their ability rather than their time in post when promotion was being considered, something the old regime had resisted and been constantly criticised for.

Senior Staff

F.W. Hawksworth, M.I.Mech.E., was chief draughtsman from 1925 until he was promoted to assistant to the CME in 1932. Mr S.J. Smith, who had been in the DO for twenty-seven years, was appointed to succeed him. Along with several of his colleagues, Mr (Sidney) Smith taught at the College in his spare time. He held the post of senior lecturer in machine drawing and design, and this no doubt was taken into account when he was promoted to the top job. Mr (Frank) Mattingley, known to all as Matt, succeeded Mr Smith, and in the 1950s, Mr Gilbert E. Scholes became chief draughtsman. In each of the three main sections of the office, the person in charge was an assistant to the chief draughtsman. 'Old Charlie Dunford was the senior of four DO clerks when I first started,' (in 1944) said George Petfield.

After the war, the 'chief', Mr Scholes, had a personal secretary, while his assistant had a registrar and two lady tracers allocated to him. Several ex-staff I have spoken to agreed Mr Scholes, who lived in Croft Road, was rather refined: 'A gentleman in keeping with his position, commanding respect without ever raising his voice,' said one. He had started in the DO in 1925, becoming assistant chief draughtsman in 1945 and taking overall charge in 1953. Both Mr Scholes and the previous 'chief', Mr Mattingly, had spent all their working lives in the office after their apprenticeship training in the Locomotive Works. Under the new grading, draughtsmen who had risen up via the shop floor became technical assistants.

Wally Harland was the senior draughtsman on the locomotive sections and he now took the old title of chief draughtsman. Like many others, Mr Harland had come up from one of the small companies (the Taff Vale Railway) when they were absorbed in the early 1920s. He would not succeed Mr Scholes as they were both near to retirement in the late 1950s. In the Locomotive DO at that time Arthur Sly and Roland Lowe were next in line of seniority. In the Carriage & Wagon DO, Jim Innes had been in charge since 1950 and Jim Rideout and George Palphramand were heads of sections. Mr Hutchins and Mr Wallington were the senior men in the General DO. Lloyd Roberts had been section leader on cranes and previously docks' sections for thirty-one years until he retired in 1960, probably a record. Mr Palphramand left to take charge of Sudbrooke Pumping Station in the late 1950s.

Experience Outside the Office

All draughtsmen had to have some previous training and experience of working on the shop floor, even if they had progressed as academics. They would often have to liaise with the person doing the work, so a good knowledge of production and its potential problems was required. In a lecture to the GWR Swindon Engineering Society in 1929 the speaker said: 'At Swindon they were rather proud that the Works [shop floor] worked exceedingly well with the Drawing Office.' This implied that that was not always the case elsewhere. In recent years some former drawing office staff even developed asbestosis, normally associated with long-term exposure in the workshops.

Young men straight from university did a tour of the shops like craft apprentices, only theirs was condensed into two years. Just as shop floor experience was required to be a draughtsman, so time in the Drawing Office was essential for engineers applying for senior positions with the works manager's staff or the divisional superintendent's staff. For example, Mr Dymond, who had worked on both locomotive and carriage design sections, was appointed assistant to the divisional superintendent for the Cardiff Valleys: a senior position in a division of lower status. Mr H. Colton, head of the carriage design section of the office, was promoted to assistant to the C&W Works' manager at Swindon in 1939.

Young graduates usually went straight into junior management after nationalisation in 1948. Having completed their degrees, they would still have to spend time on the shop floor and in the DO initially, however, to gain experience. In the late 1950s, there were seven Batchelor of Science graduates in the Works learning the practicalities of electrical and mechanical engineering. Many of the senior staff in the office had successfully completed the Institute of Mechanical (or Locomotive) Engineers examinations and became associate members of one of those professional bodies. Capable and ambitious staff presented papers to one of the institutes on a subject within their area of expertise.

Membership and participation in the Swindon Engineering Society was also readily undertaken by particularly motivated draughtsmen. Some of them taught evening classes at the College. The SES was affiliated to the railway and attended by some of the department's most senior staff as well as the presenter's contemporaries. This platform gave him a good chance to improve his standing among them. The society's lectures were subsequently widely read by Works' staff. Jack Dymond (in the Swindon DO until 1936), for instance, was respected as much for the papers he presented as he was for his impressive professional qualifications and achievements. He had been in charge of the rebuilding of the stationary locomotive test plant in the 1930s and the gas-turbine locomotive experiments later.

For a few years after the war there was little new design work in hand and consequently there was a surplus of draughtsmen. Some staff were seconded or moved permanently as a result and a number took up principal posts when the new Motive Power Department was formed. Appointments at this level were often reported in the local evening paper.

In the 1950s it was Roy Nash who took the pictures for DO use and he probably took other official Works' photos at that time, although he wasn't the only one. Roy, from Pinehurst, had trained as fitter, turner and erector in the 1940s. 'He was a nice kid,' said Ted Randell, 'but was never really accepted in the Drawing Office.'

Surviving rough books, once belonging to Alan Peck of the DO buildings' section, show that he was drawing plans of workshops, offices and buildings in 1948. This was for the purposes of calculating: 1) the electric lighting requirements; 2) the cubic areas for heating and plumbing installations or alterations. For this the Works' photographer would also be employed and the photographs submitted with the report that was sent to the appropriate works manager.

Alan Peck spent some time redrawing the internal plan of St Mark's Church and working out 'improved illumination', as stated above. This was because the contractor (GEC) had been supplied with plans of two different scales. The discrepancy was only discovered when Mr Peck queried the cost submitted. Mr Hawksworth, by then the CME and a member of the church choir, bore the cost of the work himself.

Mr Peck was sent to Newport as temporary assistant to the motive power superintendent in early 1951. By October of the following year his rough books show he was back in the Works (No. 4 Office, Motive Power Department) recording the weights of standard locos and tenders. These were 78000, 78001, 46503 and three Western Region 'Britannias'. This he did by totalling the weights on each wheel as recorded in the Weigh House. The known weight of water and coal they were carrying would then be subtracted. Such was the diversity of work for the draughtsman on secondments.

Research and Development Section

Sam Ell ran this section with his assistant 'Chick' Ockwell and later Herbert Titchener. They had about a dozen staff under them. The R&D section had been known as the 'experimental section' until the late 1940s. After a brief period in the new DO Annexe in the early 1950s, they moved out to occupy the floor above the telephone exchange. After nationalisation, Mr Ell became technical assistant to the chief mechanical engineer, although by now 'chief' was dropped from the title.

This section of the Drawing Office are perhaps best remembered for recording the data from steam locomotive testing on the stationary test plant with the aid of a long, mainly home-made instrument panel. The official interpretation was that they were analysing 'draught arrangements, maximum evaporative capacity and establishing the relationship between the coal rate, steam rate and power at the cylinders and drawbar'. The tests could not be completed without running the locomotive under normal conditions, known as 'controlled road tests'. With both methods the engine was connected to instruments in the Dynamometer Car. This work is particularly remembered nowadays for the way it led to the redesigning of the draughting of express locomotives so effectively after the war.

An official portrait of the experimental carriage No. 2360 in the 1930s. This vehicle was unofficially known as 'the whitewash coach'. It has been strategically placed outside 24 Shop. With the bank down to town level behind, the sky makes the subject of the photograph stand out. Staff from the experimental section of the Drawing Office went out on this specially converted Churchward 'brake third Toplight' carriage throughout the period covered by this book. It would be attached to the rear of normal service trains to gather data regarding the riding qualities of the bogies, as well as the condition of the permanent way.

'Hall' class locomotive No. 4930 outside A Shop in 1931. It is fitted up for indicating tests that will determine the efficiency of steam distribution by the valve gear. The wooden surround at the front of the footplating protected the operators of the experimental section of the Drawing Office, who monitored the instruments when out on the road. The dynamometer car, on the right, carried various recording instruments but its main purpose would be to measure the speeds of the test train accurately. The figures obtained would be meaningless unless the graphs produced showed the speeds at which the coal rates, drawbar effort and train resistance were recorded. *GWR*

One of the staff, Ken Ellis, told me about a discussion he had with Sam Ell in 1956, concerning a delay in taking him on. When Ken mentioned his letter of application he was taken into his office and asked: 'How am I supposed to keep track of such things.' Ken said it was floor to ceiling with plans, letters and paperwork: 'You could hardly move in there.'

Technical assistants (draughtsmen) in the R&D office in the late 1950s included Alan Fairbanks, John Smith, Mike Casey, Maurice Herd, Ron Lucas, Bob Hancock, Doug Stagg, Ken Ellis and Ernie Nutty, the 'senior TA'. Mr Harland had a son who worked for Sam Ell too, but he may well have moved on by this time. Most of these draughtsmen had progressed quickly to become professional and technical grade B staff while still quite young. In the past a person would have to be 'in post' for a set period of time and a P&T B, or equivalent of, would be at least forty years of age. With these senior posts came first-class concessionary rail travel too.

Staff from this office would go out to depots to evaluate complaints about locomotives and rolling stock. Sometimes the complaints were in the form of performance limitations. They would, at the request of the Running Department, travel on the footplate or in the train to investigate and, if necessary, redesign the offending parts.

A problem was realised when the GWR Automatic Train Control and passenger communication (cord) application apparatus came to be fitted to the diesel-hydraulic engines entering service on the Western Region. The German railways, for which the diesel equipment was designed, did not use these same systems. The DO therefore had to design, and the workshops produce, a device to 'marry' the two together. On the steam locomotive, the pump that maintained the vacuum in the brake pipe, keeping the brakes off, was automatically isolated when the brakes were applied, including when the ATC was activated. On the diesels, exhausters created the vacuum but they could not be isolated using a similar valve.

George Connell worked with the R&D section for a time and remembers Mr Ell spending a lot of time on a design for this emergency automatic brake valve. The problem was eventually overcome. Not only that, but the new Swindon adaption also incorporated a means of overcoming another long-standing braking problem. It allowed for a graduated brake application of the ATC or the 'deadman control': whichever was automatically selected. One of the advantages of graduated braking was the elimination of 'bunching' with diesel-hauled, unfitted goods trains. The other advantage was that the 'passenger-goods valve' was now obsolete. This was a control that, if not set correctly, could have serious consequences.

The science of slowing trains on the move, by friction braking, was something of a speciality for Mr Ell. He had been given the task of improving the efficiency of locomotive and rolling stock brakes in the 1930s. The obvious solution was to increase the area of the block face, which would require a larger block brake and hanger. However, he calculated that vibration was having a significant effect on efficiency, so he redesigned the brakegear to improve its stability. This reduced the vibration caused by the friction on application. Not only was efficiency improved but the rate of maintenance and failures was reduced too.

Another problem that the new lightweight D800s had in slowing heavy trains was that their small wheel mass reduced heat dissipation and the brake blocks and tyres became very hot. This was not unduly troublesome with the heavier D600s and their slightly larger diameter wheels. Several options to remedy this were considered, including fitting double brake blocks at each hanger: something that was being incorporated in the larger D1000 class locomotives now under construction. The problem was solved by running a few braked vehicles in unfitted trains until the latter became obsolete.

A new mathematical formula, to determine economical timing and loading of trains, was being tried in the office with a view to extending it throughout British Railways. In connection with this Ken Ellis was working on accelerated timings for 'class C' freights in 1957. Using gradient profiles and working timetables, he mapped out paths for the future diesel hauled trains.

Social Life

By talking to ex-staff so many years after the events, it was only possible to obtain first-hand recollections from those who were young at the time. For them at least, the social side of the Drawing Office seemed particularly well organised and supported. Beryl Stanley (nee Hunt) summed it up by saying 'it was a wonderful life':

Pat Williams and I joined the Railway Debating Society at Paddington and became associate members of the Swindon Engineering Society. Few females were eligible to join the latter. As well as the regular meetings in the lecture hall [at 2 Emlyn Square], the SES also organised factory visits, both local and further afield, in the summer. It was on a visit to the Crown Derby Works that I met my future husband, Don Stanley from the Tool Room. Sometimes in September we got concessionary rail travel to the Continent. In 1957 we went to the SNCB railway workshops in Brussels, which had to be rebuilt after the last war.

Technical Assistants Ron Lucas left and Martin Lloyd at their desks, sometime in the late 1950s. This was the R&D section, whose office was above the automatic telephone exchange at this time. The man in the background is thought to be Ernie Nutty. *Ken Ellis*

Beryl Hunt was presented with an illuminated address and a set of cutlery by colleagues of the Combined Drawing Office when she got married. With her here are fellow tracers, from left to right: Andrea Hewlett Carriage & Wagon DO, Pat Williams, Beryl Hunt, Christine Fleming, Maureen Downey and Alison Ridgeway. Alison's father became Locomotive Works' Manager about this time 1960. This photograph was taken by Roy Nash of the DO survey section. *Courtesy of Beryl Stanley*

Four of us, Pat, Patsy, Christine and myself, all loco side tracers, stuck together. We went dancing on Thursdays and Saturdays: in winter it was to the Majestic Ballroom at Milton Road baths but in summer they took the floor up for swimming, then we went to the Regal Ballroom in the Mechanics' Institute. There was always someone in the office going to the pictures or arranging to play tennis and inviting us to join them. I can't speak for the men but none of us girls had any romantic expectations when invited out like this.

An office walk to a nearby village and an outing to the seaside were arranged every year too. On the first Friday in January we were allowed to leave work early and go to London to see a show. We had an office newspaper called 'Bloggs Weekly', for which I was the token lady reporter. It was full of humorous and interesting snippets about life in the office. Christmas Eve was a special time and anyone who could play an instrument became part of an orchestra. One year the men got a piano up four flights of stairs to the office, and we all sang carols. We were also members of the BRW Staff Association. They organised all sorts of games: we liked to play putting in the summer and skittles in the winter.

The men's annual outing had started in the 1920s and was well attended each June. Beryl remembers the ladies' outing was in May during her time. Some of the outing committee were allowed time off to go to the destinations in advance and make bookings for meals and perhaps a show. Nearly everyone went from the 'chief' down.

Surviving programme cards show that in 1955 the men went to Bognor via Hogs Back and Hindhead and in 1958 they went to the Isle of Wight. By this time several staff had motor cars and they held an annual car rally/treasure hunt. Manfred (Fred) Spindler said that on one occasion he and his navigator, Dick Eatwell, got lost and ended up on the runway at Kemble airfield. It was around this time that Fred won the Works' annual chess tournament, held in the Mechanics. Fred had to beat off stiff competition, especially from other DO colleagues.

Many in the office were, of course, naturally artistic. Fred said Phil Nethercot and others would produce humorous sketches and present them as part of an illuminated address when someone retired. Beryl said George Connell was another one particularly good at penmanship: 'I received a lovely address upon getting married in 1960: everyone signed it and contributed towards a gift.'

Sometimes a person was found out for a misdemeanour or else some other incident worthy of gossip. Then someone known for their cartoon ability was called upon to record the event in a humorous sketch. The *Swindon Railway News* referred to the handiwork as an 'illuminated crime sheet'. This type of mockery and high spiritedness was traditional and even encouraged from above, but there was a limit. Reg Willcocks remembers one of the female tracers, who was a good dancer, showing off outside the chief's office one day: 'Mr Scholes called her in and she came out in tears.'

8
CME Dept Management

Works' officials and others of a certain means often chose to live on the far side of Swindon hill in the Westlecot, Okus and Marlborough Road areas, along with schoolmasters and business owners. It was generally accepted that the air up there was more conducive to good health, away from the fumes and noise of the Railway Works. As a consequence, there were few upmarket homes incorporated in the planning of New Swindon. Before the war there were no designated car parks in or outside the Works, so car owners would drive down and leave them in the Fire Station Yard.

GWR Chief Mechanical Engineer

G.J. Churchward resigned as CME at the end of 1921. His successor, C.B. Collett, remained head of the department for the next twenty years. It was the board of directors who had decided upon the choice of the new CME in the years leading up to the change, just as they did for all senior GWR managers. No doubt they took into account the views of the general manager and the outgoing CME. The younger a man was when he was promoted, the further he would go because of the policy of promoting from within the department.

A good example of the flaw in this method is the well-known story concerning the popular and capable W.A. Stanier. Mr Collett's appointment, it is said, was greeted with hushed amazement because WAS, the popular locomotive works' manager, showed more potential. However, Mr Collett had remained one step ahead in seniority because of his age. Therefore Mr Stanier had little choice but to take the top job on the London, Midland and Scottish Railway when it was offered if he wanted to progress. He was only slightly younger than his boss, and would be too old to succeed him at Swindon when the time came.

Charles Benjamin Collett, GWR chief mechanical engineer from 1922 until 1941.

The chief mechanical and electrical engineer was the full title of the head of the department that dealt with all the GWR mechanical work, including that of its docks. The responsibility for all electrical equipment had also been amalgamated into this department shortly after Mr Collett took over. Most of the manufacturing was centralised at Swindon. However, the majority of this department's work was maintenance and repairs, and some of the more routine work was divided up among the various operating divisions. The Signal Works at Reading was a separate department and they carried out their own mechanical engineering and repair work with little co-operation from CME Dept.

By the 1930s, Mr Collett's standing within the company had been reduced somewhat as he reported to the general manager, Mr (later Sir) James Milne, at Paddington. His predecessors had direct access to the board of directors and attended board meetings.

Senior departmental officers met regularly to discuss, among other business, ongoing work proposals. The CME chaired these meetings and he decided whether the work should go ahead. In the case of expensive new work, Mr Collett would have to submit his recommendations to his superiors. He did this by asking whichever assistant had been tasked with investigating its viability to join him at the monthly managers' conference at Paddington. With the aid of plans and estimated costs, they would make a case for proceeding with it.

Most of the expenditure, including that of buildings and machinery, would eventually be recovered from the department's own budget. Even so, authority from the general manager and the board had to be obtained for work that was estimated to exceed £100, rising to £250 in 1944. This did not include the anticipated costs of repairs and planned maintenance. Company publicity from Mr Collett's term says that the CME's plans were rarely opposed.

The CME was also responsible for more than 16,000 running shed grades, enginemen, carriage & wagon maintenance staff and cleaners. However, Mr Collett extended the title of his outdoor assistant with the addition of locomotive running superintendent, and left him with a greater share of the responsibility for that side of the department. The company docks were managed jointly by the chief docks manager, Cardiff; the chief civil engineer, Paddington; and the CME, Swindon.

C.B. Collett gained extensive shop floor experience before he took over at the top but he was rarely seen around the factory or even in the Drawing Office after that. With so many fine engineers from the shop floor up, it is misleading to attribute all the designs to the chief directly. Some historians even go as far as to claim that the CMEs who came after Mr Churchward were no more than figureheads. As a trusted head of department, the CME was given almost a free hand to decide whether new designs or modifications went ahead. In that sense at least, Mr Collett can take the credit, or blame, for the developments during his term of office.

By the 1930s Swindon had become very good at rebuilding earlier locomotive types. The '3200' or 'Earl' class was a good example. They were successful engines but no effort was made to bring their Victorian appearance up to date. The story of the naming of some of those being outshopped in 1936 and 1937 says something about this enigmatic and dogmatic CME.

An example of one of the nameplates relating to the story of C.B. Collett's practical joke. So that the plates would sit on the larger diameter splashers of the 'Castle' class engines, the radius of the base had to be enlarged. This made the arc of the name less than concentric, as can be seen here. *Courtesy of Trevor Dale*

Some of the GWR directors had been complaining that their titles were not being used as locomotives names. This had been the policy on other railways and the CME was well aware of the dissatisfaction. It seems that Mr Collett did not hold the dignitaries in high regard as his solution was to use their names on some of the quaint-looking '3200' class. When they saw where their titles had been displayed, they were not impressed. As these types of locomotives would not normally be named at this time, it is likely that this was Mr Collett's stand against the directors' expectations. With his point having been made, the nameplates were transferred to new 'Castles' being built at the time.

At the time of his retirement in July 1941, Mr Collett was past his best. That's what Mr Cook, the loco works' manager at the time, said in his book. The chief was in his seventieth year, but was still reluctant to leave. It was his principal assistant, John Auld, who determined events in this matter: he was six months older than his boss and refused to be talked into staying on any longer. This meant that Mr Collett could now no longer claim he was not the oldest at Swindon. The story of his successor, F.W. Hawksworth's, term of office, is recorded in other sections.

Principal Assistant

Mr John Auld, M.I.Mech.E. (Member of the Institute of Mechanical Engineers), was the most senior 'foreigner' to arrive at Swindon as a result of the grouping of the railways in the early 1920s. Just prior to the takeover he had been carriage & wagon superintendent on the Barry Railway. After other high-ranking positions on the Great Western, he became principal assistant to the CME. This came about when Mr Stanier left to become CME on the LM&S Railway in 1932. To fill the void, the highly regarded young chief draughtsman Frederick Hawksworth was moved straight up to assistant to the CME. This is thought to have been done to prepare him to succeed the CME when the time came.

The principal assistant would share the running of the department, sign documents and deputise for the CME when necessary, chair meetings, deal with union deputations, and have influence over new designs and modifications. Great importance was placed on supporting the cultural and leisure pursuits of the workforce, and the principal assistants of the 1930s and '40s, presided over the Mechanics' Institute council.

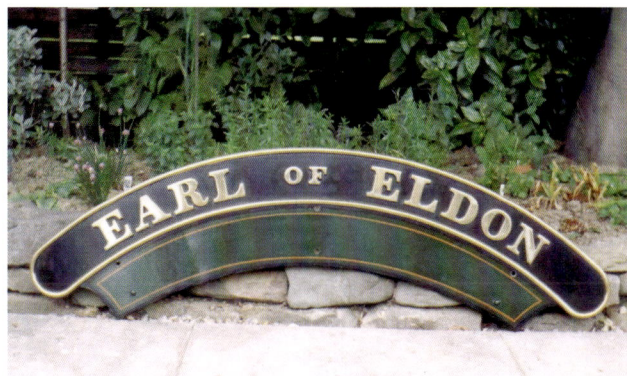

Part of the announcement of his retirement in the *GWR Magazine* in 1941 makes reference to Mr Auld's dealings with the workers. It states: 'In his negotiations with the representatives of the men, he always displayed a keen understanding of the problems presented, combined with a sympathetic appreciation of the human side relating to conditions of working. In this direction, as principal assistant he gave very able support to the CME.' Not retiring until he reached the age of seventy, Mr Auld might have expected to enjoy less time to put his feet up. And so it was: he had just short of six years of retirement at his Marlborough Road, Swindon, home.

Locomotive Running Superintendent

There was nothing more important than the job of making the most efficient use of the company's locomotives and rolling stock. Consequently, the position of locomotive running superintendent was set aside for the most experienced and highly regarded engineers in the department. Locomotives were the most important asset and they needed constant attention, which was expensive. If the fleet were not kept in the best state of readiness the company reputation would suffer and the business could even collapse altogether. Mr Hall succeeded Mr Crump as locomotive running superintendent and outdoor assistant to the CME, when the latter retired in 1931: his assistant was Mr Simpson.

In the early 1930s, the GWR consisted of 6,411 route miles, including lines that were jointly owned. For its efficient maintenance and administration, the network was divided into eleven operating divisions, later reduced to nine under the Western Region. Each one was overseen by a divisional engineer based at the principal loco depot. In his office he employed an assistant, a clerk and an inspector.

The running superintendent, based at Swindon, would co-ordinate his divisional superintendents' and inspectors' reports. He would work with the CME and a designated draughtsman to improve efficiency and influence new designs. Whether stock was withdrawn, repaired or rebuilt was also decided upon in the same way. Mr Churchward had summed up the role of his outdoor assistants and inspectors by saying 'they are my eyes and ears', referring to the evaluation of locomotives and rolling stock performance in traffic.

The CME's Personal Staff

All the senior staff in the department, except the docks assistant and the divisional engineers, were based at Swindon Works. They included the electrical assistant and technical assistant, and all had deputies who were expected to succeed them upon retirement. The company nearly always adopted the controversial system of promoting staff at all levels by seniority regardless of capability.

The offices of the CME's assistants, together with the chief draughtsman and chief clerk, made up the CME's personal staff. The CME's chief clerk oversaw offices, sometimes referred to as sections, dealing with correspondence, staff and machinery records, and until the 1950s, the loco and the carriage & wagon sections were on separate sites. The chief clerk, Mr Kelynack; chief draughtsman, Mr Smith; assistant chief draughtsman, Mr Woolacott; and chief chemist, Mr Dawe, all reported directly to the CME.

The Role of the Works' Managers

The offices of the locomotive and the carriage works' managers, which comprised themselves and their personal staff, worked to find ways of improving efficiencies. This they did by: 1) reducing the time plant and machinery were left standing idle awaiting repairs and maintenance: 2) improving the layout of the workshops to speed up production: 3) evaluating various alternative methods of production, to save costs: 4) overseeing the suitability of applicants for employment.

At a Swindon Engineering Society lecture in 1929, Mr Evans, the C&WW Manager, said of his men: 'There is a great deal of the animal in their make-up. They can be led, but they cannot be driven: good men worked willingly.' The conduct of the staff was the responsibility of the foremen and office chiefs. If managers saw breaches of discipline, it was not seemly to confront the person direct. They would speak to their subordinates and they went to the accused person's overseer. By the 1930s, it was the works' managers who were also expected to deal with labour disputes. In this capacity, Mr Cook and Mr Evans headed the company side of the Joint Works' Committee from its inception during the war.

Locomotive Works' Manager

The position of locomotive works' manager was considered to be of a higher status than his counterpart on the carriage & wagon side. He had five assistants to manage his various factory and outstation work commitments. Although the other main GWR works had their own managers, they were answerable to the loco works manager' at Swindon. Occasionally the boss would visit the other works if, for instance, major changes were made to production facilities. Incidentally, when senior positions became available at Caerphilly and Wolverhampton, experience of working at Swindon was an advantage for potential replacements. Several of their works' foremen and managers were ex-Swindon men.

Some managers were very resourceful and designed aids to improve ways of working. One was C.T. Cuss, who was assistant to Loco Works' Manager Hannington until he retired in 1936. Mr Cook called him 'very ingenious'. It was Mr Cuss who made the case for bringing in glass-lined tanks for the bulk conveyance of milk. He also invented several fire-fighting aids in his role as Works' chief fire officer.

```
                        Chief Mechanical Engineer
                                   |
                          Principal Assistant
                                   |
    ┌──────────┬──────────┬────────┴───────┬──────────┬──────────┐
 Assistants   Loco Works   Carriage & Wagon   Chief      Chief      Chief
to the CME    Manager      Works Manager      Draughtsman Chemist    Clerk
   x 3           |              |                |                     |
                 |              |                |                     |
        Loco Running  Asst. to the   Asst. to the   Section        Office
        Supt. and Outdoor Loco Works   C&W Works     Heads          Chiefs
        Asst. to the CME Manager       Manager
           |             |              |
        Divisional L,C&W  Chief Foremen  Chief Foremen
        Superintendents
                         |              |
                      Foremen        Foremen
```

GWR CME Department Management

and Supervisory Staff

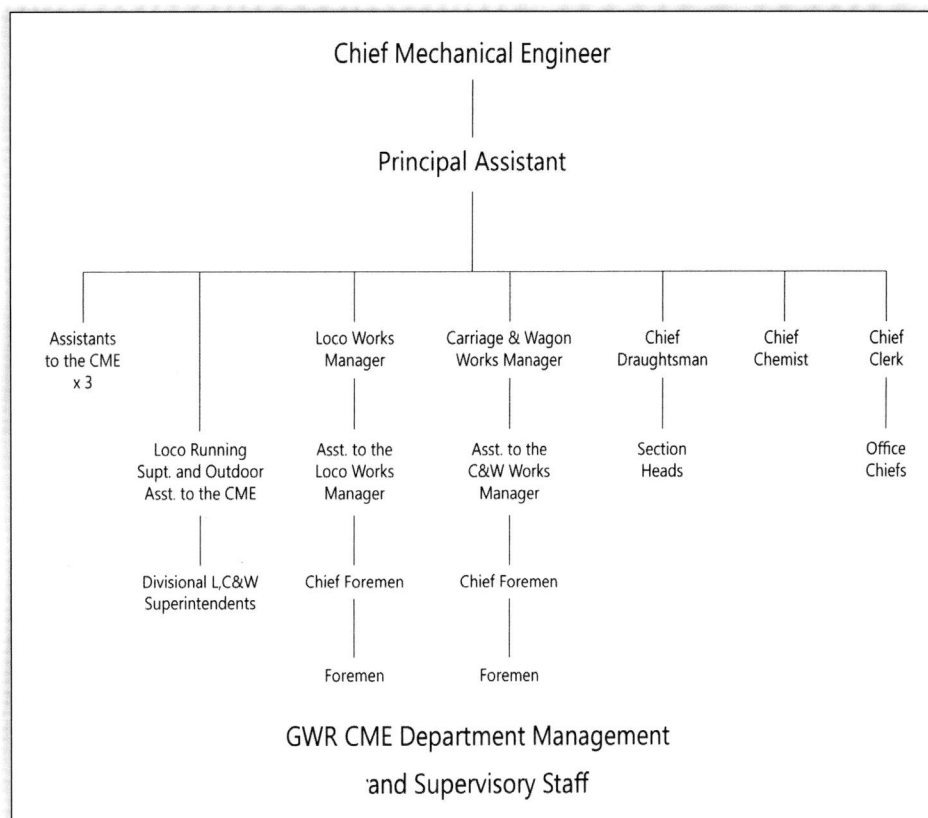

Mr Hannington had been locomotive works manager but his premature death in 1937 meant that his place was taken by his assistant, K.J. Cook. The other assistants to the loco works manager at that time were Mr Johnson, Mr Lawson and Mr Grainge, who was electrical assistant. The loco works' manager's office was in the south-east corner of the managers' office building behind R Shop. He and his assistants used the ground floor while the loco wages sections occupied the first floor.

Selbourne Smith got the job of loco works manager' in 1956 at the age of forty-seven. His route to the top was fairly typical of those with exceptional ability. He distinguished himself as an apprentice on the loco side and had gone on to further education at the College. He then went into the Test House and then to the Drawing Office. Promotion took him through a number of locomotive positions at divisional level before becoming assistant loco works manager at Swindon in 1948.

Carriage & Wagon Works' Senior Staff

Mr E.T.J. Evans had been C&WW manager from 1922. He came from a Swindon family with working roots in the railway factory of the nineteenth century. Mr Evans lived in a large house in Bath Road and, like other senior officials, his home phone was connected directly to the Works' telephone exchange. It was the works' manager who oversaw production and repairs in the Carriage & Wagon Works and at depots around the GWR. Like his

assistant Mr Randle, who would succeed him, Mr Evans had trained and come up through the ranks in the Locomotive Works.

The head of the C&W Works was also expected to take part in the administration of staff welfare and recreational activities to some extent. Mr Evans chaired the general committee of the GWR Athletic Association, Swindon branch, upon its formation in 1931 and for long periods was vice president of both the Medical Fund Society and the Retired Worksmen's Association. He retired in 1946, fifty years after starting his apprenticeship.

The other senior staff in the C&WW Manager's Office in the 1930s, starting with the most senior, were: two assistant managers, Mr Dawson and Mr Hurle, the latter also responsible for train lighting; assistant to the C&W works manager, Mr Randle; chief clerk, Mr Ford and storekeeper, Mr Faith. Next in line were the heads of sections dealing with outstation, staff, costing, repairs, design and special loads.

Whenever any senior position became available, there would have to be several changes in a department as subordinates were promoted, moved or retired. Just occasionally the reason was less conventional. One such case was Mr G.W. Tew, A.M.I.Mech.E., who became assistant to the carriage & wagon works manager in place of Mr Colton. It has been suggested that Geoffrey Tew, who worked on the locomotive testing side of the Drawing Office, had upset Mr Hawksworth by working on ways to improve the performance of his express engines. The chief, some have claimed, moved him to the C&W side as a consequence.

In this official staff photo are, in the centre of the front row, the two works' managers, Mr Evans and Mr Hannington; assistant to the CME, Mr Hawksworth; and the principal assistant to the CME, Mr Auld. The only other person positively identified is Bill Harber, second from the left, middle row. He was, by this time, a chargeman fitter in AM Shop. It was unusual to photograph management and lower grades together. Perhaps the latter had achieved some distinction in their working lives. Bill was a part-time Works' fireman and a first-aider, so maybe this photo was taken at an awards' presentation. The date can be narrowed down to sometime between 1932 and 1937. *GWR*

Training

The position of chief foreman was the highest position attainable by a tradesman without the additional qualifications that he was unlikely to be in a position to pursue. Before the 1930s, when further education courses were less well established, this did not necessarily hold back someone with potential. Indeed, the general manager of the GWR from 1929, James Milne, had started his career as a pupil in the locomotive shops at Swindon. He was promoted to ever higher positions on merit and seniority. Apprentices who had shown particular academic distinction would spend time in the Drawing Office soon after their initial training and could go all the way to the top. All the most senior men in the DO in the 1940s and '50s were ex-Swindon Loco Works apprentices. The CME in 1941–49), Mr Hawksworth, also came up through the ranks via this route.

By the 1930s engineering apprentices who excelled might still be offered a three-year studentship, a small number of which the directors offered free each year. The object was to raise the general standard of technical training among those who might be capable of higher positions in engineering. However, a career in management would now require a degree of bachelor of science in engineering, or the equivalent.

After the war, university graduates with technical engineering training could take up junior management positions in the department. Their training included working alongside gangs in the workshops, and prolonged periods away at college.

Salaries

All salaries, wages and expenses paid to non-productive workers from the CME down came under what the company called 'establishment charges'. This was the part of the department's budget that paid everything that was not directly attributable to the work produced; what we would know better nowadays as running costs. There is no mention of the 'special classes' in the National Union of Railwaymen pay rates for salaried staff before nationalisation, so it is likely that these rates were paid to lower management in the GWR and anyone promoted above grade 1 was presumably expected to sever all union loyalties. Only senior management were above a 'special C' grade and only they were not paid in cash. They received an annual salary by way of a bank cheque sent down from Paddington with a representative of the chief clerk.

Alan Peck noted in his rough book while working in the Drawing Office that the vacant post of outstation materials' assistant to the loco works manager was being offered with a starting salary of £650. This was in 1949 and presumably this position, which interested the twenty-nine year old Peck, was then the minimum starting figure for senior staff.

The CME's chief accountant, Mr Gardner, said in his lecture to the Swindon Engineering Society in 1929: 'The salaries figure is of course subject to constant scrutiny in that additional staff are only appointed after careful consideration and advances [increases] in salary are only made as authorised by the Board of Directors.' Established management positions were rarely, if ever, considered dispensable on the Great Western but there would be questions asked about increases in personal expenses or why certain sections of a department wanted to increase its manpower.

The workforce faced their first wage reductions in the late-1920s due to the worldwide depression in industry and its effects on railway receipts. Similarly, officers and staff with salaries of £350 or more per annum had their normal pay increases deferred, with the possibility of a reduction at a later date. At the start of the voluntary reductions agreed jointly by the companies, trade unions and other staff organisations, the directors had their fees and salaries reduced by 2.5%. It is almost certain that GWR managers had to make financial sacrifices too.

Nationalisation

Following the change of ownership at the end of 1947 there was an overriding need to bring the constituent regions of the newly formed British Railways together as one coherent operating system. All aspects of design were now in the hands of Mr R.A. Riddles, the CME of the new regime. His assistant at the headquarters of the British Railways Board in London was Mr E.S. Cox. They visited all the major drawing offices, including Swindon, regularly, to see how their ideas for standard locomotive and rolling stock designs were progressing.

Managerial staff would now move between regions and works to take up promotions. Other successful businessmen were also now coming in from outside firms. Senior staff, who had always expected to have to move around within their own company, were now moving throughout the mainland UK to give them wide-ranging experience. One of the first things that the new BR administration, the Railway Executive, did was split up the CME Dept after Mr Hawksworth retired at the end of 1949.

The word 'chief' in the title of the CM&EE was dropped because the Carriage & Wagon Works as well as outdoor machinery were no longer under the control of that person. Mr Hawksworth's successor, Mr Cook, was to be known as mechanical and electrical engineer. Mr Pellow, who had been loco running superintendent and outdoor assistant under the previous CME, was now to be known as motive power superintendent. The MP Dept became more closely connected to the operating side at Paddington. Its head (W.N. Pellow) now had an office there, as well as at Swindon, until the department moved to London in 1956. The other change was that the MP Superintendent was no longer answerable to the chief at Swindon.

Mr Randle, who had been works assistant to the CME, took up the new post of carriage & wagon engineer. The new head of the C&W Dept was now to be considered equal to his counterpart on the locomotive side. He was installed in an office near the M&EE in the east wing. H.G. Johnson took over as C&W works' manager from C.T. Roberts in 1948. As head of department, that person continued to be responsible for the production side of the C&W Works. Mr Creighton was made electrical assistant to the M&EE, another new post due to the reorganisation. Jack Hartley, a clerk on the personal staff of the M&EE, said:

> Just as the former head of department's position had much of its responsibility stripped away, so we, as his personal staff, felt aggrieved at being, in theory at least, equal only to our counterparts on the C&W side. They had always been seen as the poor relation.

F.W. Hawksworth was unique among the senior staff in that all his working life was spent at Swindon. He rose from a lowly apprentice in the Locomotive Works to become head of a department employing 37,000 staff. Swindon locomotive design work was all but complete before Mr Hawksworth took over at the top. His best work was done in the Drawing Office during the Churchward and Collett periods. However, F.W.H. is best remembered for the developments during the turbulent years 1941–49, which was his term of office. *Author's collection*

In 1951 it was all-change again. The chief, Mr Cook, who had been at Swindon all his working life, moved to Doncaster on the Eastern Region and was replaced by Mr Smeddle. Ethel Panting was Mr Smeddle's personal secretary; she did all the typing for her boss including a good deal of his private correspondence, said Jack. Tommy Turner was chief clerk to the M&EE, and he dealt with all correspondence and matters relating directly to Mr Smeddle: they both shared No. 101 Office, which was next door to their boss. Carriage & wagon engineer Randle moved away and was replaced by C.A. Roberts (not to be confused with C.T. Roberts). In 1952 the post of loco works manager went to Mr Finlayson, who came down from Scotland.

Jack Dymond had become an eminent engineer in the Works by the 1940s, having transferred from the Taff Vale Railway upon its amalgamation. In 1957 Mr Dymond made a very unconventional move from assistant to the mechanical engineer to taking control of the Supplies and Contracts Dept. The Western had always placed great importance on an efficient Stores Dept, now called the S&C Dept, but had never installed an engineer quite this senior to run it before and it was probably done on account of Mr Dymond's advancing years.

9
Other Work

Internal Transport

A good deal of the work done by the Internal Transport Dept involved moving materials and components between workshops during the various stages of manufacture. There was also all the supplies to be moved to and from the various stores, warehouses and the Central Laundry. They would move incoming goods from wagons, such as timber and other raw materials, plant and machinery. They also moved machine tools into position, ready to be bedded in by the bricklayers, as described later in this chapter.

Before the war, factory transport, as it was also known, could be divided into three distinct types: railway wagons, mechanical trollies and hand bogies. The choice of haulage carrier depended on the size and weight of the load. It was uneconomic and could lead to disciplinary action if, for instance, an open railway wagon towed by a tractor was used when a trolley and trailer would have been adequate for the load.

Petrol-electric trollies were the most common method of moving materials and parts between workshops at that time. Although they had a carrying deck behind the driver, the trollies were designed to tow one or two two-wheeled trailers, each of 2-ton capacity. Some had a clutch and gearbox giving them a greater tractive effort. You did not need a road licence to drive vehicles 'inside' but drivers had to be twenty-one years old or more.

Tractors usually hauled larger loads up to 20 tons, such as locomotive cylinder blocks and frames, on specially constructed trailers. Heavy and bulky loads were also moved in railway wagons that were towed between shops by tractor or locomotive. Limited use was made of horses for pulling rolling stock around the Works. Before the 1950s one or two horses were also used to haul single wagons where locomotives couldn't, off of capstan turntables for instance. An elderly resident told me that when not working, horses, including those owned by the railway, were kept in Gorse Hill, where Tiverton Road was later built.

It is possible that those used around the Works' were taken to be used on the land during the Second World War.

It is recorded that a total 1,145 tons of items were transported around the Works each day in the 1950s. This department was also responsible for some outside jobs. They took coke, for instance, to the Mechanics' reading rooms in Gorse Hill and Rodbourne Road, and to the Luggage Office under the junction station. Gordon Turner joined the factory transport in 1947 as a labourer. His first work was unloading scrap metal at the Foundry, which was destined for their furnaces.

Another job Gordon remembers from his early days was collecting horse manure from the stables at the Transfer Goods' Depot, about a mile east of the Works. This, he then took to a brick-built bin outside the Foundry (it was used in moulding as described in Chapter 2). Every so often, Works' transport men went outstation digging and loading red sand at the company's own quarries in Kidderminster. The sand was calcinated by plant installed in the early 1930s, before being brought back for use in the Foundry.

The 1926 additions to the CME office building's north range incorporated an area for the storage and maintenance of factory or internal transport. Sometime after 1935 it was given the name Z Shop. It should not be confused with The Garage, nearby, used by the Road Transport Dept. Of his working life in the 1950s, Gordon remembers:

There were 30 drivers and 20 to 25 labourers. We had thirty-four tractors of various types, supplied by the Mercury Truck and Tractor Co. and Fordson. We had six petrol/electric mobile cranes, four rigid lorries, four forklift trucks and a large and small loading shovel as well. Another tractor did nothing else, on the carriage side, but move batteries between the Battery House and the sidings where they were fitted onto coaches.

Some tractors were fitted with towing plates, front and back, and they shunted wagons in and out of 21 Shop. They also moved coaches and non-passenger vehicles in and out of the various sections within 19 Shop. Gordon remembers the names of factory transport men: Harry Stiles, Percy Smart, Derek Johnson and Clem Manning. Gordon's brothers also worked on the transport; Stan joined in 1950 and Ivan in about 1954. Teddy Rowe was internal transport foreman in the 1940s and '50s, and Reggie Hinton took over from him in the 1950s.

After nationalisation there was a growing realisation that the storage of raw materials and finished components by thoughtful utilisation of the storage space available could keep costs down. An investigation over several months by the works' study people concluded by making several observations: one was that moving internal consignments by railway wagon was slow and costly compared with the use the latest industrial transport vehicles. They found that, as well as congestion, wagons were not being used to capacity and far more reliance should be placed on the more manoeuvrable internal road vehicles. The accessibility of stocks and keeping handling to a minimum would also increase productivity, said the investigators. Stockpiling stores and materials had been seen as an investment by the old Great Western: they would buy in bulk when prices were low. The new state-owned railway saw that as tying up capital that was not then available for other purposes.

Based on the findings of the study, a range of vehicles for handling materials were brought in. The latest forklift trucks for stacking, withdrawing and moving loads over short distances were purchased. Larger forklift carriers for stacking and transporting long lengths of timber and wagon solebars in the Carriage Works were also introduced. This work had formerly been done by various stationary and travelling cranes, then moved by railway wagons. Four standard sizes of wooden pallets were introduced along with purpose-built four-wheeled trailers to stack them when not in use.

For moving loaded pallets one at a time, hand-operated trucks were brought in. They worked by jacking up the two forks a few inches from the ground to lift a pallet and manoeuvre it. The various types of powered aids were adapted in different ways to suit the requirements of each workshop. Instances include:

1) The handling of swarf in the A Machine Shop was much reduced by 'palleting' it; 2) In the Grease Works, a forklift with a boom attachment enabled two oil or grease drums to be carried at one time; 3) Similarly, in 16 (Carriage Wheel) Shop special attachments enabled a forklift to move two wheelsets at a time.

Watchmen

Outsiders coming on to Works' land uninvited were usually just young men trying to 'spot' locomotives. However, crossing the busy running lines could be very dangerous and the authorities naturally took a dim view of it. This was a time when people took responsibility for their own actions and expected to face consequences designed to deter. The company would have been particularly concerned about adverse publicity and an inquest that would result from an accident. Much of the Railway Works was surrounded by high brick walls but there were places where iron railings no more than 6ft high formed the boundary. The latter could be breached, especially with the help of a mate or a wooden box.

The duties of the watchmen were of two main types: 1) patrolling the shops and yards between 6pm and 7am on weekdays and throughout weekends and public holidays; 2) to act as gatekeepers at the Works' entrances. They were required to apprehend trespassers and look out for fires. The premises were divided up into a number of areas to be patrolled and each watchman was responsible for one round, each turn of duty. Each round took about an hour and had a number of 'stations' that had to be visited. To prove he had covered the rounds as required, each station had a fixed key that, when inserted into a clock he carried around his neck, recorded the exact times he was there.

Mick Fisher was warned not to put shop lights on at night when he first became a watchman on the loco side. He had heard about a manager who had seen workshops that didn't have a night shift lit up from his home overlooking New Swindon. The following day questions were asked. Jack Fleetwood said: 'I remember two distinct types of men employed to maintain security around the Works: some were overcome with a sense of self-importance in the uniform, while others were quite agreeable.'

THE RAILWAY EXECUTIVE
Western Region.

SWINDON WORKS & OFFICES

All persons, with the exception of the Executive's Officials furnished with Periodical Passes and others holding Special Permits, must enter and leave the Works or Offices by the authorised entrances and exits for their particular place of employment.

They are not allowed to walk along or across the Lines or to enter or leave the Executive's premises by other entrances or exits.

Watchmen are instructed to see that this Order is carried out.

BY ORDER.

H. RANDLE,
Carriage & Wagon Engineer,
SWINDON. *May*, 1950.

K. J. COOK,
Mech & Electrical Engineer,

A watchman's key for the Beatrice Street entrance, which was just north of the five Whitehouse bridges and next to the Central Laundry. By the 1930s all the external door locks on Works' buildings and gates were standardised and designated staff carried keys or a master key. The Works' Fire Brigade also held a full set but part-time fireman Ian Sawyer said that he filed one of the keys into a master to save taking the heavy bunch on a call out.

A third duty of the Works' watchmen was to act as guides on Works' tours (see also Chapter 20), although this was not exclusively their job. Bert Stratford was a watchman in the 1940s and '50s, and he would cycle in from his home in the village of Wanborough. Bert had worked in the Boiler Shop and when war came he spent four years in the RAF. He was then invalided out with a back injury and could not return to his manual work. It was probably Bert's upright and imposing stature that got him a job as a Works' watchman. When Bill Leader retired in the 1950s, Bert was promoted and became the senior watchman on the loco side. The office where he was based was to the right of the tunnel entrance. Bill Poolman was his opposite number on the carriage side.

Bert used to recall an incident that happened when he was accompanying a group around, probably on a Wednesday open day. As often happened, once visitors got into the Erecting Shop some wandered off to try to spot a locomotive or take a picture and the guides usually turned a blind eye. On one occasion Mr Hawksworth came out of one of the foreman's offices upstairs and shouted at the offenders. He then told the guides what he thought in no uncertain terms.

At the entrances, the watchmen were conspicuous to deter intruders and notice suspicious-looking activity. Workers leaving before their normal finishing times were required to present a pass out to the man on the gate, who would endorse it with exact times of leaving and re-entering. Goods and the accompanying paperwork arriving at or departing from the Works was initially dealt with by the watchmen; they also received the post from the Royal Mail. In addition to the watchmen on the gates, others were stationed at some railway crossings, which gave access to the Works via the railway lines. For instance, there was a wooden foot crossing in regular use between the up main platform (5) at the station and the Works.

George Petfield told me a story about an unofficial visitor at the Running Shed in the late 1940s. When approached by watchman Frank Cottrell, the engine spotter decided to make a run for it through the Works. Short, burly Frank pursued him for some considerable distance but the intruder easily kept ahead of the watchman. He was, however, caught after others joined the chase. In court the villain was fined and when asked if he had anything to say, said: 'I should like to apologise for the distress I caused to the short fat man who chased me.' The other watchmen who were present with Mr Cottrell ensured the apology passed into Works' folklore.

The Central Laundry

The company's laundering had been centralised in the Trimming Shop basement alongside Sheppard Street from 1893. Before it was moved, there were thirty-six laundresses employed, and the facilities included five washing machines, four hydro-extractors (driers) and three large ironing machines. The laundry's workforce was almost entirely female and presumably always had been. The *GWR Magazine* reported in 1931 that a Mrs Robinson, one of the laundresses, had worked there for thirty-four years. The only man employed was the foreman, who probably also carried out maintenance on the machinery.

Wicker boxes filled with used laundry came in from the company's hotels, refreshment rooms, sleeping cars and camping coaches. Towels made up the biggest proportion of items dealt with. Linen, blankets, doilys, dusters and antimacassars were also laundered and starched, then sent back.

The go-ahead was given to finance a new laundry for the GWR in the 1930s. Swindon was again chosen as the site because of its central geographical position within the company. It would have to be close to the station for easy delivery and dispatch of consignments. The only suitable space available was in the C&W Works, alongside Whitehouse Road. Being right on the edge of the Works' land, there was a steep bank down to town level. The only practical way of building here was to excavate and build hard up against the perimeter, at the lower level. So this is what was done.

In 1938 the new purpose-built Central Laundry took over. The washing, drying and ironing machinery was, of course, increased and in addition there was now a dry cleaning machine and a proper sewing machine section for repairs. Fifty staff worked in the new laundry, including a resident engineer in charge of the machinery and water-softening plant. Baskets were dispatched and returned via Swindon Junction station. They were loaded into and out of travelling stores' vans.

Machine Tool Installation

Bringing in new machinery or replacing what they had was a regular occurrence in the Swindon workshop due to a policy of continuous renewal. If either of the works' managers could show that production was being affected or that costs were excessive because of outdated machine tools then it was likely to be acted upon. The preferred manufacturer depended on reputation and any previous experiences with them. The shop floor supervisory staff would usually have an opinion on this too. Makers' catalogues, showing the latest products, had been received and retained as a matter of course. The model chosen would depend on the type of work to be undertaken and price. Whether it could be modified to suit certain requirements might be another factor. For the purposes of accounting and administration, the paperwork was handled by the Stores Dept.

At the chosen site in the workshop the floor was prepared. This may or may not have been the site of an outgoing machine (some men who worked at the company's other works have said that machine tools previously used at Swindon would turn up in their machine shops on occasions). Works' bricklayers, with advice from a machine tool fitter, excavated a space for the baseplate using a template made by a D Shop

carpenter. Next the 'brickies' laid a suitable foundation of brick or concrete, or both.

Machine tool manufacturers had their own rail access and would dispatch direct to the receiving workshop in sheeted open wagons. The main component parts of the machine were lifted from the wagon at this end by crane. They were moved into the shop by the 'heavy gang' using rollers, ropes and levers. Under no circumstances was a crane to be used to winch the loads along. Once on to its foundation and loosely bolted down it was fully assembled. Wedges of steel and timber were then driven under and around the base to bring the structure into alignment using plumb lines and a spirit level. The bricklayers then prepared a strong mortar mix and poured it into the cavity around the base.

This type of work was often done after the Friday day shift had finished or during the annual holiday shutdown. A general arrangement (blueprint) drawing and a manual would accompany the cargo as aids for future maintenance by Works' fitters. An export packing list of parts was also included with machinery to be assembled on site. Every machine tool in the Works was given a number, which was fitted to it on a cast plate. This identified it for maintenance and for company records.

The Laboratory and Research Dept

The company's laboratories occupied two early Works' buildings in the south-west corner of Fire Station Yard. By the 1930s they had evolved to enable an ever greater range of chemical, metallurgical and bacteriological work to be carried out. Scientific analysis and the testing of materials used in manufacturing was undertaken. This work was separate from the testing of general stores coming in from suppliers under contract. Other work here was involved with goods handled by the GWR.

A diagram of a machine tool from the makers' handbook: one of which was delivered to the Carriage & Wagon Works' Smithy in 1932. It would have been used to forge relatively small masses of iron and steel into parts for carriage and wagon drawgear, brakegear and carriage bogie frames. The hot metal to be shaped was held on the anvil pallet, while the tup pallet rose and fell as either a single blow or as continuous automatic blows.

Apart from being ahead of its time as regards operating versatility, there was nothing remarkable about this particular piece of machinery compared to others being erected in the Works regularly. However, for some reason the paperwork that accompanied it from B. & S. Massey Ltd of Openshaw has survived. From this it can be seen that: the machine arrived towards the end of July 1932 in thirty-three separate parts; it cost the GWR £306 16s 6d; its height above ground was 9ft; the drive was powered by a 17hp electric motor. Inside the cover of the handbook someone has written 'A.H. Munden, 15 Shop' and I assume he was the machine tool fitter responsible for maintaining this equipment at some period. *Author's collection*

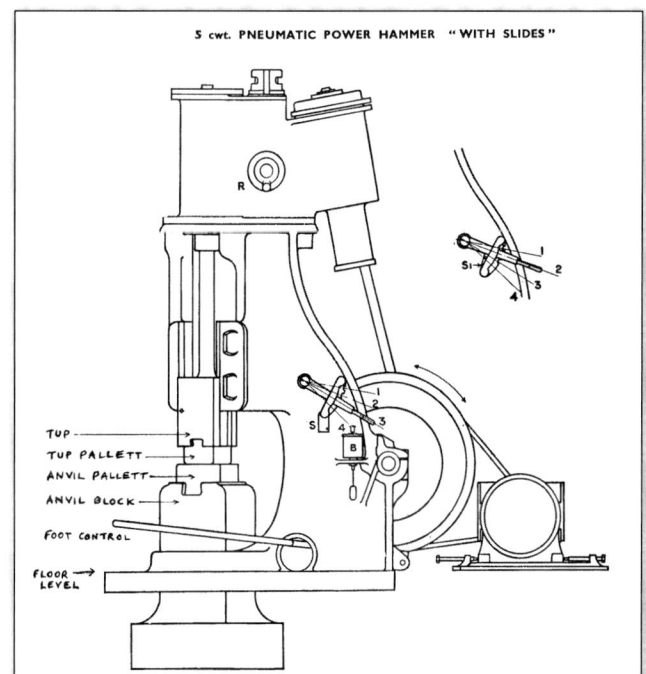

One end of the chemists' and metallurgists' laboratory at Swindon. Some of the staff based here would have been out working on site, testing and assessing materials and goods. *Author's collection*

Mr Dawe was the chief chemist and chief of research for many years; he had succeeded his boss Mr Davison in 1935. After the war, Mr Tidball was his assistant and Gordon Packer was their clerk. Fifty or sixty people worked in the chemical section. Analysing water and oil samples used in the Works and throughout the company took up a lot of their time. One section was made up of assistant chemists who did nothing else but analyse water supplies. If they encountered a problem they would, under the direction of the chief chemist, find ways of improving the quality of the water. They might for instance increase chlorination to destroy harmful bacteria.

The Works at Swindon was supplied with Kemble water, which was abundant and soft. Soft means containing low amounts of minerals (salts) such as calcium and magnesium and little or no corrosive acids. Water in this state would minimise the problems associated with heating it for power. Some areas of the GWR only had water that was of inconsistent quality or hard. Water-softening plants that supplied the boilers in hard water areas had to be visited and the composition of the treated water checked. Samples from all sources, for industrial use or for drinking, were regularly tested chemically and bacteriologically. They were usually collected in Winchester quart bottles filled right up to the glass stopper to exclude air, then labelled with date, time and location.

Chemical and physical tests were carried out to determine the quality of crude oils arriving at the company's Oil Works at the eastern end of the site. The Works' chemists wanted to know the percentage of say, paraffin or asphaltic hydrocarbons, and whether more than one chemical element was present. Later, after refining, further tests would be done to establish specific gravity, flash points and viscosity.

Works' chemists were also involved in deciding the classification of rates charged by the company for carrying goods. These were worked out depending on whether the commodities were dangerous (poisonous or hazardous), valuable, ordinary or perishable. One or two assistant chemists spent all their time outstation investigating claims of deterioration or mishandling made against the Goods Dept.

Other investigative work involving this department was wide ranging. For instance, Jack Hartley remembers when the slope up from the tunnel entrance could be very slippery in winter because of the smooth surface of the engineering tiles: 'The chemi lab staff made up some acid, which attacked the glazed surface and cured the problem.' Bert Harber, a part-time Works' fireman, told me that laboratory staff would sometimes be asked to help investigate serious fires. If company premises required de-infestation, it was these people that made up suitable preparations.

Steve Bond became a trainee metallurgist in 1952 or 1953. By this time the Works' metallurgists had moved into a building behind the CME offices, on the ground floor. As a trainee he had a day release to do a Bachelor of Science degree course in London. There was no set syllabus for his practical work 'inside'. In his second year Steve proved that he could be left to do skilled work without direct supervision.

Works' metallurgists spent a good deal of their time on what was known as failure analysis. This involved taking samples of such things as locomotive motion parts and boiler tubes that had failed in use due to stress, corrosion or fatigue. They would be looking to determine whether there was a design or a manufacturing fault. Random testing of metals cast in the Works' own brass, cast iron and non-ferrous furnaces were analysed here too.

Metals used for railway equipment such as bridges, rolling stock and rails were also analysed for quality and therefore reliability. The properties and composition of samples were checked under a microscope, reports were written on the findings and recommendations made. They would also investigate metal that had fractured unexpectedly while being machined. If the operator had been injured as a result, the metallurgists report would be important in a compensation claim. A foreign body in the eye was not an uncommon injury in these cases.

Other work included checking pyrometers on the wrought iron puddling plant in the Rolling Mills, analysing sodium cyanide concentrations (used in the case hardening process), and structural analysis of welded seams.

Personnel remembered by Steve Bond in the metallurgists' sections during the 1950s were John Hardy, who was regional works' metallurgist. Next in line of seniority was Ray Westney and later Bill Wilson, who were works' metallurgists. Then there were two just classed as metallurgists; they were Eric Mason and one other, until Steve finished his training. Later Mr Hardy moved to Derby Works but continued to live in Swindon.

The Work of the Test House

Physical tests on materials were carried out on the loco side in a separate shop using purpose-built machinery. This workshop was clean and quiet compared with the smiths' shops that surrounded it. Here in the Test House they were mainly concerned with the preparation, maintenance and testing of iron link chain and steel or hemp rope lifting tackle, together with its accompanying hooks and rings: a good proportion of which had been made in nearby workshops. The staff also checked over the hand-operated chain pulley blocks (used with block and tackle equipment).

The Chain Testing House. On the left can be seen the Buckton load testing machine; in the centre, the Ransome chain-tester; while partially visible on the right is a machine for testing the steel chains used with the 100-ton cranes. This equipment remained, and in working order, right up until closure in the 1980s.
The British Machine Tool Engineering Magazine

Sets of lifting tackle used by the GWR came in a range of standard types. They were listed in Works' catalogues by: 1) the type of lifting attachments fitted; 2) the length of the chain; 3) the lifting capacity. They were proof tested in a machine of 100-ton capacity when new and at regular intervals thereafter. A pre-determined force or load was applied to the item under test, if known. Otherwise the operator had to calculate it using mathematical formulae.

When chain links were formed, a number of separate samples from the iron bar used were tested for elasticity. They were produced to set sizes to be loaded into a Dennison 10-ton testing machine. One sample was elongated (in tension) and another of the same batch would be shortened (in compression). From the results, given in pounds per square inch (psi), and the pre-determined sectional areas, the metal's elasticity could be worked out.

New and used iron link chains were despatched and received via the Stores Dept. They were used extensively with cranes for lifting loads. Chains were returned to Swindon at intervals to be checked for wear. The links could 'go' at the welds but usually they wore and stretched at the points where they made contact with each other. When the diameter was reduced sufficiently from its original size, the links affected were condemned and replaced. If there was excessive general wear the whole chain could be annealed again by heating and slow cooling. This would improve its ductility (its ability to withstand tensile stresses under strain). An independent source stated at the time that: 'A good chain, properly looked after, will make from 100,000 to 150,000 lifts before it is entirely worn out.'

If passed as OK, a small cast iron identification label was attached to weight-bearing equipment, with an identifying number stamped on. Heavier loads were lifted by chain, or later steel cables, and they would also have plates attached to the frame of the crane or machine, giving 'load not to exceed' details.

Three Test House labels that had been attached to chains and other lifting equipment after being tested satisfactorily. They were then sent out to workshops, warehouses, yards and docks, throughout the company. Every item tested had a number that was recorded so its past history could be traced. The maximum working load of a chain depended on whether it was used singularly or together with others.

Wire and hemp rope was another means of transmitting power when lifting lighter loads. It was made in the Works in sizes determined by its circumference. Rope tackle included slings, nets and direct lift devices. Its durability was reduced compared to crane chains as it was subjected to two tensions: the working tension and the tension due to bending about the pulleys. However, the sum of these tensions would not exceed the elasticity of the rope because of the correct ratio between its diameter and that of the pulleys. A Buckton machine of 60-ton capacity was used for load testing ropes.

An Avery impact tester was used to check iron and steel for hardness and toughness. Between 150 and 200 steel and copper boiler plates were also tested on this machine each week.

The GWR Gas Works

The company made their own gas at the northern end of the Works' site. It was said that theirs was the largest privately owned plant of its kind in the world. More gas was produced than at the Gorse Hill works, which supplied the rest of the town. After the First World War the plant was rebuilt using vertical retorts, whereby gas coal was descended through red-hot retorts and converted to coke: the resultant vapours and gases rose and were then drawn off. An article in *Wiltshire Life* magazine stated that by 1946 the Works was also using modern horizontal retort carbonising plant designed by Messrs W.J. Jenkins of Retford. Its coal and coke handling plant capacity allowed the carbonisation of 240 tons of coal, giving approximately 3 million cu ft of gas. These figures were given in company publicity in 1924 and were the same as those given in 1950.

Engine or boilerhouse workers, maintained the plant, and gas or retort workers worked on production. They worked around the clock in three shifts. Throughout the Works, use was made of the temporary labour available in the 1930s due to unemployment. Bert Harber remembers that during the winter of 1937, railway wagons couldn't deliver coal to the Gas Works due to the severe weather and thirty men arrived from the labour exchange to shovel coal from the stockpile. Colin Bown was in the Gas Works during the severe weather in early 1947: 'The coal stocks froze solid so a bulldozer was brought in from Hills (a local excavating and haulage firm). Railings along Iffley Road had to be taken down to get it in,' he said.

Mr Ackroyd was the manager in 1937 and Mr Jefferies was foreman; Mr Wilcox was chief clerk and Ernie Wordsell was the timekeeper. Another person remembered by Bert was Leonard Lucas, who was a full-time painter. Len, together with his mate, painted lovely country scenes around the internal walls of the meter house. A piece in *BRW Magazine* in 1948 by R.J. Blackmore tells us that other walls were brightened up around the site too, such as those in the Governor House. Len started in the Gas Works in about 1931, repairing gas light fittings including seals and glass shades sent in from all over the GWR. This work was decreasing as electric lighting gradually replaced gas and so Len took on any painting work that needed doing. This led to him painting the well-known murals.

Bert Harber told me of his time as a Gas Works' office boy in 1937:

> There were three clerks: a chief and two. I had to take paperwork to other offices and deliver messages to people who could not be contacted by phone. These were the usual duties of the boy. I also wrote out coal tickets for the staff and assisted with the labelling of coal wagons before they were returned to the collieries. Copying letters for the clerks was tricky: you had to place a damp tissue over them and put the two under a press.

Bert's impression was that the workforce did not seem to mix with other railway workers or visit the rest of the Works. This was not the experience of John Jefferies, who began his apprenticeship in 1957. He was the last apprentice to be taken on and based in the Gas Works. John spent much of his time away in the factory or outstation assisting gas fitters.

Within the Gas Works they would maintain and repair gas- and coal-fired boilers, and John remembers testing samples of tar as well. Tar is a by-product when coal is carbonised or gasified into coal gas. They would heat it and put it in a hydrometer to test its density. Calcium carbide was also produced in the Gas Works and used in large carbide and hand carbide lamps. 'As the apprentice I was taught to clean and adjust these lamps so they gave off a brilliant white light,' said John.

Another by-product was Benzole, which was used in petrol, medicines and rubber production at the time. A new recovery plant for the extraction of this heavy chemical, and also sulphur compounds, was installed by W.C. Holmes and Co. Ltd of Huddersfield. The yield of Benzole then increased by a third to 3 gallons per ton of coal carbonised.

A scheme to modernise the Gas Works was worked out in 1957 but the 'Region' decided the costs were too high. Gas started to be received from the South Western Gas Board in May 1958. The old GWR Gas Works closed completely in early 1959 but the gas holders were retained. The gas fitters were moved to a corner of D Shop and the ordinary fitters were moved to the G (maintenance) Shop: all then came under the supervision of Mr Gibbs, the maintenance fitters' foreman.

Works' Goods' Traffic

An average of 500 wagons arrived in the town each day to be distributed between the dozen or so sets of sidings east of the junction station. That meant that the same number would have been dispatched. All incoming Works' traffic was dropped off at the Transfer Goods' Yards. Wagons were either left on the up side (north) or down side (south) of the main line, depending on which direction they had arrived from. Trains would arrive and the wagons, which should have been marshalled so that the first to be taken off were at the back, were uncoupled by the man on the ground (shunter) and moved to the designated sidings by a pilot engine. Those for the Works would be sorted into order, and again the first to be dropped off were coupled on last.

One of the main reasons why railway wagons came into the Works was to deliver materials and equipment needed for manufacturing and to carry away finished work and waste. Before the war especially, labourers emptied and refilled wagons inside the Works, often by hand, only being aided by cranes for heavy items. Lines of goods wagons containing components, raw materials particularly metals, timber and coal, machinery, wheelsets, general stores and laundry baskets were constantly being hauled one way then pushed another, as they were manoeuvred in and out of different parts of the Works.

Shunters and pilot enginemen sorted and moved the wagons according to instructions from the yard inspector's office. Not all goods arriving at 'the Transfer' was Works' traffic by a long way. But what was, had to be marshalled and moved by dovetailing it with wagon and carriage movements on a much wider scale. Wagons from vacuum-fitted trains had 'instanter' or screw couplings and they would have to be slackened by the shunter if they were to be moved together. This, together with radial axleboxes, allowed them to negotiate the curves in and out of the sidings without derailing. During all movements, the shunter would operate the point levers and if a capstan turntable was involved he worked that too.

Bob Dauris, who lived in Morrison Street, started his working life in the Yard Master's Office at Swindon Transfer Goods Yard. This was in 1956 and he was a junior clerk. Mr Hill was yard master at that time and Mr Holloway before him in the 1940s. Much of the following is based on notes Bob has made about that period of his working life.

Cocklebury Yard, on the up side between Whitehouse and Cricklade Roads, was the main sidings from where Works' traffic was initially stabled. From there it was collected by a shunting engine (the Cocklebury pilot) and taken to Loco Yard, which was the Works reception sidings, round on the Gloucester branch. Here it was marshalled before entering the various workshop sidings. The same sequence happened in reverse, using the Loco Yard pilot engine for consignments leaving the Works.

The Cocklebury pilot would take a 'stores trip', as it was called, from Cocklebury to Loco Yard a couple of times a day or as required. Included in these movements, or what the railwaymen called 'trips', was every kind of traffic: mechanical equipment of every type and in every state of assembly that could not be repaired on site. Non-passenger carriages such as stores, mess and tool vans, breakdown vans, cattle boxes, one-off vehicles such as the track testing (whitewash) coach, steam cranes, match trucks and shunters' trucks would be coupled together waiting to go 'inside' for repair or planned maintenance.

The little six-coupled docks' shunters were ideal as Wagon Works' pilot engines but most were the '5700' and later the '1600' class 0-6-0 pannier tanks. They were allocated to the nearby running shed for these duties. By the late 1950s 0-6-0 diesel-mechanical shunters were to be seen in the yards at Swindon.

Goods wagons that required works' attention or scrapping also arrived from all across the system.

The main line showing a freight train heading west on the left. Highworth Up Yard, nicknamed Spike Sidings, just east of Transfer Bridges, can be seen on the right. Among the goods that can be identified is a locomotive boiler and firebox mounted on a well wagon. Bob Dauris said these wagons, together with any contents, would be leaving the Works.
R. Dauris collection

Carriages and wagons that had been stopped awaiting attention were known as defective: the unofficial term was 'cripple'. A large proportion of the older damaged wagon stock was the result of loose shunting. With that in mind, designs between the wars often incorporated steel bodies and shock-absorbing underframes.

Wagons with hot bearings and often with a full load were common: they had usually been temporarily repaired where they stood. Insufficient oil or grease between the bearing surfaces caused friction and generated heat, which would gradually break up the white metal bearing. The load could be moved to another wagon (transhipped) if urgent, but this was labour intensive and therefore expensive. Defective rolling stock was checked by the carriage & wagon examiner, who would then label it with either a red 'not to go' label or a green defect label, which allowed it to continue and be repaired at the depot or yard at its destination.

The ex-works wagons with or without loads would pass over the weighbridge before the Cocklebury pilot formed them up. He then either made a transfer trip to the downside or stabled them for onward movement in goods trains at Cocklebury. The details of each shipment were recorded on a label on the wagon solebar by the consignee. Charges were due and accounts kept for private owners' wagons that were involved in Works traffic movements unless the costs were inclusive of transit and charged on the goods' invoice.

As far as Bob can remember, coaches entered the Works via the Water Sidings behind the station. Waiting to enter the carriage shops would be standard passenger stock including buffet, restaurant and sleeping cars, the occasional Royal Mail and newspaper vans, inspection saloons used by the Engineering Dept, Syphon Js (milk vans), horse boxes, slip coaches etc. The one and only Dynamometer Car was also the responsibility of the Carriage Works but the recording instruments were maintained by the Loco Works. Ex-works coaches were attached to timetabled passenger trains at the station or sometimes a complete rake would come from the Works and depart as a 'special' train. Some coaching stock would be sent to Marston Sidings, just east of Swindon, to be formed into trains from there.

The railway Gas Works used a lot of small gas coal in their retorts and this generated a lot of wagon movements to and from Highworth Up Yard, which was also known as Spike Sidings. Some trains would attach and detach coal and oil-gas tank wagons from there rather than from Cocklebury Yard. After supplying the Gas Works, Loco Works and the Running Shed, the empty wagons ('coal empties') were made up into trains and held in Loco Yard sidings. Later, they would be dispatched as complete special trains back to South Wales via Gloucester. This was done as and when required (not stated in the working timetable).

The costs of Works' traffic were debited to the department dispatching or receiving. New materials, plant equipment, spares and scrap were the responsibility of the Stores Dept; defective equipment and that for planned maintenance was the responsibility of the CME Dept and they would claim from Traffic Dept for its transportation.

10

The Stores Department

Introduction

The role of the Stores Dept was to purchase, store and distribute parts and materials for use by other departments within the company. Sometime in the 1950s the name was officially changed to the Supplies and Contracts' Department but, as was usual, most people continued to use the original name. Only the company's coal was bought in by another department, the CME Dept. Even then the storage and distribution at the three local coal wharves was administered by the Stores Dept.

Of course, the CME Dept, being largely made up of manufacturing facilities, also had stores attached to the larger workshops. In fact, there were two types of workshop stores, neither of which was part of the Stores Dept. There were tool stores, from which hand tools, cutting tools, measuring instruments, jigs and gauges could be borrowed. Then there were the warehouses or storehouses (see overleaf).

Charles Frederick Faith had been seconded to undertake divisional positions in storekeeping. Further promotions brought him back to the headquarters at Swindon and in 1932 Mr Faith became storekeeper in overall charge of the Carriage & Wagon Stores. In 1940, he was appointed assistant to the stores superintendent. At that time, there were three men with this title, each responsible for a different part of the Stores' activity (see text). These posts should not be confused with assistant stores superintendent, who was second only to the head of department and one position higher than that which Mr Faith now held. During the latter part of his working life he lived in Westlecot Road and was a member of the nearby bowls club.
GWR Magazine

In the early 1930s, the Stores Dept comprised of superintendent's offices; accounts' sections including a machine room; correspondence section; loco and carriage & wagon stores offices; general and traffic stores; timber stores. The latter consisted of three large sheds and a receiving yard at Rodbourne Lane down side. Most incoming timber was stacked in open sheds or on open ground for seasoning. The Sheet Works, a manufacturing outpost at Worcester, made ropes, sacks, mattresses, and sheets. Their administration came under the Stores Dept, Swindon, and they did not have a budget of their own. All their overheads were paid for and their products distributed by the Stores.

Swindon Works was the largest single purchaser from the Stores and, according to *BRW Magazine*, 90,000 items of stock were held here (this must mean types of items). Various stores were also held throughout the railway system if a particular site or sites would minimise shipment. For instance, a Docks' Material and Spare Parts' Stores was sited at the GWR Docks, Cardiff, which was best situated to distribute items to the major docks within the company. Similarly, stores for maintenance and repair of road transport vehicles were held in a building near the main depot at Slough. Raw materials too, bound for the workshops of the CME Dept, the Signal Works or the civil engineers, were usually held locally rather than centralised. It was not until as late as 1936 that the Stores had a fully comprehensive catalogue of items handled, all fully coded and described.

To attempt to minimise handling and damage, a statistical analysis of all materials moving between the workshops and stores was completed in 1955. It was compiled using punch card accounting and showed 2,000 tons was moved every day. Although by this time the Works used hoists, forklift trucks, power shovels and many types of crane, it was found that much of it still had to be moved by hand.

The GWR described its Stores Department as its 'housekeeper and universal provider'. Its importance was reflected in the fact that senior stores staff had all been selected from senior mechanical engineers. Mr Cookson was stores superintendent: his assistant and successor was Mr Boxall. Mr Webb, Mr Dashwood and Mr Willis were the assistants to the superintendent, and they were the next in line of seniority. They were responsible for either purchases and inspection; storage and distribution; or accounts, sales or staff.

After the war their responsibilities changed and, from the Works' telephone directory, it can be seen that they now dealt with: iron and steel purchases and sales; and general stores purchases and supplies. The third assistant to the superintendent position had gone and I wonder who dealt with all the timber transactions? The other senior stores' staff were the storekeepers, the chief clerk and the inspector of materials.

Stocktakers came in periodically to record the stock in hand, that which did not currently form part of an internal transaction. They were able to show that the value of receipts (or purchases) from contractors or from the company's own workshops rose steadily as the economy slowly recovered from the recession. This meant that issues, the money reclaimed from sales to the various departments, also went up correspondingly, although it should be borne in mind that both sets of figures would include rises in the cost of raw materials when compared year by year (during the early 1930s however, these prices remained almost static).

Stores' Accounts

The accounts' sections in this department were divided up into: 1) invoices, 2) ledgers (compiling data by hand, including paybills), and 3) mechanised accounts. Contracts had to be drawn up, orders placed, stores paperwork received and accounts kept, and this was the work of Stores' Accounts. Goods coming in had been purchased from contractors, and occasionally from other departments, and sold on within the company, the receiving department being debited with the cost. The Accounts' section of the Chief Accountant's Dept, based in the CME Building, did the ordering and handled the paperwork that accompanied goods received. This, the staff called 'progressing'.

By 1936 material movements started to be processed by electro-mechanical means from information on the requisition cards. When materials were moved between the Stores and the CME, or other departments, buying or selling it, it was accompanied by a requisition card. The card contained the details of the order, including the weight, the quantity, the coded charge and the signature of the storekeeper or foreman. The respective accounts' sections then evaluated the requisitions in turn. The information was then transferred to punch cards for compiling statistics and accounts.

This department did not make money when buying and selling. However, there was quite a difference in their favour between receipts and issues. In other words, they did sell certain commodities on to other departments for more than they had paid. Mr Gardner, the assistant chief accountant in the CME Dept, said in a paper he read to the Swindon Engineering Society in 1929:

> All articles manufactured in the CME's Dept workshops went into Stores at a price fixed by the CME's accounts staff and were charged back again at the same figure when drawn out for use, unless in the interim the price had been revised. I understand the Stores Dept cleared their expenses by adding a percentage to the cost of raw material which was purchased from firms and issued to the CME Dept.

The fact that Mr Gardner was a bit vague about Stores accounting emphasises the segregation that existed between the two departments, even though he had overall control.

Warehouses

Some of the CME Department's purchases from the Stores went straight into maintaining 'pools' of parts. Manufacturing workshops required an immediate supply of spare parts and they were held in warehouses or storehouses. They were beyond the control of the Stores Dept and therefore not strictly part of this chapter. The following only applies to Swindon Works and not to outstation warehouses.

The 230 staff in the various warehouses of the Loco Stores handled items ranging from copper boiler plates, heavy iron and steel sections, raw materials in the form of steel blooms, billets and bars for the Rolling Mills and Stamp Shops, base metals for the Foundry, loco wheel centres for turning and other semi-manufactured components and so on, right down to bolts and nuts. They also kept such things as paint, permanent way materials, gas and electrical fittings, and crane and turntable parts.

Another 176 people worked in the C&W Stores' warehouses. Besides every component for current rolling stock building programmes, they held road vehicle parts, oil and grease and platelayers' materials. Norman Pickett worked in the 'G' warehouse as a stores issuer. He had been there since it became the diesel parts store for the C&W side in the mid-1950s.

The Works' telephone directory shows that, by the early 1950s, workshop stores are listed as locomotive, carriage & wagon, timber and general. Each had a storekeeper and an assistant in overall charge and, as with the workshop tool stores, each store had an office run by a senior (class 1 or 2) clerk. Apart from the timber stores, each one was further divided up into various warehouses. The storekeeper was responsible for the orderly storage and handling of stock in his own areas. He had to strike a balance between supplying items without holding up production and holding only sufficient quantities to minimise loss of capital interest and the risks of deterioration and obsolescence.

When an order arrived at a stores' warehouse via head office the requested items were sent on with a charge note. It itemised each type of material or part by a requisition number, description, quantity and price. The inspector at the receiving department confirmed the order was correct or informed the dispatcher immediately. The longer discrepancies were left unresolved, the more chance there was of holding up the monthly accounts' figures of both departments.

The Metals' Section

Ordering and receiving iron, steel and alloys into the Works in a raw state was the responsible of the metals section of the department. It came in a million and one different grades, sections and sizes. Statistics released from Paddington state that in 1936 the Stores Dept issued out 3,793 tons of pig iron, just over 5,000 steel locomotive tyres and a combined total of 4,500 tyres for rolling stock. These represent approximately three times the stock held on site at any one time. Such statistics give some idea of the work involved so as not to hold excess stock, thereby keeping the costs of materials and storage space down.

'A' grade cast iron of a dense structure was used for pistons, chimneys, tender axleboxes and other engine fittings. Machining cast iron took some skill to get good surface finishes; it required drilling or turning at low speed and feed using high-speed steel or carbon steel cutting tools. From the 1930s, arc welding in particular was starting to be used to fabricate steel rather than rivet it or buy in expensive castings. In some applications fine-grain cast iron could be used but was generally inferior and difficult to weld at that time.

Steels in particular had to be bought in as there were no foundry facilities 'inside' for producing it. The Rolling Mills did have furnaces capable of melting down steel, mainly from old wagon axles. It could then be added to the mixes in the foundry furnaces where required. Carbon steel ingots and billets, steel bar and plate were brought in to be tested, inspected and either hammered, rolled, drop forged or stamped, then machined and heat treated. Locomotive and other cast steel wheel centres too were bought in from the railway works at Crewe. Open Hearth Basic or Acid steel was preferred for locomotive working parts. The plain carbon steel used for connecting and coupling rods had a tensile strength of between 32 and 38 tons psi.

The head of the metals' section in the 1950s, Mr Humphries, said of the purchasing and selling of scrap metal: 'Each day brings its quota of demands, enquiries,

phone calls, correspondence and visits from firms' representatives. Prices of the valuable metals can fluctuate considerably, and a watchful eye must be kept on the market so that, where possible, advantage may be taken of any fall in basic prices.' Inspections were carried out at firm's premises by staff of the Works' metallurgist section. Frank Webber, from G Shop, took samples from forgings such as connecting and coupling rods and had them tested for tensile strength in the Test House.

The way all raw materials reached the shop floor was by the 'slip system'. When work orders were issued by the foreman, slips or requisitions were made out by the chargeman of the gang doing the work. They were sent to the Stores Department, who issued the material and recorded details on the slip. The purchase price and handling costs were also recorded and invoiced to the CME Dept. Unused or scrap material could be sold back to the stores. Defective material, and the cost of any work done to it, was charged to the Stores Dept, who then had to make a claim against the firm who supplied it. The departmental accounts of both GWR departments were settled every four weeks.

After the war the output of British Steel could not meet the demand and priority was given to projects of national security and to exports. Consequently the Western Region allocation was limited and new building programmes were increasingly affected. Later in the 1950s, when conditions improved, the Works received around 35,000 tons per year from outside steel mills. Mr Basham, the Locomotive Storekeeper, claimed his department had 16,000 tons of steel and £1 million of scrap on the premises at any one time. These figures excluded the considerable amount of manganese steel used around the site for track renewal, most but not all of which was carried out by the Engineering Department. More steel was now needed than before the war as it gradually replaced timber in certain forms of railway engineering. Some grades of iron, copper, brass, tin, antimony, zinc and aluminium sheet were also received. These non-ferrous metals were being increasingly used in rolling stock construction.

The *Swindon Railway News* said in 1960: 'Tons and tons come in every day for the construction and repair of rolling stock. Steel for carriage underframes, side and roof panels, tyres, wheels and axles; frame plates; steel boiler tubes; gas and water pipes; conduit for cables; angles, channels, joists, flats, rounds and hexagons; steel for platers; for machinists; for spring and toolmakers.'

General Stores

The General Stores was a branch of the Stores Dept that was also based at Swindon. Its function was to supply consumable and cleaning products, clean laundry and other (household) supplies to company premises and to rolling stock of the Traffic Dept. To simplify the administration, all general stores were centralised, then distributed from one point.

Staff outside their rest room in the General Stores building. From left to right they are: 'Bamp' Shepperd, unknown, ? Davies, Alec Romans, Charlie Miles, Ernie Ruggles and Pete Aldridge. This picture was taken was because Charlie, who lived in Argyle Street, was retiring. *E. Ruggles*

The large building with the ridge and furrow roof between the Swindon Junction and the Running Shed was the General Stores. It was purpose-built and came into use in 1896. Storage areas were arranged over three floors, with some items stored outside. The General Stores differed from the rest of the Stores Dept in that it had no particular connection to the CME Department. It dealt with all the cleaning and consumable supplies required by all departments. The vast majority of general stores were bought in from outside contractors.

Staff in one section of the department perused the trade and economic journals as well as the daily press in order that the best prices were not overlooked. Raw materials in particular were subject to fluctuations in prices and these were noted. If oil, steel or leather, for instance, came down in price, the superintendent was notified and he would decide whether to authorise purchases ahead of schedule. Once the quality of the product had been established, not only cost but a reliable supplier was an important consideration. Breaking standing contracts just on the basis of costs could prove to be a false economy. Where applicable the superintendent was under no obligation to buy from Swindon Works; if he could buy in cheaper from outside he would do so.

One of the items most commonly handled was brushes of all kinds and inspector Ken Watts said the firm of Davis & Burrows was the supplier of choice. He remembers a consignment of superior brooms and brushes arriving on one occasion and a stores issuer taking it upon himself to store them on a high shelf. They were, he said, for cleaners of management offices only. He would get worked up when he discovered that people had taken them for other use on Saturdays when he wasn't there, said Ken.

At the age of fifteen, Ernie Ruggles went to work in the General Stores. Ernie, from Stanier Street, said the date was easy to remember as it was 12/3/45. His father, Arthur, had come to Swindon from Stratford Railway Works in east London in 1911 and had obtained work 'inside' on factory transport. Arthur Ruggles was for many years churchwarden at St Paul's church (behind Woolworths) and caretaker at the church hall in Dowling Street. His first son naturally took up the free trade arrangement, so Ernie would remain unskilled, something he feels bitter about:

This out of date policy of offering only the eldest boy an apprenticeship took no account of ability and split up families. I started as stores lad the only one on 'B' floor in the General Stores' building. The three floors were known as 'A', 'B', and 'C': 'A' being at the top. Within these three floors were three further warehouses: 'D', 'M' & 'O'. The clothing/uniform store ('M') was in the corner of the top floor and Comptons' factory supplied most of this stock.

The warehousemen went on strike over the right to get piecework payments. I was not yet in the union on account of my age so I worked on my own. Management gave in after a couple of days when they realised the disruption it was causing. The piecework price achievable was the same for all entries on the requisitions whether they took a few seconds or fifteen minutes to deal with, but it did make people work harder. As I was under sixteen years I was only allowed to do light work. I branded brushes and bass broom handles with a branding iron heated on a gas grill: they were made at the Institute for the Blind in Bristol. I also stamped GWR on small brush handles using a rubber stamp and inkpad. Many of these were made in the Works and were used for clearing swarf from machine tools. The department could get items ready marked but it was cheaper for me to do it. I put away incoming stock, taking care to stack it correctly so that: 1) The maximum could be stacked, 2) They would not fall out, and 3) They could be removed easily.

Each consignment arrived with three copies of a receipt. One stayed with the goods, another went to the office and a third went to the inspector. After clearance from him the clerk would release payment to the supplier. 'B' floor held life belts for the company's ships, guards' watches, sheets of asbestos of varying thicknesses for steam pipe connections. Rolls of 'balata belting' were also kept here; after riveting into loops in the Works, they transferred power to some machine tools. The belt came in thicknesses from ½in up to 6in wide. Pipe fittings, guard's lamps, fire buckets and padlocks we stocked too. We even issued out combs for stationmasters above a certain grade. From my early days there, I remember seeing stocks of wartime tin hats and stirrup pumps as well as horse shoes and stable equipment.

The laundry bay was also on 'B' floor, where hampers of clean laundry for the company's hotels and refreshment rooms etc. were held. They were dispatched to the outstation room at the junction station for delivery by stores vans. Ernie remembers that there were three or four women in 'B' packing room, including Florrie Browning and Betty Perry. The men working there were Dick Ellis, Reg Arthur and Alfie New, in charge. Heavy items and large loads were moved by a sack truck or trolley, which each gang guarded as their own.

The annual turnover of the General Stores in the late 1950s was around £171,000. This was the purchase price of the items dispensed and did not take into account the savings made from repairs. For instance, the value given for the 23,800 guard's lamps that were exchanged each year was £37,500. However, most could be 'turned around' after perhaps replacing the lens and a repaint. As a result, the majority in circulation had been patched up. The next most numerous item summarised in a Stores Department booklet for general circulation were shunters' sticks. They were used for coupling and uncoupling wagons, for which they took a lot of wear and tear. Thousands were sent back as unserviceable but the steel hooks could often be reused and the hickory shafts could be cut down and made into smaller items.

General Stores' staff are seen making up consignments to be sent out in travelling stores vans to all parts of the GWR. The vast majority of general supplies were bought in from specialist manufacturers. Although the General Stores also supplied the Works, they had no particular alliance to it or to the CME Dept. *GWR*

Distribution of General Stores

From about 1930 there were five travelling vans that were sent out weekly to all parts of the system. This was considered to be more efficient and economical than keeping stocks in each division. The vehicles used were converted brake third coaches and could therefore be attached to passenger trains. Stores van No. 2 was rumoured to be a converted clerestory royal coach. While outstation they were manned by an attendant known as a 'vanman' or 'tallyman'.

A further fleet of sixteen vans was based at the General Stores for a quarterly delivery and collection involving something like 1,100 offices, stations and depots.

A postcard sent to firms and departments that dealt with the General Stores, dated Christmas 1950. *E. Ruggles*

Wishing our Old and New Friends the Compliments of the Season and a Prosperous New Year. From Mr L.G. Eveleigh and Staff, General Stores, Swindon

They carried items needed less often, such as consumables, protective clothing and tools etc. A requisition book with the station or depot's requirements was received before the commencement of each thirteen-week period. Their entitlement depended on their category (status): the larger and busier places were given a higher category. Cotton waste for cleaning and 'lighting up' locomotives was one of the main items delivered to running sheds and it arrived in hundredweight bales.

All GS stock items were ordered by description using the authorised name, group letter, number and quantity. The orders were made up by men and women in the packing room on each floor of the warehouse. Warehousemen collected the orders in large trolleys. All loading was done outside in the Station Despatch Depot. When they were ready for dispatch the (quarterly) four-wheeled Stores' vans were marshalled into goods' trains. Very bulky or heavy items were sent direct from the manufacturers' works to the destination.

Inspecting and Testing Materials

An Inspection and Test Room was set up within the Works. Here samples of ready-to-use materials and basic commodities purchased by the Stores Department were checked and tested to ensure they were up to the job. The scientific testing of samples purchased by the Stores Dept or manufactured on site was carried out in the Works' laboratories. Stores sent there included metals, paints, varnishes, lubricants and other oils, creosote, cement and soap etc. (see Chapter 9).

Mr Phillips succeeded Henry Arkell as chief inspector of purchased materials in the late 1930s and had a staff of about twenty-seven. They carried out physical tests on random samples and visual checks for signs of damage in transit and deterioration. Machines for analysing the properties of iron and steel were used; other tests accelerated ageing or determined hardness. Large consignments of such things as steel, copper plates, wheels and timber were inspected by Stores' staff before they left the contractors' works.

Shunting poles were bought in and a random one or two from each batch was

A small brass plate from an oil reservoir can, giving the standard instruction.

inspected in the Material Stores. The hickory shafts were tested by leverage. This was done by inserting one end in a socket and, using a mid-point fulcrum, a man put his full weight on the other end. Bill Kent or his assistant Frank Smart did this and other types of testing after the war. Used poles also came back in and the inspectors would mark the metal hooks that required reshaping or replacement. Linesmen's belts, for climbing telegraph poles, were tested using another home-made rig of pulleys and weights.

Materials' Inspectors

After being wounded in Malaya in 1949, Ken Watts returned to civilian life but found it difficult to get a job. Ken, of Avenue Road, Old Town, was failing the obligatory medical examinations so his fiancée Hazel Newman, who worked in No. 48 (Mileage) Office, suggested he try the BRWR Stores. For some reason the medical examination was not being carried out on new staff and he was offered a start in 1950:

My first job was marking metal items with a vibrating pen. Then I was moved to a pattern store in the old medical fund swimming baths: one of a number of satellite buildings of the General Stores. The pool area, long since drained, was where certain patterns, moulds and templates were held. My job was to arrange to have them sent out to firms making items for the railway. There were several of each pattern and a 'master', which didn't leave the premises. The resultant castings coming in were checked by our inspectors.

A first floor had been added to the old bathes and that's where Eric King the paint inspector was based. He would coat various surfaces and leave them outside to weather, having carefully recorded when and what paint was used. Eric also sent samples to the Works' laboratory. Supplies intended for marine use, he sent down to Weymouth, where they would be painted on to surfaces and submerged to test durability.

When Mr Phillips retired in 1949, Mr Tyler became chief inspector of materials. In time his assistant, Jack Tudman succeeded him and Bill Morris became his assistant. Bill later went to the Timber Stores and I remember him telling me that they ordered wood for the Southern Region too. Other materials' inspectors I remember are Norman Raven and Ray Harris, who played in goal for Chippenham Town in his spare time. Assistant inspectors included Bill Larkin, Archie Wilson and Bill Iles, who dealt with the various types of incoming lamps, among other things.

The clothing/uniform store in 'M' Warehouse kept samples of every type of railway uniform fabric, which were sent out to manufacturers as a guide to work from. Tom Mapson, the clothing inspector, would visit suppliers such as Compton Sons and Webb, a local factory next to the Works, in Sheppard Street. They set up business many years earlier, primarily to supply uniforms to the GWR. The contact at Compton's was on the Works internal telephone exchange. The cut and finish of uniform material coming in was inspected by Tom or his assistant Gordon Hancock. They would also check samples of weave from each batch by counting the threads per inch.

The Stores' Offices

Noreen Harris didn't want to go to Paddington when the Motive Power Dept where she worked was relocated. Instead she transferred to the General Stores Office as a clerk dealing with purchasing and stock control. This was in the mid-1950s:

Some of the contacts I had made with outside suppliers while working at Plessey's and Vickers now came in handy when doing similar work here. Mr Curno was in overall charge and all letters and documents had to go to him to be signed. Reg Cripps was in charge of the GS warehouse floors and his assistant was Arthur Hunt. The office was very hot in summer and draughty at other times. In 1960 another girl and myself were sent on a course to Windsor in connection with our work. On the ground floor of the GS there were three coke-fired ovens that were part of the original 1896 building and were listed. When the building was demolished 100 years later they were broken up too.

Both Maureen Stokes and Margaret Eveness started their working lives in the Loco Stores Office in 1950. This was one of a group of offices on the first floor of the CME building that formed a sub-section of the Stores Dept. The clerks and typists here handled all the incoming and outgoing paperwork relating to ordering, receiving and dispatching of materials stored in Locomotive Works' warehouses. This included raw materials and subcontracted work such as electrical fittings and material; paint; non-ferrous metals, iron and steel for loco building and overhaul. Components sold back to the Stores from the CME workshops and movements of stock to outstations all made work for Maureen, Margaret and their colleagues.

Next door to them were the secretaries and typists of the stores superintendent's section. They dealt with correspondence and the organisation of the department. The Materials Inspectors' Office was another where Maureen and Margaret both spent time working later in the 1950s. Material inspectors checked samples and recorded the results from batches of items that were brought in, as already described. The resulting paperwork and its distribution were dealt with by the clerks of this office.

Maureen Stokes was fifteen years' old when she went into the Stores' offices as office girl. She lived in Guppy Street, just behind Rodbourne Lane:

A lot of workers going to and from the factory passed our house every day: little did I think I'd soon be one of them. After work I went to night school at the College and did English, shorthand and typing courses with the intention of becoming a shorthand typist. This was achieved, although

Maureen Stokes next to her desk, which has been decorated by her colleagues for her twenty-first birthday. As was traditional, she also received a large brass key made 'inside', with her name engraved upon it. This was 1956, during the period when Maureen was working in the Clothing Office. *Courtesy of Maureen Marvell*

some of my time was still spent doing clerical work. Head of section in Loco Stores was Jack Basham, at that time, and I remember Carole Paulley and Doreen West. They had both started as office girls in those early days.

Maureen's typewriter was a model called The All British Bar-Lock, of Nottingham, a type designed for business use and made about 1930. When she left the railway in late 1959, Maureen was allowed to keep her typewriter as they were all being replaced by electric models. At the time of writing she still has it and still meets up with several ex-colleagues including Carole Paulley, Mary Barnes, who had started in the Carriage & Wagon Stores Office, and Audrey Clarke, whose working life began in the Stores Correspondence Office. Like Maureen, both had moved around within the offices of this department. Other people remembered who worked in the Stores offices were Les Cox, Foster Day, Eric Cook, John 'Jack' Purdy, Joan Woodroffe, Val Bennett, Joan Bowles, Lorna Dawes, Ben Blackmore, Bob Bauld and Doreen West.

Unlike Maureen, Margaret Eveness completed her further education before going into the Works. She enrolled on a day commercial course at the secondary technical school on the Goddard estate. This was a two-year course that she started in 1947. From the Education Committee handbook for that year it can be seen that the syllabus included the main school subjects of arithmetic, geography, physical exercises and French, together with commerce, shorthand typing, craftwork and handwriting. Homework would, no doubt, have been an important part of the course as well. Margaret told me:

I came from a typical Swindon family, most of whom worked on the railway and married into other railway families. Grandfather Albert Eveness was a top-link engine driver and a big ASLEF (union) man from Rodbourne Green. My father was colour blind so they wouldn't take him on. My sister Maureen was a French polisher and my brother was apprenticed to fitting, turning and erecting. We had been bombed out of our house in Ipswich Street in 1940 and had to be moved to Beech Avenue, so I moved from Ferndale to Pinehurst School. I was eighteen when I went 'inside' but still had to do the duties of office girl along with Jeanette Absolom from Westcott Place.

As well as running errands, I had to collect supplies from the canteen for tea breaks. Mr Plyer, a tall thin man, was in charge and Mr Hobbs was the storekeeper. I used to come in through the Beatrice Street entrance and so had quite a walk to the main offices. After a few months I was moved to the Material Inspectors' Office, where we all sat in rows at high desks. Eric King and Ray Harris were the inspectors there. After a year you had to move again to either a typists' pool or the Machine Room. They offered me the latter and I went to have a look but didn't fancy it. When a job came up in Garrards' accounts, I left and went there.

In 1960, Ernie Ruggles, who was in the General Stores being paid as an unskilled worker, applied for a job as warehouseman:

Presumably because I was the youngest applicant, they offered me a position as a clerk instead. They asked me some general knowledge and maths questions as a sort of test. As was well known, if the questions were easy, and they were, they wanted you. So in September that year, at the age of thirty-one, I went into the General Stores Office, on the invoice section. There were about sixteen clerks here, of which about six were females; Ralph Butt was the chief clerk. I was put to work matching up the cleared invoices with the order forms and filing them. As with most newcomers in any department, I was not supposed to answer the telephone. Now I could join a superannuation scheme. The GWR fund wasn't taking any more so I joined the LNER scheme.

Pamela Page also worked in the General Stores Office; she had moved across from the Loco Stores Office in 1955:

It was a large office and Mr Sheward was in charge. He was an elderly man who was stone deaf. Someone told me that he had been the last male to be employed as a shorthand typist in the Works. Fred Bishop was quite senior too. I remember him because he died during my time there, even though he seemed quite young to me. Fred Lye was an ordinary clerk but insisted everyone call him Mr Lye while he used everyone's Christian names. Harold Thorpe was another clerk I can remember. He was a member of the town council (and mayor for 1956) and rode a bike very slowly.

In the late 1950s Ken Bowles' outstation section of the Loco Stores Office was spending a lot of time dealing with requests from Western Region diesel depots for locomotive parts. Roger Wise from Lowestoft Street was a junior clerk on this section at this time. This was the start of the diesel era proper. He told me:

The office would receive a phone call for a part for a diesel that had failed (very common in the early days). After ringing us and setting the wheels in motion, so to speak, the depot would be required to send in an Urgent Vehicle Standing requisition to the Stores Accounts' Office. Meanwhile, I would look up the part number in the appropriate catalogue or manual: there were dozens of makers' manuals in the office.

On a Works' bicycle, I would go to the diesel stores in 'A' Warehouse and collect a part, or parts, from the stores issuer. As a junior, I was usually the one who took the part(s) to the station, where it was handed over to an engine driver whose train stopped at Swindon. It had been pre-arranged that it would be picked up by an engine crew from that particular depot. Charlie Matthews at Cardiff Canton was one man among several I remember dealing with concerning UVS requests. As the depots became more familiar with diesel loco faults, they kept their own ranges of spare parts.

This is the Stores Accounts' Office on the second floor of the CME building in the 1940s. According to the 1935 Works' telephone directory, those with their own telephone here were: E.J. Burrington, clerk in charge; E.A. Blackman, section head of Invoice Accounts, later to be succeeded by W. Scott; G.W. Worthy, head of Ledger Accounts, which included paybills and stores sold; F.C. Tomes, head of Mechanised Accounts; and B.E. Turner, Pricing Accounts.

Irene Dening, seen on the left of the third row, was already quite senior but, assuming this was her normal place of work, it would appear not yet senior enough to have her own telephone. *B. Carter*

A tender register plate sold by the Stores Dept to a Mr Mython Hunt in 1950. The price asked was two shillings and sixpence. This was based on the scrap price of the brass at that time. A surviving letter concerning the sale advises the purchaser that the two tender plates he had requested had been 'broken up'. From that and other research I deduce that up to that time the Stores rarely had requests to buy anything other than withdrawn locomotive nameplates.

Tender number 1054 was attached to four different 'Dean Goods' locomotives between 1930 and 1940, when it was found to still be in serviceable condition. By this time many of the 'Dean Goods' locos had been withdrawn or 'called up' and sent to France, so 1054 was attached to a new '2251' class 'Collett Goods' until withdrawn in 1950.

Scrap: Disposal and Reclamation

As already mentioned, the Stores Dept dealt with the company's scrap. Residual materials were sent back to Swindon, where the department received them and reclassified them as either saleable, salvageable or for disposal. The department did not actually store or handle the scrap, apart from having a clerk in attendance when wagon loads arrived to be weighed. What they did was to acknowledge its shipment to Swindon and arrange for its onward movement. In other words, they acted as the go-between by dealing with the paperwork and chasing other departments or contractors by telephone.

Some redundant items could be reused in workers homes or gardens. An advert in the July 1927 edition of *GWR Magazine* offered 'Old railway carriage and van bodies for disposal', many of which finished up on farms as summer houses or storage sheds.

Some scrap was lucrative, such as the reclamation of metals, but other types were not. Stores' clerks had to arrange for it to be recycled, to use a modern term, or pay for its disposal. An article in a pre-war *GWR Magazine* lists old bricks, ashes, battery mud, common and hammer slag, old carriage trimmings, coal bagging, asbestos, India rubber as well as scrap metals as the sort of materials typically 'handled' by the Stores Dept. They also arranged for all of the company's paperwork, no longer deemed to be of use, to be collected and brought back to Swindon before being sold on, in bulk. The stores superintendent was particularly keen to clear old paperwork before it built up as storage space had long been a problem and, of course, it was a fire risk.

The C (cutting up) Shop area was in the Concentration Yard, at the far west or Bristol end of the Works, where all the scrap metal was sorted. The facilities here included a large corrugated iron clad building with a 25-ton overhead crane, plate levelling rolls, shearing machines and lifting magnets. Smaller buildings nearby were used for the storage of torch cutting equipment and gas bottles; they were also supplied with mains gas. In the sidings that served them, travelling Goliath cranes were used to sort and load scrap into wagons. The ground on which it all stood had been built up in the late 1920s and the C Shop

facilities became operational in 1931 and 1932. Then withdrawn locomotives, plant and machinery could be quickly and economically stripped down and sorted. Steel was cut up by oxyacetylene torch and iron castings were crushed using a drop ball and crane. It was then sent on to scrap merchants or returned to the Works' furnaces.

In 1937 there had been difficulties in obtaining supplies of materials due to a government rearmament programme and general trade requirements. Therefore the Works recycled more of the scrap that they would normally have sold. The following year the situation of supplies had improved but the market conditions for the sale of scrap materials became less favourable. The company waited for values to increase but with the introduction of controlled prices in 1939 they did not. Presumably they then decided to cut their losses and sell the stockpiled scrap. Despite the lower price realised, the annual figures for material sales didn't look too bad. No doubt the accounts people at Paddington were not fooled.

During the war the CME Dept were told to process as much of their waste material as possible for reuse on the premises. Some metals, for instance, could be melted down and recast, and if necessary rolled in the Rolling Mills. Wood shavings and sawdust were burned for heating, although this may not have involved the Stores. Most timber was sold to employees or else burnt; it was not reused. Even reusing hardwoods had never been economically viable but that was not a factor while normal supplies were being diverted elsewhere.

According to *GWR Magazine*, 'striking economies in the use of materials have been effective by a variety of special means including modern methods of reclamation and the painstaking salvage of bomb damaged and worn equipment for repair and reuse'. During this period it also fell to the Stores to find suitable substitutes for scarce items.

Like all second-hand materials, wood was classified as either serviceable or scrap. The official instructions to employees who graded it were 'care should be taken that timber disposed of as firewood or refuse is such as could not be used with advantage for company purposes'. What they called 'refuse' timber was larger and of better quality for use at home or in the garden. Most of this type of scrap came from the bodies of withdrawn wagons.

The oil painting that was used for the frontispiece of the famous book *The 10.30 Limited,* published by the Great Western in 1923. The picture had been hung in the offices at Paddington, then sent back to the Works for disposal sometime after the war.

In the Second World War the cheap supply of household coal, which was not dealt with by the Stores, was stopped because of alternative demands being made on ships and trains that carried it. The demand for scrap wood then went up as workers and their families had to burn only wood in their fireplaces.

By the 1950s wood deliveries were half a crown a hundredweight and coal was a little more, presumably because it had to be bagged up. The Swindon Corporation Act of 1951 stated that wood fuel sold within the borough now had to be valued by weight alone. Railway wagon loads were exempt, so this saved the Stores Dept from having to process a lot of weights and measures forms that had to accompany the sale of 2 cwt or more.

When company premises were updated and refurbished, all the redundant furniture, fabrics and fitments were brought back to Swindon Works to be reclassified. All metals went to the loco side and timber to the carriage side. On one occasion, probably just after nationalisation, wagonloads of effects arrived from the offices at Paddington. Arthur Moody, a carriage trimmer or upholsterer, came over to see what was being disposed of. He managed to rescue a framed and glazed painting 'just before the labourer tasked to deal with the wagon contents put his foot through it'. It shows 'Star' class locomotive No. 4062 hauling the *Cornish Riviera Express* and was painted in 1922 or early 1923, see photo. (This locomotive had a life of 34½ years and was withdrawn in November 1956. The carriages of such a prestigious train were replaced a lot more often.)

The 'Western' realised the value of railway enthusiasts and invested in such things as Swindon Works' excursions and open days. Another way in which they encouraged interest was by selling nameplates from withdrawn locomotives to the general public. It was common knowledge among the men and boys who stood on the stations and watched trains

that a letter to the 'Stores Superintendent, Swindon, Wilts' could secure a nameplate for a sum that would just cover handling costs. The railway would dispatch the item requested, or offer an alternative, to the nearest station for collection.

11
Accidents: Prevention and Treatment

Education and Incentives

It is often said that what we now call 'health and safety' in the workplace was virtually non-existent in the GWR Works, but this is another myth. As well as preparing staff to deal with casualties once accidents had occurred, the company worked hard to promote awareness of potentially hazardous situations. This was part of what they called 'staff welfare'. The first ambulance classes were held at Swindon in 1882, before it became law for railway companies to educate their factory workers' in this regard. Despite this, working in heavy industry remained, for thousands of enlightened Swindon workers, dangerous. Now though, the suspicion of blame could be shifted on to a careless worker.

With the government breathing down their necks, the railway industry had to be seen to be taking all possible steps to prevent accidents. They did not want the Ministry of Health introducing further regulation and controls. Most of the safety laws listed under the Factory and Workshop Act as applicable to the GWR were reminding the worker to use common sense. Whichever way it was presented, the advice would sound patronising and therefore have less impact. Employers had to find other ways to appeal to their workers.

The Safety Movement was started in 1913 and promoted through the staff magazine. Free pocket tokens were issued to employees on application. They were embossed with slogans that the company hoped would catch on, such as 'look before you leap' and 'is it safe?' It was the GWR that first coined the phrase 'safety first' in this country. The movement was, in their own words: 'A definite attack upon the causes of personal injuries sustained by employees in their work, and a campaign designed to sharpen the appreciation of risks and to cultivate forethought and caution.'

Safety crossword puzzles were printed in the *GWR Magazine* in the mid-1920s, with prizes awarded to the first correct entries sent in. An all-line Freedom from Accident Competition was introduced to encourage staff to participate and think about accident prevention. Again the company and Works' management gave its support by providing facilities and presenting awards for teams with the best safety records. This competition began in 1926 and by 1931 the number of accidents throughout the company had fallen by 56%.

So accidents, which kept a man off work or worse, did decrease in the Swindon workshops due to organised education. When they did occur, however, they were the most effective reminder for others to be careful. Foremen and chargemen often recalled injuries they had witnessed and the reasons for them as an effective way of deterring newcomers from repeating the same mistakes.

A gold 'one in a thousand' and a silver first aid long service medal. They were awarded to Bill Bown in 1938 and 1946 respectively. The gold medal was awarded to the captain of the AM Shop team, one of five to win the all-line Freedom from Accident competition in 1938. To qualify and compete, places of work had to be assessed. Those thought to have similar potential for accidents were put into a league of fifty teams, each made up of twenty people. Points were awarded or deducted depending on injuries or lack of them at work.

The company handbook instructed machine operators about things that might seem obvious: not wearing loose clothing and keeping guards and fencing in place around moving machinery. In practice, the latter took time and reduced visibility so it was often disregarded. Therefore the penalties for not complying were publicised as being severe. Contractors too, had to be educated on safety matters before they started any work on company premises. Injuries were most often associated with lapses of concentration or haste by those doing repetitive work. It was said that if a wood machinist in the Saw Mill retired with all his fingers he was very lucky.

Works' First-Aiders

Men and women were trained to render first aid, not only to casualties who had suffered industrial trauma but also to a colleague who, for instance, had fainted or had an epileptic fit. It was the possibility of the latter that inspired office staff to take up the training too. Before the war there were 103 dressing stations (first aid posts) in the Works. The walking wounded could summon the first-aider from them with a bell. In 1931 the staff magazine reported that 270 of the Swindon workforce were ambulance trained. This was, as a percentage, among the lowest in the CME Dept.

Any Works' employees aged sixteen years and over could take up first aid training and every encouragement was given by management to do so. The training and studying were intense as well as time consuming, and some soon found out that they did not have the dedication required. There was always a need for more suitably qualified first-aiders in the Works, therefore those they had were that much more valued. As a consequence, ambulance-trained staff received certain concessions and assistance from the employer.

Ambulance training in the GWR mess rooms in London Street. A young Bert Harber acts as the casualty.
Bert Harber collection

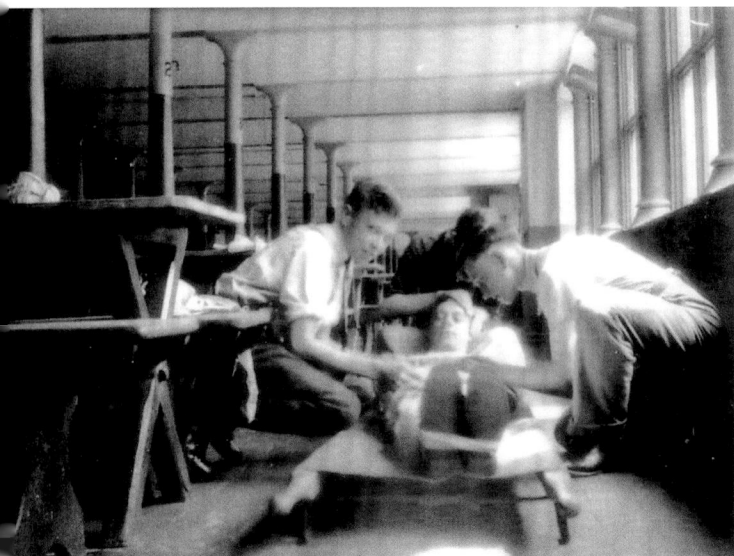

Weekly evening lectures were given by Medical Fund doctors in the Bridge Street Institute and an examination was held annually. Management allowed the mess rooms in Bristol Street to be used for ambulance training. Participants spent some evenings and Sunday mornings practising first aid and testing each other using scenarios given in St John Ambulance handbooks. If a student passed two successive examinations they were allowed to practise within their workplace, although I am told it took a while before the less experienced first-aider was summoned if others were about.

Not all first-aiders were members of the St John Ambulance brigade, only those who progressed to become trainers. They had to be assessed periodically and attend courses run by the St John Association. It was they who set the standards for teaching and all theoretical examinations were judged according to their latest published information. This changed regularly during the period before, during and after the war, and every new edition of the authorised St John Ambulance textbook had to be studied to keep abreast of current methods. The cynical among the Works' first-aiders suggested that all this did was sell more copies. What the regular updates did achieve though was to reduce the apathy that crept in once a certain level of proficiency was reached.

The Medical Fund Society doctors had overseen the GWR Local Ambulance Competitions since 1898. The annual competition allowed teams of 'advanced' and 'beginners' to play out life-threatening situations that had been thought up by medical staff. Marks were awarded by the doctors and a scoreboard was displayed for the audience to watch the progress of the team from their shop or office. This competition – there were other similar 'all-line' competitions – was held at the MFS baths. The two swimming baths in the Milton Road building could be covered over with wooden flooring and used for this and other functions.

Several first aid inspectors and team captains made names for themselves over the years. People such as Bill Bown, Gordon Culling, Fred Drinkwater, Freddie Cockhead, Bill Harber, Jack Dixon, and after the war, Jack Sutton, gained an elevated status in the Works and in their own neighbourhoods. Jack Dixon's grandson said that neighbours would call on his grandfather when someone living nearby needed medical assistance. No doubt other Works' first-aiders could tell a similar story.

Females in the shops and offices became accomplished and respected first-aiders too, none more so than Alice Sturgeon of the CME statistical (mileage) staff. A piece in the *GWR Magazine* when she retired tells us that Miss Sturgeon was a St John gold medallist and holder of the St John Ambulance Association long-service award. It is likely that she took up first aid soon after she started 'inside' in 1917. An accompanying photo shows her looking very smart in her St John uniform.

The man qualified to administer first aid in the Foundry had a reputation for being heavy handed, so the casualties would get young Jack Fleetwood to treat their minor mishaps. He could remove a particle from an eye or clean and dress a cut with the minimum of discomfort but, with no proper training, this was highly improper. Jack was eventually reported and told to stop.

Jim Lowe said Gordon Clack was the best first-aider in AE Shop in the 1950s. He worked on Lewington's finishing off gang. Fred Drinkwater in the nearby Weigh House was another who was highly regarded. It was Fred who was immediately summoned by those first on the scene when Mr Churchward was found lying by the main line after his fatal accident. Walking across the main lines was dangerous for anyone and Janet Morgan, in the CME offices, was told she had to do it: 'I was sent to the first aid post on the other side for some minor treatment. This was just after I had started in 1960. They told I had to walk across the (Paddington to Bristol) main lines and I was terrified that a fast express would hit me. One of the men working outside escorted me back so I assume it was the accepted route for staff in certain circumstances.'

First-Aider Competition

After 1945 the annual competitions were better organised and better supported; that's the impression one gets from the reports in staff magazine. Not only was there an all-line competition for teams across the GW/WR but, after nationalisation, there were inter-regional finals too. The best teams from across the country competed to become British Railways' champions. The year 1948 was the first that female teams had their own competitions. That year Swindon 'A' ladies team beat all the others and became BR champions. The winning team were all CME or Stores Dept clerks A. Dixon, J. Winchcombe, E. Couling, M. McGovern and S. Dixon. The two Dixon girls, Audrey and Sheila, were the daughters of first-aider Jack Dixon.

In the 1940s and '50s Jack Dixon's team dominated local and regional railway first aid men's competitions. The GWR/BRW Swindon District Ambulance shield was engraved with their team name year after year. Despite other teams with highly capable members, it seemed they were invincible. Jack Dixon (Captain), Fred Drinkwater, Hugh Freebury, Freddie Cockhead and H. Osborne (reserve) also won the Directors Shield in 1947, becoming the best team on the GWR.

Freddie was an 'iron dresser' in the Foundry. He had taken part in about eighty ambulance competitions, an achievement that was probably the reason his obituary made it into the staff magazine. He died suddenly in 1954 at the age of just forty-six. His ambulance teammates acted as pallbearers at the funeral. I think it was H. Osborne who claimed to have made a pattern for a replacement bell for loco *King George V* (much speculation exists about whether its bell is the original).

It would not be until the 1958/59 competition that Dixon's team were beaten in the Swindon contest, and even then in slightly irregular circumstances. While each staged situation was being judged, the other competing teams were not allowed to watch until they had performed their turn. Part of the exam on this occasion required each of the finalist teams to bring a casualty, with multiple injuries, down from a single-storey pitched roof. Dixon's team performed the tricky manoeuvre well with equipment they were allowed to borrow in advance from the Medical Fund casualty department. Then Jimmy Norton's team had to deal with the same situation (Jim was a chargeman in AM Shop and his No. 2 was Ian Sawyer, also in the AM. The other two were Charlie Gee and Arthur Mullis who both worked on the carriage side. A young chap named Yeates was No. 5, which meant his role was as reserve or to act as the casualty).

To get the patient down, Ian arranged to have two hooked roof ladders and a Neil Robinson stretcher brought over from the BRWR Fire Station. This was all standard fire brigade equipment as Ian well knew because he was also a part-time Works' fireman. They were then able to lay safely on the ladders, which were hooked over the ridge, one either side of the casualty, while they strapped him to the stretcher. All they had to do then was lower him down vertically into the care of the person on the ground. This impressed the judges enough to take their points total above that of Jack's team and make them winners.

Accidents

Before the war most machine tools were driven by electric motors via line shafting and belts (or straps). If a belt gave out or started slipping on the main shaft pulley, the man who made replacements, the 'strappy', had to be sought. (There were at least two men who dealt with drive belts on the loco side: one with a small work area in O Shop and 'Strappy Winslow' in R Shop.) When he was ready to replace a belt, the line was stopped for a few minutes. However, if a main belt had come off its track it was just a question of putting it back on to the opposing pulleys. Frequent short breaks in production for this or for maintenance was frustrating for the men because their piecework figures would be adversely affected.

Ernie Culling was a skilled machinist in R Shop between the wars. He said that one fellow became very good at replacing the belt with a pole while the shaft was turning. This was strictly prohibited, so had to be done when the foreman wasn't about. Unfortunately his luck ran out one day and he was thrown off the ladder and killed.

Two men suffered fatal injuries in the factory in 1933 according to the local newspaper, the *Evening Advertiser*. They were Gordon Kendrick, who was crushed in the X (points and crossings) Shop, and William Hobbs, who died instantly when an emery wheel burst in the AM Shop. A third incident involved a Frank Cox, who fell through the roof of 13 (wagon frame building) Shop: he survived perhaps because his fall was broken by an internal roof. Another accident towards the end of that year but unconnected to any Works' activity resulted in the death of Swindon's most revered engineer, certainly in terms of steam locomotive design, George Jackson Churchward.

Newburn House, seen here derelict after Mr Churchward was tragically killed in 1933. This view shows the proximity of the house to the Locomotive Works, seen in the left middle background, across the main line. *Swindon Society collection*

At about 10.20am on 19 December, 1933, Mr Churchward's body was found by the side of the line by a platelayer. There were no witnesses but it was obvious he had been struck by the front of an engine and the Paddington to Fishguard express had just passed. One of his gardeners confirmed that he had left Newburn, the house where he still lived, via the back gate that gave access to the trackside. It was assumed he was planning to visit the Locomotive Works. This he did regularly after he retired.

The inquest concluded that failing eyesight and hearing coupled with misty weather conditions and his preoccupation with the condition of a section of track all played a part in this tragedy. A measure of 'the old man's standing in Swindon may be gauged by the fact that the Works was closed for the funeral on the 22 December so the workers could line the route of the cortège. It was his wish to be buried in the churchyard of the parish church overlooking New Swindon.

For all patients entering the casualty department, a report was filled out on the correctly coded form. From these a summary of accidents in the CME Dept was issued quarterly to each dressing station. A surviving copy shows that for the first three months of 1927 one person was killed and 168 were injured throughout Swindon Works. These figures showed only injuries requiring an absence from duty of more than three days under the terms of the Factory and Workshop Acts. Without official figures year by year, it is not possible to say whether this level of casualties,

from 1933, were typical. Des Griffiths told me of an incident that happened where he worked (AM Shop):

I remember Jack Titcombe machining loco motion bars, on which the crosshead travelled. A shaving of hot swarf shot up into his eye. He subsequently lost the eye and badly burnt his fingers getting the metal fragment out. This happened around 1946 or 1947 when goggles were available but wearing them for this type of work was not compulsory. 'Cocker' Howell was a well-known character on the loco side and he had a glass eye. My father-in-law told me this was due to an accident at work. First aid men had taken 'Cocker' out on a stretcher and flagged down an up express [It is more likely that the signalman at Rodbourne Lane was telephoned by an official and told to stop the train] and he was taken to the Royal Westminster Ophthalmic Hospital in London. This would have been about 1936 or 1937.

Herbert Sillett's story is another particularly sorry situation: Herbert made an application for compensation after being discharged along with 820 men in August 1932. His argument was that with injuries to both eyes received in the course of his work 'inside' his chances of finding paid work 'outside' were very small. While employed as a rivet holder up in 1924, Herbert suffered a penetrating eye injury. He subsequently lost the eye and received compensation. While using a pneumatic riveter in 1931, a fragment of steel shot into his other eye. This time the sight was saved but Herbert said his ability to judge distances was now a severe handicap. This time the court turned his claim down, perhaps because he had returned to work and thus proving he was to some extent still up to the task.

The Hazards of Foundry Work

It took the heat generated from around 2½ cwt of coke to melt 1 ton of iron, and clearing out hot fuel from furnaces each evening was not without its dangers. New oil-fired furnaces were being introduced in the Iron Foundry in the 1940s and they were safer. This foundry also had an overhead crane and swivelling jibs in the heavy bay. Elsewhere, large amounts of molten iron had to be carried manually from the furnace to the mould. With this hot, heavy and unstable metal being moved and poured into moulds, the Iron and Brass Foundries could be dangerous places.

If the various methods of allowing the dispersal of gases, particularly in sand moulding, were not carefully worked out, then explosions were possible. Jack Fleetwood said: 'You never forget the details of serious accidents, even 60 and 70 years on. The most spectacular was when a 12-ton casting for one side of a large drop stamping machine, which was about the largest single work we undertook, exploded and molten iron shot through the foundry roof and set it alight.'

Jack said that the 400lb tilting furnaces in the Brass Foundry were much safer. 'The initial costs of installation must have soon been recovered as they were efficient and so much easier to use. They did away with the old method of lifting pots of molten metal up off ground pit fires which was not only strenuous but unpleasant too, as you breathed in all the fumes.' When first introduced in the early 1920s, the Morgan tilting furnace was so revolutionary that *GWR Magazine* did a piece on them. They said that the coke-fired furnace tipped on an axis at the lip to ensure a constant pouring point so that the ladle did not have to follow the stream. This greatly reduced the possibility of spillages, which had often proved dangerous. The magazine also said that all waste gases were taken out of the building through flues provided, thus helping to improve the atmosphere and comply with the Factory Acts.

Safety Precautions

In theory, the safety equipment provided was leather aprons and gloves in the 'hot shops', and welding shields and goggles where necessary. However, many men kept protective wares locked away for their own personal use and newcomers found them hard to come by. Ordinary window glass was the only suitable transparent material available for eye protection throughout the 1930s. Nevertheless, it would stop a flying particle of some force. In wartime a new potential hazard became apparent as fashions changed; female operators not tucking long hair

Moving and pouring large amounts of molten metal like this was comparatively safe in skilled hands. It was the small jobs that had proved hazardous. That was until tilting ladles or 'prams' were brought in. These aids also did away with heavy lifting and cut the time taken to produce batches of small repetitious castings. *GWR*

under a cap or net, properly. Suspended loads slipping out of slings were not uncommon and slipping on oil could be dangerous too, especially when jumping over pits. The latter could be dangerous at the best of times and everyone was made aware that it was a disciplinary matter.

Everyone knew of the dangers of loose clothing near moving machinery, especially where it was not possible, or practical, to fit adequate guards. Even so, the most educated and careful workers could become the victims of misfortune rather than negligence. This is almost certainly the only explanation for what happened to Frank Nutbeem, a chargeman machinist, who lived with his wife and family in Grosvenor Road.

Throughout the inter-war years Frank was a dedicated St John Ambulance man in the Works. His interest in first aid must have started from his time in the Royal Army Medical Corps, during the Great War, where he finished up as a sergeant. By the 1930s Frank was probably the most accomplished of all the first-aiders in the Carriage & Wagon Works. He must have witnessed many of the results of carelessness in the workplace.

One Saturday morning in October 1940, Frank was at his machine in 15 Shop. His job was the same as he had been doing for the last eighteen months, operating a Holroyd four-spindle boring mill. He was machining cast iron axleboxes, which were clamped to the machine's table. Cutting tools revolved on horizontal spindles as the table moved slowly towards them and the apertures were opened out to take the axle and bearing. Somehow Frank's clothing got caught in the machinery and he couldn't reach the stop lever.

Machining iron castings required a slower speed and feed than steel but the machine's drive was designed to keep going regardless of all but the strongest resistance. Stephen Hunt, at the next machine, heard him yell out but by the time he stopped the machine it was obvious that it was too late. The foreman Sam Owen covered the machine with a sheet and called the on-call doctor. It was Dr Frumin, from the Medical Fund, who pronounced Frank dead.

Ted Randell was in 15 Shop that morning and he told me that it was Frank's tie that got caught but the inquest said it was the long warehouse coat that he was wearing that was found wrapped around the driving spindle first. Ted said: 'The bedplate and driveshaft had to be dismantled to get his body out and remove blood and tissue.' A small section in the evening paper announced the tragedy among the headlines regarding the latest war news. As well as family and neighbours, there were a number of works' officials, NUR representatives and many workmates and first-aiders at the funeral.

Lengthman Herbert Webb was cleaning points near 'Hayward's crossing' in front of B Shop in January 1943. His mate had just gone to collect a wheelbarrow and no one saw the fatal accident. Herbert was struck by a locomotive running tender first, having come off the turntable. Mr K.J. Cook attended the inquest on behalf of the company. There it was established that the engine driver had taken the correct precautions of sounding the whistle and having a pilotman walk alongside. It was therefore decided that Herbert must have stepped backwards into the path of the engine, on the blind side, immediately before it passed him.

There were at least two further fatalities in or near A Shop that were talked about for some years after the war. Both happened sometime before my informants arrived in the 1950s. One man was climbing on to the footplate of a tender engine being overhauled and grabbed the reversing lever to pull himself up. He had expected it to be fixed tight but it was not and he fell backwards. A platform with safety rails pushed up against the back of the cab came into use as a result of that. Another poor fellow had his legs crushed by a moving wagon between A Shop and the Weigh House: 'A shunter was running alongside and uncoupling wagons being loose shunted into the yard beyond. He slipped on the steel plates that had been laid for heavy internal transport vehicles using the crossing there,' said Jim Lowe.

A 'factory' pilot engine about to tow a tender from B Shed where it has been overhauled to the reception shed, where it will be reunited with a locomotive. Jim Lowe said that the shunter on the ground is the man who had the accident on the crossing outside A Shop. *Author's collection*

Consequences and Rehabilitation

Accident reports had to be made out and sent to the CME when a worker in his department was injured at work. Where the company judged itself to have been negligent, a man would receive compensation equivalent to his wages for the period of his incapacity. This was subject to a doctor's report and sometimes the services of the company's own medical officer would be called upon to give a second opinion. If the injury resulted in permanent incapacity but he was still able to walk well, the man might be invited to return to the Works to undertake menial work. This would be dependent on whether the company had filled the number of such vacancies that they were obliged to make available by law.

Incidentally, one such fellow was employed to go round and disinfect all earpieces on the telephones. He, like others employed on a similar basis, would be paid as a labourer. From 1949, if a man who had twenty-five years or more adult service was reduced in grade owing to ill health or accident, he would receive the mean rate between that of the vacated post and the post to which he was reduced, up to a maximum loss of 10 shillings a week.

For railwaymen and women convalescing after accidents at work there was a rehabilitation workshop in the Carriage Works. This was known as 15B Shop and it opened in 1953 after a scheme had been studied at Vauxhall Motors. Under medical supervision, suitable patients were put on light production work as physiotherapy. Dr Watkins, the Swindon railway medical officer, prescribed the treatment and Micky Austin, the foreman, saw that it was carried out. Providing follow up treatment and physiotherapy got staff back to work that much quicker. Machine tools had been modified by Mr Austin, who had worked in the carriage side, to make them productive as well as therapeutic.

Aubrey Wykeham-Martin broke his leg in 1958 when a wagon door fell open on him. He later attended the rehabilitation workshop and operated a drill that he powered by walking slowly on a treadmill. Aubrey recovered sufficiently to return to the A Shop stripping gang on lighter work (his speciality was burning through nuts and bolts that couldn't be removed, using oxyacetylene cutting equipment). In 1957 two casualty centres were opened, one on the loco side and the other on the carriage side.

At this time the Works ambulance was being called out about five times a week. Some of these emergencies originated from railway premises beyond the Works. Two more shunters were involved in accidents in 1960: Charles McCord and Brian Webb suffered life-threatening injuries and underwent immediate surgery with blood transfusions, both making a full recovery. Brian, who lived in Folkestone Road, was fitted with an artificial leg and returned to work as a watchman at the tunnel entrance. Their stories were used for publicity to encourage staff to attend blood donation sessions held twice a year in the Works.

Artificial limbs had been made and fitted in a workshop on site until about 1950, after which they only did repairs. The staff magazine said in 1940 that there was an average of ninety cases dealt with each year. Although most of these were 'renovations and renewals', the majority of men affected must have been injured since the company began to make organised efforts to reduce accidents. This showed that, in most cases, there was no real alternative to common sense.

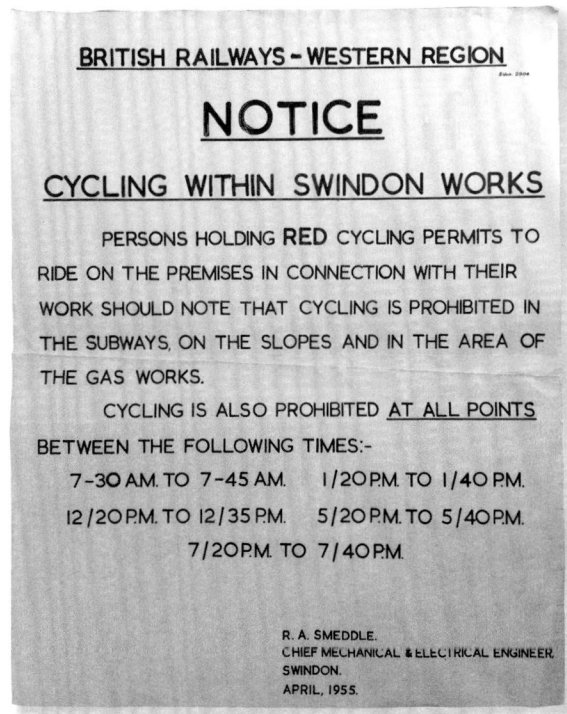

BRITISH RAILWAYS – WESTERN REGION

NOTICE

CYCLING WITHIN SWINDON WORKS

PERSONS HOLDING **RED** CYCLING PERMITS TO RIDE ON THE PREMISES IN CONNECTION WITH THEIR WORK SHOULD NOTE THAT CYCLING IS PROHIBITED IN THE SUBWAYS, ON THE SLOPES AND IN THE AREA OF THE GAS WORKS.

CYCLING IS ALSO PROHIBITED **AT ALL POINTS** BETWEEN THE FOLLOWING TIMES:-

7-30 A.M. TO 7-45 A.M.   1/20 P.M. TO 1/40 P.M.

12/20 P.M. TO 12/35 P.M.   5/20 P.M. TO 5/40 P.M.

7/20 P.M. TO 7/40 P.M.

R. A. SMEDDLE.
CHIEF MECHANICAL & ELECTRICAL ENGINEER.
SWINDON.
APRIL, 1955.

A notice inspired, no doubt, by accidents between cyclists and pedestrians, especially when leaving the premises. Once outside it was back to being every worker for themselves. *Author's collection*

12
The GWR Medical Fund Society

Organisation

The Medical Fund Society (MFS) facilities were available to company servants in the Works and their dependents, as well as retired and widowed members. Through the 1930s the number of local people eligible for medical treatment was between 36,000 and 39,000 at any one time. In 1941 the GWR said: 'The Society attends to the needs of nearly 45,000 persons.' I suspect that this number also includes all CME Dept workers, as they were entitled to be inpatients here.

A condition of employment was that employees pay in to the Fund in return for a whole range of medical, surgical and health services. Some say that no other similar scheme operated anywhere else in the country, at least not on the scale that this one did. George Petfield pointed out that Works' people living outside the town could not make full use of certain facilities, such as the dispensary and baths, therefore he thought they may have paid a reduced subscription.

All railway employees had to pay into national insurance schemes to cover them for health and unemployment. Workers whose total rate of remuneration exceeded £250 per annum in 1936, also paid for an old age pension. The National Health Insurance gave local people, including dependents, retired workers and widows, access to the Medical Fund Society facilities. A small sum was deducted through the paybill, proportionate to the rate earned, and the company matched it.

If the insured employee was a member of either the GWR Staff Friendly Society or Locomotive Running Department Staff Approved Society, they would contribute one penny less and the employer one penny more. Sickness benefit (claimable after twenty-six weeks of contributions) was 9 shillings per week for men, increasing to 15 shillings after 104 weeks. Women's benefit was proportionately less. Thus all workers in the CME Department became members of the MFS.

The book *A Century of Medical Service* shows that the subscription fees charged in 1947 had remained unchanged since the 1930s. This may be because in the later period, prior to the takeover by the National Health Service, the fee was separate from the sick pay deduction. The book also gives the company's contribution to the MFS as £1,750 for the year 1947. On top of this they, and not the subscriptions, paid the salaries of the medical staff. Later came the National (Health) Insurance, which George Petfield remembers paying as a fixed amount of 6s 9d in the mid-1950s.

The Society was managed by an elected committee of GWR workers, who exercised democratic control over the running of it. Each of the twelve or so members (numbers varied over time) was elected by ballot every two years. Every department in the Works put up its own candidate for election. The committee members were divided up into four sub-committees and each managed different aspects of MFS affairs. Senior Works' officers acted as honorary president, vice-president and trustees. The position of chief medical officer, (also known as consulting physician and superintendent) was the most senior in the Society. Dr Berry, then from 1936, Dr Lowe and after the war Dr Gibson, all held this post.

Local people not entitled to Medical Fund services were treated at the Swindon and North Wilts Victoria Hospital up on Swindon hill, and later, at St Margaret's. The Victoria Hospital relied on voluntary donations and major benefactors were listed in the end of year report. Senior Works' managers gave generously to help provide hospital services for all: Messrs: Hawksworth, Cook, Hannington and Churchward all contributed. Their workforce also got a mention as donation boxes in some areas of the Works realised significant contributions.

The Dispensary and Baths

The MFS facilities were contained within three buildings close to each other in Faringdon Street. The largest of these was on the corner of Milton Road and Faringdon Street, which came into use in 1892. This was usually referred to as 'the dispensary' or 'the baths', although it housed a whole range of medical and other facilities conducive to health. The ground floor was referred to as 'the surgery' by the locals. Most of the activity here, in the mornings and evenings, was connected with the surgeries being held by general practitioners. There were a total of ten full-time family doctors and between them they provided domiciliary visits and an emergency call out service.

The large and small swimming baths claimed to compare favourably with any in the south-west. As well as providing the health and social benefits of swimming, the baths were the venue for competitive water sports. Spectators could be accommodated in a gallery of banked seating around all sides of the large bath. It could also be covered, after hours, and used for dances, roller skating and as an assembly hall. The baths opened at 6am and some railwaymen would have a swim before work. During the war years, members of HM Forces stationed in or near the town were allowed to use them and the washing facilities too.

It should be borne in mind that most of the people using the bathing and personal hygiene facilities had no bathrooms at home. There were also facilities for hairdressing, Russian and Turkish baths, as well as a tone up under the hands of an expert masseur. A service tunnel ran under the GWR Estate from the carriage body shops, allowing water for the baths and the other facilities to be emptied and refilled by sluice gates somewhere under 3 or 4 Shop. It was heated in the boiler house in No. 2 Shop Saw Mill. The company, and not the MFS, bore the cost of supplying the water.

Upstairs in this building was a fully equipped dental department with three dental surgeons (a fourth arrived in 1947) and a dental mechanics' workshop. Dental treatment consisted mainly of extracting teeth under gas (nitrous oxide) and oxygen, and fitting full dentures, which were made on site. Dental surgeons provided their own instruments, so perhaps that applied to other specialities too. Along the corridor were the ophthalmic and chiropody departments, the laundry and a committee room. The labour room and midwives' office were vacated when Kingshill House was converted to a maternity home in 1931.

Elsewhere, all other standard medical facilities of the time were provided including pathology, physiotherapy and X-ray departments, and all were staffed by specialist medical personnel and trained assistants. There was a small additional charge to the patient for false teeth, spectacles, trusses and artificial limbs: it was about half what would be charged to non-members. Medical requisites such as invalid chairs, crutches, bed rests and hot water bottles were available for borrowing. Referrals to specialist hospitals and institutions were also part of the service with, if necessary, an accompanying nurse or attendant.

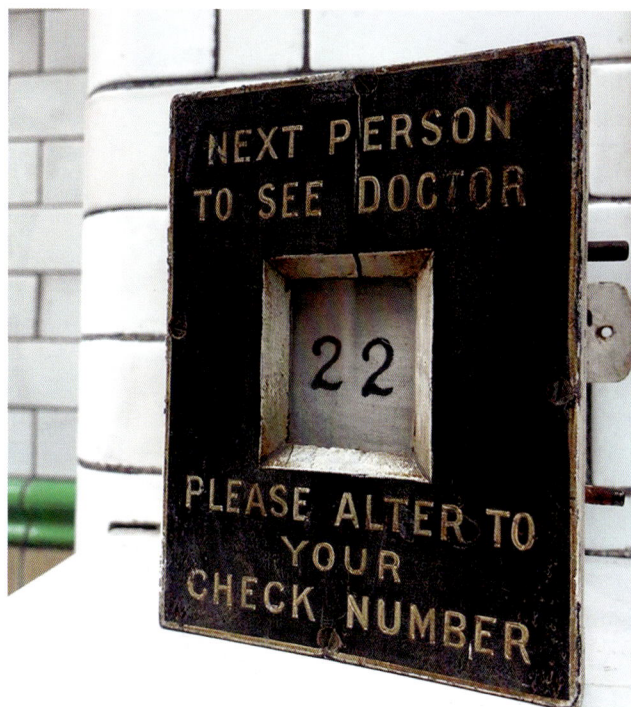

Patients wishing to see their family doctor were given a metal check with a number stamped into it. This indicator board displayed the number of the next person to go in when the bell rang. *Swindon Society collection*

Many children of Swindon railwaymen were given a regular spoonful of cod liver oil, followed quickly by the far more pleasant brimstone and treacle, to help them keep healthy. Mothers collected these preparations, which were available from the medical centre dispensary on prescription, in 2lb jars. For collection of medicines and tablets, patients brought their own containers before the war. Staff dispensed about 16,000 prescriptions annually and this did not include what was sent to the MF hospital over the road. The skilled task of making up the ointments, infusions and tonics for each patient individually was done by pharmacists. Between them they provided a service seven days a week, Sunday being one of the busiest days.

The National Health Service Act of 1946 required the county council and the local authority to provide, equip and maintain health centres for all. The following year the MFS was still the only health centre in Wiltshire.

The Outpatients' Department

In 1936 the surgical outpatients department was able to expand when it moved into the building opposite the baths and dispensary in Faringdon Street. They took over one end of a group of nineteenth-century buildings that were being used for anything that could not be accommodated by the MFS in its other buildings. There was the Lime House, directly behind Park House; a store for bath chairs; a rifle range; and an incinerator, together with its tall chimney. There was also a garage for the MFS hearse. The horse-drawn hearse,

The dental department staff in the 1940s. They were photographed on a flat roof of the baths and dispensary building. The only people identified are in the front row: Charlie Gardner in plus fours; Dr Froggatt in the centre; Mr J. Clamp, far right. Those in the back row look like dental nurse attendants and laboratory technicians. There were three dental surgeons until a fourth was taken on in 1947; Dr Froggatt was one of them. *Author's collection*

known by all as the 'Shillibier', was provided by the MFS until the late 1930s. This entitled the GWR to claim that the Society looked after its workers 'from cradle to grave'.

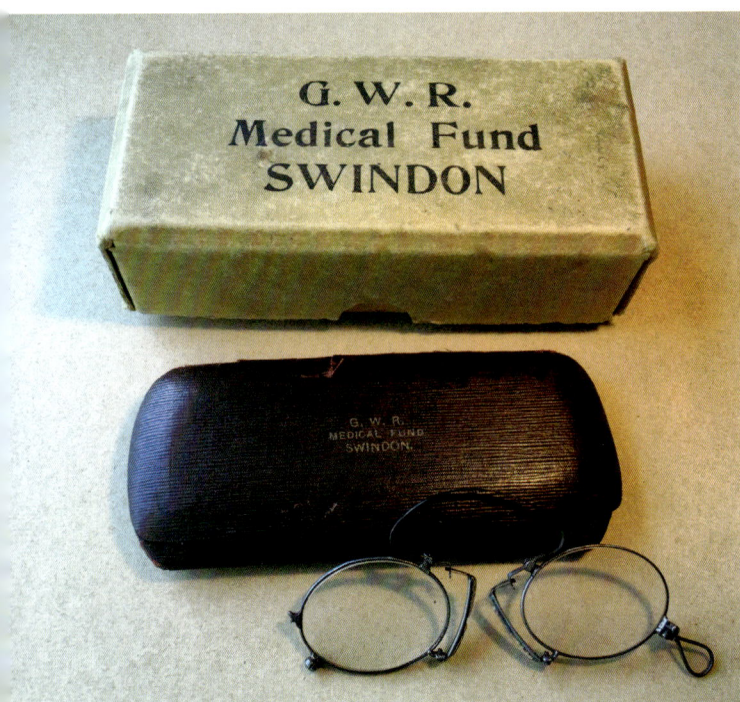

Locals then started referring to this new outpatients' building as 'the surgery' too. Woman and children were treated from 9am until noon. The only men seen in the mornings were those who had received injuries in the Works. An ambulance (first-aider) man or woman would have sent them in after having given medical assistance at the scene. Crushed or lacerated hands were common, as were burns and foreign particles in eyes. These same patients would need to return again for assessment and change of dressings by a doctor or nurse. Arthur Archer remembers being treated by a blind physiotherapist after the war, 'and very efficient she was too'. The more serious stretcher cases from the Works were also treated here before going over to the hospital ward.

Mr Greenwood, and in 1940 his former assistant Mr Schofield, were the general consulting surgeons ultimately responsible for all the treatment given. A lot of people were terrified of hospitals, as they were of dentists in those days. For this reason, Mr Greenwood encouraged a relaxed and informal mood among the medical and nursing staff. This was in contrast to the usual formal atmosphere of hospital departments of the day. The white walls were repainted with yellow above the handrail and blue below. The idea again was to try to put patients, especially children, at ease.

However, some of the medical staff remained stand-offish. Referring to a visit in the early 1940s, Harry Bartlett

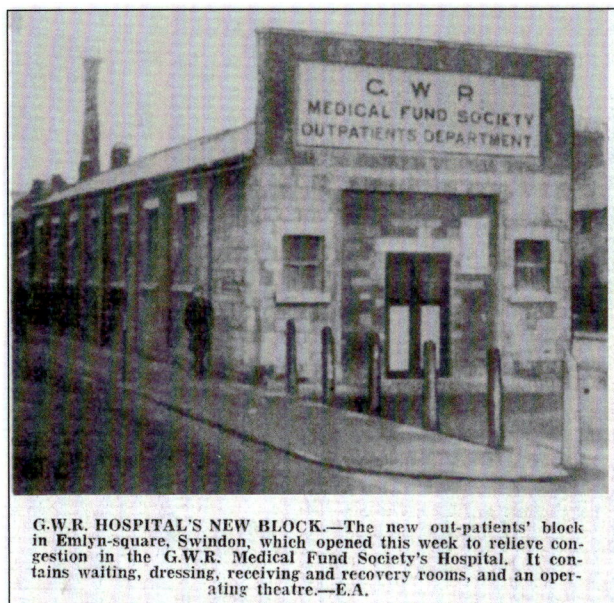

G.W.R. HOSPITAL'S NEW BLOCK.—The new out-patients' block in Emlyn-square, Swindon, which opened this week to relieve congestion in the G.W.R. Medical Fund Society's Hospital. It contains waiting, dressing, receiving and recovery rooms, and an operating theatre.—E.A.

The Outpatients Dept building. This poor-quality image is a scan of a newspaper cutting – photos of the department have proved difficult to find.

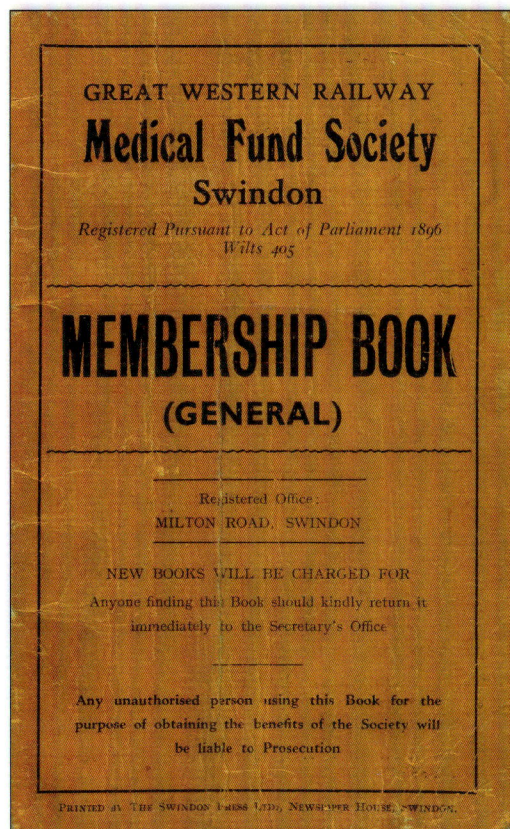

When attending the MFS as an outpatient, a personal membership card had to be presented to the person at reception. They were usually sat behind an open window of the office just inside the entrance.

said, in his book:

> I vividly remember the duty doctor, Dr Dangerfield. He was young, impatient and full of his own importance. He had dragged his desk into the waiting room and conducted his surgery from there with a queue, as you would have at the fish and chip shop. Patients had to stand in line regardless of their problem, while he dispensed a quick diagnosis and judgement, such as 'it's only a scratch, get nurse to dress it and get back to work' or 'no you can't have a certificate, you are perfectly fit for work'. He would shout at some poor wretch coughing his lungs out and point to a poster informing us that 'coughs and sneezes, spread diseases'.

The Society offered blood transfusion treatment from as early as 1923. Many of the GWR Works' people at Swindon had their blood group details registered with the Society, so if the duty surgeon required blood for a patient, a donor on the register would be called in. After giving a pint in the outpatients, the donor(s) were granted a couple of days away from the Works. The loss of pay was compensated jointly by the company and the MFS.

In April 1940 the surgical outpatients' building was damaged when a lorry with 15 tons of potatoes careered across the road and into the side of it. According to the report in the evening paper, a wall of sandbags placed there to cushion against bomb blasts stopped the lorry demolishing the building. Even so, the deputy borough surveyor had to order that the outer walls be shored up before the vehicle was removed. A Mrs Dash and Mrs Byrne, who were manning a first aid post inside, were unhurt. The lorry driver was trapped in his cab but was unharmed.

The Inpatients' Hospital

The hospital occupied an island in the middle of Emlyn Square. As well as caring for inpatients, it served as a dressing station for casualties coming in from the factory via the outpatients' department. In an article in the *GWR Magazine* in 1927, Mr Greenwood, the surgeon, said: 'As many as twenty-five accident cases have passed through the ever open door in one day.' Here too the operating theatre provided facilities for all types of surgery but they could not always treat serious injuries or provide specialised aftercare.

Jack Sutton had been an ambulance inspector at Swindon since 1944. This was probably a full-time post created during that period when the ambulance organisation was enlarged. Mr Sutton's main role was to train the Works' first-aiders, and this he continued to do for at least twenty years. A mercifully rare duty, for ambulance-trained workers like Jack, was to accompany seriously injured workers by train to one of the large London hospitals with which the GWR had an arrangement. For instance, penetrating eye injuries were taken to the Royal Westminster Ophthalmic Hospital. It was not unheard of for an up express to be stopped specially to pick up a badly injured man from the factory and an ambulance to be waiting at Paddington.

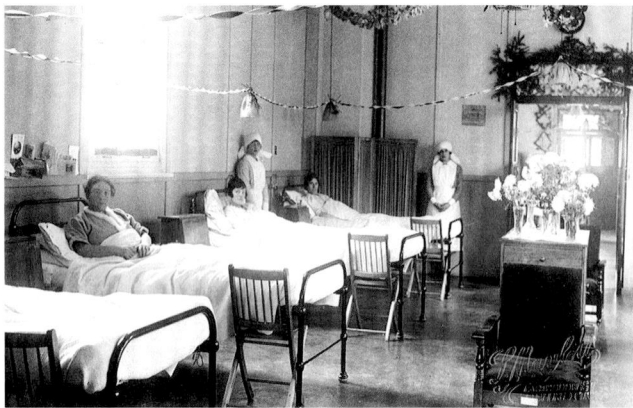

A scene at Christmas time in the female ward, dated 1927. The high ceiling and shape of the windows show that this must be the newly opened hospital 'extension'. *Swindon Central Library, local Studies collection*

This is the 1927 extension built in the front garden of the original MF hospital. Although only meant to be a temporary solution to the cramped facilities, it remained in use until the 1960s. *Author's collection*

The GWR hospital was enlarged in 1927 by erecting a prefabricated 'temporary' extension. It was erected in front of the original 1872 building, where well-tended gardens had been laid out. The MF now had facilities for up to forty-two members needing inpatient care. After other less ambitious plans had been explored, it was decided to apply to build a four-storey hospital on the site, doubling the existing capacity.

In 1930 a conference was held at Paddington with representatives of the Medical Fund Society and the GWR Company. They discussed the proposal for the new hospital, which would replace the existing one on the same site in the railway estate. The directors declined the request for a loan of £45,000 due to the worsening economic situation nationally and the idea was shelved. The existing permanent and temporary buildings would have to serve the railway community for the foreseeable future.

In 1931 there were 753 patients admitted to the hospital. Of these, 711 had 'major operations', thirty of which resulted in death. Gastric and duodenal ulcers were common especially among the men and this was thought at the time to be due to poor oral hygiene. A perforated ulcer was life threatening even with immediate surgical treatment. A very respectable figure of 1% was given for appendicitis mortality at the hospital during this period. Malignant disease was the reason for many major operations among Swindon's railway families; the use of the word cancer unnerved people and so was avoided whenever possible. The hospital authority prided itself on the regular blood transfusions given during surgery. This was due to a thriving donation programme among the community as already mentioned.

By increasing the number of hospital beds from thirty-six to forty-two and increasing the routine operating sessions from two to three afternoons each week, the waiting list of sixty was brought down to ten that year (1931). There were 2,112 minor operations for matters including tonsils and adenoids, piles injections, lancing boils and stitching cuts. Most of these cases would be given a general anaesthetic and sent home later the same day. Hazell Sheppard remembered that the hospital was scrupulously clean in the 1940s: 'The smell of disinfectant and ether stays vividly in my mind.'

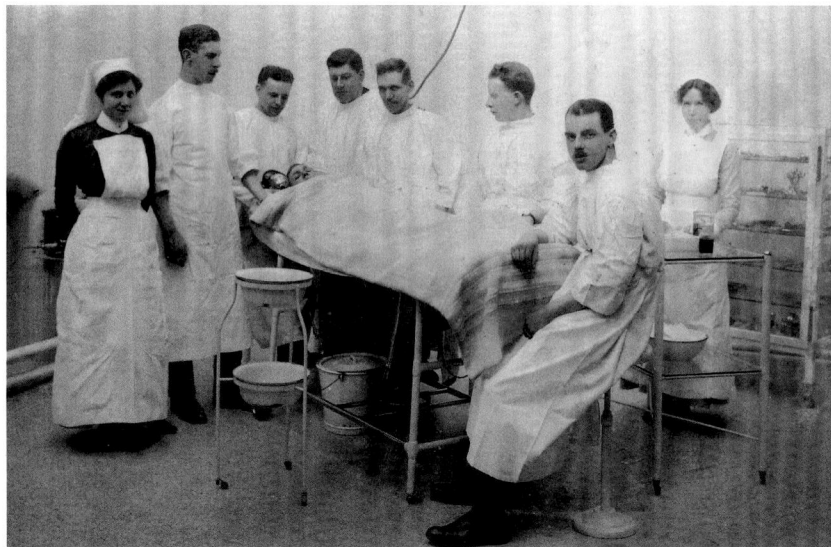

On the back of this postcard view of the operating room is written: 'The G.W.R. Hospital Nursing Staff, Faringdon Street, Swindon, Wilts. An Appendix case'. The writer also records the matron as Miss Ira Hutton and the nursing sister as Miss Mabel Woolford. The names of successive matrons from 1918 onwards are given in the annual reports but these names are not among them. A Miss Wood was matron from 1923 until 1947 but, of course, there were others to stand in or act up on occasions. There is little shown to date this photo more precisely than sometime between the wars, maybe even earlier. *Author's collection*

With honest business sense, the annual report for the year says of varicose vein patients: 'Attention is drawn not only to the suffering but of work efficiency of sufferers.' The average cost of running the hospital the previous year had been 1 shilling and 7½ pence per patient days spent in the hospital, which worked out at 14,115. The GWR directors authorised an annual donation of £50 and the company also bore the cost of gas, electric, coal, cleaning, repairs and decoration for the hospital and all MFS premises.

The depleted numbers of paying members during the economic depression caused the committee and the company a great deal of concern. The situation was made worse by another consequence of the times: a reduction in the fees received from the Wiltshire Health Insurance Committee. This led to the inevitable cuts to Society staff wages and salaries, as had happened throughout the factory. By 1935 most of these setbacks had been resolved but the Medical Fund hospital continued to have problems.

The superintendent medical officer's report for 1936 made the following observations: 1) 'Too many patients are still being sent to other hospitals due to lack of accommodation.' 2) 'It [the hospital] is situated in a very low lying and noisy part of the town and does not afford that restful atmosphere necessary to recuperation of patients.' Throughout the 1930s a large sign hung on a redundant tram line post outside saying: QUIET PLEASE – HOSPITAL. The nurses' accommodation too, said the SMO, 'left a lot to be desired'.

Hospital Patients and Staff

Kathleen Hemming told me of her time in the hospital as a child, having her tonsils and adenoids removed. This was in 1922 and no doubt her experience was typical of the whole period between the wars:

> I went in early in the morning and had to change into a gown and be put on a trolley. You were wheeled into a big room with a huge lamp on the ceiling. The nursing sister was getting all the instruments laid out ready and a doctor held a mask smelling of ether, over my face. The next thing I knew I was in another room recovering on a mattress on the floor; I remember I felt very sick. Mother came to collect me after a few hours.

Ex-patients all said the MF hospital was spotlessly clean with a strong smell of antiseptic everywhere. More than one person told me that a Dr Mac gave them their anaesthetic in the late 1940s. Unlike Kathleen, patients recovering from appendicectomy or hernia (rupture) repair were not allowed out of a hospital bed for three weeks. The local Methodist minister and the curate from St Mark's Church came round to see inpatients regularly and the Salvation Army came in to sing hymns on Sundays. Visiting was on Wednesdays, Saturdays and Sundays as well as public holidays. A period of convalescence in one of the jointly run railway homes might be considered beneficial following inpatient care.

Gwendoline Mercer began her training as a nurse at the hospital in 1944:

> I remember there were a lot of Welsh girls working at the hospital. There was a great sense of comradeship among the junior nurses (immediately after the war some patients remember there being a shortage of nurses). We used to live in the nurses home in Emlyn Square and were only allowed out on our one day off a week. There were several nursing sisters in the hospital but the probationary staff still got to do a great deal of nursing.
>
> In our second year we were allowed to put stitches in and some nights there were only two probationers on duty for the whole ward. Although Miss Wood, the matron, lived in and was our back-up, it was 'on pain of death' if you called her in the night. When off-duty we were not allowed out of the nurses' home after 8pm, unless we had special permission. That wasn't given for socialising.

I have not found it easy to identify many MFS staff by name so it is, I think, worth recording those listed as living at the GWR/BRW Hospital, Faringdon Road, in post-war electoral registers. Between 1945 and 1948 they are Gertrude Griffiths, Marjorie Barnes, Annie Mannigan, Adelaide Smith, Irene Durant, Annie Wood (almost certainly the matron that Gwendoline mentions above), Norah Kent, Ethel Hall and Dorothy Hewer. They were accommodated in a building directly behind the original hospital, other nursing staff would have made their own lodging arrangements. In 1955, after takeover by the NHS, just two staff are listed: Elizabeth and Joseph Garry.

NHS Takeover

An emergency medical treatment service was created nationally when war broke out. This provided a model for what could perhaps be continued when peace returned. The annual report for 1941 said that the GWR's health services at Swindon had begun to come under scrutiny by officials from government health departments. They were looking into setting up a welfare state for the nation after the war. The Medical Fund Society facilities started receiving visits of important deputations from medical authorities such as the Nuffield Hospital Trust. Emergency medical services' consultants were also conducted around the premises by the chairman. This attention gives some idea of how successful and highly regarded the facilities at Swindon were.

George Brunger lived in Kingshill Road and was a chargeman machinist on the loco side in the late-1930s. He had been a member of the MFS committee since 1917 and by 1940 had become chairman. He would escort the visitors who were preparing for what became known as the Beveridge Report, a blueprint for the British welfare state. They seemed to have been greatly impressed, not only by what they saw but also with their host, who would later be offered a senior position in the new

Mr G.W. Brunger, chairman of the Medical Fund Society committee during the 1940s. *Swindon Central Library, local studies collection*

Wiltshire Health Authority. In February 1944 a Ministry for Health 'white paper' stated that the intention was to introduce country-wide health service for the entire population. This was probably the first that most of Swindon's townsfolk knew for sure about the proposed changes to their health services.

Planners for the nationwide scheme continued to visit during and after the war. Mr Brunger said he welcomed Sir William Beveridge and Aneurin Bevan to Swindon, although people researching the birth of the NHS say there is no documented evidence of this. If Mr Bevan did visit, it would have been after he became Health Minister in the newly elected Labour government in 1945. The MFS chairman was also invited to visit them in London along with Dr Gibson, the chief medical officer.

In the Society's annual report for 1946 it states that a pre-eminent public servant said of the set-up at Swindon:

'It is the only current example of an attempt to provide a comprehensive health service, a service which the government hope to make available to everyone in 1948.' The positive tone in the report masked the uncertainty felt by the MFS staff, especially the juniors. In 1946 when the National Health Service Act became law the Society's committee still had no idea of how its facilities would be utilised and rumours went round that they may even be closed down.

In the last full year of its independence, 1947, the MFS had 42,656 members. The annual membership figures now included dependants who were eligible but did not include those still to be demobilised. The shortage of nurses at this time was another consequence of ongoing commitments abroad. The total expenditure for that year exceeded income by £10,018 according to the annual report (the previous year they had shown a profit of £315). The committee decided against increasing the subscription and to fall back on reserves until the takeover by the National Health Act on 15 July 1948. At the date of its dissolution, 18,000 Great Western Medical Fund Society members were entitled to a share of the assets. This amounted to just over 2 shillings for each complete year of unbroken membership.

Due to advances in diagnostic methods and the introduction of the National Health Service, some of the health care of the railway workers began to move away from what the MFS could offer. From 1950, a mobile X-ray van visited the Works for four weeks every year. The railway staff could now have regular check-ups for signs of pulmonary tuberculosis and other chest conditions. Posters were pasted on Works' noticeboards advising staff of the opportunity to participate in this 'mass radiography'. An appointment could be made by handing in your name to the shop office. Regular routine screening for TB was offered to the workforce thereafter and they would receive letters on the outcome.

A bronze tablet was fixed to the outside wall of the 1892 dispensary and baths building declaring the changeover from the GWR Medical Fund service to the National Health Service. The Swindon development plan, published in 1947, stated that hospital accommodation in the town was seriously inadequate. It said that a site at Okus was allocated for a new hospital, the first phase of which did not open until late in 1959. The original Great Western Hospital was then closed in early 1960 and the baths and medical centre continued as community facilities.

13

Fire Prevention and Extinction

The GWR took the prevention and control of accidental fires within its premises very seriously. It had been decided quite early on that the Works could not rely entirely on the town fire service and sometime before 1900 they set up their own brigade. It would cover not only the Works but also the GWR Estate, the junction station, the Transfer Goods Depot and all the yards in between.

Regulations

Not only did the company have to comply with the terms set out in the 'Factories Acts' but they also had to satisfy the requirements of their insurers and underwriters. According to the 'general regulations for the prevention and extinction of fire' issued by the general manager's office in August 1945, workshop buildings and their contents were insured for damage by fire but the permanent way was not.

It's hard to imagine steam locomotives being damaged by fire but they were insured against it in some situations: less surprisingly, so was the rolling stock. Situations where they were covered were when they were under construction or repair, or awaiting the latter. Any delays in putting locomotives and stock into traffic cost the company money. Therefore while being built or repaired, they were fully insured against damage by fire because of the possibility of burning buildings collapsing on them.

Fire regulations concerned with prevention and extinction were implemented and regularly reviewed by 'fire precautions committees', which were formed for all departments. Fire wardens were appointed for every office, workshop, warehouse, yard, dock and depot in the CME Dept and throughout the company. Their purpose was to check, at least once a month, that the regulations were being observed. One of the main duties of the works' fire wardens was to see that all first aid fire appliances and water and dry powder buckets were in their proper places. They had to be in usable condition and clean so that the instructions were readable.

Various types of hand-held appliances (or extinguishers), which contained calcium chloride under pressure, were used by the GWR. The warden would be familiar with all of them as well as others used for fighting electrical, spirit or oil fires. The warden would report any irregularities to the foreman or head of department and they would alert the Works' Fire Station. The full-time firemen maintained the fire-fighting equipment for the Works and the rest of the company.

Works' Fire Station and Water Tank

Various Works' buildings', including those making up the Fire Station, faced out on to what became known as Fire Station Yard. They were among the earliest of the carriage workshops, although their use changed regularly in the early days. This part of the Works was unusual in that it was at street level and there was no vehicular access directly into the Works. Despite its location in the carriage side, the Fire Station was part of the Loco Dept and the fire chief was an assistant loco works manager.

The station was divided into the appliance bays, a store, an office, a watchroom and, nearest the main lines, a workshop. The 50ft tower in the station yard was for hanging up the hoses after use. This allowed proper drainage so they could be rolled up and stored dry. The Works' brigade could, in theory, be called on to assist the borough brigade to fight a fire in the town. The only problem there was that the two brigades used different couplings. The Works used fittings that wouldn't couple with the local authority hydrants, and vice versa.

Of his childhood in the late-1920s and early '30s, Bert Harber remembered: 'When dad was manning the Fire Station call-board at the weekend, we would take his meal in to him. If there was nothing happening we were allowed to look round the station. The 1912 Dennis engine was the showpiece. It was said to have been the first motor fire engine in Wiltshire. I rode on it on my first call when I joined the brigade.' This vehicle went into the old Wesleyan chapel building in Faringdon Road when it was converted to a railway museum in 1962.

The water tank in the Fire Station Yard had towered over the railway houses in Bristol and Bathampton Streets since 1872. *Bert Harber*

The water levels of the Works' water tanks were all the same height above sea level. Only the 41,000 gallon Fire Station tank, when full, was different; it was 20ft higher. Because it would not fill by gravity, as the other main tanks did, a booster pump was used. The additional head and a narrower 6in supply pipe provided the Works' fire hydrants with pressure increased to 60lb psi. This enabled a jet of water from a fire hose to reach the roofs of the highest buildings, if necessary. The pump was tested every Monday morning at 9am. All the Works' water tanks were divided up to allow cleaning and maintenance work on individual compartments while the others remained full.

The Fire Brigade

Before the war all firemen had to live in the GWR estate across the road from the Fire Station. They were wired up to a bell code system between the station and their homes. After the war new recruits did not have to live in the railway estate and some existing firemen were able to move further away. The part-timers worked all over the Works, running sheds and yards. In wartime their number

was increased to twenty-four. They were normally on call every other week and would average about two call outs in each seven-day stint.

The brigade consisted of a chief officer, a second officer and eight firemen who were available for immediate call. There were six men working full-time in the station during the day; they maintained fire appliances and equipment, and practised fire drill. They were also expected to be ready to rush off at a moments' notice, if called. A further two sets of men could be assembled at the fire station at short notice.

Full-timers employed over the years included Cyril Moulden, Eric Carter, Bill Grace, Percy Moulden, Jessie Collett, Frank Baker, Sid Smith, Horace Jones, Les New and 'chief' Ray Sealy. They worked either 6am to 2pm, 2pm to 10pm or 10pm to 6am. Alan Lambourn remembers seeing Fire Officer Sealy coming to work from his house in Church Place in the early 1950s: 'He always wore a very smart dark blue suit and was one of the "old-school" who still favoured a bowler hat at that time.' Mr Sealy retired in about 1954 and Sid Smith took over. Sid had been a full-time fireman for more than twenty-five years apart from war service with the Royal Engineers. He also had a son, Harold, in the service.

William Harber became a part-time fireman in the 1920s and, together with Bill Bown, they were also the first-aiders for the Fire Station staff. Both men lived in the railway estate alongside the Works, of course, so when Mr Harber's son Bert wanted to join in 1939, it was a formality to get him on to 'the strength'. Bert said:

> There were several father and sons in our brigade. We went straight from work and did half-hour voluntary training, on four evenings a week and an hour, sometimes two, on Sunday mornings. You got 6 shillings and 6 pence a week for being on call, which paid the rent, and there was always a bit more if you had to 'turn out'.

In the 1940s and '50s the part-time firemen included Jimmy Little, who worked in L2 Shop; 'Budgie' Pretlove, who was in the C&W Stores; Ron Adams, who worked in T Shop; and 'Charlie' Bowering, the Brass Foundry Foreman. When on call, firemen who were in The Cricketers or in 'Charlie Thomas's' place (later named The Glue Pot) public houses would get their kids to stay at home in case a 'shout went out'. Bert's father was a part-time fireman when Bert was young: 'As kids we soon got used to the night alarm bell ringing and by the morning we couldn't say whether it had gone off or not. Even during the day we could not remember whether it had gone off five minutes later.' The bell was tested every day at 1pm, with just one ring, and a fire drill was carried out once a month.

After the war they struggled to keep pre-war numbers and the rule that 'A' and 'B' sets of men must live in 'the estate' was dropped. The 6 shillings on-call money had become less of an incentive, so it was doubled. Ian Sawyer was a part-time fireman in the 1950s and he still has a list of personnel from the station. It shows there were three

This 1912 Dennis fire pump was superseded in 1942 but retained as a back-up vehicle until 1956. *GWR*

regulars, nine who worked in the station workshop and another nineteen part-timers. A surviving document shows that for the year 1958 there were seventy-one fire calls.

When a Call Went Out

The full-time firemen acted as watchroom attendants round the clock, manning the telephone. At weekends they were supplemented by part-timers. When a fire was discovered, the Works' Fire Station was called on 2098 and the location given. Alternatively, the exchange was rung and the operator would take details and pass them on. There were two different ways of contacting the Works' exchange in the 1930s depending on whether the caller was using the old- or new-pattern phones.

The attendant contacted the 'fire chief' or his assistant first, then the on-call men, who were known as the 'A' list. During the working day part-timers could be summoned from their place of work via the telephone exchange; in later days they carried bleepers. Out of hours, each fireman was on call for seven days, then had seven off. The attendant pressed buttons on the call-board to alert the eight men on call in their homes.

A loud bell would go off in the appropriate houses in the railway estate, with a total of sixteen houses being connected to the station. Each had a wooden stud wall known as the partition between the two bedrooms and the bell was fixed to it. Six rings was the code for a fire. The men then had to get to the station and change into their uniforms, leather boots and brass helmets. Sometime before the war they were issued with rubber boots and black resin helmets. The ornate brass helmets were kept for ceremony and competitions. If additional men were required there was a 'B' list and, during the war, even a 'C' list of retained firemen. Out of hours, the call boy might have to cycle out to other districts of the town to knock up some of the additional men.

Early in the war when the Oil Works went up, the brigade was at the scene within five minutes of receiving the call. Although the 'A list' men must have already been in the station that Saturday night, the weather was atrocious and the Oil Works was at the other end of the site, so the short time taken to arrive was impressive. The ability to turn out very quickly had been honed over time but was not without its risks. Part of the time-saving routine was doing up uniform buttons and adjusting helmet chin straps en route. Bill Harber was probably adjusting his uniform when he was thrown from the running board as the speeding fire pump suddenly turned a corner and he landed on his back in the road, breaking a shoulder blade.

In accordance with the Factory and Workshop Act, auxiliary fire points were situated around the factory and railway estate, where pumps and extinguishers were available. Detailed maps showing the layout of the whole area, with the water supplies and the fire points, were kept in the Fire Station. They showed that each backway behind the company houses had two hydrants and the roadways had mostly firepits, sometimes called ground hydrants. The latter had a cast iron cover that was lifted off to reveal a well with a mains valve. This was turned on with a long-handled 'T' spanner and water flooded the well. Hoses with weighted ends were placed in the water and drew it up when the pump was started.

The Mechanics' Fire

Colin Bown was born in Bathampton Street in the railway estate: two nights later his father Bill was out fighting a serious fire nearby. Late on Christmas Eve it was discovered that the Mechanics' Institute in Emlyn Square was ablaze. The fire started in or near the stage of the theatre on the first floor. Later it was said that the cause was a faulty electrical fuse. Sawdust, no doubt from the Carriage Works, had been packed under the stage to dampen the noise during the performances. This accelerated the spread of the blaze and the weather hampered efforts to bring it under control.

Bill Bown told his son years later: 'It was terrible weather that Christmas of 1930. People living nearby were told to be ready to evacuate their homes. Meanwhile, they brought out hot water to try to thaw the firepit covers and hoses before we could use them.' It was 7am the next morning when the firemen from the Works and the town brigades finally left the scene. Bert Harber, who was eight years old at the time, said that the fire bell rang twenty-four times in his house that night as more and more calls for assistance went out.

The Works' fire-fighting competition team in 1953. After the war they were regular winners of the five-man trailer pump inter-regional shield and the Westinghouse cup. Right to left are: Sid Smith, Bert Harber, Art O'Farrell, Jimmy Little, Jessie Collett, Ron Adams, Charlie Bowering and Ray Sealy, the chief officer. *Ian Sawyer collection*

A brief entry in the Loco Works petty cash book shows that an outlay of 10½d covered milk and sugar for the firemen during that long night. No mention of the fire at the Mechanics' was made in the *GWR Magazine*, despite a piece about the Institute library appearing shortly after the incident. Colin remembers his dad saying that the extension and fly tower, added during the rebuilding, incorporated new fire safety features in the design.

Colin Bown's Childhood Memories

As kids we would run out and watch the fire engine turn out to a fire. It was fitted with a device which worked off the exhaust and sounded like a klaxon siren. I think it was invented by the fire chief and assistant works' manager, Mr C.T. Cuss. Later when employed 'inside' I always worried that I might be in the tunnel when the engine came through with the siren going. When the 1942 Dennis engine was new we thought there was something wrong with it. One day, as it went down Bristol Street into Sheppard Street the bell seemed to work only intermittently and the engine kept cutting out. When father, who was aboard, came home later he said Tom Kench was supposed to flick a switch to activate the siren but kept turning off the ignition instead, much to the annoyance of the driver, Mr Sealy.

The elevated water tank in the Fire Station Yard provided the water to fight fires in the estate. In wartime a lookout post was built just underneath the tank, for the firewatchers: before that they had to climb up on the top of the tank. Father told me he could see the glow from the bombing of Bristol from there one night. Sometime during the war I began earning a couple of shillings a week by cycling round all the fire engine routes in the factory and seeing that they were kept clear.

Fire Engines

Because of the area they had to cover and the particular fire risk of some buildings, it was essential that the Works had a motorised brigade. That other large GWR centre, Paddington, also had its own fire brigade. So too did the Road Motor Dept at Slough, although the facilities there would have been on a smaller scale.

The Fire Station's position at the lower level, in Bristol Street, gave no direct vehicular access to any of the Works' buildings most at risk of fire. Ian Sawyer told me that if there had been a fire in No. 2 Saw Mill, next door to the station yard, they would have had to put ladders up against the dividing wall and direct heavy hoses over the top. This saw mill and the carriage building and painting shops alongside were especially vulnerable.

The approved fire engine route into the adjoining carriage workshops was a circuitous one. That was one reason why these buildings were fitted with overhead sprinklers shortly after the Paint Shop fire of 1911. Various types were used depending on the risk, and they worked with a glass bulb containing a chemical or gas that expanded and exploded when the temperature increased. Water was released on to a deflector plate, spraying it outwards in all directions. The resulting loss of pressure in the main activated one of the alarms on the Fire Station call-board showing where the fire was.

In 1942 the first motorised fire pump was superseded by another Dennis engine of the latest type. The new vehicle could pump 450 gallons a minute. The 1912 engine is said to have last seen action when the largest of the Works' gas holders was hit during an air raid in 1942. After that it was only used for pumping water from flooded drains. This fine-looking vehicle is preserved and still in the livery of when it was the 'first-call' engine. Another vehicle kept in the station appliance bays was a foam trailer pump, which was used for electrical and oil fires. Two early horse-drawn steam pumps, probably built by Merryweather, were also garaged at the station, even though they had been obsolete for many years. They eventually went for scrap during the Second World War.

Serious Fires

The carriage side Carpenters' Shop was gutted in the early 1930s and had to be completely rebuilt in 1934. An above average number of serious fires, at the Works, occurred during the '39/'45 war. This is slightly puzzling as hundreds of men were recruited as fire guards to keep watch for fires whether caused by enemy action or not. The only one attributable to enemy action was when one of the gas holders was hit during an air raid in July 1942. This was the last time the Works' brigade requested the help of the town brigade.

As already mentioned, a serious fire took hold at the Oil Works over near Whitehouse Road in January 1940. No one was working there as it was a Saturday night. This, together with the building's effective black-out precautions, meant the fire wasn't noticed until flames came through the roof and oil drums started exploding. Then some of the gathering crowd thought it was an air raid. On the Monday, the evening paper reported that the cause was probably an electrical fault and not sabotage.

Colin Kibblewhite remembered D Shop gangs having to replace the roof timbers on several fire-damaged buildings. One of them, due to an explosion in one of the four acetylene houses, was on Easter Sunday 1945. If Colin's recollection of the date is correct, that makes at least three serious fires around that time. Surviving authorised work orders show that D Shop men had to make good damage to cupboards, lockers and tools etc., caused by fire in the AV Shop on 30 April. Less than a month later, a major fire gutted the Hair Carding and Carriage Carpenters' Shops. In each case the costs of making good the fire damage was sent to head office and they put in a claim to their insurers. The department would have to bear the cost of disrupted production.

The Works' telephone directory for 1935 shows that the Bodymakers' Shop had its own watchman. The reason for this is likely to be that more regular patrols were made here and perhaps around the other nearby shops, as additional fire precautions. The Carding Shop recycled horse hair from carriage seats using a machine that combed it out and washed it. Official figures say 338 tons a year was being dealt with in the late 1940s. The fire that started here, in May 1945, was one of the worst as it spread to the adjoining Carriage Carpenters' Shop.

It was thought that a cigarette may have been discarded and lay smouldering over the weekend, even though smoking was forbidden in and around these areas. The watchman's 'telltale' clock proved he had completed his rounds, which included unlocking the Carding House door to check for fire or the smell of smoke. When he opened the door at 2am on the Monday he said the draught ignited some horse hair. This and some of the adjoining buildings were eventually gutted and some carriages were destroyed.

Colin Kibblewhite and carpenters from D Shop spent months there re-roofing and refitting the burned-out building. The cost to put right the damage was worked out for insurance purposes to be £3,800. This did not include the costs of lost production and the use of an alternative site to continue the work. The new Carriage Paint Shop near 'Webb's entrance' also had a major fire, in the 1950s. Choking fumes from burning paint, oils and spirits used for interior wood finishes made the fire that much more difficult to bring under control.

The Station Workshop

When not out fighting fires and having fire drills, the full-timers worked in a workshop next to the Fire Station, checking and repairing fire equipment. After nationalisation, if not before, all 5,000 Western Region fire extinguishers were serviced in rotation in this workshop and all hoses were checked annually.

New, retested, recharged or repaired fire appliances were dispatched first, via the Stores Dept, to replace those due for servicing. Any that had been used or were suspected of being faulty, due perhaps to being underweight, were also sent, of course. Whenever the Severn Tunnel was closed for maintenance, the opportunity was taken to replace the extinguishers fitted to the tunnel walls and bring the old ones in. Some of the work in this workshop was unskilled and some skilled. Not all workers here were firemen. Dorothy Grimes left school in the late 1930s and worked as a shop assistant. In the early 1940s she was told she would be needed for war work:

> They offered me a start at either Vickers-Armstrongs [Phillips and Powis (Aircraft) Ltd until 1941] or 'the Western'. I chose the latter because it was nearer my home in Emlyn Square. I went into the Works' Fire Station on £3 a week replacing a Freddie Aplin, who went into the army. The station

The Platelayers' Shop women's fire-fighting team. Left to right: Doreen Guy, Rachael Scarrott, Nora Wilkins and 'Dot' Grimes. This photo was taken at a studio near Woolworths one Saturday in about 1943. *Courtesy of Dorothy Cook*

dealt with all hoses, and not just the ones for fighting fires. I was assembling new or repaired flexible train hoses and locomotive coal watering pipes which were 5ft 6in and 6ft 6in in length. The ribbed steam heating and vacuum pipes were cut to length, connections fitted and clips tightened. We rolled the diamond pattern on the brass ferrule collars using a 'honking' [knurling] machine.

The Platelayers' Shop looked after the water supplies around the Works, including those connected to the hydrants, so they had close links with us in the Fire Station. Several men in the Platelayers' Shop were part-time firemen and Ray Sealy the 'fire chief' oversaw the work there, as foreman. The administration for the five girls in our shop was done from the PL [Platelayers'] Shop Office and we had PL check numbers as well.

Reg [or possibly Les] Redwood, Sid Pugh, Doreen Guy, Jean Thorn and Rachael Scarrott were on my section and the chargeman was Sid Eburne. Vera Edwards, whose family ran the funfair business, worked with me: she was allowed to work part-time. Two of the other girls worked on fire extinguishers in Bert Speck's section. The work caused blisters on my hands and I asked the women's 'welfare officer' if she could get me moved. I wanted to be a machine operator in E Shop because they were on piecework, but I was turned down.

Fire-fighting Competition

In 1939 the Fire Station and the PL Shop formed several firefighting teams. They would practise drills designed to teach the participants what to do in air raids, should they come. Swindon was always the host for the trailer pump competitions held in the Bristol division and judging was done by Wilts Fire Service officials. An all-line fire drill competition was held annually from 1942, in London, and Swindon was always among the best. From 1944 the winners would go on to represent the GWR against the other British railway companies. 'The various fire drills were judged on speed and we had a ten-second penalty when our team was made up of full-time firemen,' said Bert Harber.

The men's teams were either three or five man. The two ladies teams only participated in extinguisher drills, they did not have to pull large pumps and equipment about. Females in the Fire Station teams were Nora Wilkins, a clerk in the Fire Station/Platelayers' Shop, and Doreen, Rachael and Dorothy mentioned above. Mr Sealy's daughter-in-law, Rose, stepped in when Dorothy went down with appendicitis. Rose Sealy drove a tractor in the Works through the war.

Additional Work in the 1950s

Erector Jim Lowe said he often saw the men from the Fire Station around A Shop in the late 1950s. They made up the coolant and antifreeze supplied by the laboratory and it was pumped into new diesel engines by the Austin Champ vehicle. They also came round periodically weighing all fire extinguishers to check for leakage. The copper extinguishers and their brass fittings had all been made in the Works. Jim also said that the managers would leave their motor cars in the Fire Station Yard. He said that fire staff would clean them and, if necessary, mechanics from the Internal Transport Depot would work on them. This area had been used for managers' vehicles since before the war and it is possible that this unofficial vehicle servicing was nothing new.

14
The Carriage & Wagon Works

Introduction

Within the Swindon Carriage & Wagon Works there were about thirty-eight main workshops. In terms of floor area this accounted for a little under half of the total. The buildings were nearly all Victorian but were kept up to date with modern plant, including electric-powered machinery where required. Most of the lighting, however, remained gas until 1948 and many lines of lathes and other machinery continued to turn by being connected to overhead shafting using a leather belt link and pulleys. The shafts were originally driven by steam. By the 1930s they took electric power from 50 or 60hp DC motors.

The workforce was almost completely separate from the loco side but the two did share some manufacturing facilities. The Foundry supplied both, so did the Spring Shop and the Carriage Blacksmiths' Shop. Some buildings on the carriage side were not involved in the manufacture of carriages and wagons at all, such as the Points and Crossings' Shop, the Oil and Grease Works, the Central Laundry and the Road Vehicle Body Shop. The sites of additional shops and facilities depended on solely on where the available land was, at the time they were planned. This was why the Works' came to be laid out in such a haphazard way over the years.

The GWR sometimes used the terms 'Wagon Works' or 'Wagon Dept' on documents and in its staff magazine when referring to the manufacture, repair and operation of its goods-carrying stock. The men also sometimes used the terms for the area in and around 21 (wagon repair) Shop. However, a Wagon Works never

A white metal toolcheck, which was exchanged for tools or gauges going from one shop to another, on loan. It would be hung up in the workshop tool stores of origin to show where the items currently were. *Author's collection*

actually existed as such. Carriages and wagons shared many similar component parts therefore they shared the same manufacturing workshops: only the assembly shops were separated. It made sense to amalgamate them under the same administration and the same title. That is why there is some overlapping in the following chapters.

Carriage Design

There was little standardisation of British railway carriages, compared with the US and Europe, until after nationalisation. The couplings and buffing gear in particular varied here because there wasn't much inter-railway working. However, basic construction showed more uniformity. British makers, including the GWR, preferred rolled mild steel sections for carriage underframes. The properties of its strength and modulus of elasticity, together with the cost, made mild steel a more practical choice over aluminium or high-tensile steels. A composite (or semi-steel) carriage of the type used on the Great Western had a body frame made of hard wood such as teak or oak covered with steel panels.

In America and on the Continent, the latest vehicle bodies were all steel and aluminium but these were not thought to be as suitable for the greater variations of the English climate. Composite coaches also gave the best results in terms of reducing weight; a standard bogie corridor coach weighed 30 to 31 tons. Tests showed that insulation and protection on impact were also within acceptable limits.

The other considerations were maintenance costs and how much service would be gained before the coach was superseded by improved designs. With the increasing proportion of metal came the potential for welded rather than riveted seams. This would give stronger joints and allow the use of thinner body sections. However. changing workshop facilities and bringing in electric arc welding machinery would take time and be costly. The Drawing Office were also still investigating the problems of contraction associated with welding, so it was restricted to use on carriage underframes before the war.

Perhaps the single most important consideration in railway carriage design was the strength of the underframe and, to a lesser extent, the body, to withstand the buffing stresses and potential impact from a collision. The American all-metal cars of the 1930s were 80% heavier than ours and carried only slightly more passengers. However, the excellent safety record of their railways was partly attributable to the materials used. The French too favoured the safer and more durable all-steel carriages. Their main-line equivalent cost more than double that of a GWR composite coach, at a time when designs were evolving quickly. Indeed, the high initial costs nearly drove some railways on the Continent out of business. The additional weight (around 10 tons above those of the GW) made fuel dearer, trains slower and needing a more substantial braking system.

Although larger sections of aluminium alloy were required to achieve the same strength, a 50% reduction in weight was possible when compared with steel. This, together with its superior resistance to corrosion, would seem to make aluminium the ideal choice of material for the underframe. In the 1930s and '40s, new carriage designs were expected to be obsolete in ten or twelve years' time. Therefore the cost, as well as the safety of passengers, was a significant factor.

Jim Innes stated, in a lecture given to the Swindon Engineering Society in 1939: 'The aim of the of passenger coaches is to secure the greatest possible carrying capacity in relation to the tare weight of the vehicle; due regard being given to the cost of production, maintenance, comfort of passengers and strength and structure under all conditions of service.' Although lighter materials were being used by the 1930s, Mr Innes, a senior draughtsman in the C&W Drawing Office, goes on to point out that the public demands for more luxurious travel as well as buffet and restaurant car services had increased the ratio of dead weight to payload appreciably. This was at a time when those same customers also expected faster trains.

Carriage and wagon development had not seen the hectic changes of designs that locomotives had. Nevertheless, manufacturing practices had to move with the times and keep pace with competitors. There was a natural prejudice against such change by coach builders in particular and long-established methods were not going to be given up easily. Sophisticated machinery was to gradually take over from the skill of working materials by hand. Within a decade, mass-produced parts using gauges, jigs and templates could be foreseen. These would do away with the preparation to achieve the correct position for machining, saving time, labour and cost. Parts were already being produced that were very accurate and therefore interchangeable. Assembly was becoming less labour intensive and less dependent on skill.

A third-class restaurant car built at Swindon as part of a new set for the Cornish Riviera Limited. These coaches were sometimes utilised for other main-line express services too. Because they were built to the maximum width, their route availability was reduced and the instructions, painted on the solebar, reminded the Traffic Dept of this. *Author's collection*

A number of these types of publicity photographs were taken in the late 1930s. This one shows a buffet car built at Swindon in 1938, when it was becoming popular to have light refreshments while travelling by train. The people used in these staged scenes were employees in the Works. Photogenic office staff were asked to participate and some people still occasionally recognise themselves or their relatives long after the taking of the photos had been forgotten.

From the early 1950s, a nationalised Carriage Works were constructing carriages for all regions of British Railways. The three main parts of carriage and wagon design were undertaken by separate drawing offices, all working towards a standard range of vehicles. Designs were to be standardised, as well as mass-produced, which, it was hoped, would cut costs still further by reducing the manufacturing facilities required. One consequence of a centralised system was that Swindon started building their first all-steel body coaches.

Existing Stock

In about 1910, GWR goods' stock was divided into over thirty main types according to their size and the load they were designed to carry. Some types were manufactured in several sizes and maximum capacities. A standard range of passenger and non-passenger carriages also evolved. The twenty-one main types included Post Office, parcels and newspaper vans, four-wheeled horse boxes, slip coaches and bullion vans. By the 1920s, most British railways used a standard range of code words for each type. They were mainly used by the Traffic Dept as a shorthand language for internal telegraphic communications.

Thanks to the company's own publicity and the histories that have been written, the GWR's main achievements in the 1930s are well known. On the Great Western, as on the Southern Railway, the CME was responsible for the Carriage & Wagon Dept as well as the Loco Dept. The state of the carriage stock was much improved during the Collett regime despite the economic depression. This was due, in no small part, to new plant and automatic machine tools, which were slowly streamlining production as outlined above.

The smooth riding qualities of various types of bogies were investigated and, from the results of the trials, an improved design was worked out and perfected. Even the third-class vehicles became far more comfortable and better air conditioned. All passenger vehicles started to receive overhauls at planned intervals too.

Of necessity, they did retain a sizable proportion of Edwardian and Victorian rolling stock, particularly carriages. Dean and early Churchward clerestory carriages were still in use in the 1930s. Although they were adequate for branch line and cross-country services, many were still being used regularly in main-line trains. These early designs were expensive to maintain and, because they were heavy, expensive to run.

A seating compartment for diners in a first-class restaurant/kitchen car, built for The Cornish Riviera Limited in 1935.
From a painting by Richard Naylor

Despite this, there was a case for maintaining some out-of-date designs, up to a point. This was probably why main-line train formations of the 1930s and '40s, were so varied.

The GWR still had over 900 non-bogie passenger coaches in use at the end of 1932: five years earlier they were using double that amount. Like a lot of early rolling stock, many of these carriages had been rebuilt and used for different purposes since first being outshopped in the 1890s and early 1900s. Some rural branch line services and Swindon workmen's trains used the last four- and six-wheeled compartment stock, while others were converted for use as camping coaches. These and other modifications were done at Swindon and Cardiff Cathays carriage works.

More than a third of the existing passenger carriages were still lit by compressed oil-gas with incandescent mantles, in the early 1930s. Although all new carriages were being equipped with electric lighting by the time Mr Churchward retired, it wasn't until the 1950s that the last of the old gas-lit carriage stock were condemned. Most gas fitters who had dealt with carriage lighting were gradually retrained but some older men continued to maintain the old vehicles until they were finally phased out (yes, the carriages and the men).

The company owned more than 7,000 carriages, two-thirds of which were passenger-carrying vehicles including dining and sleeping cars. The total stock remained fairly constant between the pre- and post-war period. Bogie vehicles were being replaced at the rate of between 250 and 300 each year.

The through working of coaches from one company to another could only be achieved if couplings, vacuum brakes and vestibule connections were the same or similar. Standardisation of carriage design among the four main British railways was increasing, in general, in the 1930s. Buckeye couplings of a style used by the LNER, but modified to fit the GW screw coupling, had been fitted to some vehicles. From the early 1930s they were being removed in favour of a standard type as they came through the Works. Great Western trains used a higher degree of vacuum than the other companies. This was not a problem for vehicles coming into its territory but those going out had to have their vacuum reservoirs 'bled' at places like Shrewsbury and Salisbury.

Repairs

More workers were employed on repairs than on new building, and the main repair shops were, of necessity, the largest of the carriage and wagon buildings. Five thousand repairs were carried out at Swindon each year, more than half of which were overhauls. Only the larger LNER did more. Passenger vehicles, including rail cars, had been brought in for repairs and overhaul, on rotation, about every two years. From the mid-1930s this method of prioritising repairs was changed and admission to the Swindon shops was on what was known as a 'systematic basis': depending on the type of vehicle and what could be done at the carriage depots.

By then main-line coaching stock, except where dimensions had to be reduced owing to through working to other railways, was standardised at 60ft long excluding the buffers and 9ft 7in wide over the body including door handles. Dining cars and kitchen cars were slightly wider as they had no opening external doors. Reg Blackmore worked in what the men referred to as '15 Shop Carriage & Wagon'. He said, in the *GWR Magazine* in 1932: 'When a coach is received for repair it first runs the gauntlet of inspectors whose duty it is to decide what is necessary. Dismantling then begins and the parts are sent to various workshops.'

Bogies, including axleboxes and wheels, underframes, springs, drawgear and buffers were dealt with by the 'lifters' of 19C Shop. The sequence was: 1) The vehicle was drawn into position inside the shop by electric capstan until one bogie was over a lift table. 2) The table was raised to about 1ft by hydraulic pressure and a trestle was placed under the headstock (there were at least two heights of trestles depending on the clearance required). 3) After detaching the bogie it was lowered into a drop pit on the table and traversed below ground level to the next parallel road. 4) Here the component was raised back up to be cleaned and then examined.

If running repairs could be done to the unit, they were done here or, in the better weather, outside the shop. Axlebox bearings might need to be demetalled and carted off for relining and white metalling in other shops. Laminated, elliptical and coil springs were sent elsewhere for testing using special machines and, if necessary, replaced. Horn blocks, equalising beams, tie rods and eyebolts were also likely to need attention. Defective parts were distributed to 19D, 13 or 15 Shops: others went to the Stores or for scrap. New or reconditioned parts were refitted if necessary to save time; all frictional parts were lubricated and axleboxes packed with grease. The bogie was then fitted back under its vehicle and the other end dealt with the same way.

Sometimes it was desirable to support the carriage or wagon body at both ends, in which case screw jacks were used as well as trestles. This avoided undue stresses on solebars and longitudinal members. With the carriage back on its feet, the bogie springs were adjusted. When banana vans were withdrawn in the 1950s, their record cards, detailing underframe repairs in 19D Shop, were simply turned over and used again. The ones I have are for adjustments made to 'Commonwealth' bolster bogie coil springs. They record the before and after readings when equalising the loading on each wheel. This was one of the last jobs done before returning coaches to traffic.

Aids used by the 19 Shop lifters and labourers included a transporter vehicle for carrying the bogies along the shop roads. This was adjustable to take the 7ft, 8ft 6in or 9ft types (only the longer goods wagons that carried heavy loads had bogies and they would have four, six, eight or more wheels to spread the load). The movement of other heavy components was achieved by raising the load using slings or chains attached to eyebolts and a Wharton 7½-ton electric walking crane, which took its power from overhead lines.

Art Fortune started his apprenticeship as a coach body builder in 1954. He was based in what was known as 4 Shop down carriage side, but was required to spend a good proportion of his time in 24A Shop working on body shell and internal partition repairs:

> Although there were six men to a repair gang over there, you usually worked on a vehicle with just one other person: even on 'smash jobs'. I was apprentice to Bert Davis, who was a bit of a plodder but a perfectionist. He always wore a collar and tie under a white apron and the men respected him. We'd have a pint together sometimes in the Cycle (Workingman's) Club in Dixon Street near to where we both lived. Other men I remember in 4 and 24 Shops in the late 1950s are Foreman George Kirkham, Junior Foreman Fred Stone, Chargeman Stan Franklin, Ted Griffiths and Ron Edwards.

Reg Dauris and NUR man Alun Rees were also coach body builders at that time.

Carriage Types

Space does not permit even a summary of all the standard passenger vehicle variants from the 1930s onward. The following are examples of the more successful production types of the period.

Two complete sets of ten coaches for the Cornish Riviera Limited were built and went into service in 1935, the company's centenary year. Amid much publicity, they replaced the coaches built just six years earlier for the same train (six of the displaced vehicles were used for a new express called The Bristolian). Each of the new vehicles was 60ft long between the headstocks and the maximum permitted width of 9ft 7in wide. The recessed external doors at each end brought the handles within the maximum loading gauge. The dining cars in the two rakes had electric lights throughout and were air conditioned, using electric fans and air extractors.

The company magazine said of the new train's third-class restaurant car, illustrated: 'It is panelled in garbon mahogany and walnut, has rayon curtains, table lamps (a new idea) and oval mirrors. There is tip-up spring seating for sixty-four diners arranged of four on either side of a centre corridor. It has 9ft pressed steel bogies of an improved design.' No mention of the Vita-glass windows 'which admit health-giving ultra-violet rays', is made (as it was for the previous CRL sets). These dining cars were withdrawn at the outbreak of war and returned to traffic, refurbished, in 1947.

A contract for 160 passenger train corridor coaches was placed with the CME Dept in 1935. Several lots were to be built over two years, comprising: sixty-eight third class, having eight compartments each; fifty-six brake thirds, with four compartments; sixteen composites, having both first- and third-class compartments; and twenty brake composites, also accommodating first- and third-class passengers. The 'compartment thirds' were slightly longer than the previous equivalent, allowing a more spacious lavatory. The company said that these new coaches would be 'used on all types of main line services and provide the long-distance travelling public with a greater degree of comfort and privacy than before'.

A Works' drawing of one of the sixty-eight third-class coaches outshopped in 1936 and 1937. This side corridor coach layout was standard for all GW main-line expresses, just as non-corridor compartment types were for secondary and suburban trains. *GWR Magazine*

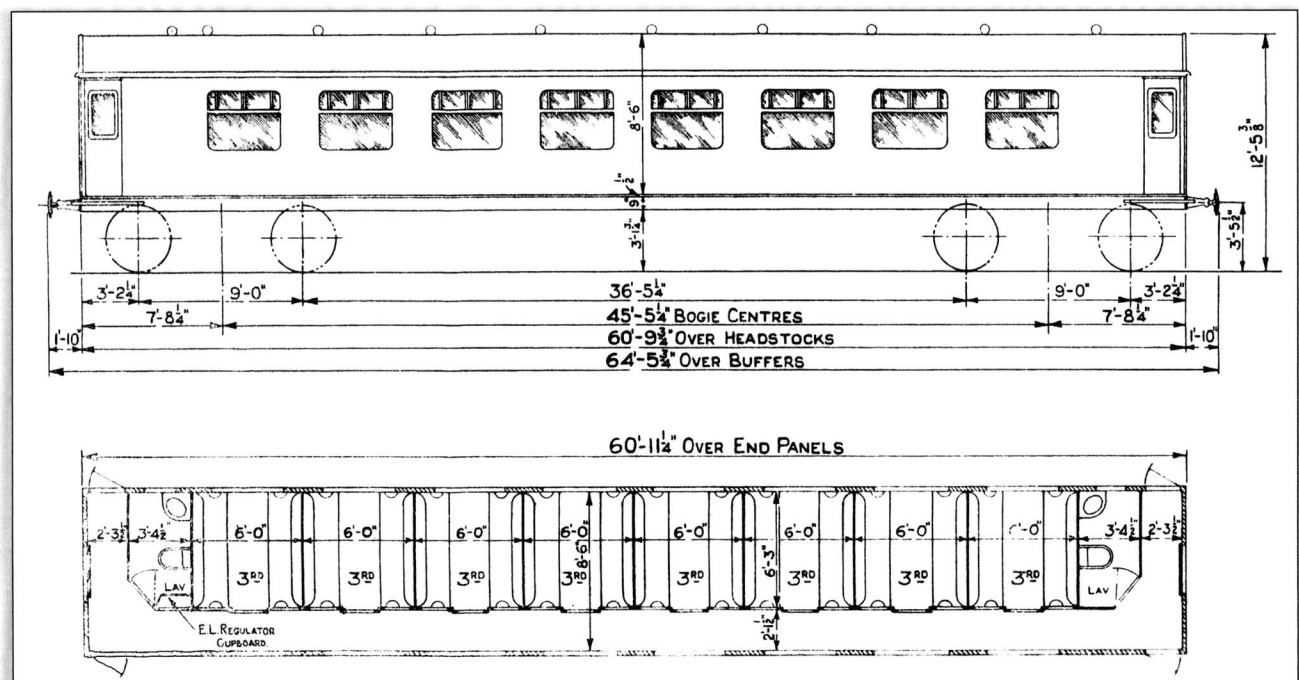

Heavy steel underframes were used. This supported the body, which was, as usual, a timber frame but now totally encased in steel. The two four-wheeled bogies had improved springing for smoother riding. Externally they were painted brown up to the waistline and cream above. The most striking new feature for the passengers was the larger deeper windows on the outer (observational) side, on the corridor partitions and on the outer (corridor) side. This gave the occupants views from either side of the train even when seated and they would gain the nickname 'Sunshine' coaches.

Glass sliding ventilators fitted with hinged vanes, above the observational windows, gave 'fresh air without draughts and made for an equable temperature,' said the *GWR Magazine*. The interior decoration of the third-class vehicles was also cream and brown with dark walnut woodwork, brown figured moquette upholstery on the seats, white ceilings, rayon curtains, Rexine blinds on the corridor side and brown cork linoleum on the floor. Rexine was a cloth coated to simulate leather.

During the war there were no new designs for main-line coaching stock on the drawing board until 1944. By then the department was planning ahead for the return to peacetime. The specification now called for many new features, which was hardly surprising since no new carriages had been designed since 1938 under the previous CME's regime. None, that is, apart from four 'special' vehicles that were ordered in 1938 and 1943 to accommodate and transport senior military and government personnel. Lack of capital expenditure after the war, the shortage of labour and then the steel shortages affected much of the proposed activity at the Works and the carriage building programme in particular. The travelling public were assured that standards of maintenance were unaffected.

The first post-war underframes were to be part aluminium because of the difficulty in getting steel, but presumably the situation eased as only the prototype was built thus. Another departure from established practice was constructing the body shell on the underframe instead of adding it when complete. The length would be 64ft, excluding buffers, an increase of almost 4ft on the immediate pre-war version. This and the deep windows would, it was hoped, create a feeling of more spacious compartments and vestibules. There was to be fluorescent tubular lighting and, most striking of all, sloping roof ends

in the LNER style. The roof label boards, with the main stopping places stencilled on, were moved down to above the windows at the level of the cantrail: a small detail, but another noticeable change, not seen previously. The internal layout was the same as the standard corridor stock of 1938 that the new 'Hawksworths', as they would become known, were superseding.

This was the first post-war design of what was to be a large contract of 260 carriages. They were due to be delivered to traffic at the rate of one a week. The first twenty Hawksworth coaches finally arrived in the autumn of 1946. They were urgently needed because a backlog of maintenance had built up during the war years and caused a shortage of serviceable stock. In 1947 a labour demarcation dispute between two trades over who did what brought work on new coaches to a standstill. This, together with the continuing shortages of materials, forced the company to look to contractors and parts of the contract were given to three private railway carriage builders.

The interior woodwork of the prototypes was maple for first class and oak for third class, with enamelled hardboard Holoplast panels and moquette upholstery. However, only the moquette was retained, and the wood finishes were substituted in favour of chocolate or cream Holoplast on the production batches. With the initial delays, an empire veneer finish did not materialise either. As time went on most of the interior finishes were considered too lavish for a railway company that was soon to be nationalised and only the prototypes or early batches received what was originally specified. The decorative metalwork would remain as it had been pre-war, oxidised bronze. The colour scheme for the furnishings was fawn and dark blue in the smoking compartments and fawn and dark red in non-smoking. A new hard laminate material called Formica, which would retain its look after numerous washes with detergent, was specified for areas of heavy wear.

The external livery was chocolate and cream with double waist lining and later crimson lake and cream, informally known by all as 'blood and custard'. The words 'GREAT' and 'WESTERN' were set either side of the GWR coat of arms in the lower panel. The pressed-steel bogies, each with a 9ft wheelbase, were very efficient and that great observer of Great Western train performance, O.S. Nock, said these coaches 'came to be accepted as the best riding that had ever taken the road out of Paddington'.

The British Railways roundel emblem introduced in 1956. It was applied to Mk 1 chocolate and cream coaches used on Western Region named expresses.

From 1950, under the newly nationalised British Railways, the planned building programmes for Hawksworths and later the BR standard corridor stock were being cut back each year. By the time the Institution of Mechanical Engineers visited the Works in June 1952 they noted that the (New) Carriage Body Shop was full of the earlier composite coaches under repair. The only new builds were those to complete the previous year's building programme.

A new range of standard main-line carriages were being exhibited and trialled in mid-1951. They were to become known as BR Mk 1 coaches. The Carriage Standards Committee, made up of engineers from various carriage works, designed the vehicles for the new owners, British Railways. Jim Innes, who was the senior draughtsman in the C&W sections of the Swindon Drawing Office, was one of the small design team. They had been asked to come up with designs that could run on routes all across the country. It was decided that they should be easy to construct and maintain and comparatively inexpensive to build. Other stipulations were that they were to have steel bodies, buck-eyed couplers and Pullman gangways.

The all-steel Mk 1s were built throughout the 1950s at Derby, Doncaster, Eastleigh, Swindon, Wolverton and York. They soon gained a reputation locally as being rough riders with rather dull interiors when compared with the Hawksworths they followed. In the latter half of the decade these carriage works built and fitted them with American-type 'Commonwealth' bogies. This improved their image somewhat.

Non-Passenger Vehicles

These types of carriages and vans have come to be known as 'brown vehicles', as a shade of that colour was nearly always used, alone, on their external bodywork. It groups together certain non-passenger vacuum-braked, bogie and fixed-wheelset vehicles, but it may well be a more modern term. 'Brown vehicles' were classed as coaching stock because they could run in main-line passenger trains. Livestock, perishables, milk and parcels were some of the commodities that could not be sent by ordinary goods trains. This was because of the extended time they would be in transit, so non-passenger vehicles were used. The company handed over 9,460 service vehicles at the time it was nationalised.

A brake third 'Toplight' passenger coach was converted in 1932 and fitted with instruments for identifying rough riding sections of the permanent way. This 'track testing car' (unofficially known as the 'whitewash coach') went out coupled to the rear of passenger trains. Other brown vehicles included passenger/parcels brake vans; newspaper and parcels vans; cattle boxes; engineers' saloons; milk, fish and fruit vans; and horse boxes.

Kitchen cars were not plain brown because they ran in the middle of the company's express passenger trains, so they were painted in the chocolate and cream shades of passenger stock. Similarly, the bullion vans that ran with the 'Ocean Liner' services between Plymouth and Paddington were turned out to match. Three were built before the Great War to carry gold bullion that was being shipped to and from the USA. The last of these was withdrawn in 1959.

Travelling Post Office sorting vans also ran in express passenger trains and they were painted in the company's colours. It saved time to sort the mail and drop bags on the route without having to stop or even slow down: special apparatus for dropping and receiving mail bags on the move was made and fitted in the Works. TPO vehicles also ran as complete postal trains carrying mail bags as well as sorting, usually at night. Three net and stowage TPO vans were outshopped in November 1933. They allowed the withdrawal of the remaining clerestory mail vehicles dating from the 1890s. The use of Royal Mail services increased considerably in the run-up to Christmas, so the Works had to maintain extra vehicles and have them back into traffic in the autumn.

Carriage Utilisation

There were significant seasonal fluctuations in the number of coaches required for passenger services and this made the storage of excess stock at the quieter times a problem. In the Carriage Works the summer holiday period was the quietest period of the year because all available passenger stock was pressed into traffic. I am told that gangs worked on some old stock, out in the open, so they could be 'patched up' with a minimum of man-hours expended. At other times the situation would become reversed as excursion and holiday traffic slackened off. Preparing extra coaches for other bank holidays and football specials also increased the activity in the Carriage Works to a lesser extent. The trouble with stabling carriages at quieter times was that sunlight and frost started a deterioration of the coachwork that, when in revenue-earning service, was considered acceptable.

The only answer was to keep them covered, so in the late 1930s a long prefabricated Carriage Stock Shed was built under the government Guaranteed Loan Arrangement. The site chosen was on some company-owned land alongside the down main lines, which formed part of Westcott recreation ground. Newburn, or Newburn House, the former residence of the Chief Mechanical Engineer, was demolished to make way for the approach roads. The CME Department and not the Engineering Department put up the building, which would house up to 265 coaches on ten roads. By the time it was completed, however, the country was on the eve of war and priorities changed. Most of it was taken over for the duration by the Royal Engineers in 1940. Later, after it reverted to its intended purpose, this carriage building was also used to store new locomotives and royal carriages at various times.

Disposal of Withdrawn Stock

Extensive sidings were situated alongside the up main line at the western end of the Works' site. They may have been laid to accommodate the influx of locos and stock from the companies absorbed at the 'grouping' of the railways in the early 1920s. By the 1930s they were mainly used to store withdrawn coaches waiting to be broken up in the Concentration Yard and C Shop area. The 'Dump Sidings', as they were known, were used as a pool so that the vehicles could be shunted across for scrapping in batches, rather than dealing with them as they arrived from the carriage depots in ones and twos.

Somewhere in the vicinity of the Running Sheds there were some withdrawn coaches, possibly grounded coach bodies. It was not unusual to utilise redundant stock in this way in railway yards. They made good rest room accommodation and makeshift cabins for groups of contractors or outstation workers working nearby. I only found about these particular ones because they are listed in the electoral registers as permanent addresses for a number of single men. In May 1945 nine men are listed; in 1947 there were thirteen; in 1955 just two were in residence and by 1960 there were none. There was a large expanse of open ground between the back of the sheds and the company Gas Works, and this seems the most likely site for these coaches. There at least it would have been comparatively quiet at night.

In the late-1950s, Bob Dauris remembers that new '9F' class 2-10-0 locos went out on test hauling heavy trains of condemned carriages: 'About eighteen old vehicles plus the Dynamometer Car were taken to Bristol via Badminton and back via Bath so that the engine didn't need to be turned,' said Bob.

The quickest and cheapish method of disposing of a Great Western railway coach body of the period was to crush, then burn the frame, leaving just the iron fittings. This left the underframes, bogies and body panels to be cut up by oxyacetylene torch, put into wagons and sent to the metal merchants. The policy seems to have been to clear all the interiors of everything that was not screwed down first though. In the early 1980s, tips of railway china and glassware etc. were discovered when some areas of this ground were being excavated. (This ground had been built up between 1929 and 1931 to increase the facilities for breaking up and reclamation.) Everything, including tea trays and crockery brought on to trains from station refreshment rooms, was thrown out into deep holes and buried.

The Oil Works

This building blended oil and grease to the required specification mainly as a lubricant for GWR rolling stock and machinery. They also used it as a fuel to fire their modern furnaces. The Oil and Grease Works, which was classified for administration purposes as 22 Shop,

The blending room in the Oil and Grease Works. Below the floor were thirteen 10,000 gallon storage tanks, which were filled by pumps from 40 gallon distribution drums. *BRWR*

consisted of two buildings and a laboratory. They had been operational at the eastern end of the site since 1915. Crude oil, or as it was sometimes referred to then, crude petroleum, arrived in drums from contractors and was held in vast storage tanks beneath the floor. In stages it was then distilled, separated, redistilled and purified to produce a range of heavy or light oils. Lubricating oils were classified according to their viscosity at 140 degrees Fahrenheit, the average working bearing temperature. Samples were tested at every stage in their own laboratory.

For lubricating steam locomotive bearings and cylinders, a paraffin based oil was used. This meant it was largely composed of paraffin hydrocarbons and wax. From the middle of the 1930s, with the introduction of chemical additives and solvents for refining, significant improvements were made to lubricating oils and methods of application. Locomotive oil was now made up of 95% mineral oils, and rape oil. Animal and plant oils had proved suitable but the costs were considerably higher. Their use was therefore restricted to additives in mineral oils, and from the 1940s, in grease compounds.

Axlebox lubrication for Great Western wagons had changed from grease to mainly oil by the 1930s because of the increased speeds of vacuum-fitted trains. However, most wagons used on the GWR were privately owned and most of them still relied on grease, which was also supplied by this facility. In the 1930s grease was made up largely of animal fats and fatty acids; its consistency depended on the amount of lime soap used and the

viscosity of the mineral oil additives. Although there were certain advantages of using grease including cost, it was not such an efficient lubricator and the company knew it cost them more in locomotive fuel to move trains with grease axleboxes. The shortage of oil constituents during the war caused a real problem in the department and circulars were sent asking users to be careful with supplies.

Used oil could also be cleaned and refined in the Oil Works. (Reclaiming it was highly specialised as even minute traces of water in the oil could reduce its effectiveness.) Axle oil from carriages and wagons in particular, but also machine tool coolant, was purified, reblended and reused. The caustic solution that had been used for cleaning the parts of dismantled underframes was also returned to the Oil and Grease Works so that the components could be separated out and used again.

Jim Lowe remembers that the used solution from the A Shop bosh tanks was pumped into an old ROD tender. Presumably this vehicle was also used to collect it from the carriage side. He said that after separation the sludge was tipped down the bank at the bottom of Redcliffe Street. Although only 4% of oil issued for carriages and wagons was reclaimed, it represented a significant saving in cost. Since 1926 specialist equipment had been used to spin the solution; the oil, water and solids separated according to their specific gravities.

Annual figures from the company in the early 1930s were 590,000 gallons of engine oil issued, 225,000 gallons of cylinder oil, 380 tons of grease for wagons and 230,000 gallons of oil for carriages and wagons. Part of the reason why so much less oil was used for carriages and wagons was because the lubricated motion parts could all be enclosed in axleboxes. All the company supplies of lubricating oil were distributed by the Stores Dept at Swindon.

The Paint Mill

A new oil paint mill was incorporated in the design when 24 Shop was planned in the late 1920s. It was equipped for the manufacture and storage of mixed paints used mainly by the Carriage & Wagon Dept. Demand was continuous but winter was the busiest time because that's when more coaches could be taken out of service for maintenance.

The GWR Magazine tells us that they made and blended paints using large quantities of linseed oil. Other constituents bought in included pigments, black japan varnish, pale and ordinary gold size, turpentine substitute, refined gum spirit, zinc white paste and certain other ingredients to give the paint body. The mixing machines were on the upper floor of the shop. When it was ready, the paint was released to run down through pipes to be strained and drawn off on the ground floor. They also prepared filling and stopping paints for cracks and uneven surfaces.

Feeding the paint mixing machines with pigments etc. on the upper floor of 24 Shop. *GWR Magazine*

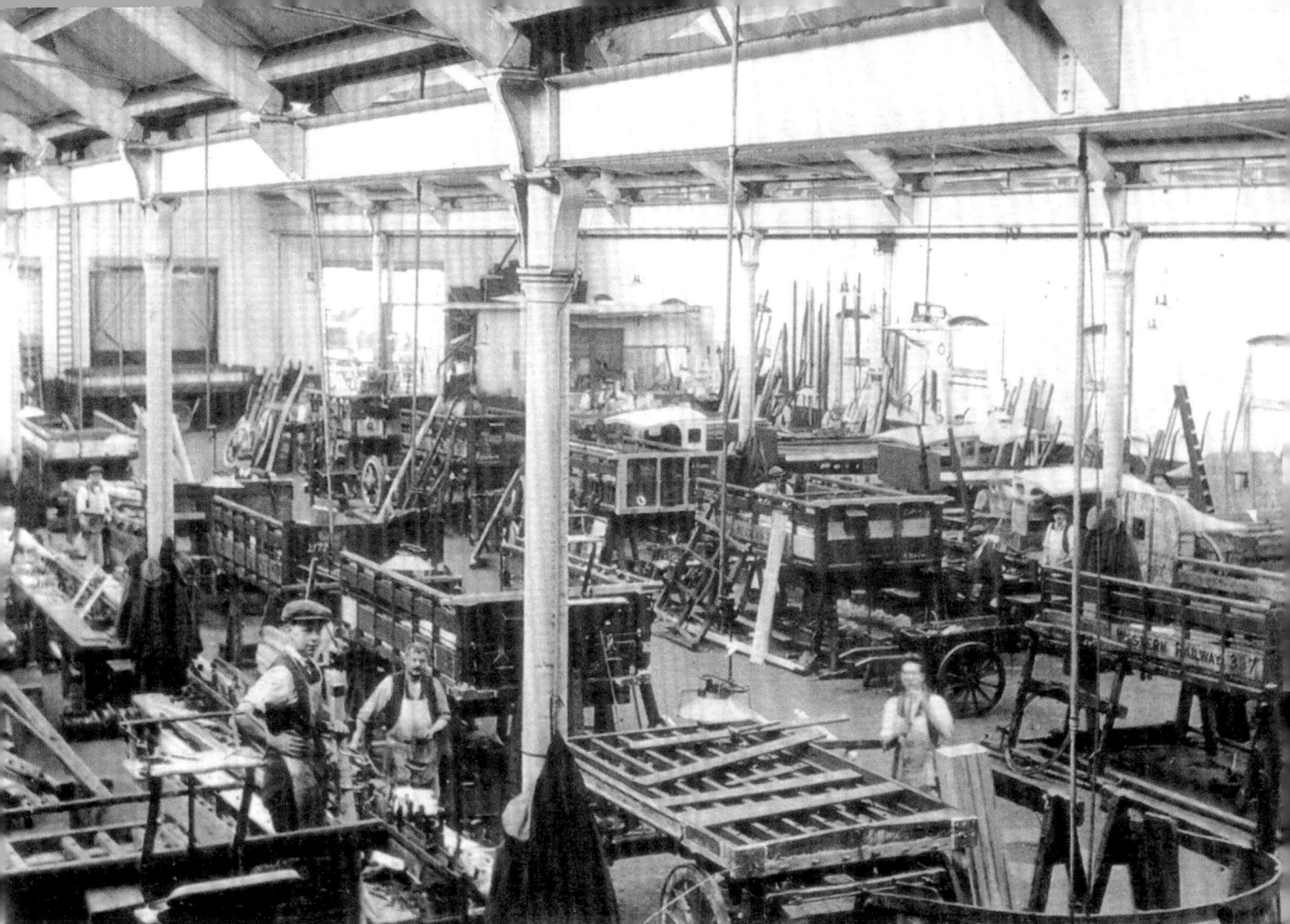

Views of the inside of the Road Vehicle Body Shop aren't easy to find. This one was a local press photograph probably taken in the 1920s. This large workshop, where lorry and van bodies were built for the GWR Commercial Department, had no rail access. *Author's collection*

17 (Road Vehicle) Shop

One of the carriage & wagon workshops that stood alongside the course of the former Wilts and Berks Canal was 17 Shop. The majority of work undertaken in this workshop after 1930 was connected with the company's huge fleet of road cartage vehicles. All the GWR's station handcarts, horse-drawn coal trailers, road carriages and motorised vehicles were built, painted and subsequently repaired here. The road motor vehicles included vans, omnibuses, lorries and Scammell mechanical horses. Their chassis and engines were supplied by the specialist builders such as Guy, Thorneycroft and Morris. According to the GWR's published statistics, they had 2,010 motor vehicles and 3,700 horse-drawn vehicles for their parcel and goods' deliveries in 1935.

The staff employed on road vehicle work, apart from the painting, came under the Road Motor Department based in Slough. There, in rather more cramped conditions than at Swindon, was the GWR's main repair depot. Engine maintenance requiring machine work was carried out on the company's road vehicles at Slough, otherwise it was done in the vehicle's home depot. Mr Coventry had been Superintendent of Road Transport since it became a separate department in 1922. He had completed his training in the GWR Locomotive Works.

Swindon would fit the bodies, cabs and trailers, and those they replaced during overhaul were repaired and repainted. The latter would then go into the pool for future use or for dispatch to various outstations. No steel supports were used in any of the vehicle bodies before the war. Instead, they used hickory, which was tough and would bend, but was expensive. Hickory and ash could also be shaped into hoops and covered in canvas. The offcuts were made into 3/8in carriage window blind rods. Elsewhere, wooden hammer shafts and shunting poles were also made from hickory. Ash was the most common wood for the superstructures; it was also used for the adjustable horse shafts along with pitched pine.

Some work was lost when the company's passenger omnibus services finished in 1933. The redundant vehicles were then converted for haulage. Trailers for the factory's Internal Transport Department were also made and repaired in 17 Shop. Their solid rubber tyres were pressed on in G Shop, on the locomotive side. In wartime some vehicles were converted for use as ambulances by swapping their bodies over.

CARRIAGE DISINFECTING PLANT AT SWINDON

Vehicles coming in for attention would often be repainted, so their old paint was burnt off and the surfaces prepared. All the painting and varnishing was done by men based in 24 Shop. Motor lorries were built by the department for the exclusive hire of firms such as Huntley and Palmer's biscuits and Coleman's (later Reckitt & Coleman's) mustard. They were painted in the firm's own style and livery at Swindon. Sometimes the company would buy fleets of complete vehicles from outside firms.

The livery of motor omnibuses was predominantly chocolate brown, with some cream above waist level. Horse-drawn goods vehicles, which the company used extensively before the war, were also brown with black canvas trim. Some received cream panels in the late-1930s with the lettering above them. I don't think that Swindon made the harnesses or horse brasses even though similar items were produced on the carriage side.

Motor goods vans were again brown and they were given medium grey roofs and wheel centres. Generally there was no lining of the panels and the lettering was cream or white. Open lorries were brown with a cream panel along the narrow sides with the words 'Great Western Railway' painted in. Open trailers usually carried their telegraphic code name upon the brown flat body sides, as well as the company name. Tarpaulins were black and had the company initials stencilled on in large white letters or, by the mid-1930s, they displayed the circular monogram.

Carriage Disinfecting Plant

Swindon was not the first railway to use this German idea for disinfecting carriages. S.A.S. Smith said someone at the Works had seen it in an engineering magazine and got the Drawing Office to come up with a design. Permission was given and a specialist company was engaged to supply the steel airtight chamber. A brick building was erected around it by the CME dept, and it was operational from 1932. The steel cylindrical chamber was 16ft 6in in diameter, inside which ran a railway track, 85ft long. This would take the latest 70ft coach or two smaller vehicles such as flour and grain vans infested with weevils. Hardly surprising then that the men nicknamed the new contraption the 'bug house' or 'bug hutch'.

The carriage doors and windows were opened before the vehicle was propelled into the chamber by a shunting engine. Once inside, the outer door was swung into place using a crane on a radial track. It was clamped tight against a rubber seal and an exhauster drew all the air out, creating a vacuum of up to 28in of mercury. The chamber was then heated to 120 degrees Fahrenheit using steam, while a controlled amount of formalin gas was pumped in through pipes to disinfect and kill any vermin and organisms.

Publicity tells us that the 'plant could also be used to wash and dry carriage exteriors by simply pressing a few alternative buttons'. It was claimed that this operation did the job much more thoroughly and quickly than manual labour, justifying the investment. Stan Leach said that: 'The disinfecting treatment was carried out by two or three blokes as and when required. Each cycle took up to eight hours.'

Also Made in the Carriage Works

The C&W Works also made all sorts of furnishings and fittings not connected to rolling stock. If it was required by the company and could be made using the skills of: electricians, upholsterers, sewers, wheelwrights, carpenters, smiths, signwriters and others, the likelihood was that the contract was given to Swindon Works. The consistently high standard of entries from the Swindon exhibitors at the annual GWR Arts and Crafts Exhibition demonstrated the range of skills very clearly. Of course, if the Stores Dept people found they could buy cheaper outside, they would, in theory.

Artists and photographers had designed those little pictures that were in every compartment on the train and they were framed and glazed in the Carriage Works. As well as constructing railway carriage and wagon bodies, Works' carpenters and cabinetmakers produced station furniture, trolleys, platform barrows, sack trucks, ticket and label racks, and miscellaneous fixtures and fittings to furnish this railway company's premises. No doubt the check boards used for determining the men's attendance had been made 'inside', and it is possible the wooden and even the marble 'roll of honour' plaques were made here too.

Fitting the upholstery in coach interiors, or to furniture, was done by trimmers. Others of that profession worked with leather 'inside', to produce such items as tablet pouches (for single-line working), despatch bags and straps of every description. Bricks and rope had also been made in the Swindon carriage shops at various times.

Until the 1950s, the top corner of 13 Shop was used to repair all the belts or straps for driving the older gangs of machine tools. Fred Parker was the Strap Shop Foreman here after the war. He lived in Northern Road, remembers Harry Bartlett: 'Bert Miles was one of his men.' The leather parts of artificial limbs were also dealt with in the Strap Shop, while the wooden parts were made by a man at a bench in 7A (Finishers') Shop. They were for workers who had been injured while serving the company.

Other places on the carriage side produced machine tool coolant, hand soap, putty, as well as oils, grease and paint already mentioned. The 10 tons of soap powder used each year in the company's laundry was also made up on the premises. It was the policy to coat all steel woodscrews used in the Carriage Works with tallow. I've heard it said that candles were produced from tallow somewhere in the carriage body shops too.

Some unlikely items were made here, including some not fashioned by the workforce at all. Birds liked to come into some workshops, especially those with high roofs, and there are stories of them building nests 'inside'. If the location chosen left the birds vulnerable, the men could become very protective towards them. The following was recorded by R.J. Blackmore in 1960 and concerned George Higgs, the New Saw Mill foreman, who retired in February 1959:

In the spring of 1958 a blue tit built a nest in a sashbox of the giant bandsaw. George, who ever loved to point out every footprint and every semblance of wild-life near his mill, was delighted. He immediately had a board of the sashbox removed and replaced by glass so that the whole business of family rearing could be observed. Bird lovers who got to hear about the tit, made a surreptitious way from nebulous recesses of the engineering shops to see the intrepid bird; far from being rebuffed by George, they were treated as if they had come from the press, and granted every facility for taking photographs if they were so disposed. George's heart was sad when the crane driver accidently struck the nest just a few hours before the whole family would have been complete.

Splicing hemp rope to make slings. *Swindon Society collection*

15
Carriage Construction

Production

Mr Johnson, the carriage & wagon works' manager from 1948 onwards, said, on the subject of carriage production: 'We like to have the (specification) drawings fifteen months before building starts. We have to order all the raw materials through the Stores Dept; alter our plans where materials are not available and prepare the jigs before the design can go down to the workshop.'

The terms 'lot' and 'batch' were both associated with production but are sometimes confused with each other. New rolling stock and locomotives were built in batches. The number within each batch depended on what the workshop facilities and labour could accommodate at any one time. The 'lot' referred to the total number of vehicles required in the contract. As mass-production techniques improved and contracts got larger, the building programme could be spread over many months, even years.

Carriages were constructed in three main parts: underframes, bogies and bodies. Operations were carried out in a set sequence that was known as 'unit assembly'. The idea was that no gang was ever left waiting on another and the sub-assemblies all came together at the same time.

As the main components were erected, pipework and fittings for vacuum brake gear, suspension gear, steam heating and plumbing were also being produced, in 15 Shop. Axleboxes, drawgear, regulating gear for auto trains and trailer cars, as well as parts for diesel rail cars and slip coaches, were all made there too. Virtually all the small brass and iron furniture (fittings) for carriage compartments and toilets were also made in this, the principal fitting and machine shop. In the mid-1950s a lot of the layout of 15 Shop was altered for production of parts for the new diesel building contracts.

A completed carriage underframe on its bogies in 13A Shop Yard. *GWR*

Underframes

Carriage and wagon underframe repairs and new builds were done in 13 (frame) Shop. Briefly the system of constructing the carriage underframes was: rolled steel main frame members had various machining operations carried out in 13 and 15 Shops, before erection. Axleguards were bolted into position before they were passed to the assembly lines. One gang would 'bolt up' the main underframe members: the solebars, longitudinals, headstocks, cross bearers and diagonal bracers. The frames were then hauled along the line after each operation, on steel-wheeled trestles. After other operations, they would be 'riveted up' by the same gang. Two gangs did this by working opposite each other on alternative frames.

Power riveters were still not fully utilised in the C&W Works as much of the work was inaccessible to the types available before the war. The slow and labour intensive manual method took one man to heat the rivet and two to form a closed head fastening. This was the way it was usually done at this time. Some rolled steel sections comprising the frame were being all welded by the late-1930s but most continued to be of riveted construction. Gordon Nash remembers his first days heating rivets:

> I was sent to 13A Shop on my first day. I thought I was going to start as an office boy so I had my best clothes on. It was March 1935 and I was put with Billy Bunce's gang fabricating carriage underframes. My pay was 8 shillings a week plus 4 shillings war wage. Tom Hart was the riveter I served and his holder up was a fellow named Baughn. Tom Ketch used the hydraulic riveter so he didn't need a holder up, just someone to heat his rivets: a boy named Scutts did this.

It was the underframe that supported the weight of the body and its load and it absorbed the stresses of braking and 'buffering up' to other stock. The carriage body would later be held by bolts through the top flanges of the solebars, cross-bearers and longitudinal frame members, and through into the hard timber bottom-sides of the body. Sometime in the 1940s fabricated steel brackets were welded to the solebars for affixing the body.

Brakegear, drawgear and buffers that had passed through 14 Shop (carriage smiths) to be forged, pressed, welded and machined were then fitted to the frame. Before assembly by jigs, a horizontal ram was used to square up the frame by sight. The solebars and longitudinal members were given a slight upward camber using screw jacks. A wire was pulled taught between the headstocks to check when the correct deviation was reached. Then the tie rods were set in place. The underframe would later become level with the weight of the body. After the war, with the use of stronger angle iron members, there was no need to compensate for sag.

Hydraulically lifting a bogie up to a carriage body in 19C Shop. The bogie had been traversed below floor level from the pit partially visible at the bottom left. *GWR*

Bogies, Including Wheels

Longer vehicle frames and bodies were supported by framed sets of wheels on a pivotal point known as bogies. The Great Western was not building any new non-bogie passenger vehicles by 1930. Their standard carriages were built on to two 7ft single bolster bogies until 1933. After that they used a pressed steel double bolster suspension type that relied heavily on jigs and templates in its production. This design remained basically unchanged until 1954. The frame of the bogie comprised of guard plates and horn block suspension brackets, produced in the press and stamping shops, and a side plate that was produced in the Loco Works.

Before assembly in 15 Shop the parts underwent various machining operations such as jet cutting, jig drilling, milling and grinding. A large assembly jig held the parts, which could then have the bolts removed and be 'riveted up'. An outer frame comprising of headstocks, transoms, longitudinals, fulcrum brackets and trimmers was also riveted up and the two were fitted together. The three bolster pressings and brackets were riveted together and the tie plates, centre casting, rubbing blocks and slings were then added. The two assemblies were then loaded on to a hydraulic machine for the steel coil springs to be compressed and inserted and all held together by suspension bolts. Brakework was fitted prior to 'wheeling' and the fitting of axleboxes and side springs.

All the machining and assembly of new steel and high-duty cast iron solid wheels and axles was carried out in 16 Shop. They also carried out repair work sent in from the Carriage Lifting Shop and 13 (Carriage Frame) Shop. New axles arrived in rough form from the forge to be descaled, straightened, centred, turned and examined for flaws. After the war two Hughes supersonic flaw detectors were used on the axles to check for cracks before they were cut to the correct lengths. The seats at each end, that were to receive the wheels, were finished turned to 5½in diameter unless they were for heavier vehicles.

Another gang bored out the wheel centres and turned the outside diameters to fit the tyres. The 'press gang' pressed the wheels and axles together using an oil or water hydraulic press (both types were in use here in the 1930s and '40s). A pulley, which had been made in the same shop,

was pressed on to one set of wheels per coach at this stage. A belt between the pulley and the dynamo, which would be fitted later, generated the current for the electric train lighting as the axle turned.

The axle with its wheels (wheelsets) then went to the tyre shop. Here previously bored and recessed tyres were heated in a purpose-built gas oven and shrunk on to the wheels and a 'key' forced into a recess where the tyre met the wheel. A retaining ring was also driven in around the outside, as it was for locomotive wheels. A lip of tyre overhanging the wheel was then 'turned over' by hydraulic rolls to hold the ring in place.

At the other end of the shop, several Craven tyre-turning lathes with auxiliary grinding heads were employed to true up the tyres by turning and grinding the profiles. Loading into a Benrath wheel balancing machine and balancing the wheelsets came next. That was followed by the grinding of the journals (the exposed section of the axle). These were the last machining operations before the wheels were cleaned, then dipped in a tank of carbon paint in an annexe of 16 Shop. Finally, the number and date of manufacture were stamped on to each axle as this would be required when the wheels came back in later for inspection and overhaul. The wheelsets were then passed to the bogie erectors in 15 Shop.

Mansell wheels, which had centres made of teak, with steel tyres and bosses, had been used extensively to reduce the noise for passengers. This practice had ceased by the 1930s and they were being replaced by rolled steel disc centres as they came through the Works. The wooden block segments were reclaimed and made very durable floors in some areas of the carriage shops. Some roadways around the site were also paved with these blocks.

Frame and Bogie Erecting

The first two roads in the south-east corner of 15 Shop were where the 'frame and bogie gangs' (about fourteen men) did the erecting. This was known as 13A Shop as it was an overflow of the work carried out in 13 (Frame) Shop, where the erectors were based. In the mid-1930s, their foreman was Jessie Farr and the chief C&W building foremen were Mr Greenwood and later Mr Garrett.

The three main components were made ready to be assembled and steam heating pipes fitted in 13A. The completed frame was then lifted on to its two bogies by the overhead gantry crane. The whole weight of the coach body could now be supported at the bogie centres by double bolster girders. It was these frame members that also checked the forces set up when braking. No. 15 Shop was the largest C&W workshop, with about 800 men employed, the majority of whom were fitters.

Bodymaking

The wheeled underframes were now shunted over to No. 4 (Body) Shop: one of a group of workshops on the south side of the main line. Up until 1945 production batches of coach bodies had been built complete before being attached to the underframes. This was because when erecting the body frame members, there was a certain amount of 'fitting to suit' at the joints and this was labour intensive. Therefore, the bodies were built simultaneously with the underframes to save time.

Through the 1930s greater use was made of purpose-built machine tools and jigs, templates and fixtures. Marking out and machining, together with the use of hand tools by erectors, would become a thing of the past. A senior draughtsman in the Carriage Drawing Office, Mr J.W. Innes, gave a lecture to the GWR Swindon Engineering Society in 1939, in which he said:

> Considerable development has taken place in the methods of production of the semi-steel or composite type of coach-body and mass-production methods of machining and assembly have considerably reduced the production time. Some difficulty in the adoption of such methods was met owing to the shrinkage of the timber, and to the natural prejudice against the application of such principles by the coach builder.

When production started again after the war, the underframes were run between platforms 80ft long made of tubular steel and 2in thick decking. The bodymakers could then work comfortably above buffer level. Timber for coach bodies was sawn from logs in the Saw Mill and further trimmed using a milling machine. The body frames were assembled using hardwood and rolled steel members.

By the 1940s, when this photograph was taken, the skeletal frame members were part timber and part steel, over which the external steel body and roof panels are seen being fitted in 4 Shop. *GWR*

Bodymakers constructing a carriage door on a fixture using jigs and cramp in 1953. *BRWR*

It was received from the wood machine shop in kit form, having been fully machined and, where necessary, shaped there. Further wood machining, if required, was undertaken in 4 Shop's own saw mill.

Continuous hardwood members formed the carriage bottom-sides with vertical teak pillars tenoned into them. Two steel angle sections known as cant rails formed the top sides and supported the ash root timbers, known as hoopsticks. Sections of wooden body and door frames were laid out on tables with jigs and hydraulic cramps, which pressed the joints together. Power tools drove in screws and iron dowels for added strength and joints were further strengthened by steel braces. The proportion of steel used in the body and frames gradually increased through the 1930s and '40s.

Steel for carriages needed to be strong, light, resistant to corrosion and inexpensive. Two main types were taking over from mild steel: low-carbon, high-tensile steel and stainless steel combined with aluminium alloy. The designers had to decide which combinations of materials to use and where, as none provided all the ideal qualities together. Impressive results with lightweight express trains were being achieved elsewhere and the GWR started to test aluminium alloys and lightweight high-tensile steel. Less credence was now being given to the idea that weight was relative to the ability of the carriage to stay on the track when running.

After the floor members were fitted, and while the body frame was being constructed, a frame of corrugated steel was laid over the floor. Later the floor would be coated in a red 'sanit' fireproofing compound. Felt, elm pads and floorboards were used to insulate against outside noise from rolling wheels and rail joints. Carpet and asbestos sheets were also used in sleeping cars and special saloons for additional insulation. Pads made in the trimming department were fitted into axleboxes to help reduce noise.

Ted Randell said there was a surplus of bodymakers by 1939 because production methods had considerably reduced the time to complete lots. These tradesmen were then allowed to learn to do their own welding, which did not go down at all well with the 'time served' welders. By 1954 the body shop was equipped with single and multiple transformer welding sets supplied by Quasi-Arc Co. Ltd.

They were used for fabricating jigged units, sub-assemblies and complete coach assemblies. For fixing studs into body frame members and around window lights they now used stud welding sets.

With the body frame finished, the outer panels were fitted and gave additional support. By 1930 steel panels were fitted to all new carriages and to those coming in for overhaul. Galvanised steel was used for this due to its resistance to corrosion from water and tannic acid in the oak. Another reason for the changeover from wood panels and floors in the 1920s was to reduce the fire risk.

A piece appeared in the staff magazine in 1932 about a worker who found a Victory Medal from the war in a coach in for overhaul. It had slipped down the gap in the window frame of a door in a non-corridor coach six years earlier. The focus of the story was how the medal's owner was eventually traced. I mention it here because it is likely that the outer wooden panels were being replaced with steel, exposing the window casing where the discovery was made.

The steel panels for the carriage sides, ends and roof were made in 3 Shop (see also Chapter 17). After being marked out by machine, 16 standard wire gauge (equal to 0.064in or 1.6mm) steel outer sheets were sheared to shape by guillotine. Holes were then punched in for fixing to the cross members. For this, specialised machinery supplied by J. Bennie and Sons of Glasgow had been purchased in the 1920s. Rolling machines and presses were also brought in at that time to shape panels where necessary. The screw heads were slightly recessed after fixing to the carriage frame because of the punched holes. The depressions could then be filled with a putty-like preparation and sanded smooth to give a flush finish when painted over.

To make them watertight, the joints between the panels had been butt-jointed vertically and those on the roof were overlaid with iron bands. In the mid-1930s this practice changed to lap-jointing, which gave flush side panels and this reduced air resistance. It also allowed for horizontal joints along the carriage waist, formed of two-piece panels that were easier to fit and maintain. Another new feature of design at this time was larger windows and they were fitted at this stage.

Before it left the bodymakers for the steam heating and plumbing to be fitted, the outer doors were hung and internal partitions and water cisterns fitted. Plumbers from 15A Shop came and installed radiators, lavatory equipment, steam hot water tanks and associated lagging and insulation. Kitchen cars took up far more of the plumbers' time, as well as that of the gas fitters, because of the cooking ranges, hot water urns, sinks and, later, refrigerators. More regular maintenance would be required and therefore these vehicles had a shorter period between Works' visits. Sleeping cars, too, would be brought in more regularly to keep the motion running smooth and quiet.

Fitting Out

Coaches under construction were shunted through different workshops connected by parallel roads. In turn, the finishers, trimmers, gas plumbers and painters would attend to them before they were fitted with dynamos, batteries and electric train lighting. Traversing tables allowed the vehicles to change roads if necessary. Later, when new building was cut back, coaches were refurbished in these shops too. Once a day, a short train consisting of two old stores vans called 'The Royal' was shunted between the two areas of the Carriage Works. It brought parts for rebuilding and took away dismantled parts for refurbishment or replacement. This provided work for the labourers of No. 11 Shop.

The coach finishers were men in white aprons who worked at benches preparing the interior woodwork in 7 Shop. They worked on such things as panels, frames for seat backs, quarter and door windows, lavatory and gangway doors. The latter had already been machined and sanded in their saw mill using edging saws, four-cutter planers and routers with jigs and templates. Some of the plywood panels were then shaped before being sent across to be painted, polished or lacquered. When the parts returned from the wood treatments, any metal fittings and glazing were incorporated.

Other finishers worked in No. 4 (Body) Shop erecting the internal woodwork. This was the partitions, internal doors, seat frames, panelling and luggage racks that came in from the finishing and polishing shops. Some tradesmen here just worked on the furnishings and windows. Later, increasing use was made of plastics and veneers for wood coverings. This was all prepared in No. 7 Shop, where a 785-ton veneer press and a glue-spreading machine were installed in the 1950s.

Male and female trimmers of 9 Shop cut and made ready the moquette upholstery, canvas roofing, linoleum, carriage blinds and the leather communicating gangways between the coaches. Their colleagues in 19A Shop fitted out the coaches, and also the road motor vehicles. Horsehair was a valuable commodity, so it was removed from old seats and reused. It was put through a carding machine over by 12 (carpenters') Shop. The machine, operated in the 1950s by Jack Huckin, pulled the hair apart or 'combed' it, then washed it. It was then bagged up and sent over to the 19A Trimmers for reuse.

A belt-driven dynamo and a battery supplied the 24 volts to light each vehicle. The dynamo produced direct current electric power, which recharged the battery so that when the coach was stationary or moving too slowly to generate sufficient power, the battery took over from it. Electricians fitted this equipment and the wooden battery boxes to the underside of the vehicle to power the train lighting. They then fitted the regulator inside, which contained three resistors and, on top, the relays. This maintained the voltage required regardless of the running conditions. Lastly, they wired it and fitted the auto and distant switches.

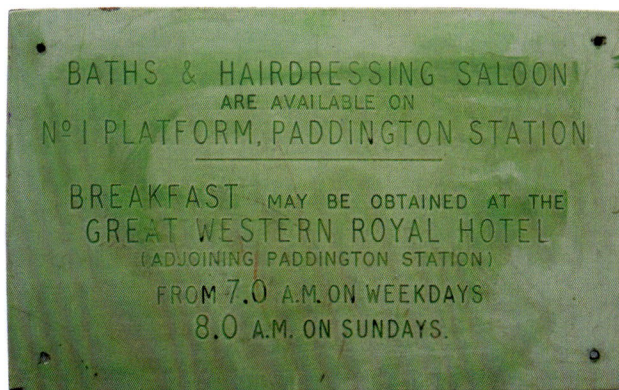

Above: A small Traffolyte or Formica notice on a thin plywood backing. These would have been displayed in the compartments or corridors of Western Region sleeper coaches. Being lime green, it may well have been from one of the four first-class vehicles outshopped in 1951, as this was part of their internal colour scheme.

Left: Engraving metal notice plates in 15 Shop using a 'master' as a template. This photo was taken in the late-1940s, by which time these Taylor-Hobson machines were being used more and more for engraving laminated plastics for carriage notices. *BRWR*

Electricians also wired up fans, extractors, refrigerators, food warmers and fluorescent lighting in vehicles that were fitted with them. The company used the Leitner electric lighting system that by 1930 was made in the Works under licence. After nationalisation the LMS Wolverton train lighting system became standard and it too was manufactured at Swindon. Batteries were brought in from Wolverton Works.

One of the last jobs before each carriage returned to traffic was clearing up the mess left by the various tradesmen. Then all internal surfaces were cleaned and polished. Finally, the coaches were shunted on again into the next workshop, the carriage paint shop. Here they might need stabling on a parallel road using the electric traverser, ready to be externally cleaned, painted and have transfers and varnish applied.

Before being taken in rakes to sidings on the north side of the Works, the kitchen cars, restaurant cars and sleeping cars had their oil-gas systems primed and their cylinders charged. Oil-gas was supplied from drums fitted to flat wagons. By the mid-1950s, new coaches of these types were being built with equipment to burn liquefied petroleum gas (propane) instead. The ex-GWR equivalents were gradually converted as they came through the Works.

8 Shop

This was the last workshop through which new carriages passed. It was noticeably quieter than the assembly shops.

The outer doors were kept closed to try to maintain an even temperature of about 60 degrees Fahrenheit. This would ensure that the paint dried evenly. It was kept clean too to minimise dust getting on to newly treated surfaces. There were a total of thirty-four carriage painters, including those painting coaches in for repairs over in 24 Shop. Each new coach received three external coats of paint and three of varnish, which took seven days to complete.

A section of this shop was set apart for cellulose spraying of panels and fittings of carriage interiors. Spray painting equipment was supplied by Aerograph Co. It was not uncommon for cleaners and painters to be still working on the interior while the vehicle was being towed away by the pilot engine.

Liveries

Until 1947 main-line coaching stock was painted Windsor or chocolate brown below the waist and cream above it. These Great Western colours had changed little over the years except that the livery was originally brown and white. When varnished, the white turned cream and this shade was adopted. Two lines of gold or yellow separated the colours at the waist and the GWR coat of arms was displayed in the middle of the lower section. The heraldic design was replaced from 1934 by the circular 'shirt button' monogram. Roofs, rainstrips, ventilators and the lettering on the solebars were white, while the ends of the coaches, including communicating gangways, were black. So too were the underframes. Luggage vans and brake vans used on secondary or cross-country services were turned out in overall brown from 1935.

In the Works, the shortages of labour and materials from the start of the war had less impact on coaches than on non-passenger vehicles or locomotives. This was because maintenance decreased as the time between Works' visits increased as the war progressed. At the carriage depots the roofs were painted over in dark grey to make them less noticeable from the air.

Ordinary passenger coaches were painted all over in grey, without lining and often without markings, during the war. Some of those used on secondary services were outshopped in 'all black' and only express stock retained the two-colour livery. With the latter the circular monogram was replaced by the letters 'GWR' and the company's coat of arms from 1943. Restrictions were further relaxed and the initials were, in turn, replaced with the words 'Great Western' soon after. The variations in colours, lining and markings were often seen in service at the same time as vehicles were only altered as they went through the Works.

After the company was nationalised, main-line coaches were painted crimson and cream (nicknamed blood and custard), the darker colour being used below the waist as before. Plain unlined crimson was used for secondary and suburban stock. Later all types received 'all over' maroon but just the main-line vehicles were lined, with BR yellow and black. From 1956, the coaches used on Western Region named expresses were turned out in brown and cream. This was very similar to the old Great Western shades but they were lined in the BR colours. Only the restaurant cars used in these sets were ex-GW, the rest were BR Mk 1s.

16

Goods Wagons and Vans

Wagon Statistics

In 1936 freight accounted for 58% of the total traffic receipts on the GWR. The Wagon Works output reached a pre-war peak in 1937 when 5,127 new wagons were built and an even higher number were given heavy repairs. The company's 86,170 mineral and merchandise wagons went into public ownership in 1948. Figures given in the 1950s show that Swindon delivered an average of 300 wagons per week back to traffic. The most numerous types dealt with were 12-ton open and covered goods wagons, ventilated vans, cattle wagons and brake vans. The wagon building weekly capacity was, by 1957, equivalent to 100 13-ton open-top types and the number of light repairs had doubled due to the improved turnaround times of lower maintenance designs. They were also busy throughout the decade converting hand-braked vehicles to vacuum-braked.

Wheels and Bogie Erecting

By the 1930s the design of wagon wheels had altered from spoked to solid castings without fitted tyres. They underwent a series of machining operations in 16 (Wheel) Shop and were the same as for carriage wheels already described, but on a slightly smaller scale. A wheelset for a wagon weighed about 18 cwt. Some non-passenger vehicle sets could weigh more: anything up to a standard set for a carriage, which was just over 1 ton. Between them about 14 tons of steel turnings (swarf) removed during machining was produced in one average week in the carriage & wagon wheel shop.

Older carriage and wagon wheel tyres were refitted then hardened after being heated and shrunk on to the wheel centres. In service they became even harder due to being heated constantly when the brakes were applied. Later, when they returned to the shop, the flanges would be checked using a profile gauge to see if the wear had reached the maximum permitted. If it had not, the tyres were 'trued up' on wheel lathes: the Armstrong Whitworth

type was preferred for this work. Hard spots on the tyre would require a 'roughing' cutting tool with the work turning slowly, after which the flanges were ground to bring them 'back to gauge'.

The axles would also be examined for defects. While in traffic, all wagons would be recalled periodically for examination and, if necessary, bogies or wheels and axleboxes would be overhauled or replaced. 'Out of date' or defective wheelsets were scrapped.

The only factors affecting wagon wheel arrangements were length and weight when fully loaded, unlike locomotives. The GWR needed a far larger range of wagon types than they would have if they were not legally obliged to carry anything that a customer wanted transporting.

An 8-ton Pooley van and its gang. They are on site to install a weightable in the North Yard: the date is about 1930. *S.A.S. Smith courtesy of Ray Eggleton*

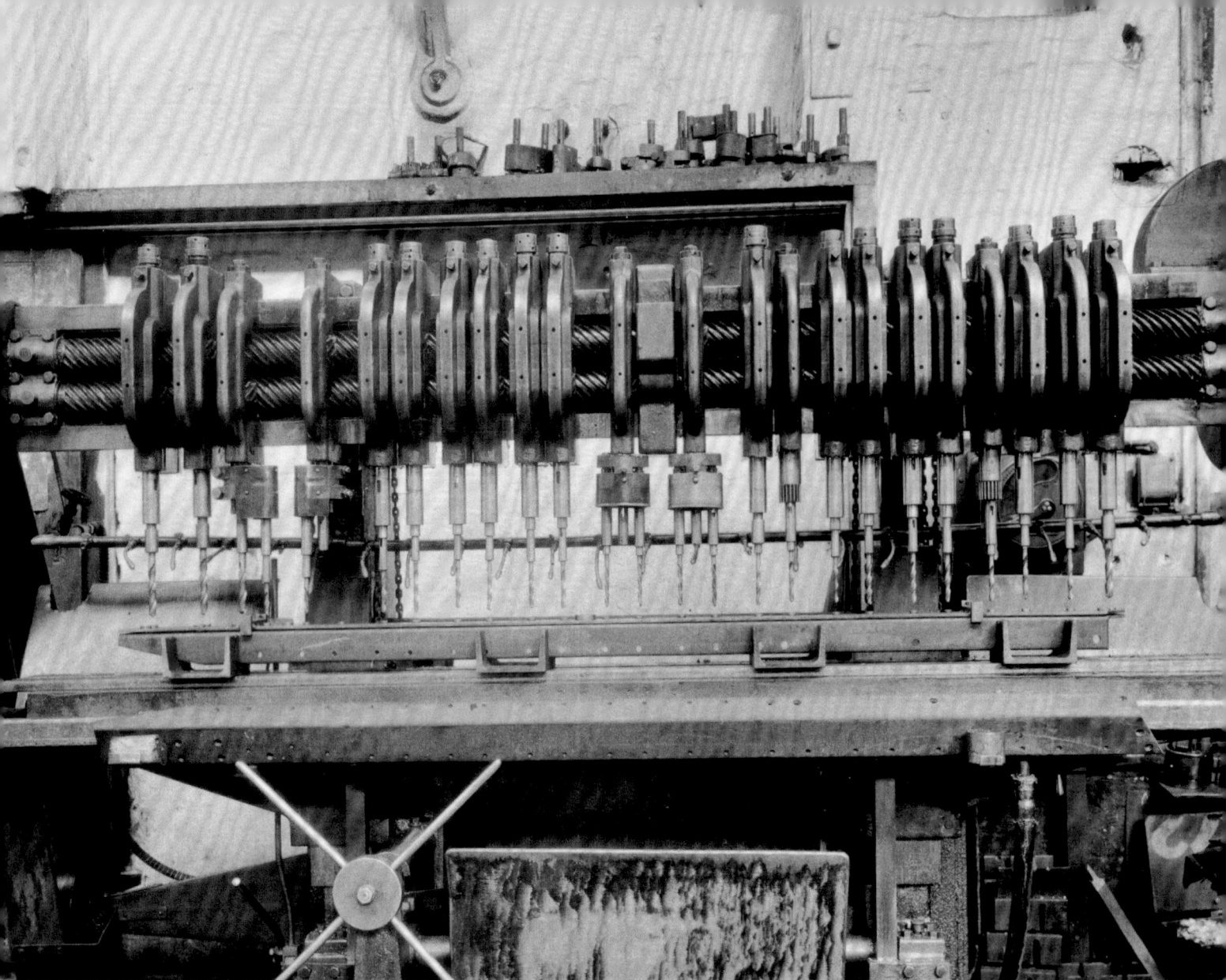

A 24-spindle drilling machine in 13 or 13A Frame Shop. These machines, there were three in the shop, drilled multiple holes simultaneously, driven by bevel gearing. The steel frame member was enclosed by the jig and template seen below. Notice the coolant pipes directed towards each drill bit. *BRWR*

Although they still had their place, the ubiquitous four-wheeled 8- to 12-ton open and covered wagons were being replaced by longer vacuum-fitted vehicles. Private wagon owners resisted the change because the longer wheelbase wagons were not suitable for the sharp curves into and out of their premises.

For long loads such as rails and timber, vehicles fitted with centrally pivoted bolsters could be used in tandem. The bolsters allowed a small amount of side play on curved sections of track. Wagons designed to handle heavier long loads were fitted with two four-wheeled bogies at each end. An advantage with the latter was that it allowed the underframes (British railway builders rarely used the French word 'chassis') to slew slightly across the inside of tight curves leading in and out of sidings. The extra wheels of bogie wagons distributed the weight of the load more evenly too and reduced the wear and tear on each of the axlebox bearings.

Frame Building

Building wagon underframes for the company and for private owners was undertaken by the 'wagon bashers' of 13 Shop. As with carriage building, once an order was placed, the parts were made in the smiths, wheel, machine and fitting shops or drawn from the stores. They were delivered to the assembly shops in sequence, arranged so that the operations were progressive and completed without hold-ups at the delivery date. A large contract for new wagons often overstretched the facilities available and 13 Shop would then work day and night.

The rectangular main frame of a wagon was made up of two solebars bolted to transoms, longitudinals and headstocks. Firstly, the steel members that would become the solebars were straightened, then milled, drilled and profiles cut on one of two oxyacetylene cutting machines in 13 Shop. The fabricated frame members were placed in a jig to be bolted together, relative to each other and to the position of the motion when fitted. Axleguards, spring shoes, stops, headstock and diagonal brackets and vee hangers were then hydraulically riveted to the solebars.

The main brake shaft was put into position between the vee hangers, before the frame was squared up using gauges and passed under a hydraulic riveting machine to be secured. The upright stanchions were usually riveted on next but that depended on the type of wagon body they would hold. As time went on more and more steel fabricated parts were held together using oxyacetylene, then later electric arc and flash-butt welding. The frame was moved along the shop and lifted by electric hoist to receive its wheels, axleboxes and tie rods, after which the drawgear (couplings), buffers and brakework were fitted. The last operation before the body was fitted was to paint the assembly with red lead. If the wagon was to have a steel body, that was also erected here in 13 Shop. Doug Webb worked there from the late 1940s onwards:

> I worked with chargeman wagon plater Mervyn Iles to start with. Mr Jordan was our foreman and Mr Dobson was the wagon builders' chief foreman. As a fitters' mate, one of my jobs was to heat rivets in a nozzle hand forge. It was very noisy in this shop, as much of the assembly was done by riveting. While I was there, a very sophisticated scissor riveting machine was purchased for 13 Shop. Only then was it found to be too heavy for the frame that was to support it from above. This expensive piece of equipment lay in a corner of the shop for years and I heard that it had eventually gone for scrap.

Bodies and Containers: 21 Shop

Wagon bodies were built and repaired in this large building, which was immediately to the north of the junction station. Completed wagon underframes were shunted into one of the six through roads. Roads 1 and 2 at the top (north) end of the shop were for 'new builds' and the other four roads were used for repairs. After the war, roads 3 and 4 were for planned overhauls (wagons were then subject to a seven-year general repair programme rather than receiving attention as necessary). The other two roads dealt with repairs between overhauls.

Each line handled certain types of vehicles depending on their lengths and the materials used in their construction. The railways had purpose-built stock for almost every type of goods' haulage including open or covered goods, fish and meat vans, fruit and banana vans, hopper wagons, brake vans, permanent way and sleeper wagons, gunpowder vans, tool vans and cattle wagons. Wagon and non-passenger vehicle bodies did not require the same degree of structural strength as carriages and so the change from timber to steel did not keep pace with carriage construction. For each order, a timber specification was sent to the saw mill. The wood arrived ready cut, sufficient for it to be marked off for final machining prior to assembly.

This wagon body shop was 700ft long and vehicles moved through the building on a belt system to emerge at the end, built, rebuilt or repaired. As with carriage body work, the lines of wagons were flanked by platforms allowing the men to work at the level of the body sides. Lines dealing with covered vehicles also had cradles suspended from above so men could work more easily on wagon roofs.

Standard open wagons passed through and were repaired in stages to emerge at the other end no more than twelve hours later. They were then ready for painting and stencilling in the area known as 21B Shop. Finally, the vacuum brakes were tested before the wagon went to the weighbridge and had its tare weight recorded. The company had to maintain a certain number of these small (short wheelbase) open wagons even though they were comparatively uneconomical. Larger wagons could not negotiate the curves of sidings and the small turntables and weighbridges of many private firms.

Steel containers that could be lifted by fixed crane from rail wagon to lorry were first introduced in the 1920s. They provided a door-to-door service for house furniture removals. Soon after, general merchandise containers were being built and repaired at Swindon too, although they were restricted somewhat by the capacity of the cranes existing at goods depots.

Timber

Before the war, this side of the Works was often referred to as the Carriage, Wagon and Timber Department on documents. In 1935, 3,170 full-size logs or flitches (tree trunks) went through No. 1 Saw Mill, twice the number that was handled in 1959 (and that was not the only way timber was supplied). More timber was used at Swindon for wagon bodies than for anything else. Despite the huge amounts needed by the CME Dept, they were not the biggest consumer within the GWR: the Chief (Civil) Engineer's Dept used more on their buildings and permanent way sleepers.

Although iron and steel-bodied wagons, vans and containers were being introduced, the vast majority would continue to be built and repaired using wood. The advantages of this material were that it was comparatively cheap. It was also light in weight and abundant. Perhaps the main reason, though, was the long-established system of production and supply. This made it impractical for factories such as Swindon Works to suddenly change its traditional building methods and materials.

Walter Timbrell was timber yard foreman until he retired in 1944. He received the incoming wagon loads, many in purpose-built wagons constructed to carry large logs. They could be up to 40ft in length as it was cheaper to buy it that way. If it still had its bark, the logs could be seasoned in the open air. Seasoning reduced the moisture content over a period of time if air could freely circulate the pile. The intention was that any distortion happened before the timber was cut to size.

At the far west end of the Works was what was referred to on plans as the Timber Stacking Ground. It consisted of sidings, timber sheds, stacks and a saw mill. The latter was No. 1 Saw Mill, seen here, or what was better known as the 'New Saw Mill'. This distinguished it from the other Works' saw mill on the south side of the main line. *GWR*

In peacetime, Swindon received a large amount of timber from abroad. Consignments arrived mainly through the docks at Cardiff or London, then by barge to the GWR dock at Brentford. It was then examined by the company's inspector before being accepted. Wherever possible the company policy was 'to utilise timber grown in the British Empire if cost and quality were acceptable'. Hickory came in from North America; pine from Canada; mahogany from Borneo and West Africa, while hardwoods, oak and teak, which were used for carriage and wagon body frames, came from Poland and Burma respectively. Logs could also be skimmed in the saw mill and artificially seasoned in the timber drying shed before being cut to manageable sizes and sent out to the shops. Most woodworking shops on the C&W side had their own saw mill and could cut the timber down further for their own requirements. Occasionally it was received from the supplier as ready-cut boards if their own facilities could not cope, or a good price had been secured.

One of the few woods used at Swindon for its engineering qualities was lignum vitae, a wood so dense it won't float. It was used to make brake blocks, bearings, shafts and pulley sheaves. Hardwood blocks, including lignum vitae, were kept in the guard's van of a train along with the jack, so as to secure a temporary repair to axle boxes, excluding the locomotive, where the white metal bearing had broken down.

Mr Bezzant, the timber storekeeper from 1933, placed the orders from his office in 4 Shop. Before they became area inspectors in the mid-1950s, the company's timber inspectors were based at Swindon. They would go out to inspect the orders before they left the merchants. Gabriel Wade & English Ltd, who had a depot (Baynes) in County Road, was one local timber merchant that supplied the factory from its earliest days. Imported shipments were checked before they were brought ashore. The inspectors were looking for water and other damage, fungus or disease. Gordon Nash trained to be a Works' timber inspector in the late 1940s:

Foreign exporters could not afford to have timber shipments returned so their inspectors checked it over before sailing. It was the home-grown consignments that were likely to cause problems, if any. Sometimes different types, or different grades of timber, were mixed in to make up a load. There were several similar types of Douglas fir, for instance: I would view it close up using a small lens. Sometimes I would refer to the grading manual or to illustrations of wood structures known as the 'lens key'. I also had to check the dimensions and calculate the quantity in square feet against the order. When I was satisfied I would stamp it with my personal ink mark.

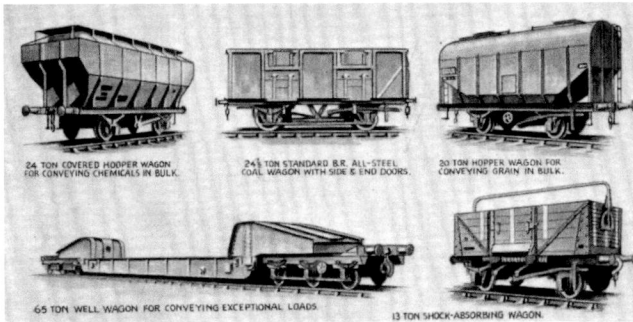

Examples of special-purpose wagons built at Swindon during the 1930s and '40s; most would be vacuum-braked. Increasing numbers of vacuum-fitted stock were coming out of the Works but with so many privately owned loose-coupled wagons still being handled, the proportion of unfitted and partially fitted freight trains remained high. *GWR*

Colours and Markings of General Stock

With so many slight variations, it is only possible in a work of this kind to give a general overview of this subject. Goods wagons' colours hadn't changed much since the 1890s, when the standard became lead grey bodies and underframes for all new stock. Repainting was often omitted altogether in the austerity of the 1930s. All lettering was white with the exception of insulated meat containers and refrigerated vans: they were given white bodies therefore the lettering was black. By the mid-1930s, the larger GW letters on each side had been reduced to 16in high but this lasted just a few years. If designated as 'RETURN TO G.W.R NOT COMMON USER', this was painted on a small rectangular piece of tinplate fitted each side on the lower right of the body.

Bogie vehicles classed as passenger stock such as Siphons, fruit vans, horseboxes etc., were painted brown with black ends and underframes, and white or sometimes grey roofs. Their lettering was yellow in the style and layout of goods wagons. In 1934 the circular 'shirt button' monogram used on passenger stock also appeared on non-passenger carriages. It was never used on wagons but was stencilled on to all containers over time. From 1936 'XP' denoted that the vehicle was 'fitted' (with vacuum braking gear) and long wheelbase measurements were given if applicable.

In wartime, vehicle roofs, containers and storm sheets were darkened to disguise them from above. From 1942 a new specification for lettering was introduced similar to the 1937 style: open wagons had 'G' 'W' and the vehicle number in 3in block letters on the bottom plank. Also painted on were the maximum load and tare weight details together with the wagon number. The latter together with the name of the owning company were embossed on cast iron plates fitted to both solebars. The telegraph code, if there was one, was stencilled on to van body sides too.

There were two types of cast numberplates used during the period, depending on whether the wagon was built or registered by the GWR. A third, rectangular type, seen on stock in the 1930s and '40s, had been fitted to wagons and vans that were built earlier. These plates were fitted to both solebars, allowing the Works and goods' depots to identify the vehicle and refer to its history card details. The background was painted the same colour as the underframes. The embossed vehicle number and the carrying capacity were highlighted with white paint; so too were the company initials, as the builder or as the company with whom the vehicle was registered.

The new owners had to standardise the different railway company colours and markings after nationalisation. Steel framed/wooden body-fitted vans were painted in what the railway called orange brown, while non-fitted bodies were given a topcoat of dark grey. The underframes, wheels and running gear were painted black and the lettering white.

Wagon Writers (or Signwriters)

Ron Harper started his working life in the Wagon Works as an office boy in 13 Shop. His father worked as a labourer in the AE Shop bosh and they lived in Harding Street. After six months Ron went out into the shop to heat rivets for wagon frame building. During the six months he spent there he was asked to choose what he wanted to do when he reached sixteen. The choices were wagon building, blacksmithing or painting and Ron chose the latter. He would, in time, become a semi-skilled wagon writer. A lot of the time he would be painting instructions and lettering on to wagons and containers coming out of the Works new or having been repaired.

Ernie Stowe did the rewriting or over-painting and Ron would go over and watch him while still employed on rivet hotting. He wanted to get an idea of what to expect. On the appointed date he was instructed to report to Bill Richens' gang in the south-west corner of 21B Shop. Other writers remembered by Ron are Ken White, Fred Gwillam, Dick Sturgeon, Den Carter, George Hobbs, Albert Brown, Len Blackwell, George Luckman, Fred Watson, Bob Jefferies, Phil Sargeant and Chargeman Bert Barnett. Ron thought Phil was the most accomplished wagon writer. The foremen were Reg Sheppard and Ralph Stowe (no relation to Ernie).

There was no training given: Ron learned by watching, copying and trial and error. They used sable chisel, sable point and stipple brushes, a mahlstick to steady the hand, a palette, chalk lines and bags of pounce for surfaces where the paint might run. For small jobs the pay tins made by Works' tinsmiths were used as paint pots. Work included painting the 1ft × 2ft CME panel on the end of the wagon. On it they had to paint the wagon number, specification, the date it arrived and the date it was expected to return to traffic. Other details that were written on certain wagons were tare weight, telegraphic code and logos (on private vehicles such as Birds Eye and Fyffe's Bananas). Wagon writers might also have to add 'Empty to' followed by the goods' yard it originated from.

Smaller dairy farm suppliers used 17-gallon milk churns. They were loaded into these vans, which had been built in the Works in 1930. The milk was kept cool by using ice boxes instead of the old method of having slatted or louvred panels in the body sides. Their telegraphic code was 'Syphon J' and this particular 50ft vehicle only worked between Carmarthen and Paddington.
Author's collection

The long wheelbase wagons such as 'crocodiles' and 'macaws' were 'written' in 21A Shop, known to the men as 'the extension'. They were normally parked just south of 21A in sidings reserved for 'special load' wagons and known as 23 Shop. Tarpaulin sheets used to cover open wagons were 'written' using stencils they had made. In the Container Shop they labelled the bodies that were to be chained on to flatbed wagons too. Ron told me:

A typical day for me once I had 'found my feet' was to meet at the annexe in 21 Shop, which we shared with the wagon roofing gang, and collect our paints and equipment. Six of us would work on the thirty odd, mainly mineral wagons, on No. 1 road. They had to be finished before the 10am break to get our piecework (bonus). Next we would go onto No. 2 road to work on covered and open wooden wagons. There could be just as much work here but, as before, it depended on whether it was 'new writes' or 'rewrites': the latter involved painting over existing figures and letters. After dinner, if the weather was dry, two of us would go over to the Transfer Goods Yard and put tare weights on wagons that had just been on the weighbridge. Or else we might be sent up to the sidings at Pressed Steel (motor car plant) to write on weather sheets covering car bodies waiting to go out. For this we used a scaffold.

Special-purpose Vehicles

Space permits the description of just a few types here in detail. There was a range of notable vehicles built for the GWR to accommodate what they called 'exceptional loads', including 'out of gauge' loads due to their width. They would require special train working, which was carried out on Sundays.

A one-off special trolley or wagon was designed at Swindon to meet the requirements of the Central Electricity Board. They would occasionally need to move very heavy transformers and the only way was by railway. The one-off wagon that was designed and built at Swindon, for the purpose, was known by the code name 'Crocodile L'. It had an interchangeable straight or well girder to support a load measuring up to 24ft in length and weighing up to 120 tons. Having a low girder supported by a twelve-wheeled articulated bogie at each end allowed it to negotiate curves of a radius no less than 1½ chains.

Either-side and screw brakes were fitted that would hold the trolley and its load under normal conditions. Its tare weight was 75 ton 19 cwt and the length between the buffers was 89ft 6in. The first load carried was a 63-ton transformer to be moved from Hayes to Yorkshire in 1930. The loading and unloading was supervised by men of the CME Department. 'Crocodile L' was still in use on the Western Region in the 1950s.

Banana traffic was very important to the Great Western. Like other perishables, such as flowers, vegetables and milk, such fruit needed transporting carefully and quickly to ensure it arrived in good condition. Trains of four-wheeled, 8-ton tare (10-ton maximum load) banana vans were kept at Avonmouth Docks to meet the ships arriving from Jamaica. This fruit, which was imported all year round in peacetime, had been refrigerated on the ship. A white disc was painted on the railway van bodies for the onward journey. This indicated that the contents were being gently steam-heated to fully ripen them.

Surviving wagon stock index cards show that each banana van spent between ten and fifteen days in the care of 19D Shop when under repair. I'm not sure why these comparatively small (16ft between headstocks) vans are recorded as being in the workshop for so long. I think that the shop clerk must have included the time each was 'stopped awaiting works', which would account for it. This average time span remained the same for the period covered by the cards: 1936 to 1956. This included those converted to meat vans when imports of bananas stopped

An official photo of a 3,000 gallon milk tank wagon owned by the Milk Marketing Board. Swindon designed, built and maintained the underframes, wheels and cradles. *GWR*

during the war. The time between heavy repairs varied from two to six years, presumably depending on the maintenance and repairs received elsewhere.

Milk traffic was very important to the GWR and they provided the best means at their disposal to convey it. Main-line milk trains had to be worked to fast timings to keep the milk fresh. They were often as heavy as the longest passenger trains and covered the long distances from West Wales, the Midlands or Cornwall to London. For that reason four-cylinder locomotives were usually used.

It was the introduction of glass-lined milk tank wagons in 1927 that greatly improved the conveyance of large quantities of milk by train. United Dairies owned the first batches of these wagons, which had metal outer casings. Another company that purchased them was the West Park Dairy Co, Market Lavington, in 1931. The 18ft × 6ft diameter cylindrical tanks, which held 3,000 gallons of milk, were manufactured by Enamelled Metal Products Ltd of London NW1. They were insulated with a 2in layer of cork and were glass-lined for hygienic reasons. Swindon Works fitted them on to steel underframes supported by six wheels and secured the tank in a cradle.

A long-distance milk train might also include one or more 2,000 gallon trailer tanks with pneumatic tyres, for transporting milk over routes where part of the journey was by road. Again the Works built specially adapted flat wagons to carry them. Complete with their tanks, these vehicles had the telegraphic code name 'Rotank' or 'Rotruck'.

As each vehicle was fitted with vacuum and either-side brakes, screw couplings and a through steam pipe, they could also be coupled to coaching stock in fast passenger trains. They were given the same axleboxes and bearings as passenger coaches and the wheels had to be balanced to avoid wobble at higher speeds. The glass tanks only had a limited life but were, for other purposes, perfectly serviceable. The railway would sometimes buy them to use as water-carrying vehicles.

With private motoring becoming more popular, a motor car carrier was introduced in 1930. Morris Motors at Cowley near Oxford and Rover at Solihull wanted vehicles moved from their factories to the distributors and to the docks. This new type of railway van carried two cars and had a wheelbase of 22ft. Its telegraphic code name was 'Asmo'. It had double doors at each end and a flap that dropped down to rest on the buffers. This formed a horizontal bridge so that road vehicles could be driven off and on to a loading dock or through from another van coupled to it. As these and the one-car types went through the Works in the 1940s their internal gas lighting was converted to electric.

Looking much like the standard GW ventilated van, this was actually a single road motor vehicle carrier. This design was built from 1933 until 1936. *GWR*

The C&W Works at Swindon also designed and built non-standard wagons, usually in small lots, specifically for the conveyance of such things as aircraft propellers and fuselages, rail sleepers, gunpowder, theatrical props and scenery, glass, meat, livestock and circus animals including elephants, provender and manure. That's not to mention the dozens of different types of merchandise containers manufactured. They were carried by flatbed wagons and would be transferred to road vehicle or ship by mobile or fixed yard cranes at the other end.

23 Shop

At what was usually referred to as the 'London end' of the Works' site, between the Oil and Grease Works, was 23 Shop. This title was misleading as it was actually a Platelayers' and a special loads' yard with two small buildings for the platelayers' foreman and clerk and the special load inspectors.

The yard sidings were mainly used to hold 'special load' wagons: the long and/or reinforced vehicles for carrying heavy and oversized loads across the company's territory. Because of the 'common carrier' obligation, imposed upon the railways, they could not refuse to take loads on account of their nature or weight. All the planning for these journeys was done in the Special Loads Office in the C&W office building. A Mr Hext was the clerk-in-charge of this work and he was succeeded by Mr Juggins. In the C&W Drawing Office there was a sub-section for these non-standard wagons.

17
Carriage & Wagon Workers

Out of a total workforce of between 10,000 and 13,000, depending on the period, about 40% were employed on carriage and wagon work. Of that figure, about three-quarters were manual workers and it is some of them that this chapter is concerned with. It is impossible to divide numbers further, as already stated, as so much carriage and wagon work overlapped.

Carriage tradesmen, who were bodymakers, carpenters, trimmers, polishers, electricians and coach finishers, built and repaired everything above the buffers. This included the hard timber frame, roofsticks, steel panels, partitions, windows and sliding ventilators, external and internal doors. (It is important to make the distinction between the doors.) Others fitted out the interiors with seats, panelling and upholstery. Erecting wagons was centred on Nos 13, 15 and 21 Shops, with some parts coming in from the smiths, springsmiths and wheelwrights. Iron and steel parts would have passed through 16A Shop to be heat treated. Careful heating and cooling would improve their resistance to wear while maintaining toughness.

There were gangs of lifters, labourers, painters (or signwriters), fitters, machinists, carpenters, sawyers, smiths, and riveters etc., and not all of them worked on rolling stock either. The Works needed carpenters, electricians, plumbers and gas fitters for workshop and building installations too. Among their own, each profession was known by more basic terms according to the types of work performed. He or she might be known as a: 'rubber', 'flatter', 'shingler', 'fettler', 'straightener', 'pressman', 'clothier', 'saw doctor', 'dings separator', 'knocker up', 'holder up', 'hooker on' and other mysterious titles.

Conditions in the Saw Mills

The men in the saw mills learned on the job, there being no formal training until after the war. Labourers and timber porters were paid 32 shillings a week exclusive of piecework earnings. They could apply to learn to do jobs for which experience was necessary, enabling them to become semi-skilled. For instance, becoming proficient in the work of the saw doctors in the adjacent workshop would get them the 40 shilling rate. For that they would have to learn to sharpen, tension and set saws and cutters.

Gordon Nash moved from 13A Shop to No. 2 Saw Mill in March 1936 to become wood machinists' boy. He was allocated to Jack Panting's gang, who did the initial machining of timber. Besides Jack the chargeman, there was Bert Clark and two other 'boys'. Jack's daughter, Ethel, was secretary to one of the works managers and Bert, who came from Blunsdon, later became a prisoner of war.

After a bit of guidance from Bert, and because he was now sixteen years old, Gordon was allowed to operate machinery unattended. Guards' flag sticks, trenails (rawlplugs), axlebox shields, handles for hand tools and later ferrules for track chairs were among the things he worked on here. Gordon moved around the workshop and operated most types of machinery over time. They did miles of matchboards for coaches on a tenoning machine and also a lot of sanding work using the two drum sanders, which could handle work up to 3ft 6in wide.

As already stated, wood machinists who operated the lathes, shapers and spindle moulding machines in the saw mills were not recognised as skilled tradesmen. They could, however, be paid skilled men's rates in time, which were 38 to 46 shillings a week in the 1940s, depending on whether they were grade 1, 2 or 3. In the 1950s, Gordon, who was by then a timber inspector, played a big part in getting these grades recognised. However, some of the older men were not happy with this. They pointed out that, in the past, when the Works cut back on numbers, they had been retained to work as labourers and they said this would now no longer happen.

By this time the men in the saw mills were becoming highly regarded. Art Fortune, a coach bodymaker, had nothing but praise for their skills and resourcefulness: 'Whenever we needed a replacement wooden part for a coach under repair, the (saw) mill would make it. Some of

A general view of No. 2 Saw Mill showing timber in the advanced stages of being prepared to go for carriage and wagon body building. Rail keys were produced by the wall over on the right. *BRWR*

A radial arm routing machine is being used here to cut wood panels for carriage interior partitions. This is No. 2 Saw Mill at the west end of the new carriage shops. *Author's collection*

the vehicles were very early and we couldn't get hold of jigs, templates and engineers' drawings but, with a brief explanation, they always came up with what was required.'

Some men who deserved promotion were overlooked because someone else was in favour with the foreman. They may have gone out of their way to strike up a friendship with the gaffer in the Workingmen's Club or at his place of worship. Gordon thought men known to be in St Mark's congregation generally got on better in the shops too. Jim Lowe said there were quite a few Salvation Army men 'inside' and a greater proportion of them seemed to become chargemen, then inspectors, then foremen.

Men related to the foreman might well be given posts they did not deserve too. It was a situation that persisted throughout the period apparently, as described by a disgruntled 'workshop scribe' in a letter to *The Swindonian* magazine in June 1959: 'Promotion for tradesmen is simply a racket. An inspector falls sick and someone is appointed by the foreman to act in a temporary capacity. When the vacancy occurs this temporary man, in nine cases out of ten, obtains the post despite a promotion scheme which invites applicants from all.'

Workers' Conditions

Men from the same workshop would speak if they passed one another in the town except for the foreman. If he was a churchgoer he might speak only to men in his congregation or in his choir. Stan Leach, like Gordon, went into the Carriage Works in 1935 and he remembers that some men would try to win favour with their foreman. This was in the days when the latter could hire and fire people:

Some of these 'hopefuls', as the men called them, would leave a box of vegetables or eggs outside their gaffer's front door with a note wishing them well. This was more common when orders were down and men were being discharged. I remember the chief foreman coming round with discharge notices before the war. The men knew a lot would be going on the carriage side but until the boss stopped and handed out the envelope, no one knew who. It seemed to be mostly the last in that were selected and as apprentices we knew we were alright. Everyone was surprised to hear that Jack Hext got an envelope: they said he went as white as a sheet. He was a left wing union man on the Works Committee, and generally kept in with the right people. When he opened it, all it said was 'evolution not revolution'. This was the foreman's idea of a joke.

A lot of carriage bodymakers and upholsterers wore their white aprons home of a dinner time. Being as only tradesmen wore them, I think they wanted to show off. Before the war some of the older men wore bowler hats to and from work. Nowadays you hear people say that this was forbidden unless the wearer was a foreman but this was not so. I think that the supervisors were wary of a confrontation with some of the older hands if they challenged them.

Guillotining steel body panels in what Ted Randell thought might be 13 Shop. The official photographer was probably brought in because the machine was new. The date given on the back of this print is January 1954. *BRWR*

Here bodymakers are preparing hardwood pillars for the fitting of partition panels. Written on the mount underneath this photo is: 'The coach of the riveting dispute – iron cant rail. 4 Shop Swindon.' Although details were not always written on the backs of official prints, the GWR did not take random photographs. Therefore it is unlikely that this, the scene of a dispute, was coincidental.

Whenever production methods changed there was potential for differences over which trade did what and the price or piecework rate for the job. This picture was taken sometime after 1944. By that time disputes were usually resolved quickly by the Shop or Works' Committees. The need for photographic evidence suggests that this matter was not settled locally. The next step in the 'machinery of negotiation' for railway shopmen was for senior delegates of the Works' Committee to meet with the general manager at Paddington. *Swindon Museum and Art Gallery collection*

In 1939 the Civil Defence Organisation set up several publically owned emergency feeding centres around the town in case of mass homelessness due to the expected air raids. Stan and his father could not get home at dinnertime as they lived at Purton, so they would walk up to one of these British Restaurants: one was in Maxwell Street and there was another in Savernake Street. There they could get a reasonably priced hot meal.

Because of the anticipated run down of carriage work during 'the present emergency', Stan was called up fairly early on, in 1940, for the army. At this time apprentices were among the first to be enlisted because of their young age and because, in theory, their work could be done by others brought in. Stan was in his final year of training and doing the work of a skilled man while getting a lot less pay, of course. While he was away a canteen was opened on the carriage side: 'By the time I got back, women from the canteen were coming round the shops with a refreshments trolley during the breaks.'

There were five or six outside toilet blocks around the Works' site and in the 1930s they were very basic, said Stan:

The long narrow toilet building behind 15 Shop was made of wood and louvre panels on a brick base. You sat on a low wall, which had a wooden top with a line of holes in it. No doubt designed with the intention of stopping you getting comfortable and loitering. There were scant partitions and doors but no wash basins. A chap named Evans was the attendant: he had been injured in the First World War and retained to work in this post.

You gave the attendant your check number as you went in and he would record every visit and whether you took more than ten minutes. After which you lost a quarter of an hour. It was said that if Evans caught you smoking in there he would lock you in so you did lose time. Later, just after the war, new toilets were built by 24 Shop next to the carriage disinfecting plant. They were much better and gone too was the unpopular lavatory attendant arrangement.

No doubt these improvements came about when the Joint Works' Committees were formed in the early 1940s.

Perhaps too, the management realised such primitive conditions could not continue with more females coming into the workshops.

18 (Stamping and Drop Forging) Shop

Components for wagon and carriage frames and underframes, brakework, bogies and vacuum cylinders were worked by men in 18 Shop. They also made parts for containers and had work contracts with the Signal Works and X (points and crossing) Shop. Some smaller parts for the Loco Works also passed through this shop. After the war Fielding & Platt 200-ton hydraulic presses were brought in to form pre-heated components such as stanchion brackets and pressed-steel bogie members.

The nine Massey steam drop stamps and five drop hammers, with friction drives, had capacities ranging from 10 cwt to 2 tons. Mains steam reduced to 80lb psi powered these and two upsetting machines. It was generated by Stirling boilers at the Central Boiler Station. The supply was drawn upon as required and the pressure could drop if too many machines were working at the same time. To cure the problem, a Ruth's steam accumulator was installed alongside the shop in 1944/45. This was a large storage tank that acted as a reservoir, maintaining a constant supply, and was economical in use.

When Stan Leach was in the nearby 17 (road vehicle) Shop after the war he got to know their routine:

> Some of the men here went in half an hour early to light the many furnaces, including at least twenty that used creosote pitch oil fuel. Not surprisingly there would soon be black smoke everywhere. If the wind was in the wrong direction they, in their building, would catch the choking air from 18 Shop. If the wind was blowing in the other direction, housewives from Beatrice Street to Ferndale Road would be out complaining among each other because they could not hang out the washing.

The implementation of the Clean Air Act of 1956, as interpreted by the Western Region of British Railways, sought to improve the firing technique used with furnaces, thereby reducing the emission of 'black' or 'dark smoke'. Notices to that effect were displayed in all of the appropriate workshops at Swindon and beyond. Similar instructions were issued for workers using hand-fired boilers.

14 Shop (Smithy)

According to the company, there were 200 men employed here in the early 1930s: of those, seventy-six were skilled blacksmiths. By 1948 the number of C&W smiths had gone up to 109. Their work included fashioning parts for carriages (and later, diesel railcars) and wagons such as brakegear, drawgear, fittings for goods containers and numerous tools used in the Works and elsewhere on the GWR.

Fred Garrett was a carriage side blacksmith before becoming an inspector. In his spare time, Fred played the violin in the GWR Works' Orchestra. *GWR Magazine*

The forge ran down either side of the long workshop with fireplaces and hearths at equal distances along its length. A clean, bright fire, of the right shape, was essential for the blacksmith to work with. To achieve this, the coke had to be sifted to remove dirt and dust, and clinker was removed from the bed of the fireplace. Live coals were raked into the centre before applying the blast to raise the temperature. The blast, or air, was delivered to the fires from a fan set into the wall and driven by an induction motor. Nine steam hammers forged the larger iron and steel components and two 'hot saws' were installed nearby to cut through red and white hot metal from the furnaces (it being much easier to cut through in this state).

In the early 1930s lots of carriage smiths were engaged on coupling work. The links, including three link 'Instanter' couplings, were manufactured using a pneumatic 5 cwt hammer. They were made from grade 'A' iron bar, 1½in in diameter. Inspector Fred Garratt passed, and occasionally rejected, them. Batches of these couplings were 'on order' virtually all the time. Each sawn section was bent in a machine and hooked together before the links were closed by hammer welding. They went to be normalised (heat treated),

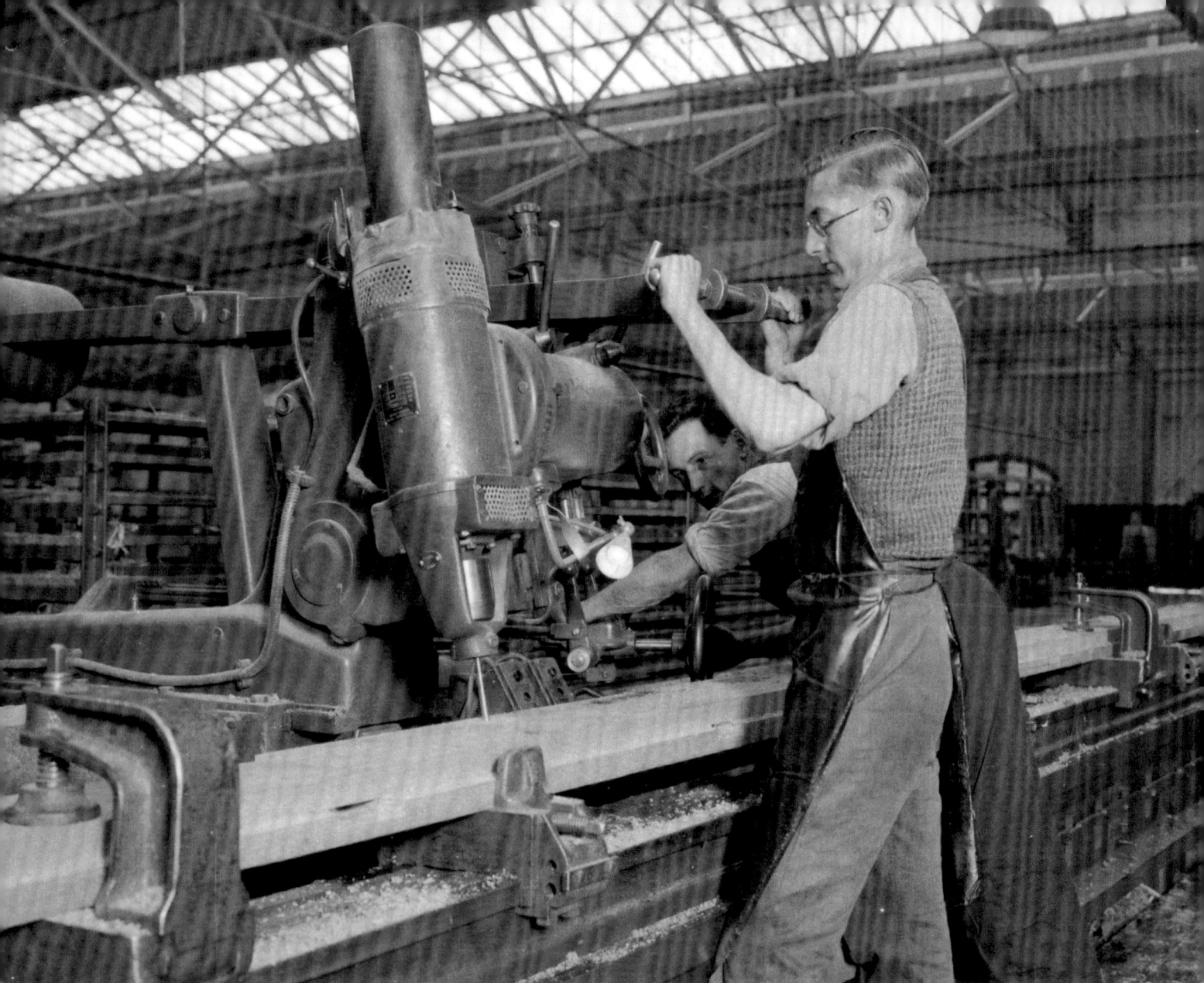

A large timber carriage body section being machined using a trenching, boring and recessing machine. Ted Randell, who spent time working here, in No. 3 Shop, pointed out that the machine tool guards were not in place, so as to show the cutting tool in action. He also said that a lot of the operators' time would have been taken up with securing the work with cramps and jigs. *Author's collection*

then samples were sent to be tested in the Test House. By 1940 the links were joined using a butt welding machine. The output for one machine was about 400 per week, more than double that achieved by one blacksmith previously.

Advancements in industrial welding and pressed steel components were to reduce the work of the blacksmith considerably. By the late 1930s the smiths' hand-forging hearths were being removed to make way for production using oxyacetylene and electric arc welding. In 1944 a further two smiths' hearths were replaced by a specially designed flash butt welding machine and electric lighting was installed to go with it. With these changes in working practices, half the labour got through the same work in less time. Some components continued to be hammer welded, such as buffers of various types and tyres for road vehicles. These tyres were still fitted in the old way on a section the blacksmiths used in 17 Shop.

Before the war there were no tea breaks for shop staff and many work-weary men took risks to get a 'drop of tea' or a few draws on a cigarette. Some smiths were allowed to take a break for refreshment, however, because the piecework time allowed for the furnaces to cool before de-clinkering. No doubt utilising the time in this way was brought up at one of the shopmen's Works' Committee meetings, part of the 'machinery of negotiation' being introduced in the late-1920s and '30s. These committees consisted of managers and men in equal numbers. They met regularly to try to resolve matters that concerned the workers and, might therefore, affect production.

Stan Leach remembered that:

14 Shop was the Blacksmiths' Shop proper: on one side it was joined to the Wagon Frame Shop and on the other, the huge Fitting and Machine Shop.

160

Bending and pressing flat steel coach panels in the fitting and machine section of 3 Shop. This 500-ton press was the first of its kind to be installed in the Carriage Works. The machine setters here were fitters, namely Keith Freeman, Chargeman Gordon 'Joey' Bevington and a fella named Sanders. *Author's collection*

I regularly went through 14 Shop in the 1930s when running errands or to meet my father at the end of the day. Mr H. Griffiths was smiths' foreman at that time: he had lost an eye in an injury at the anvil. When he retired, Alfie Godwin took over and later in the 1950s, his son Charlie was foreman there.

Carriage Finishers

Finishers prepared all the internal timberwork, glazing and fittings. Others of that trade then fitted the doors, panelling, windows and frames. In the repair shop finishers had to removed worn and damaged internal carriage fittings and refurbish then replace them. These included carriage pictures, luggage supports and nets, sliding and hinged doors, ceilings, handrails in corridor coaches, drop lights, mirrors, lavatory pans and wash basins. Of his time in 19 Shop (carriage repairs), Stan said:

> An apprentice and I would complete a coach a day if nothing went wrong. We worked on coaches on 'the bank': the roads leading in and out of the finishers' repairs' section of the shop, which were nearest the embankment. On one occasion I was trying to screw down a lavatory pan in a coach which had a special soundproofed and fireproofed floor. Try as I might I could not locate any cross members to screw into. I decided to leave it and put extra-long screws in to hold the toilet roll holder. This cured the problem as far as I was concerned because the piecework inspector, Jack Shailes, saw the screws projecting through into the corridor. He made such a song and dance about that, he missed the loose pan in the lavatory. I could rectify the roll holder in time but not the pan. This was one of the tricks of the trade. In winter with no artificial light, we had to stop work at dusk; sometimes we had a sleep in a coach till the hooter went.

The 19 Shop finishers would refurbish coaches required for the mass exodus in July that was 'Trip'. Doug Webb, formerly of 13 Shop, told me that this was done on the sidings at the back of A Shop on the loco. (Incidentally, this was also where the frames for 'Hall' class locomotive 4911, which suffered a direct hit in 1941, were stored until at least 1948, said George Petfield.) Stan dismissed the refurbishment of the 'Trip' coaches, saying: 'They didn't do much to them, just looked them over and gave them a bit of a clean.'

Ken Farncombe remembers hearing of men who, on finding a carriage lavatory in need of work to be done, screwed the door to the frame so that it could not be used. This was pre-war and I should think such 'tricks' were only tried on Works' holiday coaches that were soon to be condemned. Many of the Works' holiday trains were made up of old third-class, non-corridor stock. The overhead luggage racks had to be inspected carefully as this was a favourite place to put a sleeping baby when the compartment was full.

Occasionally finishers and other trades were paid overtime to refurbish burnt-out carriages. Stan said some of the men suspected fires were started deliberately using cotton waste soaked in turps that the men cleaned their hands with. Ron Cox was a coach finishers' foreman, later chief finishers' foreman. He originated from outside the town (Oswestry), so was known as a 'down homer'.

C&W Repair Shops

Various types of carriage and wagon repairs were carried out in outposts of other workshops. They were 13A, 21, 20, 19A, C & D, most of which were under one roof collectively known by the men as 19 Shop. Looking at Works' plans of the 1930s and talking to men who worked here in the latter half of the 1950s, it is clear that the way vehicles passed through these areas did change over that period.

'Traffic' or light repairs were done outside 'under the veranda', which was fixed to the north end of the building. Carriage work necessary because of damage or 'fair wear and tear' was not carried out here though. Attending to interior wood partitions and panelling, including surface treatments, was done by finishers and polishers in 19B Shop, which was under the same roof as 24 Shop. The reason for this was so that the vehicles could be painted and varnished externally at the same time.

Work carried out in various areas of 19 Shop included lifting vehicles, stripping and assembling bogies, overhauling brakework and replacing vacuum cylinders, oil-gas burning equipment, sanding gear and heating equipment etc. Upholstery repairs were also done at the top end of the shop by carriage trimmers. Unlike construction of new coaches, some repair work involved working underneath in inspection pits between the rails. This building was known by everyone as 'The Klondyke', a name it was given when it was the old Carriage Lifting and Paint Shop. There are differing views as to how the nickname, which goes back to at least 1900, came about.

Because of the serious decline of cattle carried by train, these shops converted large numbers of cattle wagons into fruit vans from the late 1930s onward. The carrying of fruit was a business restricted only by limited facilities. It was a straightforward job to remove the floor battens, fit louvre panels and ventilators and replace doors.

Stan Leach worked in 19D Shop from 1953: this area was known to the men as the 'buffer, brake and drawgear' shop. His gang inspected and, if necessary, removed and replaced the various types of springs, tie rods and brakegear of gas tank vehicles with Chargeman Sid Adams. The bogies or running gear, including axleboxes, were dealt with by the carriage lifters in 19C Shop. When returned to traffic the tanks were filled at the adjacent Gas Works so that carriage examiners at the depots could use them to recharge the oil-gas tanks of their passenger carriages. These vehicles, together with milk tanks, fish vans and others had brakes, bearings and motion that were suitable for them to be coupled to the rear of passenger trains.

Stan also spent time with the horse box section. Horse box bodies were nearly all made of oak, with some elm fittings as these would not give horses splinters. Stan was employed putting in greenheart timber floors with oak battens for the tough wear and tear they would receive. Later he was converting old passenger stock to outstation mess vans and tunnel maintenance vehicles. The other large repair building was 24 Shop. Here the majority of the work was external body repairs and painting. Before this shop was brought into use in 1930, a lot of this work was done on sidings in the open.

Ivor Wilkins: Electrician

A lot of the electrical work required on coaches was undertaken outside or in other carriage shops. What was done in 5 Shop (train lighting equipment) was concerned mainly with the maintenance of coach dynamos and batteries and this workshop was better known as the 'battery house'. This work could be uncomfortable and hot because the battery gang had to wear leather, and later rubber, aprons, boots and gloves for protection from the sulphuric acid that got everywhere. Reconditioning and testing of train lighting equipment was also done in one end of this shop.

No. 5 Shop, part of which was occupied by a stores warehouse, had outgrown itself by the time the diesel multiple unit contracts were placed in the mid-1950s. Ivor said that this workshop had started life as a Nissen hut in the Great War (I think he must have been referring to the adjacent electric stores building). By 1960 a new building for electrical train lighting had been proposed.

Groups of electricians were sent to Swindon Works in the early 1930s to learn about electric lighting that was being installed in modern coaches. Here is class number 30 at the start of a two-week course in May 1931. There were sixteen men in this class from carriage depots all across the system. The camaraderie must have been good as everyone has signed the back of this photograph and added the name of their particular depot. *Author's collection*

Ivor went into the Works in 1954 as an electrician. He had just finished his apprenticeship with the firm Tucker & Pearce, at the top of Victoria Road. Typically, he came from a Swindon family with roots deep in its railway industry. Ivor's father, Bill, started in the Works in 1906 and became a rail planer in the Points and Crossings' Shop, and his father's father had been a signalman at Rodbourne Lane Box until he retired in 1933. You might think that the work of a rolling stock 'sparky' was light and fairly clean but that wasn't Ivor Wilkins' experience.

They put me on Jack Cook's gang refurbishing the dynamos, which generated DC current for carriage lighting. Jack was a 'down homer' from Wolverton Carriage Works: so called because he was one of those who was fond of saying 'we don't do that down home'. I had to take each dynamo outside on a handcart as they weighed 5 cwt. They got filthy dirty under the coaches in service, so first I had to scrape the worst of the dirt off, then blow them through with a compressed air line. Occasionally bits of body tissue from suicides were mixed in with the muck that was caked on. Back in the shop the dynamos were dismantled and the armature, which weighed about 2 cwt, was put up between centres on a lathe and the brushes skimmed. The whole thing was then reassembled and tested.

My next job was in 24 Shop, where coach bodywork was repaired and repainted after overhaul. I had to scrape all the muck off of the external electric cables [in service these were plugged together between coaches]. They were then inspected for deterioration and passed or replaced as necessary. My colleagues here were Georgie Crees and Alfie Ponting, who were both nearing retirement. After seven months I felt I was getting all the worst jobs, so I applied for, and got, a move to E Shop. They installed and maintained the electrical power and lighting circuits in Works' buildings and plant.

About a year later [1955] I was temporarily moved back to refit coaches that had been used in General Eisenhower's wartime train. We were doing some conversion work, including wiring Holborn convector heaters on these former staff cars. Draughtsman Eddie Lomas came to see me and asked if I would like to work in the Drawing Office as my foreman had recommended me. The Loco Drawing Office had taken on a lot of diesel work at that time and were recruiting tradesman from the shop floor. I agreed and began working on electrical wiring layouts for the new 350hp diesel shunters. Considering I had to go back to night school to get additional qualifications, I didn't think my starting salary of £530 per annum was good enough. Therefore I returned to E Shop in April 1956 with a gang rewiring the lighting and power points in the CME building.

BRITISH TRANSPORT COMMISSION

BRITISH RAILWAYS

APPRENTICESHIP AGREEMENT

This Agreement made the **Twentyfifth** day of **October** 1954 BETWEEN **Harold Gordon JOHNSON, WORKS MANAGER, CARRIAGE & WAGON WORKS, SWINDON,**

on behalf of the BRITISH TRANSPORT COMMISSION (hereinafter called " the Commission ") of 222, Marylebone Road, St. Marylebone in the County of London of the first part, and **William Henry Percy RICHENS,**

of **165, Whitworth Road, Swindon,**

in the County of **Wiltshire** (hereinafter called " the Guardian ") of the second part, and **Dennis Arnold John RICHENS,**

of **165, Whitworth Road, Swindon,**

in the County of **Wiltshire,**

(hereinafter called " the Apprentice ") of the third part.

WHEREAS—

1. The Apprentice has completed a period of probation from the **Thirtieth** day of **August** 1954 to the **Twentysecond** day of **October** 1954 and has attained the age of 15 years.

2. The Commission are willing to accept the Apprentice to be taught and instructed in the craft of **Wood Wagon Building.**

3. The Guardian having enquired into the nature of the business conducted by the Commission desires that the Apprentice shall learn the craft of **Wood Wagon Building** in the service of the Commission.

Now it is hereby AGREED as follows :—

(1) The Apprentice, of his own free will and with the consent of the Guardian, hereby binds himself as Apprentice to the Commission in the craft of **Wood Wagon Building** on the conditions hereinafter appearing.

The front page of Dennis Richens' apprenticeship agreement. The document lays out the commitments expected of not only the apprentice, but also his father, as surety for his son. Before the war the probationary period prior to the five-year training was one month and was unpaid. By the time of Dennis's apprenticeship in the 1950s, the three-month probation period was paid. Typically his 'time' was to start shortly after the sixteenth birthday. The agreement was signed by the carriage & works' manager, Dennis and his father. It was witnessed by J.C. Morkot, a clerk in the C&W staff section. After completing his time in 1959, Dennis worked as a carpenter in 12 Shop. Here he would have made and repaired furniture and platform barrows etc., in use throughout the Western Region. *Author's collection*

Wagon Piecework

Every operation performed on component parts had a piecework price payable in full if the gang got through a certain amount of scheduled work per fortnight. A 13 and 21A Shops' piecework register for 1958 shows how much in old pence, or shillings if more work was involved, had been negotiated. Alongside the name of the item and a p/w number, the operations are described as such things as mark out, punch, shear, guillotine, bend, straighten, level, drill, joggle, rivet, grind, cut by profile machine, carry, dress down or fit up each part, or set of parts if more than one was required, per wagon. The register also shows that unskilled labour not involved in production work were, by 1958, also receiving piecework bonus rather than a fixed day rate as before.

Labourers' work in the wagon shops included drawing out smaller parts from stores or warehouses and transporting them to the shop; removing swarf from machine tools and topping up the coolant; sweeping and removing refuse from incoming wagons; keeping shop gangways clear and clean; issuing items from shop stores; cleaning and attending to hand washing troughs. One labourer was paid 4s 6d a week extra just for switching on and off all the electric shop lighting. This seems very generous for those days but he would have had to arrive and depart at least fifteen minutes before and after the shift times.

Women in the Workshops

In peacetime, female conciliation and wages' staff were employed in certain types of manual railway work. In the CME Dept they could be office cleaners, charwomen, gatekeepers, carriage cleaners, linen sewers and machinists. At Swindon they were also employed as stores' assistants and laundresses. Before the war women's pay for manual work was about half what the unskilled workshop man took home and girls were paid less again. However, the published wage tables for females that I have seen do not state whether they are for full or part-time hours. Office cleaners' hours, for instance, are known to have varied considerably. It is also worth remembering that a man's working conditions were likely to be a lot tougher.

Women ('ladies' were in the offices) worked in the down carriage side. This was the name used for the shops spread out along the south side of the GWR main line: the ones mostly associated with new carriage building. The trimmers, polishers and linen sewers sections, where women were employed, faced on to London Street. In some cases they did the same types of work as men but separate from them. Female manual workers were working 'inside' before the Great War but details are scarce. In the 1930s and after they were working with a range of fabrics or applying wood finishes to carriage interiors and furniture. For some reason the utilisation of female labour was never fully exploited in the carriage shops, in peacetime or during the war, perhaps because of prejudices and the perception of traditional family roles.

Male trimmers made ready the fabrics and horse hair stuffing for the upholsterers to fit out passenger coach seats and interiors. They also produced a range items required across the railway, articles made of leather, canvas, linoleum, felt, rope and moquette in particular. These included such things as despatch bags, aprons, coach window straps and axlebox pads. Another men's section worked over on the carriage repair side. The women's section produced cushion linings, window blinds, towels, bed linen and pillow cases etc.

The linen sewers in 9A Shop worked with a range of fabrics and leather. The majority of their handicraft was used in the fitting out carriage interiors. *GWR*

Mr Duck was the foreman over the 9 (trimmers), 10A (polishers), 9A (linen sewers) and 19A (polishers and finishers' repairs) Shops in the 1930s. No. 9A Shop was staffed entirely by women and occupied an area alongside the trimmers' section' facing on to London Street. The windows were frosted over but they did provide some welcome natural light to work by. Some of the work done in the Linen, or Sewing Room, for the company's coaches, including sleeping cars, refreshment rooms and hotels, was passed on to the trimmers for further work, or vice-versa.

Although some of their work had to be done by hand, the sewers worked mainly with table-top machines. For instance, they put seams on lace doilies, flags, tablecloths, towels, sheets, slip covers and antimacassars. Carriage blinds, axlebox pads and netting for luggage racks were also among the many types of items that passed through the Sewing Room to have work carried out on them.

A purpose-made women's rest room and mess room were provided in 1939 for employees of 9, 9A and 10A Shops. The Works had also provided a welfare section for women (and men) by the 1930s: the rest of the company did not get a woman's welfare officer until 1941. Of the 123 females in the Carriage Works in 1947, just twenty-four were under twenty-one years of age.

French Polishers

Before 1939 there were three polishing sections, one of which was staffed by women and overseen by forewoman Miss Fagin. Margaret Kirby worked there in 1941 and remembers her forewoman was Miss Warren, who lived in Princes Street. By the end of the war all three polishing sections of 10A (Polishers') Shop were staffed by women. The polishers prepared the interior carriage woodwork and practiced the art of French polishing, staining and lacquering, to produce high-quality finishes on mahogany,

oak and walnut surfaces. The displaced men, if they hadn't been called up, were presumably moved to similar work in 7C Shop or over to the carriage repair shops.

Beryl Wynn (nee Odey) came from a typical Swindon family in that the men of each generation had been in the Works and formed a lineage back to its earliest days. Her father, Albert Odey, was apprenticed to French polishing in about 1912 and stayed 'inside' all his working life. He was never put on short time or dismissed, something the company were quick to do before the war in 1939 whenever orders were down.

Bert, and others of his trade, French polished and/or lacquered hardwoods, which were used for carriage interiors and furniture. This was a slow process that required several applications of cellulose lacquer, shellac and spirit and needed skill and experience to achieve the right finish. Male French polishers worked in part of 7 Shop or, before 1945, 10A Shop on the south side of the main line. Others were in the body repair and repainting shop, where they worked on carriages in for overhaul. Beryl too, was expected to go on to learn her father's trade 'inside' but resisted it: 'I developed a loathing of the distinctive pear drop smell that was always present when dad was around. I didn't want the stained hands of a polisher either: it looked like bad nicotine stains.'

Maureen Eveness went into the Works as an apprentice French polisher in 10A Shop in 1954. She left school at Easter having just turned fifteen years of age. Her older sister, Margaret, worked in the offices of the Stores Department, as mentioned in Chapter 10. Maureen would ride in from her home in Cheney Manor Road and leave her bicycle in the racks on the ground floor below the polishing shop. She explains her typical working day:

All the internal doors [usually eight or nine], handrails, panels and wood fittings from the same coach came to us as one batch. The old finishes and polish was removed by 'pickling'. All the girls on that section had to wear rubber gloves as the chemical stripper would burn their hands. After that the surfaces were scraped, sanded and washed before they arrived at our section for treatment.

All the work was now done with the surfaces horizontal starting with a coat of 'colour', which we mixed from a powder and brushed on. Each type of wood required a different shade of 'colour'. When that was dry the first coat of a proprietary polish was applied. For this we used a pad made of wadding wrapped in old cotton material we had brought in from home, it being better than what was provided. The chargehands checked the tone and sheen at each stage. For inspection, all the work had to be positioned to catch the natural light. Once they passed it, two of us would carefully turn the doors over to treat the other side. Each coating took a day to dry so we would work on the other carriage fittings in between. Three or four further coats of French polish, which was shellac dissolved in spirit, were put on to build up to the required surface finish.

Other girls in our shop were June Allan from Gorse Hill; Edith Eggleton from Whiteman Street; Diane Inkpen from [Wootton] Bassett; Sandra Weaver from Hook; Pam Dowswell from Whitworth Road; Eva Prentiss from Broadway; Margaret Pearce; and Jean Brooks. Violet Newton was one of the two chargehands, the other woman's name I can't now recall. A chap named Reg, who lived in Whitworth Road, did some labouring in our shop and looked after the check board.

As elsewhere in the Works, females in positions of authority were of a different generation to the girls in their charge. Consequently, they felt little affinity towards them. That, together with having to justify their positions, ensured that most supervisors applied the rules ruthlessly. For instance, talking in the Polishing Shop was only allowed in the course of ones' work. 'You had to ask to go off to the toilet. The answer usually included the order: "Don't have a cigarette",' said Maureen. To be fair, anything that reduced the risk of fire in these areas had to be strictly enforced.

French polishing was very labour intensive and therefore expensive. Since the 1920s alternatives such as spray polishing were used for some applications. In Maureen's time French polishing still gave the best results but it was considered to be old fashioned. Art Fortune, who was an apprentice coach builder in 4 Shop, said: 'We were allowed five days to put a (carriage) shell together. If we finished early I would go along and watch the French polishers at work: it was fascinating.'

The Western Region wanted new modern materials such as laminated plastics and Formica that were not only considered more stylish but also cheaper, durable and easier to keep clean. As new coaches with modern interiors were introduced the remaining work went to the men's polishing section. More and more females found themselves having to clean glass, chromium plate and felt instead of the craft they were trained for but this did keep them employed for a while longer.

The Polishing Shop was finally closed in 1958 and Maureen and her colleagues were made redundant. Only Miss Woodruffe, the forewoman, was retained: she was given a position in the offices until retirement. The unions had an agreement that where men did the same work as women, the women would be first out if dismissals were to take place. In those times, everyone accepted that the male breadwinner was more dependent on long-term employment.

Royal Visit: 1950

Princess Elizabeth visited Swindon Works on the afternoon of 15 November 1950 after performing some civic duties in the morning. Her time in the Works was brief but she was shown what was considered to be the more interesting aspects of activity in the Locomotive Works. The princess also performed the naming ceremony of the last 'Castle' class locomotive to be built. The name it was given was *Swindon* in recognition of the town's fiftieth anniversary of the incorporation of the Borough.

As had happened when her grandfather George V visited in 1924, the longest-serving staff were presented to the royal guest on her tour around the workshops. The princess was naturally taken around the areas of the carriage shops, mentioned above, where the work of the female manual workers could be seen. Those who met Her Royal Highness included Miss B.J. Baden, forewoman in charge of the Sewing Room, who had worked 'inside' for an impressive forty-six years; Miss M. Webb, linen sewers' chargewoman, who had completed thirty-one years; Miss R.M. Woodroffe of the Polishing Shop, twenty-nine years; and Miss I. Newton, French polisher, twenty-six years' service.

Princess Elizabeth on the footplate of the engine that bore her name. This was at the end of her visit to the Works in 1950. The locomotive, which was named after one of her recent ancestors, was parked outside A Shop, ready to return the train and royal party to Paddington.
BRWR courtesy of The Swindon Society

18

The Telephone Exchange

An Essential Service

Immediate communication had become an essential part of the GWR by the turn of the last century. The telegraph, telephone and, later, the teleprinter, were vital to the safe and efficient working of the railway. The main centres within the GWR Company had electro-mechanical telephone switchboards by the early 1930s. They were Paddington, Swindon, Bristol and Plymouth, with two more brought into use in 1932. At each of these facilities, access to the Post Office network was available and omnibus circuits connected outlying stations, depots and signal boxes to a central switchboard. To reach points on the railway further afield, additional trunk lines were being installed so that calls could be made with less chance of the line being busy.

A booklet was issued after the war summarising the Borough of Swindon's Civil Defence Organisation. It stated that the Works' Exchange had been designated as an important report and control centre in the event of air raids and invasion. Therefore, at these most dangerous of times, the exchange operators needed to be at their posts. They were almost unique among the Works' many types of workers in that they could not go to the relative safety of the shelters and underground tunnels when 'enemy aircraft overhead' alerts were given. Their only protection was tin hats and wooden shutters up at the windows. They couldn't be spared to participate in fire drills either.

Exchange and Telegraph Office

This office was on the ground floor of the CME building. As you reached the top of the slope from the tunnel entrance, it was on the right. Until 1952 there was a manual switchboard for the internal, and another for the external, telephone systems. The old network had made intercommunications possible for around 350 Works' extensions. It was still known as the Exchange and Telegraph Office but by the 1930s the directory was using the title GWR Swindon Telephone Exchange. Up until that time the Works telephone number was 185 and the telegraphic codes were 'Loco' or 'Carriage, Swindon'.

Signalmen were advised of alterations to the operating conditions in their sections by electric telegraph. Messages between signal boxes, telegraph offices and area switchboards such as Swindon were sent and received in the form of telegrams. Phrases in common use when communicating railway business were represented by a single code word. The Swindon exchange handled a lot of this communication. This was because a great deal of it originated from or was destined for the running superintendent's section, based in the Works.

In the 1940s, local teleprinter omnibus circuits were being installed. Messages could then be typed and transmitted between two distant points on the railway system via telegraph wires much the same as for Morse telegraphy. Teleprinter machines were very similar to typewriters to operate, and therefore required little or no training. The skill came with not having to keep referring to a code book for the short-form words. This would save the operator time and the receiver's machine would print a message that was comprehensible and to the point. In Western Region days, and possibly earlier, messages often finished with the words 'walnut read', which meant 'arrange and advise all concerned'.

From the instructions for use given in the 1935 Works' directory, we know that there were two internal telephone networks in use at that time. This was because the original Strowger switch exchange apparatus could not be discontinued until the later version, with improved electric circuitry, was ready to take over reliably. The earlier telephones were the upright or candlestick pattern with a microphone and separate ear piece. They had call buttons to alert the operator so that the desired extension number could be given. The receiver was then replaced to await a connection. The so called 'new pattern' was the black Bakelite desktop type with a combination handset.

This view shows the internal 'doll's eye' switchboard in the old exchange. It must have been taken in 1952 just before the new building nearby was brought into use or during the changeover period. Peggy Wallis, in the centre, only started work here in February that year. Violet Peaple is the other operator. *Marion Reeves' collection*

Serious congestion at GWR telephone exchanges was one of the matters mentioned in the regular circulars sent out by the Superintendent of the Line's dept in wartime. Three days after the start of the Second World War, it was stated that many staff were using telephones to enquire about the altered timetable services. They should instead 'refer to the publicity available and not call the, already very busy, telephone operators'.

Direct trunk lines were provided to telephone exchanges sited at all the more important railway stations on the Great Western and later the Western Region. The busiest places, Paddington and Bristol, had two lines each. They allowed communication to be made between the departments in the Works and departments all over the system without relying on the Post Office network.

Muriel Everrett: Switchboard Operator

Muriel worked in the E&T Office for four years, from leaving school in 1944. She remembers:

The internal switchboard was split between 'carriage' and 'locomotive' sides and there were two operators manning it during the day. There was no STD dialling: when a caller picked up the receiver one of the switchboard terminal windows fell open. We put a jack plug into the appropriate socket, flicked a switch forward and asked the caller for 'number please'. They then gave you the number or the shop, office or department they wanted to be put through to.

To make a Post Office, omnibus or railway trunk call, the caller dialled '0' or, with telephones that had no dial, the hand combination was removed and held to the ear. They then had to give you their extension number followed by the number, person or department required. We then obtained the required number using telephone dials on the desktop in front of us. The external switchboard was usually manned by three operators, who would greet all incoming calls with simply 'Great Western Railway', later 'British Railways'.

When I mentioned the 'telephone voice' that was associated with telephonists, especially in times gone by, Muriel said: 'We had to speak clearly, so yes, I suppose we did sound different than normal. If we got into a conversation with the person on the other end, the tone became more relaxed.'

Muriel recalled working from 8am to 2pm or from 2pm to 8pm, five days a week. (Only men manned the switchboards at night and for them the longer night shift meant working fewer shifts per fortnight.) She also had to work quite a few Saturdays and Sundays. For this, of course, a day off in the week was taken. For instance, the people working early on a Sunday got the next day off, and those working a late got the following Thursday off. Muriel said that herself and a colleague would sometimes go to London on their weekday off, using their reduced rail fare passes. By the time Marion Davis started, in 1952, the number of starting and finishing times during the day had doubled, as a consequence of a shorter working week. This gave everyone, regardless of shift, a break at dinnertime and in the evening.

The New Exchange

A purpose-built automatic telephone exchange building became fully operational in the summer of 1952. The installation of electrical supply plant, air conditioning plant, staff amenities, cabling and exchange equipment took four years of planning. Mr Woodbridge, the signal and telegraph engineer for the Western Region, supervised the work. During the war, there was an increase in communications, in and out, via a Works' switchboard that was already working to capacity. This highlighted the fact that a new automatic exchange was long overdue. The old E&T Office now, or sometime later, became a time office.

The site of this new facility was between the southern end of the CME Offices and the main line. Excavations must have gone down well below the height of the built up land as fossilised vertebrae from an Ichthyosaurus were found. This was an extinct marine reptile, measuring up to 40ft in length, which lived millions of years ago. The top floor of the proposed two-storey building was earmarked for a section of the drawing office. An air conditioning plant where air was filtered and cleaned and temperature and humidity were controlled took up most of the basement. A passageway for access and cables led off from the main tunnel entrance into this basement.

The new exchange had an ancillary five-position manual switchboard allied to it. Lights and buzzer alerts replaced the old drop-down call indicators. It served the 495 Works' extensions listed in the 1952 telephone directory. Of these, about half could be used to make and receive railway trunk and Post office calls, via the operator. Thirteen bus circuits were also available via the switchboard operators. They connected outlying stations such as district inspectors, goods yards, booking offices and signal boxes within a 40-mile radius. Eleven post office trunk lines were brought into use via the manual side of the switchboard by dialling '0': six for incoming calls and five for outgoing calls. The new equipment also allowed for future expansion.

Polished parquet flooring was used in the switchboard area and the supervisor's desk was behind, but facing, the operators' backs. The switchboard panel was positioned parallel to the main line and behind it there was the Telegraph Office. The partition wall had what one operator called 'some very futuristic glass blocks' in it to make the most of the natural light. Other parts of the ground floor were taken up with an Apparatus Room; a Ladies Room; a Linesmen's Room and a Telephone Room. In the Telegraph Office an electro-mechanical teleprinter was installed so that typewritten messages could be sent and received between one or more points instantly, using the Telex network.

Marion Davis: Messenger Girl

Marion started work in the Works' exchange in early 1952, 'just a few days before the king died'. She recalled:

I lived in Dowling Street at the time, at the house I was born in. As I was about to leave Drove Secondary (Girls) School I enquired about becoming a telephonist in the GPO but they had no vacancies. So, with another girl I knew from school, Margaret Wallis, we applied to the telephone exchange at Swindon Works. Margaret was known as Peggy: her father owned a furniture shop in the town called Norman's.

The Exchange supervisor, Miss Gutridge, interviewed us and gave us both a job. We were both fifteen years' old and were given a six-month probationary period. She told me that one of my duties would be to make the tea and that she always had her own china cup. My new boss was coming up to retirement and I found her very nice as I got to know her better. My father Bert was a coach body builder in 24 Shop [and highly regarded according to others who remember him]. Other than that the only other people I knew 'inside' were my friend Lavinia Kibblewhite and my second cousin, Peggy Butler. They were both in CME Accounts somewhere.

You never used Christian names, it was always Miss, Mrs or Mr, and their surname. No one seemed to use job titles here but I classed myself as the messenger girl. Until the new exchange opened in July, I was based in the Exchange and Telegraph Office, to give it its full name. In here there were two telephones and two manual switchboards: one for the Works' extension lines and the other for outside lines. The office was about 15ft × 10ft with another little room, like a converted cupboard, leading off, where the two teleprinters were set up on desks.

There was also a restroom where I made the tea. I would have to make 14 or 15 cups, but only in the afternoons as there was no time deducted for a break then. Therefore the company would allow a mid-afternoon drink as long as the work wasn't affected. Even after the new exchange took over I was left to run errands for more than a year but I didn't mind. It meant I didn't have to work late shifts, which finished at 9.30pm. I just worked 8.30am to 5.30pm. Everyone else had to do their share of afternoons and evenings as well as split shifts: mornings and evenings. I always went home for lunch, as did most people, even though we only had just over an hour. When I did go on to shifts the late turn break was one and a quarter hours and I could have a slightly more leisurely meal at home.

Marion: Telegram Clerk

The teleprinter machines would start up without notice and my main duty as messenger was to cut the paper tape and stick it on to teleprinter dispatches (telegrams) then get them checked. If I was busy somewhere else I might return to find the role of tape coming from the machine all over the floor. When this happened someone would often say: 'It was like this all the time during the war.' Miss Ryman was assistant supervisor and in charge of the Telegraph Office. She usually checked the telegrams, after which I wrote the particulars in a book: where they came from and who they were destined for. XP coded telegrams took priority. If I found a discrepancy I would have to type back: 'Please repeat.' Sometimes I would be required to send telegrams too.

A lot came in from the divisional superintendent's offices and were addressed to 'Pellow GWR Swindon'. They were concerned with locomotive breakdowns, derailments and engines not adhering to their shed diagrams. I would telephone them through or take them the short distance to the Motive Power Office. This department was known to Works' staff as 'engines on the move'. After handing the telegrams to Mr Pellow [the superintendent], he would initial them in my presence.

Other staff that I remember having to visit were Mr Gardner, the chief accountant for the Western Region; Mr Squires in the C&W manager's office; Mr Fluck in the Mileage Office on the top floor; Mr Spurlock upstairs in the Fuel Office; Mr Purdy in the Loco Works Managers' Office; and Mr Chesterman in the Correspondence Office. There were two Stores' managers named Mr Webb, so that could be confusing. The Shopping Control Office and the Staff Office, both on the ground floor, also received regular telegrams.

The clerk in the Drawing Office would tell me to cut through that long L-shaped office rather than go round the long way if it would shorten the distance to my next call. Some of the staff there sensed that I was a bit self-conscious and would tap out a clip-clop sound to synchronise with my footsteps. It was all meant, and taken, as harmless fun.

Janet Morgan, in CME Accounts, also remembers being made to feel embarrassed when walking through there as a youngster.

Marion: Switchboard Operator

'Works' extension numbers could not be dialled direct [STD dialling was not possible until the new exchange took over], so the callers had to be connected via the smaller of the two switchboards. The operator faced a vertical socket panel that we called the 'doll's eye' switchboard. When someone picked up a receiver at the other end a drop indicator would 'fall down' exposing their extension number in a window that looked like a doll's eye. The

operator would plug a jack into the socket that had lit up. We would then flick a switch forward on the desk and ask the caller which number they required. Then, assuming the line wasn't engaged, we connected them.

I never worked on the larger switchboard in the old exchange as I was still very junior. The operators would later say that it was hard work, when comparing it with the automatic board in the new building. The public had to ring into the exchange and be put through to 'train enquiries' and that alone kept the switchboard busy: there was often a queue of callers holding the line.

Having been able to get out and about I learnt things that would now help me. For instance, staff and the public could ring us up on Ext. 2066 and make enquiries. The knowledge I picked up would often help me to advise them or put them through to the relevant person or department. It used to get hot and stuffy in the old office as the weather got warmer because there were windows on two sides. There was no such problem in the new air-conditioned exchange.

Once I was permanently manning the switchboards I discovered that the operators weren't so cut off from the rest of the workforce after all. When out and about, and particularly in the tunnel going to and from work, you would hear people and think, I know that voice, even though you had never met them. Mr Smeddle spoke very quietly and I always worried that I would have to ask him to repeat the request. Mr Hawksworth rang occasionally even though he had long since retired: he spoke in a very authoritative manner.

All the local signalmen would ring up on the omnibus circuit to get the exact time [the Magenta 'master' clock from the Loco Managers Office was moved into the automatic exchange]. This was so that they could, if necessary, adjust the clocks in their signal boxes. They usually rang in the evening when it was quieter unless they had any reason to use the switchboard during the day. You got to know the staff that used the telephones regularly by the sound of their voices, and you got a mental picture of them in your mind. The younger signalmen would have a laugh with us as the supervisors had gone home and sometimes a girl was asked out. Two or three operators married signalmen: Gwen Breakspear was one and I was another.

Without realising it, we became aware of the time by the passage of non-stop expresses that passed close by the exchange. The noise was amplified by the Works' buildings either side of the main line. On weekdays the Red Dragon express raced through just before midday and an increasing roar at about 5.10pm meant that The Bristolian was on time as it too made its way up to Paddington.

An amusing incident occurred during the early days of the first Swindon (main line) diesels. I took a call from Friedrichshafen for Mr Smeddle and rang his secretary. While waiting for the CM&EE to answer the other phone she enquired: 'How's the weather over there,' obviously thinking I was in Germany rather than on another part of the Works. Trying to sound 'matter of fact', I said: 'Oh it's fine and dry,' and she said: 'It's much the same here too.'

Sometimes we were asked to get somebody on the telephone, in Munich or Friedrichshafen, in connection with contracts we had for diesel-hydraulic components. The lady on the continental switchboard in London referred to international callers, held in a queue, by the country they were waiting to be put through to. When speaking to me she would say 'connecting you now Miss Germany'.

Staff

Female staff began to be employed as telegraphists from 1912: perhaps that's when the Works first had a centralised telegram and telegraph office. A seventeen-year-old Emily Gutridge was possibly the first female to be employed on this work. The GWR staff register shows that she was a 'learner' for her first two weeks, in January 1912, then made supervisor! Other long-serving GWR/BRW T&T Office operators were Ada Retter and assistant supervisor, Winifred Ryman.

Muriel Everrett remembers the three aforementioned staff from her time here in the 1940s. She also recalled Violet Peaple, Eileen Waterhouse (started in 1937), Elizabeth Smith, Pat Turner and also Joyce Brunger and Rene Newman (both started in 1933), Nell Saunders, Joan Moon and Irene Cottrell. Betty Carter was another:

she married one of the linesmen who repaired and maintained the exchange apparatus.

No particular academic qualifications were required for acceptance but a good school report or previous employer's reference was essential. Even then there was the entrance test and medical, of course. Violet Peaple started as a learner telegraphist in 1936 on a rate of 13 shillings (per week). From her seventeenth birthday, a month later, Violet was considered competent enough to be left unsupervised and her rate increased to 17/6d (17 shillings and 6 pence). At each birthday her pay rate would increase further until she reached the extent of the pay scale for her profession. Only by becoming a supervisor or training assistant would she be paid more again. The company employment records show that these figures were slightly lower than the equivalent GWR clerical worker of the time.

After the war, and perhaps earlier, the exchange was staffed by up to eleven females at any one time during the day: three seniors; two on the external switchboard; two on the 'doll's eye' manual switchboard; two or occasionally three on the telegraph side including a messenger. There would be two maintenance engineers available, who also had other work outside (and one on call at night) and an evening cleaner.

Here is the external switchboard in the pre-1952 exchange office. Like the previous picture, it was probably taken just before the new facility was fully functional. From left to right, the operators are Beryl Morse, Lizbeth Smith and Pat Chapman. *Marion Reeves' collection*

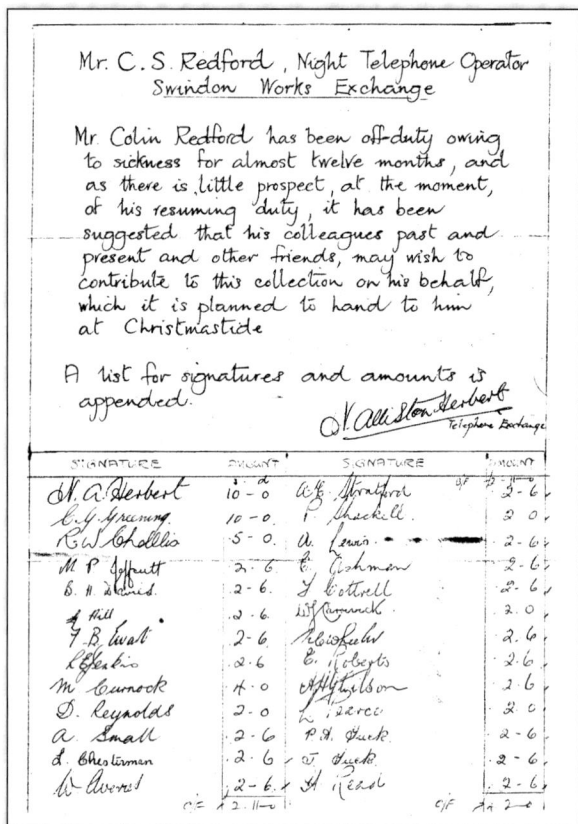

Mr. C. S. Redford, Night Telephone Operator
Swindon Works Exchange

Mr. Colin Redford has been off-duty owing
to sickness for almost twelve months, and
as there is little prospect, at the moment,
of his resuming duty, it has been
suggested that his colleagues past and
present and other friends, may wish to
contribute to this collection on his behalf,
which it is planned to hand to him
at Christmastide

A list for signatures and amounts is
appended.

Being a telephone operator at night was a lonely and isolated job. The staff in the exchange would have known Colin Redford in passing as he began or finished his night shifts. Nevertheless, he was obviously a popular member of staff. In 1955, Norman Alliston Herbert, another night worker in the exchange, arranged a collection for his friend who had been on long-term sick leave. As if that wasn't bad enough, Colin and his family were experiencing financial hardship. The well-known Swindon Works' benevolence is shown in this discourse and another list of contributors fills the back. Alas, Colin never did return to work: he died the following April. *Courtesy of Brenda Hanks*

In the early 1950s I'm told that three senior staff continued to oversee the activity during the day. Miss Gutridge and Miss Ryman were still there but now Violet Peaple had been promoted to training assistant. There were always four operators on the switchboards: only if it was very busy did the supervisor open up the fifth position. Although the new exchange building was more spacious and had a larger capacity, they still had the same amount of staff on at any one time.

With the help of several presentation photographs, Marion and others were able to name most of the switchboard operators at Swindon Works exchange after the war. They were Violet Peaple, Betty Gisbey, Beryl Morse, Jean Day, Elizabeth Smith, Pat Chapman (nee Turner), Eileen Waterhouse, Betty Carter, Liz Hancock (left c1951), Mary Lloyd, Sheila Dover, Maureen Green, Gwen Elliot, Ann Canfield, Mollie Clarke, Ann Cave, Eileen Cavill, Maureen Mabberley, Margaret Hillier and Barbara Smart.

Marion's younger sister, Ann, came to work here too, in 1958. Two male staff covered each night shift. After the war the night workers included Norman Alliston Herbert, Ron Challis, Colin Redford and Cecil Greening. A Mrs Curnock was the cleaner, who came in on weekday evenings. The telephone engineers, known as linesmen, included Maurice Jeffcutt (chief linesman and thought to have been here since before the war), ? Davies, George Hill, Frank Ewart, Ray Jenkins and John Read. They were also responsible for the common electrical wiring that regulated the 'slave' clocks, around the factory.

Miss E.A. Gutridge finally retired in 1955. She continued to live with an older sister in Burford Avenue but later she married the man she was often seen walking down Milton Road with on her way to work. Her assistant, Miss Ryman, also retired as a spinster at about the same time: her husband-to-be was killed during the war. It is thought that Violet Peaple, who started in 1936, now became acting supervisor. Marion married a Wootton Bassett signalman in 1960 and became Marion Reeves. At about the same time she became assistant supervisor and a Mrs Benson, who came from outside, took over as supervisor.

With so much reorganisation in the Works, the names of many of the extensions and the titles of the staff soon bore little resemblance to the 1952 telephone directory. Of course, the exchange had regularly revised information that their staff could refer to but if staff throughout the factory did not update their directories by hand they became unusable. Nevertheless, it is not thought that another was printed until 1962.

The presentation gathering for the retirement of Miss Gutridge, front right, in 1955. Marion is behind the woman with glasses, in the centre.
Marion Reeves' collection

19

Outdoor and Factory Maintenance

Outstation Commitments

The CME Dept installed, maintained and, when necessary, dismantled and rebuilt all mechanical equipment used by the railway company. The only exceptions were where special arrangements had been agreed with the manufacturers. Of the five assistants to the loco works' manager, three were responsible for outstation and outdoor machinery. If the equipment could not be brought into the Works for attention then the appropriate tradesmen were sent out to work on site.

In either case their base was the workshop at Swindon or other works, where spares and repair facilities were available. Their men were responsible for the electrical and working parts, while the water supplies, if any, were dealt with by men from the PL Shop. The company's docks had their own mechanical engineers, workshops and stores, but the Swindon workshops still dealt with their heavier work. Design work was also undertaken here in the Drawing Office. After nationalisation the Docks and Waterways became a separate department and this work went elsewhere.

Some Swindon men spent part of their working time away from the workshop, and some all their time away. The D Shop carpenters' and bricklayers' checkboard, for instance, continually displayed outstation checks for some personnel who were based there for the purposes of administration.

Water Troughs

Gangs of men based mainly in the L2 (tank) and PL (platelayers) Shops would go out to maintain the water troughs and with them would go the tool and mess vans. The galvanised steel plate troughs were 6in deep, 18in wide and, in sections, could be up to nearly 2,000ft long. They were fitted along the middle of the 'four foot' (track) at strategic points along the main routes allowing main-line locomotives to pick up water at speed.

With full line occupation and temporary speed restrictions on the other running lines, the 10ft sections of troughs were removed, repaired and replaced. Permanent way gangs also took the opportunity to work on the track at this time, thus minimising the disruption to train services. Trough maintenance was done mainly at night and could take up to a week before locomotives were again lowering their scoops to fill their tender tanks. Meanwhile, locomotives on non-stop trains would have to make unscheduled stops at stations to fill up at a water crane.

The Severn Tunnel

The Severn Tunnel ran through severely waterlogged ground and millions of gallons of water were left to seep into it through the bore structure, daily. This stopped the pressure building up around it but then that water had to be raised. In addition, more water ran down from the embankments on the approaches to the tunnel. Pumping stations were situated on both sides of the estuary: two at Sudbrooke on the Welsh side and two subsidiary pump houses on the English side. The four pumping shafts that had been installed in the 1880s handled up to 34 million gallons of water every twenty-four hours. Sudbrooke was the site of the main pumping plant. Not only was there the drainage water to contend with, but also an underground river known as the 'Big Spring'.

Electrical and mechanical gangs from Swindon would go outstation to do maintenance and repairs to the boilers, the old Cornish beam engines, pumps and ventilating fans. As most of the work had to be done on site they could be there for weeks at a time. The permanent staff included Mr Stephens, the works' manager, who was based at Sudbrooke, and the maintenance foreman who, from 1954, was Mr Bull: both were ex-Swindon men.

Gangs spent a lot of time underground replacing the suction and delivery valves and bucket plungers, which varied in size between 26in and 37in. Worn parts would

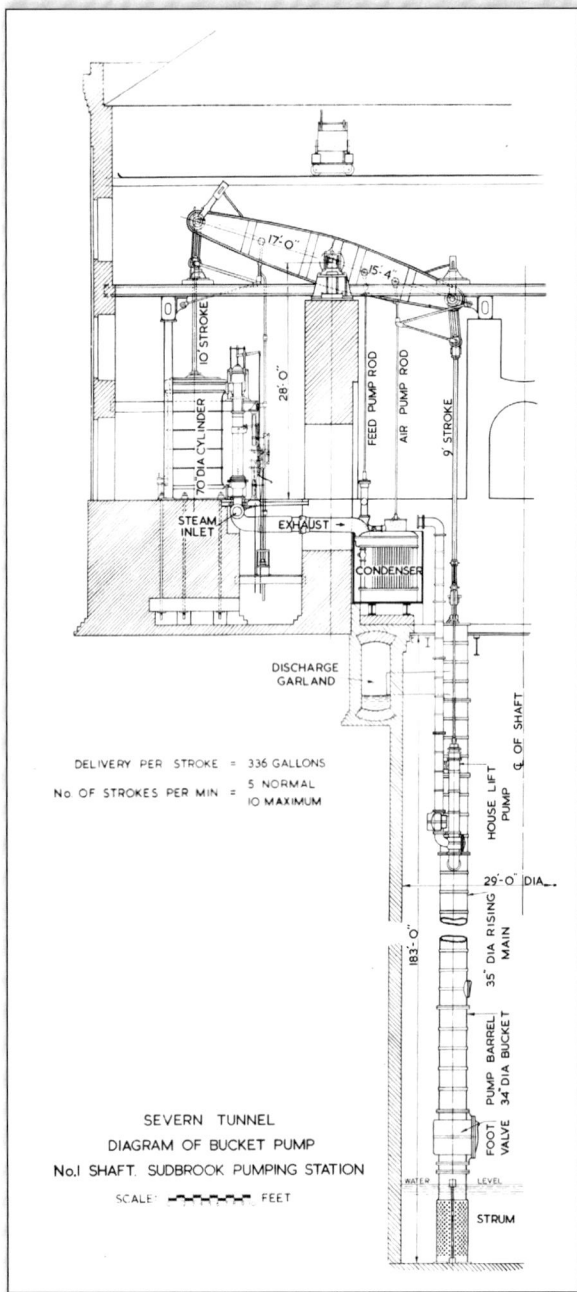

DELIVERY PER STROKE = 336 GALLONS

No. OF STROKES PER MIN = 5 NORMAL
10 MAXIMUM

SEVERN TUNNEL
DIAGRAM OF BUCKET PUMP
No.1 SHAFT. SUDBROOK PUMPING STATION

SCALE: ▬▬▬▬▬ FEET

Inside Seawall Pumping Station on the English side of the Severn Tunnel. It shows the top of a 70in steam cylinder and its valve gear (see also the previous diagram). Although there were resident engineers here to maintain the machinery, Swindon gangs came out to do repairs and new work. *BRWR*

any landslips due to leakage. Men went out daily to the electric and steam pumping station, which was just north of Kemble railway station. As the Railway Works and the adjacent Running Sheds expanded, so the wells were deepened in an attempt to increase the yield. A 24in diameter bore was sunk to a depth of 72ft in 1935. In the same year the Lancashire steam boilers and pumps were replaced by electric turbine pumps capable of pumping 75,000 gallons an hour.

A Works' maintenance gang would check, lubricate and, if necessary, replace crankshaft, crosshead and connecting rod bearings. At the bottom of the wells, the bucket plungers and valves in particular would often need attention like those of the Severn Tunnel pumps.

New seats and valves were fitted periodically to suction and delivery pumps. The cylinders, barrels and snuffing boxes of various types of these and other steam pumps were brought back to G Shop, Swindon, for turning back to true. If necessary the cast iron pump barrels were also brought in. They would be set up on a boring mill and bored out to accept the replacement gun metal liner, which was turned to suit the diameter of the plunger fitted.

Works' maintenance fitters kept the original steam pumps in working order in case of emergency. Swindon Shed would send a pannier tank loco to Kemble once a month, so that steam could be supplied to these pumps while their boilers were shut off for washing out and cleaning. The status of Kemble Pumping Station was, for maintenance purposes, classed as a Works' outpost. This meant that Swindon supplied the engineers and labourers on a full- or part-time basis as required.

be inspected and if possible the seating surfaces were turned and scraped to make them airtight and watertight once more, otherwise they were scrapped; it depended on the extent of the corrosion and pitting caused by silt and salt water.

The Cornish engines had all been replaced by electrified pumps by 1961 and again Swindon provided the manpower for the changeover. Swindon draughtsmen Terry French and Brian Stephens, son of the pumping stations' manager, had produced the drawings for the new pumps.

Kemble Water Supply

The CME Dept maintained the pumping plant and pipeline that brought the Works' water supply from a borehole in Kemble. They would also have to make good

G Shop Maintenance Fitter Norman Sanders is 'oiling round' one of the two steam engines kept in reserve at Kemble. Their boilers were no longer used, so when the electric pumps were switched off for maintenance the standby pumps were driven by steam from a tank locomotive. This photo was taken by apprentice Bob Grainger, who accompanied Norman 'outstation' on this occasion.

For short periods, the elevated water tanks at the Works ensured that disruption to the supply of water for industrial use did not affect demand. For longer periods they had access to water from the local authority (a 5in main had been laid under the railway estate and came into the Works near the tunnel entrance). Stopping the Kemble supply might be undertaken if: 1) the periodic chemical analysis was not right, 2) maintenance or repair of the pipeline joints was to be carried out, or 3) while the royal train, on its way to Cheltenham Races, ran over the route. The latter was effected in case a leak washed away the ballast and track.

If the pipeline did spring a leak, signalmen along the route were warned by a pressure gauge installed in their signal box. The reason for the loss of pressure had to be ascertained first, so the alarm in the Works' Fire Station was reset after thirty minutes. If it remained active the pumps would be stopped and the line closed. The Swindon Junction station pilot engine, together with a fitter and a mate from the PL Shop, would set off to find the leak at little more than walking pace. Part of the PL (plate layers) Shop dealt with water mains maintenance and they kept a large covered rail van stocked and ready to be taken out for emergencies.

Mechanical Maintenance Workshop

Maintenance staff worked all around the factory site as well as outstation, and could be on call seven days a week. G Shop was the mechanical maintenance workshop and the base for men maintaining and repairing all the overhead lifting appliances, cranes and pumps in the Works. Keeping the eight Stirling boilers that generated the steam for engines, steam hammers and heating in good order was their responsibility too. So were the plants necessary for the central supply and distribution of electric, hydraulic and pneumatic power and the oxygen and acetylene mains' supplies to the shops that required it.

All the heavy machinery inside the Works was cared for by G Shop men, as were internal transport vehicles and outstation mechanical equipment that could not be dealt with on site. Bricklayers from this shop had a cabin in the Rolling Mills from where they regularly had to replace the firebricks in the furnaces. This was just some of the varied and many types of work of the Works' maintenance men. Not quite everything was the responsibility of G Shop however: 'O' Shop maintenance fitters overhauled and repaired the smaller machine tools in W, L2 and K Shops, while men from the Boiler Shop maintained the manufacturing facilities for boiler mounting and steam testing in P1 Shop.

Hydraulic cylinders were bored on Kearns or the larger Shanks boring mills in G Shop. Hydraulic rams were machined on the Tangye lathe, which had the capacity to turn work up to 50ft in length. To make room for this machine tool to be installed, an internal wall of the workshop had to be knocked through. The 9in diameter rams were used to open and close dock gates. Some rams were more than 44ft long and were made in two sections, then joined using 2ft long dowels. The bored out ends were heated and the dowels screwed in as the ram expanded. The dowel would be held tight as the ram cooled and shrank around it.

Retirement presentation for Fred Selby in G Shop, 1953 or '54. In the front, left to right are: John Brettel, Foreman Bert Price, Harry Philpott, Ernie Simpkins (chief foreman), Fred Selby (maintenance chargeman) and Charlie People (chargeman painters). 'Of the senior G Shop staff at that time, only Inspector Jack Tyler is missing,' said John Brettell. *Evening Advertiser*

Manual capstan turntables used in goods yards for turning wagons were dismantled and brought to G Shop as well. The usual type was the 'Armstrong turnover' and most weighed 1 ton 30 cwt. Setting a capstan bed plate up on a vertical table of a boring mill was a specialised job. Capstan rams were also machined on a boring mill using a special fixture.

John Brettell moved from A Shop to G Shop in 1949. At that time it was still known as the old millwrights' shop by some of the older hands. Bill Brown was head foreman at that time, having taken over from Mr Marshman in the 1930s. Mr Simpkins took over from Mr Brown, then by 1954 Harry Philpott had become the G Shop and Wire Rope Shop foreman. It was not unknown for Mr Philpott to turn up in the workshop in the middle of the night if he could not sleep and was preoccupied with some work-related matter. There were some who said he was just checking up on what the night workers were, or were not, doing. John's first job was as a fitter in the shop, then late, an outstation fitter. After that he became a crane tester. Of the latter he told me:

Les Humphries and I would go all over the Western Region to supervise the regular loading tests that had to be carried out. My next move was to grade 2 workshop inspector before becoming assistant engineer (cranes) in the Drawing Office. All the electrical, boiler and crane inspectors now came under me: a combined total of ten or twelve men at Swindon and others throughout the Western Region. I, in turn, was answerable to the assistant mechanical and electrical engineer for outdoor machinery.

Each division would send in a report when they required work to be carried out. I would meet the engineers involved and submit a report to the head of department, detailing the conclusions reached and how best to apply the department's plant and resources. I also had to decide which depots should take on the work. The 'chief' (Mr Smeddle) never once questioned or changed my proposals.

Electrical Maintenance

E Shop was the electrical maintenance and installations' workshop for the factory and outstation. Like G Shop, they too had sections in some other shops. Carriage lighting and batteries were dealt with in 5 Shop. Most machinery was supplied with its own electrical motors, wiring and fuses, so it was just a case of stripping it down in conjunction with the fitters, cleaning and testing it periodically. Electric lighting equipment was also manufactured and installed by specialist firms in the first place. Any outstation maintenance that could not be done on site was brought back to E Shop. Bert Harber became an apprentice in E Shop in 1938:

There was no set programme of training: I gained experience with each gang in turn as determined by the foreman. There were about sixty men based in E Shop then; the two foremen were Mr Sutcliffe

The site of a former level crossing and crossing keeper's cottage at the end of Broome Manor Lane. It was listed in the electoral registers from 1945 onward, as 'GWR bungalow'. The single-track railway between Chiseldon and Swindon Town used to run across the road that led to a farm, immediately behind these buildings. Bell signals were received at the cottage to warn of approaching trains. GW Gas Works' staff maintained and repaired the gas plumbing here and presumably other trades from the Works looked after the other mains' services and building repairs. *Author*

and Mr Hugo. There were seven gangs and my first was with chargeman George Dan. There were also seven of us apprentices. [For this information Bert referred to a list of personnel he made at the time.] In 1942, our workshop was moved from a corner of O Shop, to take over a part of D Shop, over by the Running Sheds. It was about this time that I finished my training and was immediately called up. When I returned in 1947, the foremen, who had stayed on passed their normal retirement age, had been replaced by Mr Money and Mr Hewitt.

Bert told me that during the war electricians from E Shop worked outstation on new cranes being built at various South Wales docks. Two or three men, and sometimes himself as the apprentice, worked from 6am until 8pm under licence to Stothard and Pitt. They came home every other Saturday and returned again on Monday morning. On the other weekends they came back just overnight, for a bath and change of clothes.

Ivor Wilkins transferred to E Shop from electric train lighting work in November 1954. He remembers that there were seven sections or gangs there in his time too. They were three wiring; one high tension; two fitting; and one armature rewinding. There was also a lamp-cleaning gang made up of grade 3 men (unskilled). They would remove glass lamp covers hanging from roofs and ceilings with long poles, clean them and replace them the same way. Grade 3 men often went on to become fitter's mates with gangs of electricians.

The chargemen that Ivor remembers are Arthur Johnson and Bill 'Butty' Butt, on fitters' gangs, and Ted Sancto on the armature rewinding gang. The foremen were Les Money and Arthur Adams. Another E Shop electrician was Percy White. Ivor worked on Stan Hall's gang maintaining the DC motors that powered the old belt and shaft drives. This form of power was proving very uneconomic compared with the independent three-phase electric motors that were being installed with new machine tools.

The electricians had an ongoing programme of servicing plant and machinery with the fitters and this included working while production stopped for the annual holiday. For four years running in the 1950s, each one of the 100-ton overhead cranes in A Shop was overhauled in turn. Access to the cranes was via the stairs that led up to the men's toilets. Bert remembers the work started at 5.20pm on Friday as the day shift left for the two-week shutdown: 'We removed all the electrical gear as well as the motors and control gear then we stripped it down. The day before the end of the holiday, everything had to be back together ready for the testers to move in and do the load tests.'

There was no safety equipment available for those working high up in workshop roof spaces. Carpenter Arnold Woolford fell from an A Shop crane gantry about 1949. He had been replacing some duckboarding when he lost his balance. He broke both his ankles but it could have been a lot worse.

Other Outdoor and Outstation Work

Works' staff often went out just to evaluate the condition of mechanical equipment before a programme of work was authorised. In the summer, men worked away at carriage depots, removing the steam heating hoses from stock. They were then sent to Swindon for testing and repair or replacement by the 'steam gang'. This gang dealt with all the steam heating apparatus used on rolling stock. G Shop maintenance men periodically inspected the hydraulic capstans used in shunting yards. With these they would dismantle them to clean and grease the moving parts. The trunion valves too, regularly needed replacing: new ones were turned in G Shop and fitted on site.

Where changes to machinery and plant were necessary, draughtsmen would go out to make notes, take measurements and perhaps photographs too. The resulting drawings were used by the CME staff and/or contractors who were to do the work.

Permanent way work had become more mechanised by the 1950s and a corner of B Shed nicknamed 'the cage' became the track maintenance section for the Western Region. Ballast cleaners, tamping machines, track-laying machines and excavators were overhauled here, while intermediate repairs were usually done on site.

John Jefferies from Albion Street started an apprenticeship in the Western Region Gas Works in 1957. While waiting to reach the age of sixteen he had been 'rivet hotting' to 'Nobby' Clark in 21 Shop. John's father, Henry (Harry) Jefferies, worked in B Shop as a chargehand labourer. Although based in the Gas Works, John's work would take him all round the factory and beyond. Mains gas and water, as well as coal, were also provided for railway premises such as the Medical Fund, St Mark's Church and Vicarage. All had to be maintained. He remembers:

On one occasion after working on a dual-fuel [oil and gas] furnace in the Rolling Mills, the Gas Works' foreman Mr Ellison arrived to see it tested. A small leak caused a fine jet of oil to squirt over his light coloured and recently pressed smock: that was about 1958. Another time I was called out to an emergency in the Mechanics' Institute with a couple of gas fitters: probably Chargehand Jack Hedges and Ian Ricks. A coke-fired boiler had reached a very high pressure and the [weighted type] safety valve wouldn't lift. We had one chance before clearing the building and waiting for the explosion. I hit the valve as hard as I could with a large hammer. There was an almighty noise of escaping steam and the pressure slowly came down.

Replacing oil-gas lead seals on dining cars and their supply equipment took men from the Gas Works all over the Region. With each coach seen to, the system was tested to 150lb but worked at about 100lb psi. For this and other outstation work John usually went out with gas fitter Ernie Webb and sometimes fitters' mate Bill Tyler, as well.

One of the last jobs Gas Works' apprentice John Jefferies was involved with was renewing gas pipes and some gas fires at Old Town station in about 1960. John was made redundant upon completion of his time in 1961. Swindon's other railway station was called Swindon Town but everyone referred to it as 'Old Town' station because it was situated in that part of Swindon.

Bicycles were used at the Works and at regional depots by those employed to knock men up in the early hours, or by clerks collecting paperwork from outlying offices. Works' bicycles were made to a GWR specification. They were designed, perhaps at Swindon, to withstand being ridden over rough ground and withstand general wear and tear better than the average models of the day. As they were mechanical equipment the CME Dept was responsible for maintaining them. A circular sent out from Swindon in 1927 shows that one of Mr Collett's assistants was involved in mustering all the GWR bicycles to identify losses and under-utilisation. Redundant machines were to be sent to Swindon for overhaul and redistributed to where best employed.

Travelling Steam Cranes

I have met several Swindon railwaymen who were fascinated by steam cranes just as others were, and still are, by steam locomotives. The Swindon factory looked after the maintenance and repair of all the travelling cranes: those that ran on rails. After overhaul they were load tested using flatbed wagons filled with cast iron weights and fitted with lifting slings. There were various types of cranes in use around the Works and Running Shed yards of different ages and lifting capacities.

Travelling cranes awaiting Works' attention were held on sidings that curved around the east side of the CME offices alongside the Gloucester line. These sidings had pits, so that work could be carried out there as well as in part of B Shop, which was manned by G Shop personnel. In the 1950s this was Chargeman Ralph Angold's section.

The Locomotive Department's crane drivers carried out their own routine maintenance back at their home depots.

Loading and unloading timber in the yards around the Saw Mills and moving assembled trackwork in and around X Shop occupied a lot of the crane gang's time. A lot of the time cranes were standing idle during the week, but were sent out in goods' and breakdown trains at weekends to do routine engineering work.

George Petfield remembers Harold Couling from the early 1950s: 'He could drive anything.' Harold was G Shop chargeman responsible for allocating the labourers to their work routine. Other Swindon-based crane drivers remembered from the 1940s and '50s were Jack Norris, Claude Prince, Bill Ireson, Eddie Jones, Bob Waite, Norman Smith, Sam Jones, William Holden, Albert Crighton, Dick Selwood and Les Smart. Les later went into A Shop and drove one of the 100-ton overhead cranes. Not all these men were passed to drive the larger cranes.

Cranes on their own wheels, lifting loads, could be unstable, especially without the careful use of extension girders or outriggers to stabilise them. Dick Selwood had to jump clear when the ground gave way while he was working on the construction of the new Points and Crossings Shop in the mid-1950s. If a 4-6-0 locomotive had overrun the turntable road and the bogie had dropped over the pit, it was one of the big breakdown cranes that lifted the front end so it could be hauled slowly back and rerailed.

Swindon had, I think, three 6-ton and one 12-ton travelling cranes, and some of these smaller-capacity cranes were hand operated. They had a long life but few had many original parts in their later days. Other travelling cranes such as hand (manual), hydraulic and electrically powered types also came into the Works for repairs but the smaller types were likely to be maintained at the home depots. Swindon had built their own cranes but the GWR relied on specialist builders such as Stothard & Pitt, Ransome & Rapier, Cowans Sheldon and Smith Rodley for the larger types.

A 45-ton-capacity crane, lifting the jib of another back into position after overhaul. Dave Viveash, who worked on the cranes' section of the Drawing Office, thought the crane on the left was a Booth's diesel hydraulic 10 or 15-tonner. 'There were five on the Western Region, but none were based here,' said Dave. The crane sidings ran parallel with the Gloucester branch as it curved away from the main line. This area of the Works was known as the 'triangle' or 'angle'. *R. Grainger*

Cranes and Breakdown Trains

Steam cranes, together with their match trucks, formed part of the breakdown train; the rest was made up with mess/sleeping and tool vans and a guard's van. The largest engine depot in each division would have a 45-ton or a 36-ton crane, or both. Swindon was the exception as it was not the principal depot in its division; that was Bath Road in Bristol. Two large cranes were kept in G Shop yard. For many years they were No. 2, a 36-tonner, and No. 19, a 45-tonner, both built by Ransome and Rapier of Ipswich. The 45-ton crane was one of four ordered by the Railway Executive for the GWR and delivered in 1941.

During the passage of a royal train, the depots along its route kept a crane in steam, together with breakdown vans and gangs. A prepared locomotive would be on standby too. The code word for the royal and special trains was 'deepdene'. The crews liked them because they usually got overtime for doing next to nothing.

The Swindon breakdown cranes were based in the Works, not in the running shed as was usual. When surplus to divisional requirements they might be dispatched to assist cranes elsewhere, perhaps to where the Engineering Dept was working on the permanent way or installing a prefabricated girder bridge. Then the position of the 'foreigner' on site had to be such that if called away, it was not 'boxed in'. A full crew went out with the breakdown train, even for routine work, in case they were called away to an accident or derailment.

The Swindon crew would be made up of the supervisor, who was a G Shop foreman, the crane driver and four or five groundsmen. The latter were general assistants who went out with the crane and were paid a little more than the labourers' rate. During the week, if not required to go out, groundsmen worked in G Shop as fitters' mates. One of them would be responsible for seeing that all the tool van equipment was present and in working order, ready to go out at short notice. Items such as hydraulic jacks, oxyacetylene cutting equipment, first-aid boxes and contents, gas cylinders, chains, hand tools, a stove for cooking and heating in winter were all carried.

Cast iron instruction plates fitted to the crane body sides gave the safe loading details on a level road. It also reminded the crews that, when working, the extension girders should be fully out and clips secured to the rails. The exception was when they were required to move slowly with suspended loads; the capacity then was a third of what it would be when stationary.

During working hours the outdoor assistant to the CME, Joe Clarke, would often see the breakdown train

Another photo taken on the same day as the previous one, 22 July 1962. The day's work is now complete. The crane men identified are, left to right: unknown, Vic Corbett, unknown, Sam Jones, Fred Archer and Jack Bates. *R. Grainger*

away. He would always remind the crane driver of 'no more than 10% overload mind'. This meant that the driver should be mindful that, with the jib lowered, the lifting capacity was much reduced. But often there was no choice, said John Brettell. 'The large cranes were often lifting more than they should because of the need to lower the jib further to reach an adjacent load.'

The dangers of crane work were perhaps offset by the opportunity to earn good money through overtime, as crews could expect to be away for long periods. On the rare occasions that George Petfield, in the Wages Office, was questioned by his boss as to why a man was receiving so much more than his normal money, it was usually due to a timesheet submitted by a crane driver or his mate.

During the war, the cross-Channel guns that were aimed at the Germans in occupied France had to have the 16in barrels bored out and relined. Swindon's big cranes were sent down to Dover to help remove the barrels, which were then brought back to Swindon Works for machining. The gun barrels were then returned accompanied by the cranes and lifted back into position.

20
Other Aspects

Applying for Work

Applications for employment on the railway had to be processed thoroughly to try to secure the best candidates, but with the minimum of expenditure. Signs outside the Works' main entrances directed all people looking for work to the employment exchange in Regent Street. If the prospective employee found that the Works were 'taking on' and he or she felt they were suitable, a clerk at the exchange would go through the application form with them. The forms of successful applicants were retained in the Works records; those I have seen show that the selection process varied little until nationalisation.

The clerk would find out whether the criteria required could be met while at the same time assessing their general intellect, approximate build and demeanour. There were upper age limits for new staff joining the GWR: in the CME Dept it was forty-five years. The applicant had to: 1) be able to read and write 'with reasonable facility'; 2) provide two testimonials of character, which had to include the last employer or last school, whichever was the most recent; 3) provide their certificate of birth.

If all these conditions could be met the form was filled out in the applicant's own handwriting. Besides the usual personal details, the company wanted to know about close relatives in the service of the GWR, if any. The completed application form was left unsigned and undated at this stage and sent up to the staff sections at the Railway Works. Before the Second World War they were addressed to either Mr Richens or Mr Franklin, who headed the staff sections of the carriage and loco sides respectively.

If the Works were satisfied with the candidate's submission, a medical certificate with their name and temporary ticket number typed on to it was prepared. An appointment was then made for them to be examined by the company's surgeon at Park House. The medical certificate made it clear that a company official should avoid referring a candidate to the medical officer who was

Thomas William Harry had 'served his time' as fitter, turner and erector in the Loco Works. Five years after receiving the usual notice: 'your services will not be required after...' he was applying to come back. This letter implies that Mr Harry had been injured, leaving him with a physical disability, during his time away. The Ministry of Labour had, therefore, issued him with a green card, which confirmed to a potential employer that he had the disability claimed. Thomas Harry was successful in his application and went back to work 'inside'. By the start of 1929, the railway factory claimed to have fully recovered from the arrears of maintenance and material shortages caused by the General Strike.
Author's Collection

unlikely 'to attain the requisite standard'. If the 'general health and physical condition' were acceptable and there was no personal or family history of certain medical conditions, the certificate was stamped 'suitable for railway service'. Only now would the employer send out two forms to the appointed referees. Assuming these came back to the satisfaction of the staff section, the candidate would sign to show that they had made themselves acquainted with the terms of engagement.

Forms for wages grades and salaried grades were slightly different and there were some concessions made to disabled men and ex-servicemen. The Ministry of Labour set up the National Scheme for Disabled Men after the First World War and those eligible were given a green (disability) card by the labour exchange to present to the employer. Anyone wanting to return to the Works, having been employed there previously, could deal directly with the staff department 'inside', but unofficially.

There were, it seems, some exceptions to the rule that 'green card men' were to be put on to lighter work and paid less. Thomas Harry wanted to return to the Loco Works in 1929. Presumably he had been dismissed following his five-year training in 1923. A surviving letter (see scan) shows that an application for work was made by someone at the employment exchange on Mr Harry's behalf. The reply informs the applicant that 'the Manager, GWR, Swindon, is prepared to take you on as an erector in the Loco Dept. The wages are the same as paid to similar grades.' This man must have impressed them as 1929 was not a time when labour was in short supply.

Boys leaving school at fourteen years of age and hoping to go into the Works had to find temporary work until their next birthday. Hugh Freebury says in his book that the minimum age for acceptance was fourteen years and eight months, but most say they went in upon reaching fifteen years, or soon after. Frank Cockayne from Pinehurst, for instance, had been a bread van boy for the New Swindon Industrial Co-operative Society in Fleet Street. In 1938 he applied for employment in the railway factory, where his father worked, now that he was old enough. They offered him a start in No. 17 (time) Office, on the carriage side. Frank's application papers give no indication as to whether he was destined for the shop floor or whether he was to become a clerk.

Getting to, and from the Factory

Before the war, most Swindon railway workers walked to work. Around the 326-acre Works site there were numerous entrances, fourteen of which had gatehouses. During normal working hours, each person was required to come and go via a certain gate. This was usually the one nearest to the shop where their checkboard was located. All men working nights and shifts booked on and off at entrances with gatehouses, where their name was recorded in the register. If they wanted a pass out they got it from one of the time offices that were staffed around the clock.

Men are seen leaving the Works by the main tunnel entrance. If the date given on this postcard view is correct, 24 October 1928, this must be dinner time. The finish of the afternoon shift that day would have been after sunset. *Author's collection*

George Petfield told me that the only gates manned and open all the time were the main tunnel in London Street; the west gate, in Rodbourne Road; Beatrice Street entrance, in Whitehouse Road; and the Gas Works (also known as Bruce Street bridge) entrance. All of these provided access for road vehicles.

Beatrice Street was the main entrance on the eastern perimeter. The next one round was known as Osborne Terrace and then from 1940/1, Short's entrance. This one was used exclusively by the aircraft workers, at least that was the arrangement initially. Carriage, wagon, running shed and CME office workers living in the east and north of the town used these gates or the foot gates along the old canal path. Jack Fleetwood told me: 'The routes to the factory were always covered in spit and they used to hose out the tunnel leading into the Loco Works every day. The state of the average workman's lungs was very bad.'

This was one of the workers' 'foot gates' into what was still known as the canal-side workshops. The path ahead took the worker up between 17 and 24 Shops. Notice the early wooden railway vehicle body being used as a gatekeeper's cabin. The photo is one of a large series used as an ordnance survey mapping record at the time, March 1953. *Local Studies collection, Swindon Libraries*

If you didn't know someone by name then 'hello brother' was the usual acknowledgement before the war, said Doug Webb. Many of the older men touched their caps to the foreman if they passed him on the way to and from work, hoping to get a nod in return. One route that workers used to get to and from the Works included a long flight of steps alongside William Street School. Carriage side worker Reg Blackmore, who lived nearby, wrote a piece that included reference to these steps in 1960. Here is an extract:

> I never traverse the steps in William Street without the feeling that I am brushing shoulders with the ghosts of an obscure succession of people who, from the earliest days of New Swindon, have trudged mechanically forth and back on their drab domestic rounds, or made their way with dour regularity to and from the grim precincts of the Railway Works. To the driver of the Goddard Avenue bus, which has an infuriating habit of alternating routes, the steps signify just another stopping place. But to me the steps appear as the narrow channel that bridges the gulf between the satanic mills and the residential retreat.
>
> Away down below, the ugly outlines of the railway factory stretch from the unimaginative pile of the Station, to the outposts of the Concentration Yard and the New Saw Mill. The New Saw Mill; how curiously the appellation 'new' remains in currency in local speech. Once it was 'The New' but then came 'New Swindon' to be followed by the 'new line' [via Badminton]; the 'new shop' [A Shop] and the 'New Saw Mill'. But the 'new shop': prominent from the top steps, was laid down before the First World War, and the New Saw Mill pushed its way out towards the Shaw Road about the same time.

After work a lot of younger men ran out of the Works to get ahead of the plodding mass. People standing just outside the main tunnel said the sound of pounding feet coming towards them gradually built up to a thunderous roar. Leaving times were staggered slightly, with office and other salaried staff coming out five minutes earlier. Most workers went home for dinner if they lived close enough. Otherwise they took food in and ate at their station or else in the mess rooms. Before the war the wall of workers on foot, and later cyclists too, that spilled out of the main exits was formidable; it stopped all other forms of life dead in its path. Motorists and pedestrians in the know avoided certain routes at certain times as a matter of course.

In the 1930s, bicycles were not permitted on the premises, so for a small fee some people who lived near to the entrances allowed workmen to leave them in their gardens and side alleys. Doug left his bicycle, complete with acetylene lamps, at the first house in Redcliffe Street. The going rate before the war was 3d a week, or 4d if the cycle was kept undercover. Mr Knee, the newsagent opposite the London Street entrance, also made a few extra coppers by allowing cycles to be stored in his shop.

According to entries in the new work order books held by the Steam Museum, preparations were in hand for the accommodation of workers' bicycles at various Works' entrances by 1939. In or shortly before 1941 cycle permits were introduced for anyone storing or using a bicycle on the premises.

A report in the evening paper in 1950 said that the Swindon Accident Prevention Council was trying to involve local rail union officials in discussions about how accidents due to the Works 'spilling out' into the town could be avoided. Dave Viveash said his chargeman on the finishing off gang, Stan Lewington, rode a horse to work: 'He came across the fields from Lydiard and left the horse in an outbuilding at Even Swindon Farm, which was near the entrance at the bottom of Redcliffe Street. Then he would work all day in his riding boots.'

The Swindon Corporation trams ran for the last time in 1929 and double-decker motor buses took over the local services. Some single-deckers were already in use and they worked the routes that ran via the low Bruce Street Bridge. After the war, and perhaps before, Swindon Borough Transport ran early morning buses on weekdays only. No times were given in the public timetable, so perhaps they were workmen's buses. The other major bus company was Bristol Tramways, better known as The Bristol Bus Company. They definitely did run buses for the railway workers; after the war the timetable stated 'from Emlyn Square – GWR, on days when the BRWR (British Railways Western Region) are open.'

Workmen's Trains

Quite a number of men and some women too travelled in to the factory by workmen's train. Services converged on Swindon from five different directions: Wootton Bassett, Chiseldon, Purton, Highworth and Cirencester.

Elderly ex-workers still talk about the scramble to make the connection at Old Town station in the 1950s. The Chiseldon train arrived from the south then, two minutes later, the train from Cirencester Watermoor pulled in from the opposite direction. The railway workers from the Cirencester train had just a few minutes to cross the footbridge and pack themselves in with the Chiseldon people, before continuing on down to Swindon Junction station. In the evening the same scramble was played out again. The Cirencester train had first run in 1925 when the Midland and South Western Junction Railway Works there closed and the workers transferred to the GWR Works.

The trains ran from Monday to Friday, and Saturday too if the Works was on a five-and-a-half day week. They also ran during the summer shutdown. The last Christmas before he left school (1943), George Petfield was travelling from Wootton Bassett to Swindon to work as a temporary postman. He would catch the workmen's train, as members of the public were entitled to do. George was surprised to find it ran Christmas morning, and was quite full too! Later when he worked 'inside', George caught the 7.25am workers' train from Bassett regularly to get into work.

Some 'factory' workers travelled up the old 'MSWJ' by the early morning timetabled train from Marlborough, calling at Ogbourne and Chiseldon. Here the train has been stopped at Chiseldon Camp Halt, just south of the village. Works' Technical assistants were compiling information for a report as to the viability of using diesel multiple units and possibly four-wheeled railbuses on this route. The photographer, himself a technical assistant, thought the fellow in the light overalls, Doug Stagg, was checking the platform clearance. Notice the fellow passengers looking on. *Ken Ellis*

One morning George's train suddenly came to a halt in the cutting. From the window a bull could be seen walking along the track towards them: 'The animal ambled passed the train, allowing it to proceed without too much delay but I heard later that a "2800" class locomotive, taking coal empties back to South Wales, had to follow the Bull all the way to Bassett at walking pace.' Peter Reade also used this service: 'I cycled down from Broad Town and met George Evans, a bricklayer in the factory, and we travelled in together.'

There were women on these trains going to Wills's, Compton's, Garrard's, Nicholson's and the Cellular Clothing Company Ltd, as well as to the Railway Works. The trains were pulled by one of the modern pannier tank locomotives, usually a '5700' class, and two, three or four non-corridor coaches, depending on the service. 'The secondary stock that was used was still gas-lit up until about 1945. There would be four on from Bassett and it was usually pretty full. The Purton train only required two coaches,' said George. Stan Leach and his father travelled in by the workmen's train from the village of Purton. Alf Tutt travelled in with them; he lived near Stan and worked in the N Shop. Stan said:

I'd been using the train since I was a telegraph boy. When I went 'inside' [1935] I think a three-monthly season ticket cost about 3s 11d. In the morning the locomotive brought the train into the platform and went down to the brickworks siding to 'run round' its short train. It then ran to Swindon bunker first. Coming in from Purton, our train was rarely ever late but the Chiseldon people weren't always so lucky. Their train had to cross the main line at Rushey Platt and could be held up. A chap named Roy Green was the regular driver on our train for years; 'old Greenie' was also a union man down the Running Shed.

Virtually every traveller was a regular and they tended to have the same seat in the same carriage every journey. This was human nature but was bound to cause the odd dispute and, by the 1950s, some younger men began to challenge this ritual. The coaches were stabled near the station ready to take us home in the evening. After the war a Bristol Omnibus Company vehicle was waiting to take people on from Purton station if they needed it. Previously dozens of bicycles were left at the station.

Call Out Arrangements

The Fire Station watchroom was also used to summon breakdown crews and maintenance men out of normal working hours. A list of the various tradesmen on call, together with their address, was displayed there. If, for instance, a plumber was required during the night because of a leaking pipe or a crew was needed to take out a breakdown train, the call boy or one of the on-call firemen, was sent off on a bicycle to knock them up. It wasn't until the 1940s that a motor vehicle was available to bring on-call staff into the Works.

Several bicycles were kept in the Fire Station for the knocker-uppers. A young Colin Bown was one person who was rostered to cycle round and knock up staff on call. He would also have to wake the early turn footplate men on his round, too, anytime from 4am onwards. Adult knocker-uppers were used for midnight to 4am calls. Fred Kirby lived at 1A Emlyn Square, which was over Knee's shop opposite the Mechanics'. Up until the early 1940s he was a fireman on the footplate. A cast-iron pipe ran up the outside of the building past Fred's bedroom window, which the call boy would tap on. 'Mother would shout "Come on Fred, the call boy's knocking", said his daughter, Margaret. Colin remembered:

Mr Philpott, the G Shop maintenance foreman, who lived in Dean Street, told his men to call him as well if they were required. We were always told to rap the knocker several times but he always seemed to have the front door open before you finished knocking. As a senior first-aider, my dad [Bill Bown] would be called if a medical emergency occurred in his part of the Works. After hours he also took his turn on call with the motor ambulance and a driver. Most of the firemen were ambulance trained and some went out on medical emergencies in turn. The bell code put out for them, by the Fire Station, was two rings, a pause then two rings. In the days before they had the

Ford ambulance, a stretcher mounted about 4ft off the ground on cane wheels called a 'litter' was taken out. For me to remember it, this appliance must have been in use well into the 1930s.

If a person was killed under a train locally, by accident or suicide, the fire brigade would have to retrieve the body. In the 1930s the 'first call' fire vehicle was the 1912 Dennis Bros fire engine. A motor ambulance complete with trained staff was also on standby for medical emergencies and also for fire calls if requested. The Fire Station register survives for 1956. It shows that in the first week of December, the ambulance went out on four occasions; a fitter or electrician was called out three times for the Central Boiler Station and twice for the Oxygen Plant; Manager Smith was taken to the King's Arms Hotel; and the 1912 fire engine was dispatched to the Curator of Historical Relics, Clapham.

If an accident or subsidence damaged the track somewhere on the system, it needed immediate attention. The permanent way and civil engineers' people in the affected division would repair the main line but they might have to ring the Works at Swindon to supply points and crossing trackwork. An incoming call would be received stating a code for the type of assembly required. The man in the Fire Station would call the X Shop foreman, who would go and open up the shop while his on-call men were alerted. Mr Hobbs, the foreman until the war finished, lived at the top end of Jennings Street, which was no more than ten minutes' walk away from his shop.

Once the trackwork assembly was ready (as a set of parts), the crane drivers and road transport driver would be called. This type of work was usually only carried out as an emergency during the war years because of bomb damage. Depots too would sometimes need wheels or axleboxes due to loco or carriage breakdown. These could usually wait until they could be sent by rail.

The Mechanics' Institution

All local railway workers were eligible for membership of the GWR Mechanics' Institution for a small subscription. Besides the most popular attraction, which was the 'free' holiday travel, membership offered a range of recreational and educational facilities as well as those provided at the GWR Athletic and Sports Club behind Shrivenham Road. The lending and reference library within the Central Institute was always well used. It was the only one in the town until 1943.

Before the war the subscription was 10 pence, then a shilling a quarter for the lower-paid wages grades and for retired workers. The higher earners paid up to half a crown (2 shillings and 6 pence) depending on their salary. People not employed or laid off by the GWR could also join but their rates were higher and payable in advance. Widows whose husbands had died in the service of the company paid nothing. After the war, membership subscriptions, which were deducted through the paybill, increased a little. However, to try to attract members they were not increased proportionately with earnings.

X Shop, where the points and crossings' trackwork assemblies were made up, was at the northern end of the Locomotive Works. The layouts seen here are complete, so were presumably awaiting inspection before being partially dismantled and transported to site. *BRWR*

The north-west corner of the Mechanics' Institute main building in the 1930s, after the rebuilding. *Author's collection*

The GWR's chief mechanical engineer himself lent his name to the post of MI president in the 1920s and '30s. In practice however, it was Mr Collett's principal assistant who chaired the full council meetings and the AGM. The vice-presidents were, almost without exception, the most senior CME and Stores departments' managers, three of whom were also trustees. The treasurer was works (chief) accountant Mr Kelynack, and the secretary was the company secretary, Mr G.R. Davis. Organisational matters were the responsibility of around thirty elected council members and the trustees. The MI received an annual grant of £750 in lieu of 'free services' from the directors and management of the company. This amount remained the same through the decades covered by this book.

The GWR Swindon Mechanics' Central Institute was in the middle of the railway estate in Emlyn Square. This grand Victorian building had very churchlike architecture on the outside and a well-known weather vane on top of the west pinnacle. The latter stood nearly 4ft high and was quite clearly recognisable as the outline of one of Mr Dean's handsome 'single' locomotives. Unlike the one seen on the borough coat of arms, this loco was complete with its tender.

Above the doors just inside the main entrance was a nameplate from an old 'Dean single' locomotive. On the ground floor there was a large reading room supplied with an extensive range of current newspapers, magazines and journals. Men in particular would sit in a cloud of smoke quietly studying them. One of the tables was reserved for wives and daughters of members. There was also a 'fine

dance and lecture hall', a smoking room and rooms for billiards, table tennis and board games such as draughts and chess.

Visitors remember the sense of quiet and tranquillity in these parts of the building, contrasting with the din from the railway factory outside. With its polished tables, ornamental ceilings and classical plaster busts, the interior resembled a grand country house rather than an industrial education and social centre.

What was known as the Assembly Hall was downstairs. It catered for gatherings such as the Amalgamated Engineering Union No. 2 branch meetings, (No. 1 branch met at The Eagle Hotel and another at The Cricketers Arms) hobby groups, lectures and exhibitions. Before and after the war the Staff Association indoor activities were, in the main, held here; the annual GWR Arts and Crafts' exhibition being one of the biggest and most popular.

A Swindon Amateur Light Operatic Society production at the Mechanics' Playhouse in the 1950s.
Alec W. Hemmings courtesy of Swindon Central Library, local studies section

The MCI lending and reference library held around 40,000 books and included a juvenile department. It operated an open access system from the early 1930s, allowing users to go directly to the shelves and select their own books. There was an arrangement with the Corporation whereby it was open to certain non-members. Des Griffiths said that his school, Sanford Street, was included in this arrangement and their pupils could use the Mechanics' library. No doubt other local senior schools were included as well, at least until a public library opened in the town.

By all accounts, this library, as opposed to the smaller branch facilities, was not short of staff. Ernie Ruggles left school in the summer of 1943 and got prior notice of a vacancy coming up as a library assistant. Gordon Clack was leaving to take up an apprenticeship in the Works, so Ernie applied and got the job. Pete Heavens and Frank Gearon were also assistants in the library at the time and Stan Jarman was librarian. The chief librarian and secretary of the MI was Mr Phillips, who had his own office: Dorothy Palmer was his secretary. She lived in Aldbourne and would cycle in after the weekend if the weather would allow.

Beryl Hunt worked in the library for a short time in the mid-1950s. Another girl who worked here for some time, before she got married in 1960, was Iris Dabbs. Beryl said: 'On Wednesdays or Saturdays I worked a late shift on my own. At 8pm when the last visitor had left I had to turn the lights off at the far end and walk back through. As it was such an old building this felt very eerie.'

Upstairs there was a theatre hall large enough for 800 people. It was used for concerts, shows, dances and larger public meetings. Some people remember this was called the Sunshine Ballroom in the 1950s. The annual general meeting of the MI council was also held here. This part of the building, together with the boiler room, had suffered considerable damage due to the fire of December 1930. When it reopened nearly two years later, the hall had been enlarged, modernised and renamed The Playhouse.

As well as the main building, there were two small branch rooms in the suburbs. They were north of the Paddington–Bristol main line, in Gorse Hill and Rodbourne Road. Both had reading and recreational rooms for billiards, table tennis and darts and a small library. There was a third branch, which was smaller again, in Bath Road, Old Town. As far as I understand, it was used mainly by retired members who could not get across town to the other facilities.

After 1945 the Mechanics' Institution, which had been designed for the expectations of Swindon people 100 years earlier, was struggling to attract sufficient membership. Some sports and games rooms continued to be utilised, while some areas were left unused except for storage. The library closed for good in 1959 or 1960. Certain parts of the main institute building were renovated at this time to improve the facilities and try to reverse falling attendances.

Stealing

Around the railway town, people were generally community minded and respectful of others' property. Dave Townsend, a chargeman in W Shop, told his workmate Peter Chalk that he had lost his bike. Peter asked where he last remembered seeing it: 'Oh last week I cycled to the Co-op in Fleet Street.' Peter suggested that he 'go and see if it is still there, perhaps you walked home without it.' He had, and it was still there, unlocked and untouched. There are stories of petty thieving, most of it from the employer, and no doubt it was a widespread problem for the company. The Stores Dept was allowed costs for the secure storage of materials and general supplies against theft. Theft went on at all levels, so it cannot be associated solely with hardship, even before the war.

Everyone was made aware that the penalties for getting caught stealing were summary dismissal, or even prison if the theft was organised. Facing the grim prospect of being unable to earn a living during the economic depression did not deter everyone. By the 1930s, unless a person was caught red handed, the railway unions had negotiated for a hearing in each case. Even if that happened, the accused would have to show convincing evidence that he was innocent.

Art Fortune was still an apprentice coach builder when he went into Handy's, the ironmongers in Old Town, to buy some wood screws. He bumped into one of his workmates in there, who couldn't understand why Art didn't just take the screws from work. On Monday everyone got to hear of Art's honesty and they all had a good laugh about it.

For those who did a bit of model engineering or carpentry at weekends and supplemented the materials from their workplace, there was a constant risk of police spot checks. Tins of paint or tools were often seen hastily deposited along the approaches to the exits when word came back that searches were being conducted outside. At some point the men's side of the Works' Committee had somehow managed to successfully argue that they should receive prior warning when security purges would be carried out.

When the royal waiting rooms at Slough station were no longer required for that purpose, several gangs of different trades on the carriage side were sent to strip them out. This was in about 1950, said Doug Webb, who recounted the story. The royal furnishings and decoration came back to Swindon for disposal. Anything that had royal markings upon it could not be sold on to the workers. This included a regal carpet, to which someone fairly senior took a fancy. After having it cleaned, it was carefully folded and packed on to a handcart, then covered with some purchased wood. The paperwork handed in at 'Webb's entrance' described it as a pile of scrap blocks.

Occasionally criminal activity was on a larger scale. Around 1951 some men employed to sort scrap and load it into wagons were redirecting it to a scrap metal dealer in Bristol. Brass and copper in particular was going out over the high perimeter wall into the 'backs' behind Redcliffe Street. Because of the high value of what was taken, the men were sent to prison, said Bert Harber, who was a magistrate and also worked 'inside'. Jack Fleetwood told me that tobacco or snuff would occasionally disappear from a line of jackets hanging up in the workshop:

> Anyone caught would be outcast and have his working life, and possibly his life outside, made unpleasant by his fellow workers. If a man claimed to have lost his wages, a whip round was organised and would virtually cover his loss. Sadly, as time went on, it was suspected that this goodwill was being exploited and the practice gradually died out.

Jack remembers that most of the men in the shops were very honest and a story in the *GWR Magazine* in 1942 is an example: it said that a female carriage cleaner at Old Oak Common had lost her wage packet down the gap where the leather strap lifted and lowered the window in an external carriage door. She reported the matter but, after inspection, was told that it was not possible to retrieve it. When the coach went through Swindon for overhaul, however, the packet and contents were found and returned to her.

After demobilisation, Doug Webb returned to the factory, stripping out coach interiors. Of course, he kept the coins found down the backs of the seats to supplement his labourer's pay. On one occasion Doug found a gold cigarette case in a royal coach and handed it straight in. 'Never thought of doing anything else,' he said.

Discipline

According to the NUR conditions of service handbook for railway employees (1937), a man charged with misconduct, neglect of duty, or other breaches of discipline, would be forewarned in writing of the nature of his offence and the punishment he was likely to receive. He or she was given the opportunity to call witnesses and state any extenuating circumstances in the presence of company officials, prior to a verdict being arrived at.

At the interview the accused could be accompanied by an advocate, usually a representative of his union. Where doubts arose or where the case(s) was sufficiently serious, it could be heard by a more senior official. If they were found guilty of a serious offence, there was the right of appeal, to a superior officer. It was usual to allow a standard day's pay in cases of men attending disciplinary inquiries.

Although the railway companies must have agreed to the above, the wording in the GWR's *General Rules and Regulations* of the same period gives a different version and offers the accused little chance of a fair hearing. It states that they may at any time 'dismiss without notice'

or 'suspend from duty, and after enquiry, dismiss without notice'. No doubt the company assumed that the tone was sufficiently forthright to deter serious breaches of the rules in the first place.

These then were the official processes but by the 1930s, from what I've heard of the period up to the Second World War, a man's whole livelihood was at the mercy of the foreman or overseer's frame of mind. Some wrongdoings were handled with compassion. According to local folklore, when a Swindon engineman was called to account and his story seemed far-fetched, his foreman, who had himself come up through the ranks, said: 'You tell me the truth, and leave me to tell the lies to the superintendent.' Another unconfirmed story, heard by George Petfield, concerned a worker from the carriage side who was unhappy about his pay. He arrived at the C&W Wages Office drunk, caused a scene and threw a punch at George Tomes, the senior clerk. He missed and ended up on the floor. At this time, the late 1940s, Mr Tomes was allowed to exercise his authority: he summarily suspended the man for a week but asked that he not be sacked.

Jack Fleetwood said that in Great Western days the local newspaper, *the Evening Advertiser*, was regularly taken to the manager's office and scrutinised to see if any of the men had been up in front of the magistrate. If they had, their names and details were recorded in a 'black book'. The book of names survives today but Jack could only speculate as to whether any further action was taken against those recorded.

Electric Power
(Excluding carriage lighting and ATC apparatus)

Swindon Works was receiving some of its electricity supply from the new power station at Moredon from early in 1929. The following year another turbo alternator and water tube boiler to supply the steam to drive it were installed. This increased the capacity to 15,000kW and the

This is the Power House in the 'New Saw Mill' showing one of the first gas-driven DC electric generators. Some of this plant was retained as a back-up in case of interruptions in the supply from Moredon Power Station. *Author's collection*

Works was then able to buy in all the electricity it required. The CME's electrical assistant was responsible for the purchase of electricity for the Works and for the rest of the company.

Two high-tension trunk mains cables came in from the power station, which was about 1½ miles north-west of the Works. Each of the three-core cables delivered 6.3kV to the HT (high-tension) switchgear in 'M' Power House. The railway works had generated their own electricity in M Shop, which had been built into the south-west corner of the R Shop building, many years before. This was then converted to become the Works' main electricity substation. Besides the switchgear, which was made by the British Thomson Houston Co. Ltd, plant in the 'M' Power House included three step-down static transformers made by the Hackbridge Electric Construction Co. Ltd. The switchgear, mounted on large slate slabs, may well have been built by the GW Company's own staff at Swindon as they are recorded as having built the one in the Wagon Works Power Station in about 1914.

The AC (alternating current) was then converted to 220 or 440 volt DC (direct current) by 2,000kW capacity rotary converters in 'M' PH or sent on to the two smaller substations – one in AM Shop and the other in the Wagon Works – to be converted. Each substation had a driver, who kept his eye on the meters and kept the places clean and tidy. As the government contracts for war work started to be diverted elsewhere from 1943, the ongoing machine tool renewal and the conversion of gas lighting to electric gathered pace. Later the factory was busy converting electrical equipment from DC to AC. Much of the electrical work was subcontracted but the expected benefits were hampered because the supply from the corporation power station could not keep pace with the growing demand.

A number of 50 and 60hp DC electric motors were gradually replacing steam to power gangs of machine tools via revolving line shafting, pulley wheels and leather belt links (or straps). Each machine had different-sized pulley wheels on its drive and on a countershaft above. Moving a second belt between the opposing pulleys acted as simple gears, allowing the operator to change the cutting speed. This could be done using a pole and sometimes a ladder between machining operations.

Stan Hall of Salisbury Street was chargeman of the E Shop gang who maintained the motors that supplied the power for the old main-line shafting. This mechanism was now considered to be unreliable and uneconomic by comparison. As time went on, much of the new machinery would have its own three-phase 7½hp electric motors, but not all. Throughout the 1930s some replacement machine tools continued to work by indirect electric power transmission.

Ivor Wilkins, a 'sparky' (electrician) in E Shop in the 1950s, told me that Len Stacey was the driver in M Shop at that time. Len was a 'green card' man, so he had either been invalided out of manual work or, less likely, he had mental health problems. The HT (high-tension) gang was one of seven in E Shop and they maintained the Works' substations. In Ivor's time, the mid-1950s, Tommy Cook was chargeman of this gang. Works' electricians were based in either 5 Shop or E Shop. Neither place was very big as most of their work was done outside, in other workshops or outstation.

After the war the Works was consuming 17 million units of electricity per annum. The cost of powering its electric lighting, machinery and heating would have been between 1 and 4 old pence per unit. However, a special tariff for large consumers brought the price down significantly.

Publicity and Works' Tours

Great Western publicity and advertising had become highly effective by the 1930s, and on a scale that has since required whole books to do the subject justice. The main themes of the company's efforts to sell its services to the public were fast trains and the wonderful geography through which they operated. Swindon Works, it seemed, offered only limited potential for publicity, but as the birthplace of the 'Castles' and 'Kings', there was some.

Former general manager Sir Felix Pole said in his autobiography that it was Gordon Selfridge Jnr who first suggested showing visitors over Swindon Works. The latter told the GWR (London) Debating Society: 'You have just sent one of your engines to America and people are talking about it. Don't you think a large number of people would like to see where it was built?'

And so excursions for the general public were run from Paddington to visit the Works. Tickets costing 5 shillings for adults had to be booked in advance, and the afternoon trips were well patronised. With the organisation and the large numbers of half-price fares, I doubt whether the company made any profit out of them directly. These special trains had restaurant cars and were usually hauled by 'King' class locomotives there and back. Publicity literature and merchandise, such as jigsaw puzzles and colour reproductions of the famous engine *King George V*, were available to buy on the journey.

Handling large parties of schoolchildren visiting the Locomotive Works and having weekly open days became important to the company in the 1930s. They found that feeding the appetites of 'boys of all ages' for steam trains brought in custom and would later attract some to seek employment on the railway. Works' watchmen and senior apprentices acted as guides. They made sure that none of their group straggled behind or wandered from the route. The apprentices liked the authority it gave them but there was always a fear that some 'smart Alec' would ask an awkward question.

The route around the Locomotive Works took them through the main workshops. The visitors would be shown some of the more interesting workshop practices, such as a tyre being shrunk on to a wheel centre and a steam hammer in action. The highlight of the tour was the AE (Erecting) Shop, of course. If you were lucky you might see

Visitors waiting outside the main entrance to the Works in London Street. This must have been a Wednesday just before 2.30pm, sometime in the early 1960s. *Dave Stratford collection*

Some staff, like Bert Stratford, second left, and Stan Morris, third left, became celebrities to many of the regular visitors to the Works. With the promise of receiving a print, they would happily pose with enthusiasts. As foreman of the Works' enginemen, Mr Morris could, and did, sometimes have locomotives positioned for the picture-taker. The date of this tour was 28 July 1957 and included the Running Shed, where this photo was taken. *Dave Stratford collection*

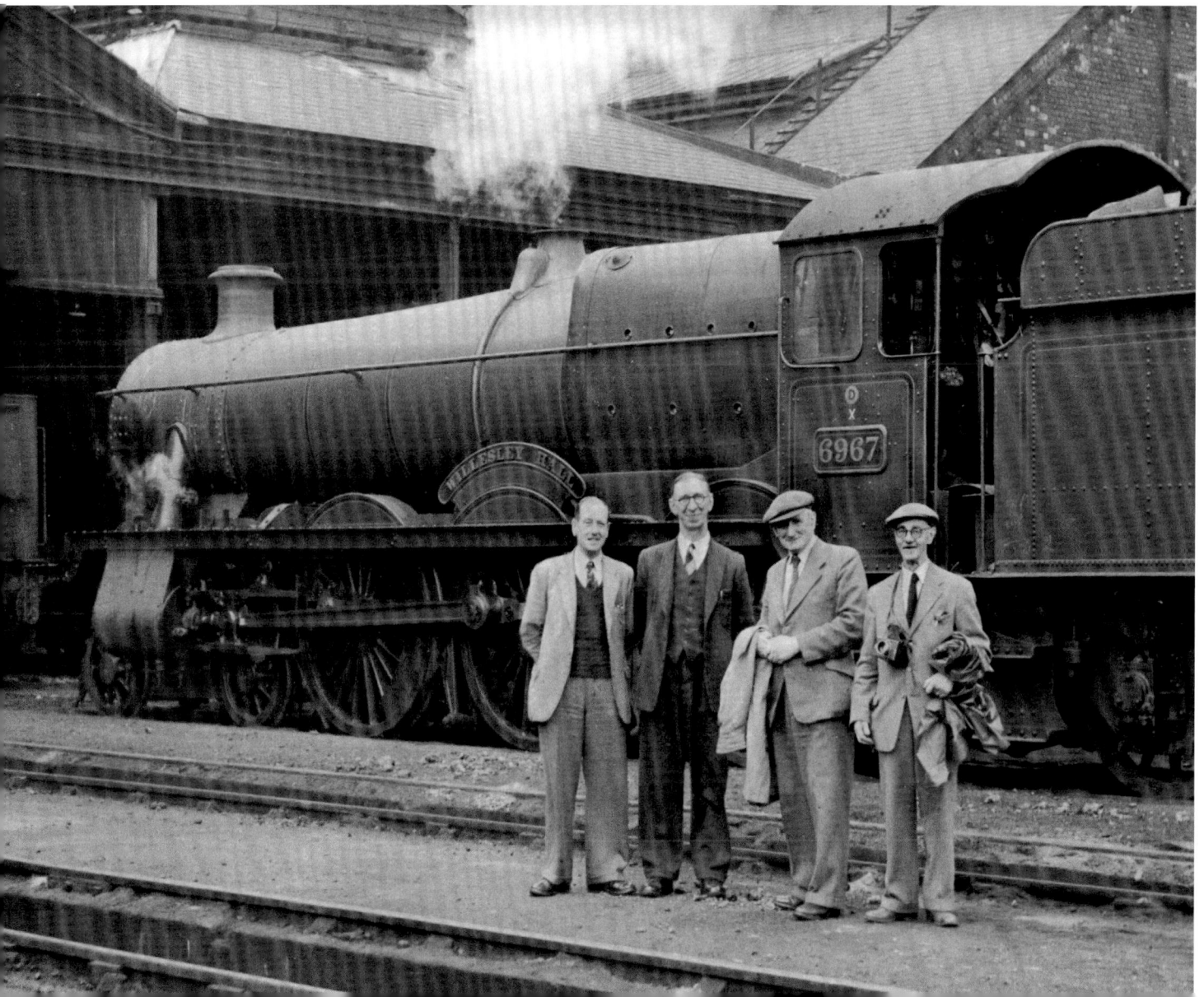

a locomotive, complete with its wheels and boiler, gliding through the air: to keep up with it you would have to break into a trot, which was strictly forbidden.

Bert Stratford was the chief watchman on the loco side and his assistant was Mr Cooper. Bert is remembered by many who visited back in the steam days. His imposing stature, yet friendly manner, is what sticks in people's minds. As a watchman, Bert would often accompany groups of visitors around the Works in the 1950s and '60s. It was made clear in the tour guide that persons attending did so at their own risk while on company premises.

Several major postcard companies issued photographic cards in the 1930s showing Great Western engine portraits. The photographs used were from the official GW collection. For one particular series of postcards, the GWR employed a company themselves. The views were again main-line locomotive portraits. Some were painted light grey and black, which the company thought suited them, for photographic purposes, at the time. A respected authority on railway postcards told me that he thought these cards were for sale at Swindon Works, perhaps exclusively, when groups were taken round.

With the worsening economic situation nationally and then the war, it wasn't until the late-1940s and '50s that special trains to the Works became popular again. Some were now arranged by railway enthusiasts' organisations. Between the wars, parties and individuals arriving by train for pre-arranged visits were not charged admission. This would normally be a shilling a head. Every Wednesday afternoon at 2.30pm, except during the July shutdown, a tour of the Locomotive Works was offered to the general public with no permit required. This had been a tradition since well before the turn of the century. The admission after the war was sixpence without a current railway ticket.

A good proportion of the visitors were schoolboys and young men taking engine numbers. The dilemma for them was deciding at what stage the stripped down or partially reassembled components could be counted as the actual locomotive and crossed off in their *Ian Allan ABC* books. Free leaflets explaining the route taken and some of the shops visited were available on the way in. In the mid-1950s the admission charge was dropped altogether. The number of visitors to the Works in 1956 was 16,300 and revenue raised by visitors' rail fares was £3,635.

Open days often followed events in the Works, such as the visit of Princess Elizabeth in November 1950. Three days after that, 20,000 members of the public were taken through the same workshops. Unlike the royal guest, the public didn't see working demonstrations as their visit was conducted on a Saturday. The publicity generated over the naming of the last steam locomotive in March 1960 was also capitalised upon, with special trains and Works' tours for the public.

Park House

The name Park House does not appear on early plans. It seems likely that this name was not used officially at least until the park opposite was renamed as simply The Park, sometime before 1900. After George M. Swinhoe died in office in 1911, the building became the residence of the assistant medical officer rather than, as before, the chief medical officer. Dr Berry resigned from the post of CMO, sometimes known as consulting physician to the Medical Fund, in 1936. He lived in Devizes Road near to the Victoria Hospital, where he was also the senior member of their medical staff. Drs T. Percival Berry, J. Lowe and A. Gibson all served as the senior MO of the Medical Fund at various times after that.

On the first floor, medical and 'educational' (written) examinations were undertaken by staff seeking employment in the CME Dept. A clerk from the CME's staff section dealt with the paperwork: in the 1930s this was Arthur Holloway. Footplatemen applying for promotion would be required to attend from all over the system. Most of them would be checked over by the MO, more than once in their careers. These examinations were particularly important as the safe running of trains depended on men with good eyesight who were not colour blind.

Muriel Summers, who was in the Works' telephone exchange in the 1940s, said her father, Edward Everrett, spent some of his working time at Park House: 'He gave the engine drivers and firemen their eye tests.' After which, the results were presumably sent to a suitably qualified person in the ophthalmology department. Muriel said that she thought her father was otherwise based in the 'office of the running superintendent'.

Park House was built in the 1870s, for the company's chief medical officer and his family. Happily little has changed today, externally at least. The substantial building survives, overlooking The Park at the southern end of Church Place. *Author*

Another man who worked here, from the early 1940s onward, was Fred Kirby. He lived nearby in Emlyn Square, above Knee's corner shop. The company gave him a job as a runner. This involved taking medical reports and appointments to and from the factory and Medical Fund departments. Fred, or 'Shiner' to his mates, from his days as a conscientious engine cleaner, had been a fireman on the footplate. During an air raid near Birmingham, 'Shiner' had been injured on duty. Under the national scheme to help disabled men, the company found him suitable alternative work once he had recovered sufficiently.

In 1945 a 57ft coach was converted in the Works for staff welfare. It took the chief medical officer around the GWR system to examine staff, although some still had to make the journey to Park House. Enginemen, for instance, were required to have a medical check-up and eyesight test, as already stated, when they started. When they reached a certain age, the tests had to be carried out periodically from then on.

Annual Holiday Preparations

Throughout the company, employees received free holiday train travel. This reinforced loyalty and the additional costs borne were negligible. In most cases the workers' holiday periods, which were unpaid until 1938, could be staggered and the service maintained. This meant that those who travelled could be accommodated by timetabled trains. For Swindon railway workers, however, the holiday trains were not 'free'. They had to pay a nominal amount to be members of the Mechanics' Institution. Although membership also entitled them to an impressive range of recreational facilities, many only joined to take advantage of the holiday trains.

Only at Swindon was it possible, as well as beneficial, to have a shutdown. This was because if all plant and equipment was stopped at the same time, for essential maintenance or replacement, it had less of an impact on production. Considering the sheer numbers involved, all travelling at the same time, there was no choice other than to provide trains exclusively for the Swindon workers.

The Superintendent of the Line's Dept produced and distributed these comprehensive booklets each year for railway officials. They gave details of each Works' holiday train to be run and operating instructions for its working over each section of the various routes. This particular booklet was issued to the signalmen at Ponsandane Signal Box, Penzance, in 1946. *Author's collection*

There were other financial burdens that the company had to bear too, such as the disruption to their goods and passenger services for the duration of the Swindon holiday period. No doubt some of the travelling public would feel inclined to travel by the Southern Railway or another road or rail company competing for holiday traffic, rather than share resorts crowded with Swindonians. At least the GWR got this mass exodus out of the way before the main holiday season began.

The 'arrangements' by which thousands of Works' trippers had to comply, had been honed over the years so that by the 1930s they ran like clockwork. No doubt there were administrative and operational hiccups but to a large extent the previous years' arrangements acted as a template: the only variables being dates and numbers travelling. I have seen notices that have been amended in ink. These were, presumably, the previous years' copies that had been sent to the printer so that updated copies could be provided.

The first sign that 'Trip' arrangements were under way in the factory was when the application forms were distributed and the 'Application for Tickets Etc.' posters started appearing on notice boards. The posters stated that employees intending to travel must return their completed forms to their shop office or designated clerk by the end of May, or in some years early June. Details required on the forms included destination, numbers of tickets required and whether the family would be away for the day or the whole week. Once compiled, more preliminary details were made public. The local paper then printed the details of numbers travelling and how the anticipation in the town compared with previous years.

The application forms were sent on to the clerks, who administered the free and privilege tickets in each of the three Works' staff sections. The publicity and bookings were overseen by the Mechanics' Institute 'trip committee' and the cost of all the printing came out of Institute funds (this amounted to around £121 in 1929). In the week leading up to the holiday, the passes (tickets) were to be collected from the Mechanics' Central Institute. Any tickets for relatives and friends of employees, not entitled to free or privilege travel, were also to be collected at this time. The elderly and frail would be advised to go and 'take the sea air', which would restore health if they were 'out of salts'.

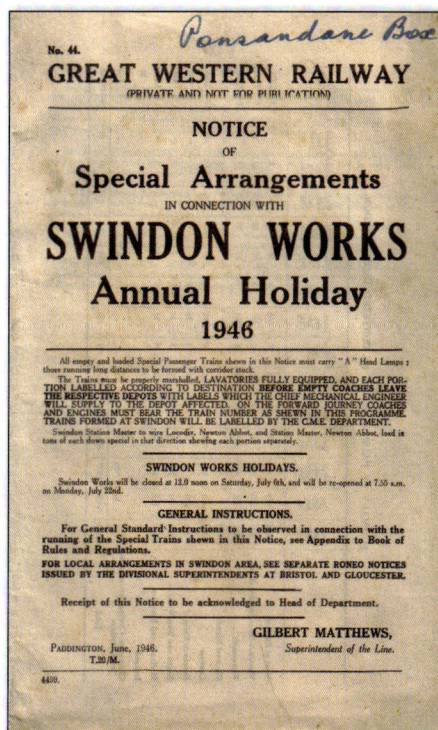

No. 44.

Ponsandane Box

GREAT WESTERN RAILWAY

(PRIVATE AND NOT FOR PUBLICATION)

NOTICE

OF

Special Arrangements

IN CONNECTION WITH

SWINDON WORKS

Annual Holiday

1946

All empty and loaded Special Passenger Trains shown in this Notice must carry " A " Head Lamps ; those running long distances to be formed with corridor stock.

The Trains must be properly marshalled, LAVATORIES FULLY EQUIPPED, AND EACH PORTION LABELLED ACCORDING TO DESTINATION BEFORE EMPTY COACHES LEAVE THE RESPECTIVE DEPOTS WITH LABELS WHICH THE CHIEF MECHANICAL ENGINEER WILL SUPPLY TO THE DEPOT AFFECTED. ON THE FORWARD JOURNEY COACHES AND ENGINES MUST BEAR THE TRAIN NUMBER AS SHEWN IN THIS PROGRAMME. TRAINS FORMED AT SWINDON WILL BE LABELLED BY THE C.M.E. DEPARTMENT.

Swindon Station Master to wire Locmdiv, Newton Abbot, and Station Master, Newton Abbot, load in tons of each down special in that direction shewing each portion separately.

SWINDON WORKS HOLIDAYS.

Swindon Works will be closed at 12.0 noon on Saturday, July 6th, and will be re-opened at 7.50 a.m. on Monday, July 22nd.

GENERAL INSTRUCTIONS.

For General Standard Instructions to be observed in connection with the running of the Special Trains shewn in this Notice, see Appendix to Book of Rules and Regulations.

FOR LOCAL ARRANGEMENTS IN SWINDON AREA, SEE SEPARATE RONEO NOTICES ISSUED BY THE DIVISIONAL SUPERINTENDENTS AT BRISTOL AND GLOUCESTER.

Receipt of this Notice to be acknowledged to Head of Department.

GILBERT MATTHEWS,
Superintendent of the Line.

PADDINGTON, June, 1946.
T.20/M.

4459.

21
National Emergency

Pre-war Preparations

K. J. Cook, who was locomotive works' manager at the time, said in his book *Swindon Steam 1921–1951*: 'When war broke out, our locomotive and rolling stock position was well under control.' The 'chief' (CME) naturally wanted to keep it that way by retaining all the facilities of the department for railway purposes in view of the uncertain times that lay ahead. So Swindon managed to avoid taking on munitions work at first and they got on with adapting the railway for the expected conditions of war.

Before war was declared, the Carriage Works started altering some rolling stock based partly on experiences gained in the last war. For casualties from air raids, some 'Siphon G' milk vans and 'brake third' coaches were converted and made up into evacuation trains. The idea was that if local medical services became overwhelmed in one area, these trains could move casualties to hospitals elsewhere. The Railway Executive, the government's controlling committee for British railways in wartime, required the GW to convert six train sets for casualty use. Eighteen LMS coaches also arrived at the Works to be turned into ambulance trains for use at home and overseas.

Three fire-fighting trains were made ready, again by converting ordinary stock. As part of the anti-gas measures, other passenger coaches were converted into mobile decontamination units. These were painted yellow and fitted with steel shutters. All were fitted with steel brackets, six to a solebar, which caused quite a bit of speculation in the Carriage Works until it was revealed they were for lifting the vehicles in and out of ships' holds. There was a real fear that the Germans would use gas against Britain but, in the event, this did not happen.

Passenger coaches had to be made to blend in with the scenery from above and not show any lights after dark. To this end Swindon men, working outstation at the carriage depots, blacked out windows or fitted blinds to ordinary passenger stock. Roofs, normally white, were painted over in dark grey and carriage blinds and metal lamp shades were turned out by the Carriage Works in their thousands.

Because much of the Works was built on land higher than the town, an extensive network of pedestrian and service tunnels ran between the two and beneath the railway, which divided the site into three. Those working near to a suitable tunnel used it as a shelter, for others brick blast-proof shelters were built. Blacking out the workshops commenced shortly after war was declared. The blackout precautions caused problems because, as well as the windows, there was a lot of glass in the roofs, so as to make the most of the natural light. A black paint was used for the workshops, and not just those that had a night shift. So everyone now worked under dimmed lighting. Later some of the paint was removed in favour of blinds, which could be opened during the hours of daylight.

A slogan daubed on the outside wall of the Pattern Store during the last war. It summed up the general feeling of Swindon people, threatened with invasion. It was still readable in June 2001. *Author*

An LMS 57ft 'corridor-first' coach converted for use in an ambulance train. This vehicle was then classed as an administration car, No. 6204, for home use rather than in one of the sets going to the Continent. *GWR*

At depots, locomotives that had cab side windows had them plated over. Tarpaulin sheets too were fitted between tender and cab roofs to stop glare from the fire after dark. The materials were prepared and sent out from Swindon Works.

Early Days

In accordance with arrangements made for a national emergency, the government's Ministry of Transport took control of all British railways as soon as war was declared. The Transport Minister appointed what was called a Railway Executive Committee, made up of senior management from the four main railway companies. This had been done in the 1914–18 war and had worked well. The general manager, Sir James Milne, was the senior GWR representative on the committee and, in a message printed in the *GWR Magazine*, said he 'had every confidence in the staff of all grades, in the strenuous and difficult days that are ahead'.

'Dean Goods' 0-6-0 tender locomotives were to be made ready for the War Department to send overseas with the British Expeditionary Force. Nine of the class that had been recently withdrawn were also included in the plan. The work required the removal of the automatic train control apparatus and the replacement of the vacuum brakes with Westinghouse air brakes. Fifteen were converted at Eastleigh and eventually more than ninety at Swindon. The same class had been chosen to be sent to France in the First World War and some of the same engines were to go again! It had also been planned to build a large batch of the '2884' class locos to send to the Continent but with the fall of France in 1940 the order was reduced and none were sent. This Churchward design, modified by Collett, was the company's principal heavy freight locomotive.

The CME Dept relied heavily on suppliers of raw materials and early in the war it became increasingly difficult to get enough to cover existing contracts. This was because materials were being diverted elsewhere for war production. A Ministry of Supply Order was sent out to manufacturers stating that they must collect their own redundant and residual materials for salvage. Swindon still dispatched scrap iron, steel and non-ferrous metals to the usual contractors but they reused a much higher proportion than before for their own needs.

As part of a national drive to aid the war effort, the GWR salvage vans travelled the system collecting textiles, rags, sacking and paper, as well as metals. It was then sorted and sent on internally or externally by the Stores Dept. The *GWR Magazine* reported that incoming supplies of quarto and foolscap paper were severely disrupted before war started. It wasn't long before they were using the blank reverse sides of documents that would normally be filed away.

From 1940 blood collection centres were set up periodically in workshops and offices. At this time the demand from regional hospitals was great and so was the willingness to give. Dr Darmady from the Army Blood Transfusion Service in Bristol wrote to Mr Collett and Mr Cook. Part of his letter said: 'I am informed that the number of donors obtained (at Swindon Works), 3,443, shows a greater proportion than any so far obtained from a large works anywhere in the south-west of England.' Under Civil Defence measures, local factories, including the Railway Works, could be used as makeshift mortuaries if large numbers of civilians were killed by enemy action.

Arrangements were made for roof spotters to be positioned on top of Works' buildings as part of the ARP measures. Anti-aircraft posts fitted with mounted machine guns were set up on suitable flat rooftops too. Four hundred workers volunteered for Works' ARP duties. They were allocated to different parts of the site on a rota, day and night. Their primary task was to warn of incendiary bombs falling on buildings, materials – particularly timber piles – and rolling stock.

These are 1,000lb bomb cases almost ready for shipment, photographed on 1 June 1941.
GWR courtesy of Swindon Society

A view from the back of the engine sheds showing where the bombs fell in the air raid of July 1942. The Works' cameraman is pointing his camera due north showing 24 Shop in the background. The area in the foreground was known as 'Lapper's Hill'. Notice the blast-damaged buildings, which would be quickly repaired.
GWR courtesy of The Swindon Society

Armaments' Production

Representatives and prominent industrialists from the Ministries of Supply visited the Works to assess its potential for manufacturing armaments. They were, according to company publicity published after the war, amazed at the range of engineering facilities available. One of them said the Tool Room was: 'second only to those of the tip top aircraft firms'. Additional work to help fight the war would have to be done by cutting back on important railway work already under way. Mr Collett, the chief mechanical engineer, believed the importance of maintaining an efficient railway should not be underestimated in times of war. However, the Works' facilities were considerable and vital armament and ammunition production had to go somewhere.

Other railway factories were taking on war work and their men were earning overtime payments. Therefore the Works' Committee as well as the government started to 'lean on' Mr Collett to conform. This, together with the desperate situation unfolding in 1940, would overcome any resistance and Swindon Works would soon be producing armaments, bombs and ammunition. It was a full twelve months into the war before contracts and drawings started arriving at Swindon from the Ministry of Supply. Much of the war work was to be making parts or carrying out specialist operations on components for outside firms.

From 1940 bombs were manufactured here too and the *GWR Magazine* says of the types made:

The general trend was a progressive increase in size to keep pace with the advancing technique of aerial warfare. At first two classes of bomb were undertaken: one was a 3in trench mortar bomb, forged from steel bar and machined in the Carriage Fitting Shop, very largely by women workers. Of these, 60,000 were high explosive and 11,000 were smoke pattern bombs. The other type was a 250lb high explosive bomb, of which 33,000 were eventually manufactured. Each line of production for the larger bombs comprised of: five lathes, two other machines, a varnishing oven and assembly benches. Suitable machines were selected from various depots and works and brought to Swindon for tooling and fitting up. One plant was erected in the Points and Crossings' Shop.

By 1942 the Works were making all sorts of parts to help fight the war including shells, bombs, searchlight projectors, cutting tools for use at home and for outside firms, parts for aircraft and radar equipment. Perhaps the largest single work undertaken was a complete platform mounting for a 13.5in hyper-velocity cross-Channel gun.

A gauge, or part of a gauge, used on the turret rings produced in 1941 and 1942. This was a large contract undertaken for the Ministry of Production, one of the first at the Works in this war. The rings were turned on wheel lathes in the A Wheel Shop, then went to the Tool Room for gear cutting. The gauge has 1.4 +.197 stamped on another face. This is its length in inches on the Vernier scale. Presumably this was an upper limit allowed on a turned recess cut around each ring. If the gauge fitted into the recess, too much had been taken off. It was found in the Works in the 1980s at the back of an old locker.

Probably the most complex war work to be undertaken
at Swindon was the two-pounder multi pom-pom guns
for the navy. Some of their components were supplied by
the Southern and London & North Eastern Railways. *GWR*

When fully assembled, it covered a large area of the boiler
shop floor. Some of its design had to be worked out in the
Works' Drawing Office.

Machine tool chucks and tooling were altered on the
loco side for operations necessary to convert rough
forgings into fully machined shell cases. In the event,
shells of 9.2in calibre were produced to high standard,
according to government inspectors. Orders from ICI
(Metals) among others required the Works to produce
copper bands that would cause the shells to spin and
keep them on a true trajectory. The copper tube normally
used could not be supplied, so discs of ½in thickness were
heated, pressed and cold drawn, then parted on a lathe.
Two production lines were set up in 24 Shop, where
further operations were carried out on shell bands and
25lb shell cases. This work was done using female labour
working under a foreman.

Tank Turret Rings

An early undertaking for the supply ministries was also one
of the largest production contracts. It was for the
manufacture of tank turret rings for armoured cars and
tanks. The Wheel Shops worked continuously, finish
turning at least fifty a week. When they were passed on to
O Shop [Toolroom] for the gear teeth to be cut, apprentice
Maurice Parsons was one of the machine operators [see
photograph] involved. George Smith, the Works'
photographer, records him working in O Shop using a
specially adapted gear cutting machine. Maurice would
'centre' each ring and clamp it down. The arbor moved on

a vertical plane and the milling cutter produced the gaps to
form the teeth on the internal diameter. After each cut the
work moved round by automatic indexing until 392 teeth
had been cut. Once each ring was set up and running there
should be no need to do anything except make sure it
didn't come loose or a milling cutter break, or both.

The operation took four or five hours depending on
the size of the turret ring, and Maurice was sometimes
moved to other work while each was being machined. A
'dilutee', or a less-experienced apprentice, was left to
watch and hit the 'quick stop' lever if something went
wrong. At the end one of the men would slide the mild
steel ring towards them and lift it down to the ground by
their shoulder and roll it away. A new milling gear cutter
was then fitted before starting the next.

Doreen Dominey had been an evacuee from London
and took employment 'inside' when she left school. She
was often required to watch the 'hobber', as the gear
cutting machine tool was known. The trouble was, said
Maurice, 'She did not work nights so then I had to watch
the work throughout, myself: very boring.' On one night
shift he arranged to meet Doreen outside and take her out
after setting a turret ring up and running. Being a
motorcycle dispatch rider in his spare time, he had his own
transport and took her up on the downs, to Uffington
White Horse. I said surely someone must have been
keeping their eye on the work, but Maurice said not!

Accounts vary as to how many turret rings were
manufactured here but they were being machined day
and night from 1941 to 1944. Depleted numbers of
carpenters boxed up the finished rings and they were sent
to Birmingham for assembly. Mr K.J. Cook, the loco works
manager at the time, said:

> The cost of gear cutting with full toolroom
> overheads was £2 9s 6d per ring. In order to get
> the production up to the tank builders'

Cutting gear teeth on a turret ring for an armoured car.
There were two sizes of the mild steel rings: 4ft and 5ft in
diameter approximately. They had first been finished
turned in the wheel shops. Apprentice Maurice Parsons,
who has removed his glasses for the photograph, watches
over the machine in O Shop in 1942. Like many of the
machine tools engaged in war production, this gear
cutter had been specially adapted in the Works. *GWR*

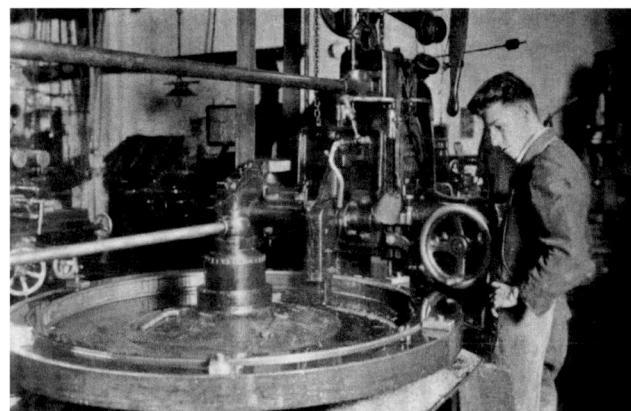

requirements of fifty sets per week, it was necessary to place subcontracts and the lowest quotation obtained from an outside firm was £11, ultimately reduced under pressure to £9 per ring.

Short Bros Ltd

When Short Brothers Ltd of Rochester was bombed in 1940, they started producing aircraft parts again in 24 Shop. Because of the potential for supplying engineers, carpenters and unskilled labour, the Ministry of Aircraft Production already had this part of Swindon Works in their sights. Planning of this kind was made in case essential war factories were put out of action in this way. The newly formed Swindon division of factories, all building different parts for Shorts' aircraft, were sited in and around the town at South Marston, Blunsdon, Sevenhampton and Kembrey Street, as well as 24 Shed (or Shop).

This massive building was completed in 1929/30 for carriage bodywork and painting repairs and could accommodate up to 160 coaches. The railway work normally done here was considered low priority during wartime, so just two through roads were retained for essential carriage repairs. Another part of this shop produced shells and the rest was adapted for production of parts for the new Stirling bombers. Much of the aircraft work carried out here was, like other war work, kept secret. Shorts were supposed to have been isolated within the Railway Works' site and their workers were issued with ID cards.

A separate entrance was built for the new aircraft plant that required large-scale earthworks to provide a ramped roadway across Ferndale recreation ground and up to 24 Shop yard. Heavy vehicles towing trailers with aircraft wings and tail sections would soon be rolling down this road and it gained the nickname 'The Burma Road'. In time some of the aircraft work was being done in railway workshops on the other side of the fence, while Great Western labour was being used in 24 Shop. One of the things people most remember about this displaced factory was the strong smell of dope. What everyone called 'dope' was cellulose acetate, a lacquer that, when brushed on to the fabric skin of the airframe, tightened it and made it waterproof.

Historian Alan Peck said in his book that 24 Shop was 'handed over to Spitfire aircraft production' but this was not true. Harry Bartlett was an aviation enthusiast and worked on the carriage side during the war. He pointed out the error to Mr Peck, who immediately realised his mistake. Harry was an office boy delivering and collecting mail around the Carriage Works and was one of the few outsiders to be allowed to go into Shorts in 24 Shop:

It shouldn't have, but their mail would get mixed up with ours because it was often addressed as 'Swindon Works, 24 Shop' instead of 'Short Bros. Ltd, 24 Shop'. Their temporary factory was so different to the railway shops, with their bright modern lighting. There was a distinctive smell from the light alloys and adhesives used in aircraft manufacture. I could see the wings and engine nacelles of the Stirling bombers being produced and assembled.

By the time they began to move out, towards the end of the war, they had been taken over by Armstrong Whitworth Aircraft Ltd. Even so, their former gates in and out continued to be known as 'Shorts entrance'. In fact, the name stuck right up until the Carriage Works closed in the 1960s. Between the 'Burma Road' and Osborne Terrace entrances there was a Prisoner of War camp put up on the green just beyond the northern perimeter fence. Italian POWs held here were put to work 'inside' the Works as labourers. Selbourne Smith said they could fashion cigarette lighters out of dessert spoons from the canteen.

War Work on the Carriage & Wagon Side

On the south side of the main line, Mr Bishop had been chief foreman of the coach finishing and bodymaking shops since they were amalgamated in 1934. Mr Barrat took over from him in early 1941, by which time the chief foreman also supervised three sections of polishers, a small stores and one of the saw mills. There were junior foremen but Mr Barrat oversaw the whole of the building and internal furnishing of carriage bodies and their subsequent repairs. In wartime these workshops took on more and more carriage work connected with the extraordinary 'fitting out' for total war. Mr Barrat's men and women were now converting carriage interiors to form ambulance trains for use at home and overseas. They provided mobile fire-fighting vehicles and US Army HQ personnel vehicles, as well as rebuilding carriages damaged by enemy action.

Most non-railway war work was of iron and steel manufacture; the limited wood work that was undertaken was mainly confined to the Carriage Finishers' Shop. New coaches were not being built from 1942 and this shop, No. 7, which normally fitted out new coaches with the internal timberwork, was turned over to war production. Carriage craftsmen built wooden models and superstructures for the Admiralty. These included the now well-publicised midget submarine superstructures and a full-size replica of a Besa machine gun made in wood. The latter was a complex assembly of a 95mm turret gun for a tank with the Besa (Birmingham Small Arms Company or BSA) gun mounted co-axially with it. Official photographs of the finished articles give some impression of the degree of engineering skill needed to produce them. At the time, this work was secret, particularly that of the submarines.

Upon Mr Barrat's retirement after forty-six years' service, it was stated that he had 518 men and women in his charge. This was in January 1945, when numbers were depleted due to men being away on war service. (The building of the diesel railcars is covered in Chapter 24.)

Where carriage underframes and bogies had been assembled, field gun carriage assembly lines were now laid out. Axles and brakework for the 25-pounder guns were made in the Carriage Fitting Shop and special grade cast iron brake drums were made in the Loco Works' Foundry. After he retired, Mr Johnson, the C&W Manager, would tell a story on occasions about artillery guns that were made at Swindon during the Great War, but never used. He said they were discovered and sent back to Swindon for the fitting of recoil and non-recoil mountings and used in the Second World War.

To the north of Swindon Junction station were the wagon shops. They were building up to 4,500 new wagons a year and repairing another 20,000 by the middle of the war. The availability of wagons had been a headache for the authorities from the start and they were now all classed as 'common user': non-requisitioned private owner wagons excepted. This eased the problem by allowing wagons to be reused after arrival at their destination, regardless of who owned them. If they were not to be refilled immediately they were placed at the disposal of the divisional rolling stock controller. The GWR's road vehicles were similarly pooled for collection and delivery services.

Swindon was required to speed up the turnaround time of goods wagon repairs and they introduced a 'green card' system. After careful inspection, only essential work would be carried out. This in turn simplified the paperwork and accounts, which helped the depleted numbers of clerks. Three roads alongside the huge 21 (Wagon Builders) Shop would be used for light repairs to bodywork and flooring; each held thirty wagons. Inside, the five long roads could hold twenty-five open or covered vehicles and heavier repairs would be done here.

On the south side of this wagon workshop a further nine roads ran through what was classified as 21A Shop. Here complete overhauls were done as facilities for lifting and re-roofing wagons had been installed. The restrictions that had already been implemented regarding the repainting and lettering continued. This was done for two reasons: 1) some pigments in paints were scarce; and 2) many painters had been called up or transferred to other work. Now priority would be given to vehicles needing light repairs. Up to 500 wagons of all kinds were soon being 'turned around' each week under the 'green card' system.

Boiler Shops

Mr White, the chief boiler shops' foreman, was in overall charge of the locomotive and stationary boiler work at Swindon. He had been foreman in the AV (boiler section) prior to taking over from Mr Higgs in 1937. Under him there were 1,343 workers such as boilersmiths and their assistants, including females, platers, riveters, apprentices, labourers, shop clerks and junior supervisory staff. They were spread across six workshops and, as in most areas, not all boiler workers remained on railway work during this time.

The Boiler Shop had no backlog of work at the start of the war and the Ministry of Supply were quick to take advantage of this. They negotiated a large contract of armour plating for Daimler light-wheeled tanks and Hotchkiss naval guns. Jigs were produced to drill the steel plates. They were then heated and quenched in oil to make them tough enough to resist bullets. The tricky part was to avoid them becoming distorted, because once hardened they could not then be easily corrected. The contract stipulated that they be tested on site using a rifle range and this was set up near the V Boiler Shop.

V Shop and the A Shop boiler section (AV Shop), in particular, cut back on their normal work programmes to make way for armaments' work for the various government war ministries. Initially plant and machinery were installed in V Shop to produce 2,000 and 4,000lb bombs. They were the first of new types still in the experimental stage in early 1941. The mild steel barrels were to be produced in the same way, but on a smaller scale, to loco boiler barrels: rolling plate rather than by casting the cases. The larger bomb casings were manufactured in L2 Shop alongside the normal tank and structural steel work.

L2 Shop had supplied every signal box on the Great Western with an air raid shelter. They were just large enough for one man to sit down inside so the larger boxes, where more than one signalman was on duty at the same time, would require more than one shelter. Hundreds had to be produced and because they had to be fabricated from boiler plate, Reading Signal Works could not take on the contract.

The semicircular mounting platform for a 13.5in calibre cross-Channel gun, already mentioned, was assembled in V Shop. A Works' photograph shows that it must have been all of 30ft in diameter when fully assembled. One of the last contracts undertaken for the Ministry was for 5,600 shackles for the Merchant Navy. This was in October 1944, by which time a lot of munitions were being supplied by specialist firms here and in America and the associated production plant had started to be taken out.

For the way the boiler shops adapted so well to this work while still fulfilling their commitment to essential railway work, Foreman White was awarded the British Empire Medal in 1945. No doubt, the way female labour was applied so successfully with little of the anticipated integration problems played a part in his recognition. Mr White was also cited as playing a big part in perfecting new techniques for manufacturing bombs.

Locomotives and Rolling Stock

Some batches of mixed traffic and light passenger locomotives were built during the war but the '8750' class of 0-6-0 pannier tank engines were the only GW engines built throughout the war years. Not surprisingly, the '2884' class of heavy freight engines continued to be built well into the war. It was not until the government wanted a common type of freight engine that production of this forty-year-old design was stopped.

By 1941/42 it was becoming increasingly obvious that Britain had a serious shortage of freight locomotives. The Ministry of Transport decided, therefore, to place orders for the LMS 8F 2-8-0. This type was the most up to date and reliable, and offered good route availability. It would be universally built by the largest British builders, including Swindon. Here they built eighty 8Fs between 1943 and 1945: the LMS built 205 and the other companies built a further 165 between them. Locomotives did not generally stray from one company's territory to another, but with the railways now under one organisation, this was not Swindon's first experience of these LMS engines. Twenty-five had been loaned to the GWR earlier in the war and they had converted others to burn oil in 1941 for use in the Middle East.

A wartime curiosity: a brass worksplate from a Swindon-built but LMS-designed 8F 2-8-0 locomotive. *Author's collection*

Although the existing stock had to be patched up and sent back out, new wagons were built in large numbers throughout the war. Others were adapted to carry special loads. When 14in and 16in naval gun barrels were brought to Swindon from the south coast for relining, wagons code-named 'Pollen E' were used. Four of these six-wheeled trolley wagons were coupled together to spread the load. The breech end of the barrel was supported on a trestle and the muzzle on a raised chock.

In February 1944 the Goods Dept issued new instructions relating to 'special wagons'. The 'common user' policy applying to all British standard goods' vehicles would now also cover certain types designed to carry wartime loads. They included: 1) Four-wheeled wagons fitted with trestles for carrying one or two cases of three-bladed aircraft propellers, code name AERO. 2) Iron or steel vans lined with wood for conveying explosives, code name CONE. 3) 50-ton, bogie flat-topped wagons, on loan from government departments, for carrying military tanks, code name WARFLAT. These, and others, would be pooled to be available for loading with legitimate traffic in any direction, irrespective of company of ownership.

Construction of new coaches was limited and then stopped altogether in 1942. Many of those that came through the Works were not repainted, and that went for locomotives too. It became difficult to obtain sufficient quantities of the constituents to mix their own paint. Considering this, and a lack of labour to carry out the cleaning, stripping and repainting, it is surprising that Swindon did as much as they did at this time. The external appearance of its locomotives and rolling stock was one area that could be temporarily neglected with little effect on the ability to meet its obligations.

If engines and carriages were attended to by the few elderly men still working in the paint shop, they would often get just a partial repaint. Locomotive brasswork and copper was painted over and engines with side window cabs had the glass plated over as a blackout precaution. A few 'Castles' and 'Kings' were painted and lined as they would have been normally, during the first half of the war. From 1942, the express engines were painted in unlined green, and all other locomotives, when they did see a paintbrush, were painted black.

Where cross-country, suburban and main-line coaches were repainted, it was in overall brown. Only the chocolate-and-cream-coloured coaches for the Cornish Riviera and the Torbay Express were unaffected. In 1943 some other corridor stock used on principal services was also repainted in the old colours. Vans were painted a dark red, insulated vans were given a stone colour and open wagons were not painted at all. A reddish-brown area was applied to the bottom left of each side of the open wagons, on to which the vehicle's details were stencilled in white.

With the preparations for the invasion of Europe, some of the LMS coaches that had been converted to form ambulance trains in 1939 were modified again for use by the Americans. The US Army took possession of a set at a small ceremony at the Works in 1943. Until it was needed on the Continent, this train set was parked on one of the outer roads at the back of the Carriage Works. It was fully equipped, manned and on standby twenty-four hours a day in case air raids overwhelmed the existing services.

This mobile hospital had its own mail service but, as with Shorts' mail, some got mixed up with that coming in for the GWR due to it being incorrectly addressed. Fifteen-year-old Harry Bartlett would have to take it over to the administration coach: 'It was staffed by female officers. They gave me tips in the form of money, cigarettes, sweets and chocolate: this made me very popular with the other office boys,' said Harry.

Some ambulance trains that had been sent overseas had been captured by the enemy. However, by the autumn of 1944, most had been recaptured. The damaged coaches were inspected by REME and replacement parts were requested. Surviving new work orders tell us that 15 Shop built nine pairs of bogies for transhipment and 16 Shop provided twenty-seven pairs of wheels and axles. A different kind of wartime job at this time was to be done in 19 Shop, according to the same source. They were to prepare a condemned goods brake van for use as accommodation for Italian PoWs at Exeter Goods Depot. The cost of this was estimated to be £17. These are just two contrasting examples of the many types of work required to adapt the railway for the conditions of war.

Ted Randell, a senior apprentice in 15 Shop, was due to go into the navy with some of his workmates, but at the last minute he was turned down because of eyesight problems.

As the war work contracts were completed or diverted away, the carriage men were being moved, temporarily, to the loco side. Ted was moved to the AE Shop in July of 1944 because so many fitter/erectors had gone to war. Here all engine pits were kept fully utilised despite the shortage of manpower. Only now locomotives were given minimal attention based on a mechanical inspector's report, keeping them running without becoming too unreliable. 'Patching up' rolling stock and locomotives would leave the company with an increasing number of vehicles that would eventually need heavy repairs or withdrawal but in the short term it served its purpose.

Canteen Facilities

The government introduced a number of schemes to improve the nutrition of the nation's workers. One was the expansion of industrial dining facilities. A contract catering company ran the Works' canteens early in the war and the largest was set up in the Pattern Store basement. Fifteen-year-old Margaret Kirby was among the first to be employed there but she didn't like it: 'I had to make a big vat of custard every day and peel lots of vegetables.' Margaret remembers a Jewish man named Joe Hansen being in charge: a Mrs Tylee and Iris Clapham (nee Cotton) worked there too.

The workers soon started to complain about the standard of cooking, in particular. It was brought to the attention of the Joint Works' Committee but the situation did not improve and, perhaps out of frustration, management said: 'If you can do better then get on with it,' so the men organised the catering themselves. A canteen sub-committee was formed and Gilbert Luker, as a prominent and respected member of that committee, was allowed to oversee the hiring of staff and the ordering of supplies.

This canteen was opened in the Locomotive Works early in the war, in the basement of the Pattern Store. Margaret Kirby, who had just left school, thinks she is the girl at the far end. The prices on the blackboards show that soup was 2d, two slices of bread were 1d, roast dinners were 9d and tea 1d. *Ray Eggleton collection*

Ray Eggleton came into the Works as an apprentice coppersmith in 1942. He told me that his father, Joe, was appointed to be canteen manager. Proper catering equipment was installed under the Pattern Store during the early part of the war with seating for up to 300 people. From early 1942, female staff were employed to cook and serve the day and night shifts. Until meal tickets came in Joe also acted as cashier. The meal tickets, or tokens, became available from automatic machines so as to avoid too much precious time queuing during breaks. Other refreshments and cigarettes were sold, although smoking was prohibited in the canteen, as it was on the pattern floors above.

Ray said his father had learnt the trade of boilermaking 'inside' and was one of the first to weld copper fireboxes. However, this is thought to have caused a permanent strain injury to his wrist and he was invalided out: 'In his new work Dad dealt with the suppliers' paperwork and the delivery lorries. They would park outside in Rodbourne Road and unload supplies through a door in the pattern building. He also collected groceries himself, from a warehouse in Bridge Street. His Ford 8 was probably the first private car to go into the Works proper.'

Peter Chalk told me that when it was very dark, during the blackout, the night shift did the 'crocodile walk' to get from the AM Shop to this canteen: 'We all walked in single file with one hand on the shoulder of the man in front. The man at the head shone a dim torch and thus we avoided walking into batches of components or falling into the engine and turntable pits.' This makeshift wartime canteen remained in use until the early 1960s.

The Pattern Store canteen was centrally situated for all but the carriage and wagon repair shop workers. A completely new canteen building was erected for them, between 15 and 21 Shops, and it came into use in 1943. A young Harry Bartlett would go there sometimes and have lunch for sixpence: 'On a couple of occasions we [two other office boys and himself] were lucky enough to see the BBC Workers' Playtime concerts. These were half-hour programmes broadcast every weekday from works' canteens throughout the country. They would have a top-class comedian and singer from BBC radio performing.'

The smaller existing facilities and mess rooms, which had served refreshments at the start of the war, were retained. Prior to that there was no food or drinks available to purchase 'inside'. Fewer workers now went home 'middle day' for what was always referred to as 'a bit a dinner', as it was always a bit of a rush, no matter how near they lived.

Some of the staff could play musical instruments or sing and entertain in front of an audience, and turns were put on in the new dining halls over the Wednesday dinnertimes. In the early days especially, people were worried about the way the war might go. Live entertainment raised morale and created a sense that they were all in it together. Enid Hogden sang in a choir and they toured the workshops, singing during the midday break. This was, she said, also designed to lift people's spirits. By 1944, manual workers in the Works, and elsewhere in heavy industry, were allowed extra rations of such things as tea, sugar and cheese.

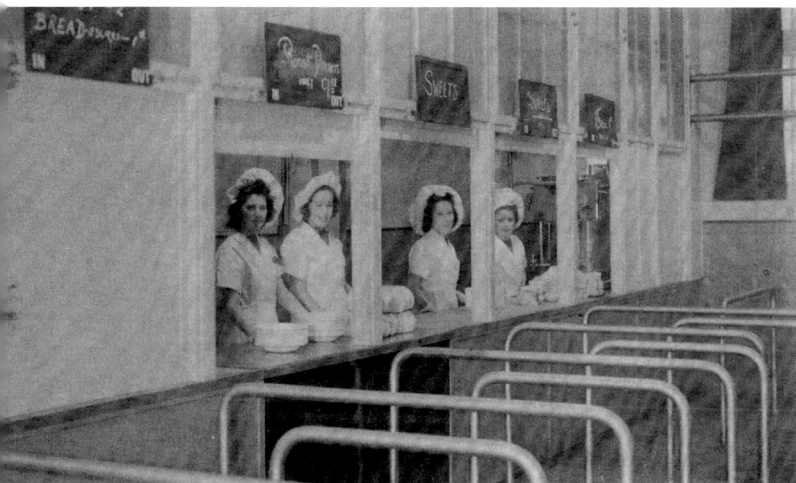

Jack Fleetwood remembered his mother saying that: 'It is a sin to give away your sugar allowance: people are dying bringing that across the sea.'

Air Raids and Precautions

The Works' steam hooter was a pair of single-note whistles giving a very deep hollow tone, similar to a ship's horn. It was perfectly audible throughout the town and beyond, alerting the workers to the approaching start and finish times of the shifts. In wartime the hooter's role changed to warn of enemy aircraft in the area. Mr Millard in the Hooter House claimed that, between 1940 and 1944, it was activated nearly 1,000 times. Klaxon horns were installed around the site and a system of wall-mounted coloured lights were rigged up in workshops and offices. A blue bulb lit up when the hooter blew. If it changed to the red bulb alongside, lighting up, it meant that enemy planes had been spotted and everyone was to go to the shelters.

The GWR Gas Works and the northern end of the Carriage Works' yards were attacked from the air by a 'lone raider' in July 1942. This incident has been described several times in books but some details from the Fire Station register add further to the story. On 27 July an 'air raid message red' was transmitted to all local emergency and ARP services by the civil defence control centre. They were acting upon information phoned in from roof spotters. The alert was received at just after 6am at the Works' Fire Station watchroom. The attendant would have then called the 'senior fire officer', followed by the 'A list' firemen on call that week.

For this type of emergency the attendant would then have to contact the 'knocker-uppers' to go out on bicycles to alert extra firemen and first-aiders, some of whom lived beyond the railway estate. Another caller at 6.48am told the attendant fireman of fires at No. 5 gas holder due to machine gun strafing from the low-flying enemy aircraft. By 7.37am, when the all-clear was given, '27 firemen were assembled' (changed and ready) at the Station. The town brigade too, would have been asked to standby.

Meanwhile, the ambulance crew were busy too. They were called out at 6.15am to take a Mr Vance, a railwayman from Beatrice Street, to the GWR hospital: the reason given in the register is that he had been knocked down by the ambulance! They were out again at 7.10am, this time to the east end of the Stamping Shop, to take a Mr Dixon to the hospital with head and leg injuries caused by bomb blast. The ambulance and first-aiders were called upon twice more that morning to take casualties of the air raid to hospital.

The major fires expected when the Gas Works was targeted did not happen. Flames shooting out of holes in the gas holders were quickly extinguished by plugging them. Locals said that Jimmy Simpkins used clay and tar as temporary plugs, something he was taught in ARP lectures for gas works' staff perhaps? Nevertheless, he was recognised by his employer and given an award or commendation of some sort. I have heard stories of men having to take cover under their machine tools or workbenches. Whether this was because the Works' alerts had not been activated, I don't know.

Maurice Dunscombe, who worked in the AE Shop, was fire-watching one night in the Works' yards when bombs started falling. He told his daughter: 'There were five of us in a coach having some refreshments. The explosions got louder and I counted six: the seventh, I felt sure, was ours. The others with me were all "tabernacle people" and were praying out loud. It worked as no more bombs fell: I must have miscounted.'

The Germans would have known Swindon was an important railway centre from flying overhead and they are known to have taken aerial reconnaissance photographs. But they almost certainly didn't know the extent of the Works' contribution to the war effort. At first they put all their efforts into attacking the means by which the British were attacking them: the shipbuilding yards, ports, aircraft factories and aerodromes. The railway factories were, by comparison, considered less

An anti-aircraft emplacement on top of the station at Swindon Junction in March 1941. There was another on the top of the coal stage water tank and one on Compton's flat roof. Each was fitted with a mounted light machine gun and telephone. Two specially trained Home Guards manned each post. At night they were used for fire-watching.
GWR courtesy of The Swindon Society

important. Later, the enemy's targets were the big cities, particularly those with ports, and again the large manufacturing plant in Swindon was spared.

Post-war Preparations

The war situation by the middle of 1944 had changed considerably from a year earlier. Now the company, like everyone else, was starting to plan for the future when peace returned.

In August of that year the huge modern carriage repair and painting shop that had all but been given over to aircraft production in 1940–41, was to be returned to its former use. At the same time, the opportunity would be taken to update the pre-war facilities. The initial work overlapped with the aircraft facilities being moved out and lasted twelve months. Firstly, trackwork was put back or altered and some smaller outbuildings demolished. Internal walls were removed and some of the original outer doors were reinstated.

Colin Kibblewhite's gang made and fitted the new doors, which were approximately 14ft square, to allow carriages to once again pass in and out. The aircraft plant had been fenced off from the rest of the Works and the original toilet block was outside beyond their fence and continued to be used by GWR workers. So the temporary indoor toilets put in for the aircraft workers now went, along with the additional fencing. Offices and washing troughs were put in, steam heating and water supplies reconnected and additional electric lighting installed. The last job for D Shop carpenters Arthur Halliday, Roy Windsor and Colin was to put up two large 'roll of honour' plaques on a single brick dividing wall. 'They were to go one either side, and I said it won't hold them, but it did,' said Colin. It was not until the old adjoining carriage washing shed was converted for roof and panel repairs in 1948, that the 24 Shop rebuilding was finally complete.

Work to remove brick shelters in R, A, J and V Shops was authorised in March of 1945. In May other ARP

From early 1944, it was becoming obvious that the country was on the eve of major military operations. The public began to see signs and hear rumours about an invasion of mainland Europe. This appeal was issued to every GWR man and women in March 1944, reminding them of the hazards of careless talk. Details of their day-to-day work, especially the movement of government goods traffic, might be useful to the enemy, it warned. This particular copy was issued to Peter Oland, who worked in the A Shop stores. *Author's collection*

measures were to be dismantled at the Works. First aid posts, decontamination stations and static water tanks were to go; steel shutters were to be removed from control rooms and the telephone exchange; emergency telephones were also to be taken out; and glass was to be replaced and/or black out paint removed from various loco and carriage shop roofs. Twenty-four restaurant cars were reinstated in May and June 1945. The Works stripped them out and contractors Hampton & Sons Ltd refitted them. They also added fibreglass insulation, double-glazed windows and lined the roofs.

Aftermath

Since 1940 there had been a few isolated attacks on the town by single enemy aircraft. Most were probably on their way back to their bases when they strafed random targets or dropped their bombs from high altitude. Official sources say the railway town as a whole suffered 158 bomb alerts, 104 bombs dropped, forty-eight people killed and 105 injured, of which thirty-three were seriously hurt. Fifty houses were destroyed or had to be pulled down and another 1,852 suffered damage to some extent. Remarkably no Works' buildings, where people were working, were hit, although some suffered blast damage. The only major remedial work that had to be carried out was the filling in of bomb craters in the yards and the relaying of some damaged trackwork.

A lot of skilled men from the Works were retained in the army after the war, particularly with the Royal Engineers. At home their places had been filled by unskilled labour brought in. The company had secured the 'class B' release for some trades such as wagon builders and boilersmiths, but not others. To get released from war service you had to convince the authorities your skills were better employed at home than overseas. Both had railways and infrastructure in desperate need of labour to get them back to some sort of normality.

The Amalgamated Engineering Union district secretary Dick Pearce wrote to the MP for Swindon in an attempt to get men discharged and back into the Works. All efforts fell on deaf ears once their plight reached the War Office and demobilisation took eighteen months, or more in some cases. Some workers who had been loaned to Short Bros aircraft factory in Blunsdon found their prospects had been better than in the GWR. *The Evening Advertiser* reported that they were reluctant to return in August 1945.

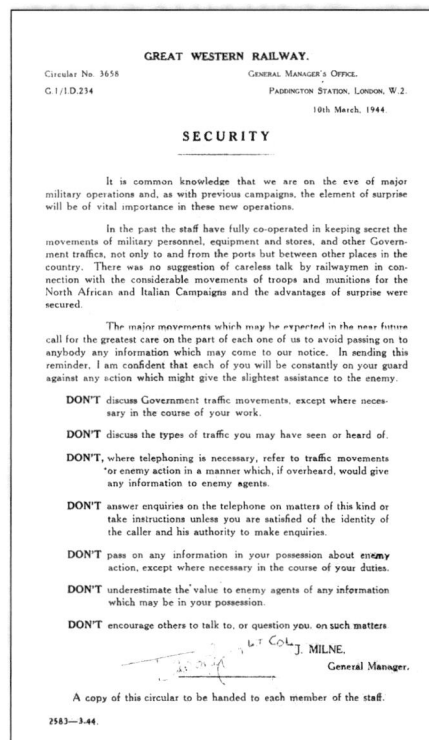

22
Workers in Wartime

Conscription

Both sides of the Works were taking on again in 1939 after a bad 1938. Immediately before the war there were 12,000 on the payroll. Of the large number of discharges announced the previous year, many were rescinded or the men taken back. Males called up for war service were drawn indiscriminately from shop and office, depending only on age. The first to be conscripted were men up to the age of twenty-five whose work could, theoretically, be absorbed by the remaining workforce. They included apprentices, labourers, clerks, vehicle drivers, shunters, and later anyone whose work could be done by female and male dilutees.

Young single women were also called up and a few of those already in the company's employment from before the war were drafted into the Women's Auxiliary Air Force (WAAF), the Auxiliary Territorial Service (ATS), or the Civil Defence Services. Presumably their railway work, mainly clerical, was done by hastily trained exempted persons brought in. Colleagues of those departing temporarily would often buy gifts and have a presentation to wish them well, particularly in the offices.

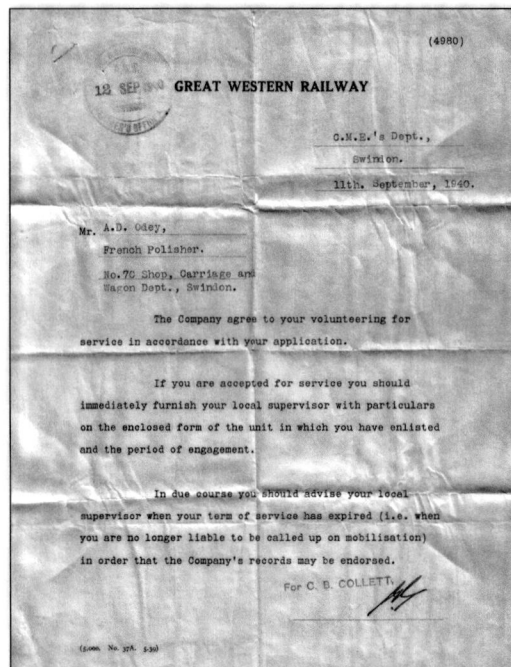

French polisher Albert Odey wrote volunteering to go to war in 1940 and here is the reply he received. Although the men in the Works would soon find themselves in a reserved occupation, the country needed more and more men and women for war service. The Ministry of Labour, therefore, amended the schedule for reserved occupations. They increased the maximum age of call-up by one year from the beginning of 1942, and the minimum age was lowered to seventeen and a half soon after.
Family of Mrs B. Wynn

One way the works' managers offset the effects of the labour shortage was to gradually reduce and then stop much of the planned maintenance programmes.

Works' men on active service made up a sizable proportion of the Royal Electrical and Mechanical Engineers (REME). Their particular skills would, wherever possible, be utilised in their new deployment, as had happened during the last war. Some men, not surprisingly, felt a strong moral dilemma between doing their duty and potentially having to kill someone. This may, or may not, have been due to their religious beliefs. Pay clerk George Petfield said of the ones he knew: 'They went off to war in non-combatant roles, and acted very commendably.' There were also pacifists among Swindon clerks. Some were sent off to work at the Ministry of Munitions at the relocated GWR Audit Section, Aldermaston.

Railwaymen talk about a bond that existed between themselves and how it was stronger than ever during wartime. Jack Fisher was a rough painter in the Erecting Shop before being called up. In the army, he found he couldn't let his family know where he was for months on end. Occasionally, however, his unit passed through

Swindon by train and he would throw messages tied to a weight on to the platform. They always reached his home in Ipswich Street but he never found out who delivered them.

As time went on, the government had to face a dilemma. The criteria for retaining many skilled and trained railway staff within the 'reserved occupations' had to be amended to allow more men to join the forces. However, the importance of maintaining an efficient railway system at home was starting to be acknowledged by the Ministry of Labour.

Roy Bown had become a skilled blacksmith in the Works during the early part of the war. Like many young men, he wanted to go and fight for his country. Many of his workmates had been swept along on a wave of patriotism and joined up but Roy suddenly found himself in a reserved occupation. His father had been a pilot officer in the last war and no doubt his stories impressed the youngster. Mr Bown senior wrote to the Air Ministry on his son's behalf. This did the trick and Roy joined the RAF as air crew. Later, when they found out about his occupation in Civvy Street, he was grounded and had his blacksmith's skills put to good use on maintenance work.

Holidays at Home

The Works' holiday trains were cancelled at the last minute in 1940 and until further notice. Then there would be no fixed holiday period in July for the duration. This was another reason to stop planned maintenance programmes as certain plant and machinery could normally only be stripped and repaired during the annual shutdown.

So as to discourage unnecessary train journeys, the Borough Council had the job of persuading local people to spend their summer holidays within the town. The *GWR Magazine* said at the start of the first 'holidays at home' season in 1942: 'Swindon has become the playground of Wiltshire.' The Council arranged an impressive programme with orchestras, brass bands, open air shows, variety concerts, music festivals and sport. Swindon's famous Edwards' Fair spent six weeks in The Park in 1942 and returned again the following year.

A programme for the local Musical Festival of 1943 survives with the scores added in pencil. It shows, as you would expect, that the majority of classes were for schoolchildren and women. Only one section (mixed vocal soloists) included men and they were members of HM forces based locally.

Programmes of events for the annual 'Holidays at Home' season. They include details of concerts, dances, community singing and games organised for and by the town's folk. Church halls, parks and open spaces were utilised throughout the annual five-week period.
Author's collection

The mayor and mayoress presented the prizes on the third and final day. The adjudicators, stewards, committee members and officials amounted to fifty people, some acting in more than one role. The same names of competitors and organisers turned up regularly over the years, giving the impression that such events were of a high standard and well organised.

Bert Fluck, a senior clerk in the Mileage Offices, had a daughter named Diana. By 1943, the 'Fluck girl', as she was known in her neighbourhood, was already showing that she had her father's natural ability for performing in front of an audience. Diana was entered for just one class in the Musical Festival that year: 'recitation for girls 8 and under 13 years'. The eleven-year-old beat all the other sixteen competitors with a score of 95 out of a possible 100. This talented youngster's film career began before the end of the decade, her name having been changed to Diana Dors.

Fred Drinkwater, a chargeman in the Weigh House, was the town mayor in 1944. He wrote a forward for the 'holidays at home' programme that year:

> My Council are again providing attractions and entertainment with a view to encouraging the people of Swindon to spend their holiday at home. The restrictions on travel are well known, particularly in a railway centre such as this, and it is hoped that the public will readily respond by avoiding unnecessary travel and thus release rolling stock for essential war purposes.

The Works' outings were also discouraged by the management, but smaller parties of railwaymen and women were still getting away. Peter Reade got three free passes a year and unlimited quarter-fares by the company's trains. With some of his workmates from the Loco Smiths' Shop, who now included females, he would often go up to the West End and see a show.

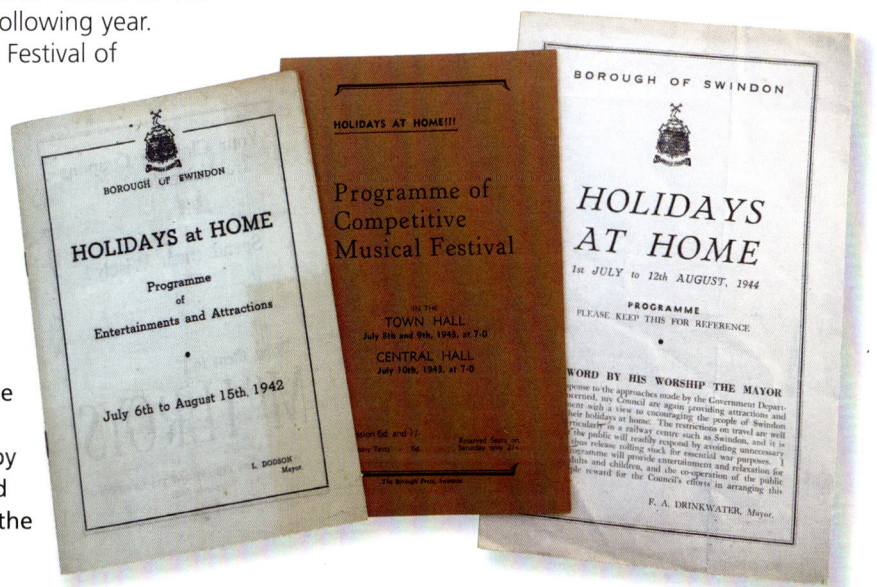

Temporary Female Labour

For some reason the CME Dept had been slow to start using female labour to replace men who were being called up. The fault probably lay more with the Ministry of Labour than with the Works. Before 1942, women were coming on to the GWR as porters, van guards, carriage cleaners, ticket collectors and other positions usually filled by men. Many of the females, when they did start working 'inside', had relatives there. This helped them settle into the alien environment and break down any animosity towards them. At first they were put on light labouring and repetitive munitions' work on the day shift. Soon though, they were doing semi-skilled machining and fitting, and some were put on to railway work proper. They proved to be equally capable of light coppersmith and tinsmith work or the heavy work of boilermakers' and blacksmiths' assistants.

Following conscription for women aged between twenty and thirty years, at the end of 1941, they came into CME workshops in much greater numbers. Females made up the labour shortage due to men being called up and the extra war work commitments. The general role of this new source of workshop labour was to supply and assist the skilled men and, with a few exceptions, they exceeded all expectations. Some went on to drive walking cranes, steam hammers and traversers, and later, the larger-capacity cranes that ran up and down the length of some shops by overhead carriage.

Phyllis Saunders and Peggy Thompson were just two of those tried on various types of work in the two Boiler Shops. This included cutting the flue tubes to length and expanding them on to tubeplates, or removing and replacing boiler stays. Much of the boilermakers' work required the use of specialist heavy machinery. From the age of twenty-one they would be receiving more than £2 per week in pay. This was more than most of them would have received previously, although those on repetitive production work would tell you that 'you earned it'. Later women were put on the night shifts as well. It was soon acknowledged that the women who complained the most were the rivet hotters, hardly surprising as this was particularly hot, noisy and dirty work.

Two sisters from Percy Street went 'inside' in 1941: Elma Howard was put into the Boiler Shop and Phyllis into the Smiths' Shop as a steam hammer driver. A third sister, Violet, worked out on the permanent way, cleaning then oiling the points with the Engineering Department. With the integration of male and female workers, there was bound to be some lasting relationships formed. The staff magazine reported that L. Collard and Miss Durbridge, both working in the Iron Foundry, were married in 1943. Another was Reg Arthurs, a coremaker also in the Foundry, who married an overhead crane driver named Violet.

Some of those who opposed women in the workshops would point out that as soon as they became useful most left to be married. In actual fact, most of those who did marry in wartime stayed on. Each family's circumstances were different of course: Fred Kirby from Emlyn Square still had four children at home when he was injured on the footplate. There was no choice but for his wife Ella to go and work 'inside'. She was placed in AM Shop working on bomb cases. Looking back on that period, Fred's daughter Margaret said: 'Thank God for company wood and coal.' This meant that they could keep the range lit in the kitchen for cooking, heating and washing.

Jack Fleetwood said that the women made good overhead crane drivers but one of them needed to get her confidence. The loco works' manager asked her foreman to put her on to nights, where it was quieter. She told Jack she once moved a locomotive boiler in V Shop and clipped another, sending a row of upended boiler shells over like skittles. Facilities to accommodate women were provided and later expanded between 1941 and early 1943. Cloakrooms, lavatories and mess rooms were installed in the following shops: boilermakers, boiler repairs, points and crossings, brass finishers, steam hammers, oil works, coppersmiths and tinsmiths and all three foundries.

A female doing the job of hammer boy in this photograph dated May 1942. Twenty-year-old Phyllis Bezer controls the hammer blows being delivered to an axle, which Mr Davis, the smith, moves and turns between blows to achieve the desired form.
GWR: courtesy of The Swindon Society

After the war a lot of women in the workshops were kept on due mainly to the slow process of getting men demobilised. They had initially been treated with suspicion and sometimes hostility but 'when the men did get back from the war it was the unions and not their male colleagues who wanted them out,' said Alan Lambourn.

Colin Kibblewhite: Carpenter

At the start of the war I was in B Shop, which was still called by its original name of B Shed by most of the men. I worked with a gang of three boilermakers as rivet boy on small engine and tender tanks. Harry Harris and senior man Sid Eatwell were the riveters, Walter Ford was the 'holder up' and I heated the rivets on a small forge. Another job I remember was helping Freddie Cockhead fit stiffening plates or patches to the horn ways of locomotive main frames. Cracks sometimes appeared from the corners where the axleboxes were held after being in service for a time and seemed to be a weakness peculiar to GW engines. We fitted the horseshoe-shaped plates around the gaps with cold rivets or threaded studs.

In December 1939 I signed my indentures, witnessed by Mr Gee, the Works' Manager's Secretary. I then started my apprenticeship in D1 Shop. D1 was near the Running Sheds and was home to one of the three types of Works' carpenters. D2, better known as Mason's Yard, was nearby and home to the Works' bricklayers and stonemasons. The CME Department carpentry work, excluding carriage building, was divided between D1 Shop and 12 Shop. The types of work allocated to each changed just before the war. No. 12 Shop was divided up as areas known as 12A, B and C. The cabinetmakers here would manufacture and repair furniture, ticket office cases with roller shutters etc., while their general carpenters dealt with platform trolleys, barrows, seats and wooden fixtures etc., throughout the company. D1 men would look after all the Works and mechanical outstation carpentry.

There was not normally any night-work for Works' carpenters, even in wartime. Fred Gooding was our foreman and Bill Harper was the Bricklayers' [referred to as masons by the company] foreman. I remember that carpenters Joe Prater and Jack Weston and cabinetmaker Dennis Jefferies were all 12 Shop men. Jim Hayward had recently taken over from Joe Boots as head foreman. Apprentices with me in our shop were Arnold Woolford, Bill Maynard, a lad by the name of Swatton and Arthur Halliday. D Shop carpenters were divided into five gangs. I was put with Bill Ayres' gang, who normally refurbished the offices in the CME building. Bert Selwood was my mate for a short while, until he retired. He used to tell me about his time in South Africa during the Boer War.

Chargeman Fred Keen's gang had been doing a lot of work in No. 8 Office. This was the loco works' managers office building, which included the Loco Wages Office on the upper floor. Repairing the desks, cupboards and fitted cabinets as they did was among the many types of non-essential maintenance that was put on hold so that internal and external war work could be undertaken. One gang did carry on as normal but with fewer men; they worked with the loco erectors fitting the wooden floors on locomotive footplates. They also fitted elm boards into tenders in B Shop, on to which sat the tank before it was bolted to the frame.

When I first arrived some carpenters were fitting roller blinds in the offices as part of a programme of air raid precautions. The following year, I remember, we had to crate up some machine tools that had arrived from Avonmouth Docks. They had been en route from America to France but the French surrendered before they got there. I think the machinery had some water damage, so the Works were asked to check them over before sending them on to factories up north [Des Griffiths said that a machine tool from a ship's cargo was collected by his father who worked on the Internal Transport. This was, he said, bedded down in the Tool Room during the war, so perhaps it was from this consignment.]

In Ayres' gang, Bert Selwood and his half-brother Cecil, Charlie Humphries, Bill Prior and myself stripped and refurbished several offices upon the retirement of Chief Mechanical Engineer, Mr Collett, in July of 1941, including his former office. After the decorators had repainted the window frames and walls, we assessed the furniture, fitted cupboards and panelling and repaired or replaced what was necessary. My job was to remove all the brass draw pulls, handles and locks, clean them and replace after the French polishers had finished. [It is interesting to hear that this type of work was still being done when so much mechanical maintenance work was being put off.]

During late 1941 and into 1942 Colin Kibblewhite was spending a lot of time making and packing wooden cases for shells, bombs and armaments. Where possible, they reused material from incoming cargoes. Another job for the D Shop carpenters was making long wooden tables for production lines dealing with shell cases in 24 Shop. Only once did Colin go outstation during the war, when he assisted a gang overhauling portable platform bridges at Fishguard Harbour. These wooden structures allowed people and cargoes to cross between the quay and station platforms quickly. They could be raised and lowered for storage by a jacking mechanism.

The O Shop Tool Room needed more space because the government Machine Tool Control wanted to place additional machinery here. They did this for balancing purposes, to get the most out of the plant already there. The electricians had occupied the area where the new machines were going, so they were moved into part of D1 Shop. Because of this, the carpenters' end of the shop was extended, which provided Colin and some workmates with work: they fitted the roof timbers.

Towards the end of 1942 I spent three weeks with the 'house maintenance gang'. They did any carpentry work required on the company houses and Medical Fund buildings. I made or repaired some 2ft diameter covers, which sat on top of kitchen coppers, in their workshop on the estate. One of the gang was making backrests for hospital beds, I remember. In 1943 I was back in the Works, this time with Jim House's gang. They normally dealt with structural timberwork such as roofs, window and door frames. However, with the ever growing numbers of women coming in, this gang were often employed on alterations to provide restrooms for them. The rest of the time they were packing goods ready for dispatch.

It was at this time that we built crates for machine tools bound for America. I remember this because they had to be made watertight.' [A round up of war work undertaken at Swindon was published in the *GWR Magazine* just after the war. One part said heavy plant had been installed in the Works for forging shells, but just as it became operational it was decided to uproot it all and send it to America. This is no doubt what Colin was referring to here.]

Later in 1943 I was transferred to [Fred] Keen's gang and sent to the Steam Hammer Shop with a carpenter: I think it was Harold Llewellyn. A large hammer and steel block was being bedded into reinforced concrete. In preparation for this we put tapered beech blocks around the base and steel wedges were driven into them. Towards the end of 1944 the overhead crane in the New Saw Mill was dismantled. We renewed all the timber packing while the fitters adjusted the track to the gauge and rebuilt it.

Workers' Conditions

The Works' day shift continued to end at 5.30pm in the shops with the option of a couple of hours' overtime in the evening. To encourage men to stay on, the smoking ban was lifted from the start of 1940, but only after 5.30pm and only in the shops where it was safe to do so, of course. As the factory took on outside contracts for the Ministry of War Production, everybody, including apprentices, started working twelve-hour days. Where the delivery time was short or where the order was large, the work continued day and night, the night shift also being twelve hours long.

The Ministry decided that bank holidays were to be normal working days starting from Easter 1940. The men were then able to take another day off instead, when mutually convenient, or be paid. The extra man-hours created would not only assist war production, it would help the railway production and repair work, which was soon feeling the effects of an ever-diminishing workforce.

The rules on smoking in the workshops were becoming more inconsistent. Some men permanently employed in the shops could smoke but most could not. Men not based in a particular workshop didn't seem to attract the attention of the foreman if they had a cigarette in their mouths. Those working in the yards outside would come in smoking without fear of being apprehended, as would visitors and others passing through, such as shunters and pilot enginemen. However, after 5.30pm and on Saturday mornings anyone could now 'light up', as already stated.

A production line making 1,000lb high-explosive bomb cases in the old Points and Crossings' Shop. Peter Chalk worked on what they called the 'bomb plant' before starting his apprenticeship. He remembers that a gang of women operated lathes here, 'parting off' copper shell bands while others varnished the cases. Part of Peter's job was to see that the varnish was bake dried. This made the cases resistant to chemical reaction, which could cause the detonators to become unstable. *GWR*

In March 1941 the *Evening Advertiser* reported that the men had announced plans to defy the daytime 'no smoking' rule: 'At a specially convened meeting in No. 5 Shop, representatives of the rail unions agreed to wait until the Federation of Railway Trades' Unions had put a proposal to the GWR management.' This would first have to go through the machinery of negotiation required by the recently formed Joint Works' Committee. The men, at least the majority who smoked, wanted the ban lifted for all, except in areas where there were explosive gases and inflammable substances used. The matter was, of course, settled in the only reasonable way possible.

Where the Works were doing government work, tighter conditions were observed. A person who was persistently late or absent would be given a warning by his shop committee. If this didn't work the Ministry of Labour could take him or her to court under the Essential Work Order of 1941, and this did happen, albeit rarely. On the other hand, skilled workers were needed like never before and were therefore not easily sacked. *The Evening Advertiser* reported that a machine setter 'struck his foreman across the face' in 1943. He was arrested by the Works' police and received a £2 fine, but not dismissed.

As a result of the extraordinary conditions brought about by this war, many traditions were discontinued, never to be reinstated. The foreman could no longer summarily dismiss a man, although, in practice, the unions and shop committees had this stopped in the 1920s. The dreaded mass discharges were also never to return, although no one knew it at the time. Promotions came along much quicker for those not away at war.

Even fashions seemed to be changing. Most of the official photographs taken around the Works' are from the 1920s or before, when everybody seemed to wear ties and waistcoats, including the manual workers. Jack Fleetwood said that, apart from supervisory, office staff and management, most of the men were wearing their shirts collars open by the early 1940s, although photographs tend to suggest this was only the younger ones. 'One-piece overalls were becoming popular by then too,' said Jack.

Direction of Labour

Workers approaching retirement had been asked to stay while colleagues were away in the armed forces. The EWO Act allowed the authorities to direct skilled labour to wherever it was most needed, so yet more skilled men were away, having been loaned to outside firms.

D1 Shop men Fred Keen, Burt Bryant and others were sent to make concrete pillboxes and defences somewhere down south. As carpenters, they made the wooden formwork or moulds to contain concrete until it set. For some reason Colin, who was still a junior apprentice, was given the task of telling them of their impending transfer. Reg Bullock had just started as an apprentice coppersmith in September 1940. At that time he remembers that quite a few of the men in his shop were being loaned to the

Gloucester Aircraft Co. or sent down to Falmouth, presumably to work at the docks.

Even though new carriage building had stopped, there was plenty of alternative work on the carriage side. Nevertheless they too were required to loan some tradesmen to outside firms, temporarily. South Marston, on the eastern outskirts of Swindon, was chosen as an aircraft factory site in the late-1930s. One of the reasons for this was the availability of tradesmen in the Railway Works, with the right skills, should they be needed to relocate to aircraft work. Reg Dauris, a carpenter in the Coach Body Shop, was one of a number of Works' carpenters sent to the South Marston factory (initially it was a shadow factory for Phillips and Powis, then it was taken over by Vickers Supermarine).

Some apprentices and labourers who had not yet been called up were sent across to help in the erecting shops. Others arrived at the Works for the first time and a post was set up outside the junction station to direct incoming war workers to their lodgings. Some civic and church buildings, left empty for the duration, had been converted to provide accommodation for government war workers. The Mission House in Rodbourne Lane, for instance, became a hostel for thirty-six females, most of whom went into the GWR.

Later in the war it was noticed that some skilled men were doing menial work with the forces, while their places on the railway were filled by 'dilutees', outsiders with no experience. Men taken away from the department could apply for a 'class B' release, and those back home with influence would, in some cases, write to the authorities on their behalf. After the invasion, however, the War Office also needed railway workers to rebuild and maintain the railways on the Continent and an early release became very difficult to obtain.

After the war, the slow demobilisation of workers continued and consequently the temporary female workers were compelled to stay on. Dorothy Grimes, in the Works' Fire Station, for instance, continued working until she got married at St Mark's Church in 1947. This enabled her apply and obtain a 'release', at the end of 1947.

Joint Works' Committee

From 1943 the men's, and now also women's, concerns were aired at regular meetings of a Joint Works' Committee. Their side was represented by elected members of the NUR, the craft unions and also non-union men. The company were represented by an equal number, made up of supervisors and managers. Mr Cook was loco works' manager at the time and sat in on the JWC through the war. They met once a month to negotiate matters arising. That could be anything from how best to use the resources to increase efficiency, to claims that some groups of men were being unfairly treated. The only subject not negotiable was standard rates of pay.

Incendiary bombs falling on the factory were a constant worry but, if spotted and extinguished early, presented much less of a threat. With this in mind, men in the GWR Home Guard were rostered to patrol the site or man fire-watching posts in the evenings and at night. One of the first matters that came up for discussion was the men involved, including office staff and managers, complaining about fatigue. Lack of sleep was, they said, affecting their work during the day. By now the threat of air raids had diminished somewhat and the amount of work being done at night had increased. Therefore it was proposed that some of the increased numbers of night shift workers be used for fire-watching duties. This was democratically endorsed by the JWC.

Mr H.C. Horrell, a patternmaker, was the first JWC chairman: (in the 1950s he had become secretary of what was then called just the Works' Committee). By June 1944 boilermaker Gilbert Luker had become chairman of the Committee. A cross-section of influential British railway workers including Gilbert were invited to a large meeting in London addressed by Field Marshal Montgomery in the run-up to D-Day. The theme was the vital importance of keeping supplies for the second front moving and the significance of railwaymen and women in achieving this.

In exceptional circumstances, such as if the matter in question affected the company at large, the committee was invited to send a deputation to meet the general manager at Paddington. With the need for co-operation being in the national interest, the local meetings are remembered for the amicable way decisions were reached. This was interpreted by some workers as their negotiators becoming passive in the presence of 'the gaffers'.

GWR Home Guard

In May 1940 the Secretary of State for War appealed for able-bodied men aged between seventeen and sixty-five to give their names in at their local police station. They would be signing up for what was initially known as the Local Defence Volunteers, guarding factories and key points of communications against invaders. A good many of those eligible in Swindon were railwaymen and they would have their own units. Most of the men in this close-knit community felt strongly about 'doing their bit' and protecting their town in its time of crisis, even if the

thought of having to change into a uniform and 'turn out' again, after a quick evening meal, was a daunting prospect. After all, they had been working 'inside' all day and many of them were middle-aged or older.

On Sunday mornings and weekday evenings, recruits received instruction on using weapons, when they became available. They also learned about such things as sabotage and concealment as well as having rifle practice, marching and inspection drills. Some, but not all, of the activities were carried out within Works' premises. These men then had to turn up for work the next morning having been patrolling the Works and the railway yards half the night fire-watching and looking out for enemy agents.

A lot of the elderly recruits who grew up in Victorian times had a strict Christian upbringing. A small number openly objected to Home Guard methods designed to defend their homeland. These men, if they refused to train, were called to account. In 1943 the local evening paper reported the hearing of a GWR Swindon man who objected to learning how to kill or take part at all on Sundays. He said that 'quiet on a Sunday was necessary to building up of the Christian character'. He failed to gain exemption.

Mr S.A. Dyer, a member of the CME's personal staff, commanded the GWR HG Company as lieutenant colonel. In 1943, on account of its growing strength and importance, the GWR Coy broke away from the 5th Battalion to form the 13th Wilts Battalion. Their headquarters were at 3 Emlyn Square, with hutments in Church Place. The GWR now had 640 men to guard Swindon Works and the junction station. Separate from the 13th was 'C' Company of the 11th (Factory) Battalion, who had their HQ in 24 Shed. The number of railwaymen recruited continued to rise in 1944, and these statistics do not include the significant numbers in other Home Guard units.

According to the official history, the GWR Home Guard's primary objective was: 'The defence of the Railway Works against attack. Its operational role was somewhat limited, but as the perimeter of the Works, Station and yards was, to a large extent, the north and west perimeter of the town, it was possible without difficulty to incorporate it into the general town scheme.' The new battalion (13th Wilts) never lost its identity as the GWR Battalion. A report in the local evening paper said the 13th Wilts had its own brass band made up of thirty-four railwaymen and one woman, Miss Iris Rainger. She was a Home Guard auxiliary and Works' clerk.

A GWR Home Guard parade inside the Works. They were held on Sunday mornings and Wednesday evenings. The site seen here was on the south side of the main line between the carriage body builders' shop, on the left, and the carriage finishers. According to 'Art' Townsend's diaries, these parades were held at any one of a dozen different areas around the Works or other railway premises locally.
GWR courtesy of D. Everett and R. Townsend

The GWR Home Guard Battalion annual summer camp at Lydiard Park in August 1944. This photo shows Major Porter presenting prizes at the sports' day, which rounded off the week. The corporation bus waits to return the men's families back to Swindon in the evening. *Swindon Central Library, local studies collection*

Art Townsend: Home Guard Duties

William Arthur Townsend, known to his mates as 'Art', was a member of the GWR Home Guard from its earliest days. He was a boilermaker by trade but, by 1940, had moved to the C&W 'T' (Timber) storehouse, as a warehouseman. This move, and the fact that his application for National Service had been declined twice, despite him being relatively young, seems to suggest that 'Art' might have suffered some ill health or industrial injury in the past. However, he was a participating member of the Swindon Athletic Club in the 1930s and possibly beyond, so perhaps not. 'Art' kept a diary during the war and the entries relating to his Home Guard duties are a rare first-hand account of the role these people had. The following is based on extracts:

On 4 January 1941 the air raid warning was sounded at 10.40pm and the all-clear was not heard until 7am. During one twelve-day period in March 1941, Art wrote that the town was subjected to ten air raid warnings with just two nights' respite. The day 12 April 1941 was typical: 'I went to bed early as I was on night patrol at the GWR Transfer Goods' Yards from 1.15am until 5am.' On 18 August 1942 he records that bombs fell on Kembrey Street and he was directed to go and clear up debris there. His son told me that their own house in nearby Cricklade Road was damaged by the same blast and the clear-up included Art's own roof slates and glass.

No. 5 platoon, GWR Home Guard, Swindon. William Arthur 'Art' Townsend, whose diaries are referred to in the text, is third from left, second row.
Courtesy of D. Everett and R. Townsend

The diaries show that turns of duty guarding the GWR premises during the night came around every ten days for Art Townsend. With another HG member, he patrolled the Transfer Goods Yards for four and a quarter hours from 9pm, or from 1.15am, on alternate turns. Later, presumably when the threat of invasion was well and truly over, Art's diary entries for night patrols become less frequent. At this time he was assigned to guard the GWR Gas Works against sabotage and report any fires in the vicinity, due to air raids.

23
Post-war Developments

Steam Locomotives: 1944 to 1946

The story of post-war developments in the CME Dept begins before the war ends. Mr Hawksworth had the misfortune of becoming head of department in July 1941, a time when scope for new designs was almost non-existent because of wartime conditions. Three years later, however, after the successful invasion of Europe, a return to peace became only a matter of time. Plans could now be made for post-war requirements. As drawings for a new generation of passenger coaches were being finalised, locomotive availability was becoming a problem. This was to pre-occupy the Loco Works and the Running Dept in the autumn of 1943, and particularly throughout 1944.

The effects of the lack of scheduled maintenance had begun to have a negative effect on engine availability. The reasons for the deteriorating motive power situation, given in the *GWR Magazine* were: 1) the movement of civilian and service passengers, coal and merchandise was higher than ever before; 2) the flying bomb menace had made significant demands on the operating department; 3) American 2-8-0 freight locomotives working on the 'Western' had now gone to the Continent. This last point was partially offset by the GWR receiving an allocation of British 'austerity' engines. The *GWR Magazine*, the mouthpiece for the company, does not mention the lack of routine maintenance.

Despite the staff and material shortages, the GWR CME Dept delivered eighty new locomotives to traffic in 1944. The types outshopped were: 0-6-0 pannier tank engines ('5700' class) for shunting and light freight work; 0-6-0 tender engines ('2251' class) for lighter mixed traffic services on mainly secondary routes; and 2-8-0 Stanier LMS 8F's for heavy freight work and on loan to the GWR until after the war. The other type was a 'mixed traffic' 'Hall' class 4-6-0 with modifications ('6959' class) sufficient to be considered a new class. The Chief Mechanical Engineer, Mr Hawksworth, with the help of the Running Dept and the Drawing Office, made some

major design alterations. These engines were universally known as 'Modified Halls'. This prefix was probably unique in the company despite many locomotive classes having been altered and returned to traffic over the years.

The main design differences between the 'Modified Halls' and the original 'Halls', which were being outshopped up until a year earlier, were: 1) Steel plate frames throughout, doing away with the extension frames bolted onto the front end. 2) New pattern cylinder blocks and smokebox saddle castings which would now be fitted separately. 3) Larger three-row superheaters and header regulators were fitted into the standard No. 1 boilers, on most but not all new engines. 4) Plate frame instead of the bar frame bogies, with the load being supported on four laminated springs and a longer wheelbase. It is likely that Mr Hawksworth had some of these ideas in his mind before he left the Drawing Office.

The first twelve to appear in 1944 also had certain temporary modifications to suit wartime conditions: the cabside windows were not yet fitted, as an ARP measure, to stop flying glass and glare from the fire; no nameplates were fitted; and the livery was unlined black. The Works stopped making and fitting nameplates to new locomotives in 1941. The 'Halls' and then the first of the '1000' class of 1945 eventually received their names as they came in for overhaul from 1946 onwards. As these engines went through the Works some modified parts were interchanged with parts from the original class. For example, some earlier boilers with two-row superheaters were soon being carried by the new engines: presumably because of post-war austerity. A little later, new Hawksworth straight-sided tenders went into traffic with new 4-6-0s but were often paired up with earlier engines after their next works' visit.

The CME and the locomotive committee wanted to build a new type of express locomotive, probably a Pacific (4-6-2), but the directors would not sanction it at that time. Latter-day historians cannot agree upon whether the new 4-6-0, the '1000' class', was a forerunner of something larger or a compromise. Neither is there consensus about whether something larger like a 4-6-2 was ever a serious consideration.

The first of the new '1000' class engines was outshopped in August 1945. It alone was fitted with an experimental double chimney. The class incorporated several features that were a departure from the Churchward/Collett designs, which were generally thought to need very little improvement, even by 1945. Perhaps the biggest difference between the new engine and its predecessor was the use of two cylinders rather than four to keep the cost of building down and make maintenance easier. They were given new straight-sided tenders with a 7-ton coal capacity, a ton more than the other types of 4000 gallon tenders.

Their power was increased compared with similar GW types by giving them slightly smaller-diameter driving wheels and increasing the boiler pressure. However, the hammer blow on the track was heavier by having two cylinders instead of four, and they 'rode rough'. A maximum speed on all but the major (double red) routes, was imposed. Until adjustments were made, the '1000' class were not popular with footplatemen.

So the proposed successor to the GWR express classes never came about after the war, although, with hindsight, it is difficult to imagine anything significantly better than the modified 'Castles' and 'Kings' that were relied upon instead. The '1000' class were later named after counties through which the company operated. Don Woodley, a Swindon engineman at the time, told me of an incident that happened when No. 1000 was still fairly new:

> The prototype hit a locomotive jack that had been left upright on a sleeper at Knighton Crossing, causing severe damage to the outside motion. One of the nameplates was also badly twisted and this was considered a bad omen at the shed and in the Works.

Recovery in Adversity

When peacetime returned there was little sign of any improvements at first. Docks, transport and miners' strikes caused a fuel crisis and made

the shortages of raw materials worse. This in turn led to a twelve- to eighteen-month waiting time for the supply of new machine tools. No less than anywhere else, the CME Dept was now struggling to catch up following the years of disruption to maintenance. The company were also being cautious about their ambitions due to the possibility of nationalisation with the new labour government.

Getting skilled labour demobilised and back into the factory was frustratingly slow. Therefore staff that should have gone years before could still not be retired off. Rationing continued and in some cases was worse than it had been during the war. Bert Harber said that there was a general feeling that the depressed economy that the war cured would now return. On top of all this came the worst winter in living memory, at the beginning of 1947.

The railways, however, carried more people than ever before and Swindon Works had more orders than it could cope with, although with a further reduction in hours of the working week, the department's aggregate production was, not surprisingly, down. The *GWR Magazine* tells us that for 1947, skilled labour 'inside' was down and semi-skilled labour slightly up on the previous year.

As had happened following the First World War, memorial services were held in workshops on Sundays for workmates who never returned. Works' officials, the mayor and church dignitaries conducted services and would unveil memorial tablets, with colleagues and relatives making up the congregation. To perpetuate the spirit of comradeship, local railwaymen who had served in the Home Guard had a weekly get-together at the Staff Association club.

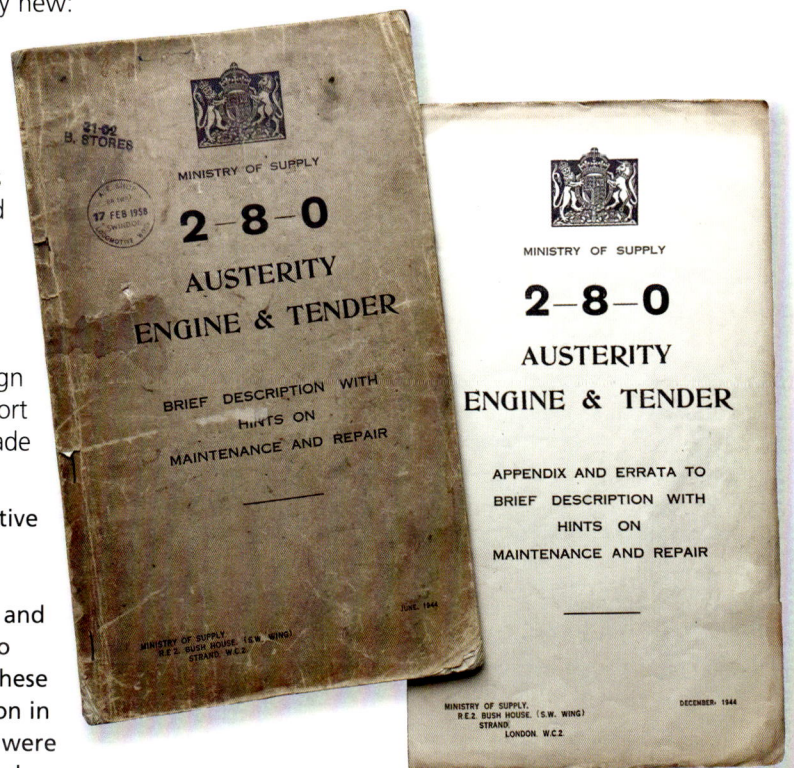

In wartime and after nationalisation, locomotive works would need to keep handbooks for 'foreign' locomotives passing through their erecting shops. Sets of engineering drawings and probably specialist tool equipment would also have to be supplied by the original builder. These two books would have been issued to Swindon in 1946 when eighty-one heavy freight engines were loaned to the GWR to balance locomotive stocks following the war. *Author's collection*

On the back of this drawing office photo is written: 'Bogie oscillation test, B.R. brake third.'

Rolling Stock

The Works had been heavily involved with reverting back from large-scale wartime ordnance manufacture since early 1944. Fifty-eight coaches from ambulance trains returned from the Continent to be made ready for ordinary peacetime traffic. Mobile firefighting vehicles were also converted back to their former purpose. The first of a further ninety restaurant cars were stripped at Swindon and reconditioned. Some had already been dealt with, as mentioned in the last chapter. The work started in 1947 and contractors refitted them internally, as the labour shortage still persisted. Two sleeping cars and a composite coach were also rebuilt inside as part of the same contract.

A case for the replacement of ageing carriages, and making good losses suffered during the war, was made to the Materials Committee by the Railway Executive. New wagons, they said, were also required in large numbers, to modernise stock and reduce the false economics of continuous repairs. The MC was formed in 1947 and its chairman was the Economic Secretary to the Treasury. They determined how much steel, timber and other raw materials each industrial department received.

Supplies allocated to the newly formed British Railways were woefully inadequate and, as a consequence, building programmes proposed by the Western Region, and the other regions, had to be cut back drastically. Loco, carriage and wagon building was 50 to 70% less than the annual average. In 1948 it was lower again, so the increased 'patching up' and conversion of existing stock had to continue. This state of affairs did not significantly improve for another four years.

Oil Fuel Instead of Coal

Supplies of coal of the right quality became a bigger problem for the railways at the end of the war than it had been for the duration of it. The Great Western decided to experiment with firing some locomotives using oil fuel, which could also cut the time they spent being serviced. Their engineers and management had been in talks with the Anglo-Iranian oil company for some time and the tests and demonstrations given were encouraging. It would initially be a regional scheme, tried in areas where coal consumption per train mile was particularly heavy.

Eighteen '2800' class heavy freight locomotives and their tenders were to be converted to start with, for working to and from South Wales. This gave the Swindon Drawing Office some work in late 1945 and conversions started in the Loco Works soon after. Each converted engine was given a different number, so new numberplates were cast in the foundry. The *GWR Magazine* announced the scheme in October 1945 and explained the way oil would be burned to produce steam:

> Oil fuel is fed by gravity to a specially designed burner located at the front of the firebox and atomised by a steam jet incorporated in the burner. The position of the necessary controls in the engine cab has been selected to enable them to be easily operated by the fireman. The fuel tank, holding 18,000 gallons, is mounted on the tender. Steam heating coils are provided to ensure that, despite varying atmospheric conditions, the oil flows readily and reaches the burner at the temperature best suited to its proper combustion.

One of the last Swindon designs was the '1500' class, introduced in 1949. Only ten of these 0-6-0 pannier tanks were built, partly because the diesel equivalent was proving successful. The '1500' class were to be a 'no nonsense twenty-four-hour shunting engine' with a short coupled wheelbase for the sharp curves in and out of sidings. The cylinders and valve gear were on the outside, a departure from the GW practice of concealing the clutter for aesthetic reasons. This, together with the absence of footplating along the sides, allowed better accessibility for maintenance and oiling of interconnecting parts. They would be used for empty coaching stock movements between Old Oak carriage sidings and Paddington, or similar work elsewhere. *GWR*

A thermometer on the tank enables the fireman to keep a check on the temperature and to maintain it at the correct level by regulating the passage of steam into the heating coils.

Modifications also had to be made to the ashpans, dampers and brick arches of conventional coal-fired locos.

The department was also involved in the design and installation of oil-storage plants at depots in Wales and then in the south-west. Some 'Halls' and 'Castles' were also converted to test the scheme on the West of England main line. These modified 4-6-0 locomotives had 4,000-gallon tenders, and one 3,500-gallon type that had oil tanks mounted where the coal was normally held. They steamed well when crews got used to them and savings were made when compared to coal, especially on the heavily graded Cornish main line. However, because foreign exchange to buy in oil was in short supply, the government-backed scheme became unviable. The whole idea was therefore not taken any further and all the engines affected had been converted back by 1950.

Bob Dauris, who worked in the Yardmasters' Office from 1956, remembers two tank engines running on oil fuel: 'They were used as pilot engines in the Swindon goods' yards but were unreliable because the oil feeds would become blocked and this could not be remedied with the engines "in steam".'

Steam Locomotives: 1947 Onward

The book *Next Station* set out the GWR's immediate post-war plans. Of new locomotive construction, they said that, for the moment, they were pursuing the restoration of standards being achieved immediately before the war. Looking ahead, the company estimated that 'to overtake arrears of renewals and to continue the work of current renewal at its appropriate rate, seven hundred new locomotives will be needed in the five years to 1950. At the end of 1946, 546 locos over forty years' old were in daily service, compared with 450 in 1938.'

Despite the restricted supplies of steel and other raw materials, the Loco Works manufactured a total of seventy-five new locomotives in 1949 and undertook heavy and light repairs of more than 1,000 others. GW loco designs continued to be built under British Railways, for a time, until new standard designs could be worked out for all operating requirements. Some small GW 0-6-0 tanks were built until October 1956 but these were exceptional. Trials took place between locomotives from each of the four former railway companies and from these a range of hybrid types were developed. The first of Swindon's BR-designed locomotives, the 4-6-0 Class 4s, were completed in May 1951. They then built batches of 2-6-0s, including some of pure LMS design. All were classified as 'mixed traffic' types.

Comparative trials had taken place in 1949 and 1950 between a Dean Goods 0-6-0 (2579) and an LMS 2-6-0 (46413). They were tested in the Works on the stationary test plant and under controlled conditions on the main line. A young Ken Ellis photographed the Dean engine at Steventon between trial trips and wrote on the back of the print: 'The only one of the class to be fully lined out.' In April or May 1952, Ken's father accompanied his son to Swindon Works to try to secure a position for him in the Loco Works. Mr Ellis senior had recently retired from the position of station master at Steventon and the family moved to Whitworth Road, Swindon.

Having the required qualifications, Ken was hoping to take up a five-year sandwich course in Mechanical Engineering. They were shown an LMS 2-6-0 tender engine (43094) being evaluated on the Testing Plant in preparation for Swindon building batches of these class 2 engines. Ken got talking to one of the test engineers, who said: 'Come and work for us.' Later he was told by someone in the staff office that there were no vacancies at the time, so Ken went and did his training at W.G. Bagnall, a locomotive builder at Stafford. During his time there he studied steaming characteristics of locomotives on the stationary test plant at Rugby. A few years later Ken found out that the engineer who had invited him to come and work at Swindon was the highly respected Sam Ell.

Some of the LMS 2-6-0s, numbered 465XX, that Swindon subsequently built were sent to work on the Cambrian route in north-west Wales. The drivers started complaining that they didn't steam as well as the Dean Goods engines they had replaced, although they did like the enclosed cabs. Sam Ell, technical assistant to the CME, was asked to investigate this and he and his team came up with drawings for an improved front end. As the locomotives came through the Works they were fitted with modified boilers and smokeboxes, which solved the problem.

A hybrid BR 2-6-0 was built at Darlington at about the same time and some of them were sent to work on the Western Region. Former loco erector Jim Lowe assumes these engines were built with the Swindon improvements because his notebooks only record them coming to Swindon for the fitting of the Automatic Train Control apparatus. The draughting of the 'Manor' class 4-6-0 engines was also improved considerably in 1952. Ken, who later came back to work at Swindon, told me what Mr Ell said about it: 'The optimum proportions of the blastpipe and chimney are not mine, they are pure Dean.'

Nationalisation

The chairman of the newly formed Railway Executive was bound to try to preserve morale on the eve of taking the British railway companies into public ownership. He said: 'Every one of us railway men and women is now working in the direct service of our country, and all that Britain means to us and to the world is something worth working for.' It did little to alleviate the bewilderment and sense of loss felt by those who were fiercely loyal to the old Great Western.

Having all departments concentrate on different aspects of a standardised railway network was sound practice. All drawing offices would now specialise in different areas instead of designing four or more versions of the same thing. Mass production could be exploited as never before and a streamlined management would oversee one big organisation. In the event, the standardisation of the various forms of rolling stock, and particularly locomotives, had scarcely become effective when the BTC announced a policy of electrification and modernisation.

Senior positions would be filled more and more by outsiders, a practice that was alien to Swindon, which had thrived on a strong sense of loyalty and tradition. For instance, the top job on Western Region, of mechanical and electrical engineer, went to Mr Smeddle in 1951. He had always been an LNER man before 1948 but under the new regime he was sent to the Southern Region, then on to Swindon. Mr Finlayson arrived from the Scottish Region to be loco works manager in 1952 before moving to the London Midland Region.

Men have told me that the quality of some materials coming in was inferior or not what they were used to, due to alternative suppliers. Jack Fleetwood, in the Foundry, remembers:

> The GW mixes we used to produce alloys were 'light' on tin. This did not adversely affect the castings and tin was expensive, but no, the people at the top wanted the correct amount of tin. This in itself was OK but now it did not suit the 'runners' and 'risers' in our moulds. The size and shape of these channels, which let the molten metal in and the hot gases out, had been carefully worked out according to the original consistency. The altered mix with our moulds now produced inferior castings but that was progress.

As the 1950s progressed, various ideas were being put forward that might make the railways more competitive and improve their image. After trying to standardise the railways, one of the ideas implemented was an increased regional autonomy. All WR passenger locomotive types were to be outshopped in lined green as they came through the Works. Previously only the 'Stars', 'Saints', 'Castles' and 'Kings' were painted green and black with orange and black lining.

When the chairman of the Western Region board, Mr Reg Hanks, first took over, he had the livery of some principal passenger trains restored much like he remembered them on the old Great Western. He had been an apprentice at Swindon many years before and remained enthusiastic about the traditions of the old company. Swindon got several new contracts as a result of this. These trains would have sets of BR Mk.1 coaches, including some ex-GWR kitchen-dining cars, all repainted in brown and cream livery. An attractive new design of roundel transfer was applied to each vehicle too. Their roof label boards were repainted to match and the Swindon signwriters used a different typeface to spell out the train names.

One of the recently repainted BR Mk 1 coaches showing the elegant new roundel design. Carriage boards stating the destinations or train names were well known to the travelling public of the time. The wooden boards were known as 'roof label boards' by the carriage signwriters in No. 8 carriage painting Shop. *Ken Ellis*

Ray Ault servicing a cylinder head from a British Railways' diesel railcar in BD Shop in 1960 or 1961. *Swindon Society courtesy of Bob Townsend*

These principal trains would receive names, if they hadn't got them already. New headboards were cast too (as described elsewhere) to fit onto the front of the loco smokebox and complete this impressive-looking style of train. Old and new names such as the Torbay Express, the Red Dragon, the Inter-City and the Mayflower undoubtedly had the desired effect on the travelling public.

Richard Woodley, an authority on Western Region steam trains, told me that the cost of building engines in Swindon was far higher than elsewhere. This only came to light because various works were now sharing the building of batches of the same classes. The reason, he says, was due to shortages of skilled labour and a reluctance of some of the older hands to accept British Transport Commission changes designed to speed up production.

'Working to rule' was usually sufficient to get the Wiltshire railwaymen what they wanted, so Swindon remained expensive to run. Richard said that although the loyalty and discipline of the old company had gone, the finished article was as good as, if not better than, the same product built at other railway works. The feeling among the men was that contracts were being diverted elsewhere, mainly to Derby, due to the influential ex-LMS (some at Swindon called this company 'ell-of-a-mess') officials on the BR board.

The Late 1950s

In 1957 a dispute over piecework caused the supply of components to the AE Shop to be held up. As a consequence, some partly rebuilt locomotives were stuck there for extended periods. No. 5024 *Carew Castle*, for instance, went into the factory in April for a 'heavy general' overhaul. As with any class of overhaul where the boiler was taken off, this engine should have been outside again,

ready for trials, after no more than eighteen days, but 'fifty twenty-four' did not emerge until five months later!

In 1956 Swindon completed the first heavy-freight class 9Fs. This Works would get to build a total of fifty-three of the large 2-10-0s. Of the last of these, Bob Grainger, a first-year apprentice on the loco side, said: 'The highest number allocated to one of the third batch of engines was 92220 and that one left the Erecting Shop on the afternoon of 1 February 1960 to undergo trials.' Bob still has all his notebooks, which show engine movements around the Works at this time. They record that this locomotive was painted in unlined black (and nameless) and was back 'inside' the same day with axlebox problems, presumably overheating.

Freight engines were not normally named but, because it was the last, 92220 would be an exception. The name was chosen from suggestions invited through the staff magazine. The very first locomotive on the GWR's books was *North Star*, so it made sense to name this, the very last steam locomotive built for British Railways, *Evening Star*. In another rare break with tradition, the locomotive was given embellishments reserved for express engines. It was outshopped with a copper-capped chimney, a green and black, fully lined livery and two nameplates with GW style lettering. A naming ceremony was arranged inside the AE Shop in March 1960 and the whole of the workforce were invited to attend.

I have heard it said that British Railways wanted Swindon to stop building steam locomotives by 1956 because Crewe Works could build them quicker and cheaper. That would explain why this works had so many diesel contracts put their way. The unions resisted and they got to build the last steam engines at Swindon. This would temporarily reprieve some steam trades such as foundrymen and smiths, and perhaps offset some of the sagging morale.

The naming ceremony of the last new steam locomotive outshopped from Swindon and the last anywhere in the country, March 1960. *Ken Ellis*

The only electrical parts on a steam locomotive were the automatic train control apparatus, but the new diesel building programmes meant recruiting electrical fitters. As part of the government overspill scheme, the first of seventy or eighty extra 'sparks' arrived from London and the Midlands during the initial stages of diesel building in the mid-1950s. Some went straight over to the carriage side for work on the diesel multiple units. The Electrical Trades Union was quite militant, or well organised, depending on your point of view. Consequently, pay rates for electricians in industry were higher, making them expensive to employ. Tony Huzzey, a prominent union man 'inside', told me about some of the others:

> Danny Lee and George Hall were the ETU shop stewards at that time, with 'Nobby' Clark representing the electrical storemen. For other trades, Mervyn Hayward and Gordon Ing represented the coppersmiths and tinsmiths; Edgar Major, the boilersmiths; Bill Peacey, the vehicle builders; and Jim Masters and Les Bates, the fitter/erectors in the Amalgamated Engineering Union. Terry Larkham was the National Union of Railwaymen steward in the stores, and internal transport man Gordon Turner was Works' convenor for the Transport and General Workers' Union. A chap named H.S. James was chairman of the Transport Salaried Staffs' Association. He worked in the Audit Office in the late 1950s.

On the carriage side George Scotford, Harold Seeley and Norman Piper represented the trimmers and upholsterers (Norman would later become grandfather of actress Billie Piper); Reg Clark was a steward in the C&W stores; and Les Bates and Reg Clark had, in turn, been full-time chairmen of the Works' Committee. Jim Masters was on the AE Shop Committee and the Works' Committee. Typical of many active in union affairs, Jim became a town councillor and went on to serve as mayor. Bob Grainger remembered that: 'You were in for a long sermon when "Brother Jim" stood up at union meetings.'

The Labour Situation

The GWR and later the Western Region trained engineers at Swindon Works from the developing countries of the Commonwealth. They also sent trained engineers out to work on railways abroad under something called the Empire Scheme, which started in the 1920s, if not before, although surviving details of this seem to be scarce.

In 1950 there were seven other major employers in the area, including four engineering firms. Over the next ten years the railway factory found it increasingly difficult to attract and retain skilled and unskilled workers with yet more firms coming in. The compulsory two-year conscription didn't help either.

George Petfield, in the Wages Office, remembers allocating a new pay number to a Ukrainian with the surname Lenik: 'He was the first immigrant worker that I can remember and was "given a start" in the Iron Foundry about 1951.' Unskilled foreign workers were brought in, mainly Poles, Italians and Ukrainians, under the government's work permit scheme in response to the shortage of labour. Jack reckoned that more immigrants came into the Foundries than into other areas, and said: 'At first they worked hard. We had two West Indians who were good workers but unfortunately one of them went mad and murdered his landlord, so we lost him.'

The government's London Overspill Scheme also brought some skilled and unskilled workers to the factory from the early 1950s onwards. The Londoners described their new surroundings as 'out in the country' and they never missed an opportunity to ridicule the rural accent. In return the locals 'inside' renamed Thursdays 'pie day' in their honour.

A British Transport Commission report of 1955 said the pay of the lower grades on the railways had fallen behind comparable work outside. The majority of young family men who arrived in the town in the 1950s were attracted by better conditions in the motor car and electrical component industries, where there were also plenty of vacancies.

Peter Reade was typical of many railwaymen: he was attracted by the thought of higher wages elsewhere and was becoming worried by the rundown of his industry. 'As a blacksmith I was no longer in demand, as forgings gave way to pressings. The better money promised in the car industry never really happened because of disputes and I regretted going,' said Peter. A letter in *The Swindon and District Review* in 1960 said that many local car workers were now on 'short time' and many others had been 'laid off' through recession in the car industry. The writer also thought that motor cars of the time were poorly made and unreliable.

Men leaving the Works could find that high working standards were a disadvantage. Pressed Steel Fisher was a new plant at Stratton, which started pressing car bodies in 1956. Colin Bown said: 'Two of our sheet metal men were taken on as inspectors there and they were constantly being told not to reject such a high proportion of work. Both men returned to the railway factory in time.' While some men were leaving, others like firemen who had been on the footplate, were arriving. Fed up with the unsocial hours, a number came into the workshops; another attraction for them was the piecework money.

Some young men, yet to have financial commitments, were not necessarily attracted by the firms offering the highest wages. The railways still held a deep fascination for many who wanted to work on the railways as an extension of their hobby. Bob Grainger was a trainspotter and photographer, but his introduction to a working life in the railway factory did not come about in the usual way. He lived in Cirencester, not far from the chairman of the British Transport Commission, Sir Brian Robertson. Bob wanted to work with his beloved engines, so his mother asked someone who knew the chairman to see if he would help. After contacting the boy's headmaster, Sir Brian gave Bob a letter to take to Swindon, which of course, was enough to get him in.

Unfortunately Bob found himself in the shop offices of the Iron Foundry, then K Shop, learning to become a clerk. After much form filling and explaining, Bob was

Chief Watchman Bert Stratford, on the left, with trainee engineers from Malaya in about 1960. *Dave Stratford collection*

The constant rumours about the downturn in the railway industry wouldn't bother most of these coach builders. The majority, like Bert Davis, far right, were of an age where they would be expecting to see out their working lives 'inside'. *Collection of Art Fortune*

transferred to become apprentice fitter, turner and erector. 'All I remember about the coppersmiths' shop office was the senior clerk, Mr Phillips, getting me to write out coal and "slow combustion" tickets, which were nothing to do with the work of K Shop. My net pay then (January 1960) was £3 15 shillings,' said Bob.

We learn that all things have their day, and pass, as pass they must.

The castles and their builders each in turn must 'bite the dust'

E.W. Chappell, from the *Western Region Magazine*, 1955.

24
New Forms of Motive Power

The department under Mr Churchward had developed steam locomotion beyond that of the other British railways. By the time Mr Collett took over they had also begun to reduce production and maintenance costs too. The problem for the new regime was locomotive running costs. About 40,000 tons of coal per week was needed to generate the power required to maintain GWR train services. The cost amounted to 18% of the CME Dept budget. Anything that would reduce the dependence upon it was being looked at in the 1920s and '30s. Even before that they had tried out motorised rail vehicles but they didn't show much potential.

Shortly before the threat of another world war and nationalisation, the company did commission a report into the comparative costs of electrification of their main lines west of Taunton. One idea was that they would eventually build the electric multiple units in their own workshops, as happened on the Southern Railway. Electric traction was quickly ruled out by the Western, even though it was proven to give good acceleration, it was reliable, clean and could be operated by one man. Diesel (electric or petrol-engine) power could, in theory, more or less match these advantages and did not need costly third rail or overhead pylons as the means to deliver the power.

Great Western Railcars

Several different types of road motor vehicles, which could be adapted to run on rails, were tried in the London Division in the early 1930s. They had interchangeable pneumatic road tyres and flanged wheels for rails. Presumably these led on to the first streamlined railcar (No. 1) being purchased. This was a 130hp oil-engine car, purchased from the Associated Equipment Company, better known as AEC. The CME Dept evaluated it on a service between Slough and Reading starting in the latter part of 1933. This led quickly on to a first series, which went into revenue-earning service in 1934 for 'promoting services with limited demand'. With good acceleration

and a top speed of 70mph, they were ideal for 'all station' cross-country services.

Initially, the railcars would be built complete by AEC, based in Southall. They were best known as builders of London motor and trolley buses and they built the first eighteen of the GWR cars. Park Royal Coachworks supplied the bodies after designing the front end streamlining by using models in wind tunnels. At the sides, valance panels covered the bogies and underframe, making them completely streamlined as was becoming the fashion at that time. These were the first vehicles to be contracted out since construction began in the GWR Carriage Works in 1868. The Swindon Drawing Office would have drawn up certain design features that they wanted incorporated to suit the operating conditions on the GWR.

After completion, Swindon Works would fit the automatic train control apparatus and the warning horns to each unit. In service they would not need the heavy engineering facilities available at Swindon. The average annual mileage exceeded 50,000. Routine repairs and

A photo issued as a postcard showing the experimental No. 18 railcar. This was the last of the GWR cars built by AEC and the first to be fitted with drawgear for hauling a trailer.

No 65
G.W.R. DIESEL RAILCAR.
The Diesel Railcar is much more economical than almost any form of Electrically propelled train because of the high capital charges for track electrification. It has a cruising speed of 60 miles an hour and accommodation for 40 to 70 passengers.

maintenance could be carried out in areas of motive power depots converted for the purpose, using parts and drawings supplied. For an initial period, engineers from the manufacturers would be on hand to assist the depot fitters. Major work and overhauls would be done by the manufacturers, at first, but they did come to Swindon Carriage Works for any attention required to the bodywork. Maintenance fitters soon found it practical to leave certain lower body panels permanently off.

Swindon-built Railcars

Swindon Works got involved with building diesels in 1938. This only came about then due to the uncertainty in Europe following the Munich Agreement. Carriage maintenance and building work was put off because of the urgent need to undertake other work during the preparations in case of war. Carriage workshops were being geared up for the possibility of special contracts for their own needs. However, further batches of the new diesel-mechanical railcars were needed. A lack of suitable motive power for passenger and parcel services on secondary routes still existed, work for which the diesels had proved more than adequate. The eighteen diesel railcars already in traffic accounted for 3% of the daily passenger mileage on the GWR in late 1930s.

AEC, who had built and maintained Nos 1 to 18, for the company, were now required to build military vehicles. Therefore the next railcars (Nos 19 to 38) were built in the Swindon carriage shops. The various trades constructed the underframes complete; produced and fitted conventional buffing, drawgear and some other mechanical equipment; built the body frames and completed the coachwork; then fitted out the passenger compartments (saloons). This was all standard work for the carriage workers. The additional work involved erectors fitting and connecting up the engines, gearboxes and transmissions, which AEC continued to supply. The valance or lower body panels could be quickly removed for access to the outer parts of the mechanical gear and engines. However, because of the very limited clearance underneath, engineers also had access through inspection doors in the vehicle's floor.

This second series had a lower gear ratio and top speed, giving a higher tractive effort. Nos 35 to 38 were designed to work in pairs and at speeds up to 70mph. As with the first series, one of these was fitted out for parcel work exclusively. The standard automatic train control apparatus, electric lighting, batteries and dynamos were then fitted. The twenty Swindon railcars were outshopped between 1940 and 1942 and were noticeably different from the AEC series: rather than the gentle curves to deflect the air resistance, the wartime austerity body shape was box-like with more angular ends.

The livery, in GWR days, was brown and cream as it was for main-line coaches. Initially they had the circular monogram applied to each end. Later, this was replaced by the coat of arms crest and the words GREAT WESTERN

along the sides. After nationalisation the fleet were gradually turned out in standard crimson and cream and lined, again in the style of the main-line coaches. The two parcels' cars were the exception: they were crimson all over and lined.

No. 19C (carriage lifting) Shop was extended with another three through roads, probably post-war. One road (No. 6) was equipped with specialised lifts to support the railcar body so that its two bogies could be removed and overhauled sets refitted in one lift. The bogie transporter was used to transfer the used sets to 15 Shop, where the 'bogie gang' dealt with them. After lifting the frame off the axleboxes, the springs, tyre wear and bearings were inspected and the axles were checked for cracks. Surviving paperwork from the 1950s shows that one of the fleet would come in for bogie replacement once a month on average. All of the GW diesel railcars were withdrawn in the late 1950s or early '60s.

The Gas Turbines

Senior staff at Swindon and Paddington were optimistic that an alternative form of prime mover for post-war, main-line train services could be found: a natural enough expectation in this, the dawn of the jet-engine age. Shortly after the war A.W. (Jack) Dymond, an assistant to the CME, was given the task of analysing the options. Later, in his detailed report, it was concluded that the potential for gas-turbine driven traction came out best. This was despite there being only one other unit in existence with which to make a detailed study. Its successful application to marine and aero-engines did, to some extent, make up for the limited locomotive data available.

The principle of gas-turbine locomotion was that air was drawn into a compressor, then into a combustion chamber where it was heated sufficient to force it through turbine blades at high pressure. The output achieved drove an electrical generator, producing current that powered traction motors: two in each of the two bogies. Some exhaust air was reused by mixing it with air drawn in at the start of the cycle, thus increasing efficiency.

In making a case for the changeover, Mr Dymond said:

> The steam locomotive, despite its cheaper building cost and longer life, seems to be approaching its demise on account of its low efficiency and poor overall availability. Other clear advantages of this new motive power are: less maintenance, due to fewer moving parts and cleaner working conditions for staff at depots (it became increasingly difficult to attract men to work in steam sheds after the war).

Although the diesel-electric also offered most of these advantages, the gas-turbine principle, when applied to a locomotive, would make it lighter and smaller than alternatives of the same power. The cost of fuel was estimated to be about one third of that of steam, although this later proved to be over-optimistic. The other advantage over steam, which appealed to the Swindon

An official portrait of the 'Brown-Boveri' gas-turbine locomotive, which was delivered to the Western Region in 1950. The colour scheme was black with aluminium or silver waistband and roof panels as used on main-line diesels already in use on the London Midland Region. *BRWR*

and Paddington people, was the driving cabs at each end of main-line diesels. This did away with the need for turning to face the direction of travel.

It was, of course, essential for the Chief Mechanical Engineer to keep up to date with outside developments in railway engineering. That well-known railway writer O.S. Nock said that Mr Hawksworth had a great interest in the Swiss railways and in 1946 the CME travelled to Switzerland with Mr Dymond to see, at first hand, the performance of the gas-turbine locomotive. The Swiss Federal Railways had ordered it from Brown-Boveri of Baden, and took possession in 1941. Naturally, one of the GWR requirements was that any new form of motive power should be able to haul the heaviest trains to times at least comparable to their own.

After reviewing the Swiss engine, the CME got the support of the Locomotive Committee at Paddington and one was ordered, with certain changes to the specification, in October 1946. It would, on paper at least, produce 2,500hp. Another similar locomotive had just been ordered from Metropolitan Vickers in Manchester, which was claimed to be able to give 3,000hp. As part of the contract agreements, engineers from both manufacturers would accompany the locomotives on the Western Region for a period of time.

The 'Brown-Boveri' locomotive arrived at Swindon in early 1950 and, even though it was ordered first, the 'Metro-Vic' was delivered in late 1951. These were the names by which the two locomotives soon became generally known, although someone at Swindon thought

up the name 'Kerosene Castle' for the Swiss engine, according to Mr Nock. They were given the numbers 18000 and 18100 and both were fitted with the Great Western type Automatic Train Control equipment upon arrival at Swindon.

Extensive trials followed using heavy trains and the WR Dynamometer Car. As well as conventional train recording apparatus, precision positive oil flow meters, volt meters and ammeters were among the instruments used for 'analytical testing' with these and later the diesel-hydraulics. These 'observational trials' continued when the locomotives were first used on normal services, and the staff of the Running Department who conducted them were often accompanied by Swindon draughtsmen.

It was decided that 18000, the Swiss loco, and 18100 from MV in Manchester, should have the same limited route availability as the 'King' class locomotives. After the road tests by both the manufacturers and the Western Region, 18000 was tried on timetable services between Swindon and Paddington before progressing to working trains on the longer Paddington to Plymouth route, via Westbury. No. 18100 was put on trains between Paddington and Bristol and then on to the Paddington to Plymouth direct main line. Facilities were provided at Old Oak Common for servicing and repairs but both still visited Swindon Works regularly for inspection and due to failures. According to the official publicity, this new form of traction was for experimental use only, to assess their potential.

Jim Lowe was an apprentice on the loco side when the alien machines first arrived at the Works and recalled that:

You were firmly discouraged from getting close to them unless you were directly involved. 'Metro-Vic' and 'Brown-Boveri' would come into A Shop at the western end, on one of the three roads, usually No. 1 [Nos 2 and 3 roads were usually occupied by bosh trolleys and loco wheels]. They were then winched or shunted across to the other side of the traverser road. The locomotive body was released from the two six-wheeled bogies and lifted clear. The bogies were then rolled back onto the traverser and taken to the diesel electric shunters' gang at the top end of the Erecting Shop opposite the 'new work' section. The locomotive body was lowered on to stands where the components and systems could then be inspected and tested, either in the engine compartments, by removing body panels, or by disconnecting and lifting out whole units.

An early problem with 18000 was the fuel oil leaving deposits on the turbine blades. The turbine would need to be 'split' in the Works to decarbonise the blades. Erector Pete Brettel had knowledge of resetting the fixed and rotor blades before reassembly. He had previously worked on the steam turbine engines of P&O ships in the Merchant Navy. The Metropolitan-Vickers locomotive suffered this same problem but initially some of their own men dealt with it.

Another reason why 18000 came back into the Works on occasions was for a new combustion chamber lining due to heat damage. Initially the time spent under repair at Swindon was not considered to be excessive, especially 18100. This took account of the fact that the mechanical fitter/erectors had to work on totally unfamiliar types of components. Later, breakdowns became more common but were usually due to minor electrical faults taking time to diagnose, in which case they did not usually require a visit to Swindon. Either way, on account of costs, British Railways allowed only a minimum of spare parts to be held and no doubt this sometimes caused delays getting them back into traffic.

The rate of breakdowns did not decrease sufficiently over time so the Western Region announced that this experiment had become too costly. They used excessive amounts of fuel too, particularly 18100. Another factor was that by the mid-1950s, technology had moved on.

The gas-turbine was no longer considered the best prospect for the future of railway motive power. Even before they had been properly evaluated, the West Germans were putting their faith in diesel-hydraulics, and their V200 class was giving some encouraging data, according to Western Region management.

'Brown-Boveri' lasted until late 1959 on the Western Region. The more powerful Metro-Vic 18100 went back to the makers in Manchester in December 1953. It was to be converted to burn heavy fuel, then return. The modifications became problematic and 18100 never did return, although it wasn't for a lack of trying to retrieve it by Swindon or the WR management.

Shunting Engines

Only non-steam powered examples that had connections to the CME Dept at Swindon are included here. The department experimented with internal-combustion power from the 1920s. Presumably the footplatemen were given practical and theoretical training by representatives of the builders. For shunting at various works around the GWR, five four-wheeled locos made by Simplex Works of Bedford were brought in. They had four-cylinder petrol engines and weighed 8 tons. The Dorman-Ricardo engines were capable of developing 40bhp at 1,000rpm. These 0-4-0 locomotives occasionally came to Swindon for overhaul and, because they belonged to the CME Dept and not the Traffic Dept, they went into B Erecting Shop for overhaul.

Loco erector Jim Lowe remembers one of the Simplex shunters being left 'out of service' in the timber stacking ground sidings at Swindon. This particular diesel shunter, No. 27, had worked the yards at Reading Signal Works but was replaced by an absorbed Welsh 0-4-0 steam engine because it was becoming unreliable. No. 27 stood in a remote siding from 1950 but was not scrapped for many years. Jim said it could be seen on the embankment from the bottom of Redcliffe Street. All five Simplex shunters were eventually scrapped at Swindon Works.

In 1933 the GWR purchased a 70hp diesel shunting engine from Fowler & Co. and gave it the number 1. It was used in the yards of the Locomotive Works so that it could be closely evaluated. Early in 1936, for use elsewhere, they received their first diesel-electric shunter from the contractors, English Electric Co. Ltd and R. & W. Hawthorn

Being able to say that a British railway company used your products was good publicity. These shunting engines were painted black, while the Great Western example before it had been outshopped in lined green. They were all given GW cast numberplates as used on steam locomotives. *British Machine Tool Engineering magazine*

Leslie and Co. Ltd. The GWR gave this one the number 2. It was powered by a six-cylinder vertical engine capable of developing up to 350bhp at 680rpm.

In 1946 seven locomotives were ordered, based on the design of No. 2. They would become Nos 15101 to 15107 and were built at Swindon with power units supplied by English Electric and Brush. Brush claimed that they could haul 1,000 tons at 9.5mph on a level road and that speeds up to 20mph were achievable with lighter trainloads. The men in the Works always referred to them as 'the 350 shunters' but this Swindon batch had 360bhp engines.

After nationalisation, private industrial short wheelbase diesel shunters were also to be seen awaiting Works' attention. Jim remembers working on their wheels: 'Running in and out of sidings with tight curves put additional wear on the flanges, so we were regularly changing the tyres.' Swindon Drawing Office staff worked on a new design for a BR 'light diesel-mechanical shunter' in October 1955. Two years later the first batch of the class was completed at Swindon. They had Gardner Type 8L3 engines transmitting 204hp to six wheels via an epicyclic gearbox, a final drive and reverse unit and a jackshaft.

These Swindon and Doncaster built 0-6-0s were later classified '03' by British Railways. The Western Region did not receive an allocation of this class until the last few months of the decade. Jack Gardner said in his book: 'To start them an air cylinder could be filled with compressed air from an on board handpump, which would then turn the engine over or they could be bump started by towing them along with a steam loco.' At Swindon the new units were not only used for working the yards, they were found to be suitable for hauling worksmen's trains over the Highworth branch as well.

Modernisation and Dieselisation

In February 1951 British Railways announced its intention of increasing its fleet of diesel shunting engines. The following year they made public plans to invest in the development of multiple unit diesel engine trains for certain types of passenger services. These plans were based on a Railway Executive survey of diesel development

in France, Belgium, Germany and Ireland. The intention was 'to give the greatest efficiency and economy in working'. They stressed that steam locomotives would 'continue to form the backbone of services and that may always be the case'. Whether that was generally accepted among the planners or whether they were trying to reassure the thousands of workers, whose jobs were dependent upon steam, I don't know.

Early in 1955 the British Transport Commission set out, in broad terms, its radical plans for the modernisation of British Railways. Of course, they included extending electrification and further use of diesel traction but there was still no certainty about being able to phase out steam completely. Mr R.A. Smeddle, chief mechanical engineer on the Western Region at the time, said: 'The choice of motive power clearly lay between steam, diesel and electric traction.' It wasn't long however, before the uncertainty was settled.

Where it could compete with 'outside' British contractors, the BTC wanted to maximise the use of its own workshops for the new orders. In the case of locomotives, comparative studies had shown that British Railways' workshops could build units more cheaply than contractors, whose plant and facilities were generally more antiquated. The government had been persuaded to take the opposite view by the Locomotive Manufacturers Association. They argued that by buying more from contractors, a larger and steadier home market would develop and assist the industry's export potential.

The government's position prevailed and dieselisation, and the haste with which it was implemented, meant that the railways suddenly became very dependent upon contractors. The BTC was then committed to placing relatively large orders without the testing of a prototype and this indirectly led to too many different classes to operate and maintain. Therefore, the testing and evaluation to find a standard design for each type of work became protracted and costly.

Workshop Reorganisation

The biggest changes in the Works' history took place in the second half of the 1950s due to the British Transport Commission's (amended) Modernisation Plan. This now required that all steam locomotives be replaced with diesels within fifteen years. Swindon Works had to be completely re-equipped to manufacture, test and repair diesel-hydraulics, diesel railcars and diesel-mechanical shunting engines. Up until then they had only very limited experience of producing and maintaining the mechanical parts for, and erecting motive power worked by, four-stroke oil engines (diesel engines). The reorganisation turned out to be extensive and time consuming, and some of it went on into the 1960s.

The first alterations to accommodate the diesel building programme was an extension to the carriage lifting shop for the building of the railcars, and a testing area built nearby. The AE Shop was altered in stages for the building and maintenance of the main-line batches of diesels and 200hp diesel shunters. New sections were set up for the construction of bogies, wheelsets and final drive assemblies and the repair of transmissions.

Because of an ever greater reliance upon welded fabrications in the building of locomotives, X-ray pictures would be required to show whether welded seams were sound or whether there were any cracks due to contraction as the metal cooled. For this a new radiological building became operational in 1958 on the loco side. Plans were being worked out by 1960 for an atomic hydrogen welding section, which would require extensive alterations within the Chain Smiths' Shop (part of F Shop). They included concrete floors, new welding plant, a pillar crane, fixed hoist structures and asbestos screens.

The 'Barn', the large shop between the Works' turntable and A Shop, where tubes had been removed from steam boilers, was gradually becoming obsolete. It was therefore, completely rebuilt inside to test diesel engine/transmission units. The building then consisted of several full-load test cells that simulated working conditions out on the road. Each cell had its own soundproofed control room.

The machining of steam loco main frames, cylinder saddles and blocks was no longer required by the late 1950s as the policy was, in theory, to withdraw engines upon needing major repairs. Therefore the two large machine shops on the loco side, W and AM, found themselves with a much-reduced workload. Machine tools were moved, stored or scrapped to make way for the testing of air compressors and exhausters and various types of brake valves.

The amount of work done in the Foundry had started to decline, although this was offset somewhat by a decision to concentrate all British Railways' non-ferrous foundry work at Swindon. To cope with this, the original Brass Foundry was extended and modernised. Half the total area of the Iron Foundry would now be used, temporarily, for adjustments and painting of the new locomotives, which would relieve the congestion in A Shop. This new section was to be set up under the direction of ex-G Shop foreman Mr Simpkins. Plans were made for this building to become the internal combustion engine repair shop, in time.

The X Shop (points and crossings) moved to a new building in 1958 and the old shop was reorganised and became the ET Shop (electrical traction). It was fitted out for the repair and testing of locomotive and DMU motors, generators, dynostarters, control gear and other electrical equipment. Like some of the other new facilities, the ET Shop moved to a different building in the 1960s. Since October 1956 classes had been run in Emlyn Square to teach drivers and workshop staff the principles of the new motive power. Mr Clark, the first tutor, said the courses for fitters were the longest and most involved.

The Post-war Railcars

This new generation of rail cars were designed to run in sets comprising of driving trailer and motor brake vehicles. They became known as diesel multiple units or DMUs. Swindon was one of three works that were required to

An Inter-city railcar underframe with one driving bogie and final drive/reversing unit visible, on the wagon turntable. *R.J. Blackmore collection, courtesy of Andrea Downing*

A leading 'motor brake second' from a Swindon-built Inter-city DMU. *BRWR*

start building single and multiple-unit railcars. They were classified as 'Cross-country' and 'Inter-city' diesel sets, depending on the type of work for which they were designed. The first diesel sets began appearing from the Works in 1956. Initially these were two sets of three-car trains designed here and built in the Carriage Works for long-distance express passenger services.

Each vehicle built at Swindon, as well as those built elsewhere for the Western Region, had bodies of 64ft 6in long × 9ft 3in wide. They had a diesel engine and transmission on each of the two bogies. Another feature of these three-car multiple units was that two sets could be coupled together and driven from the leading vehicle's driving cab. Most of these new trains were gangwayed within each set, with the guard's and luggage compartment at the inner end of the motor brake car. Swindon did not build any single-rail cars.

In 1958, the Works was building batches of three-car Cross-country DMUs, designed for fast passenger services with more frequent stops. After that came another batch of Inter-city sets, with modifications. Servicing equipment was designed and partly manufactured at Swindon for installation at the principal WR depots. One of the first to use DMUs extensively was Bristol, Bath Road. By the start of the summer timetable in 1959, almost all local passenger and parcels' services in the Bristol division, which included Swindon, were handled by DMUs.

Not all Swindon-built railcar units were used on the Western Region. In 1960 the Works built the 'Trans-Pennine' six-car DMUs and used Leyland Albion 230hp engines to cope with the steeply graded route across the

Pennines. All the variations of DMUs would prove to be ideal for stopping trains on suburban services. They had good acceleration and did not need to be turned between duties; the same qualities that the designers had strived for in the large 2-6-2 'Prairie' tanks that they were replacing. This was a time when statistics and comparisons with the equivalent in steam power were being made known to justify the colossal investment and upheaval taking place in the industry. For instance, with steam, frequent fire and boiler cleaning was labour intensive and reduced availability by 25%. The equivalent maintenance of a locomotive powered by an oil engine reduced availability by just 5%.

BD Shop

In preparation for the overhaul and repair of diesel engines, part of B (tender) Shop was partitioned off in 1956. It was planned that a good deal of the repair work would eventually be undertaken outstation and facilities were duly installed at depots on their routes. Initially though, all but the minor maintenance work was to be done at Swindon, in what would be known as BD Shop. Local and regional diesel training schools were set up for CME staff from mechanical foremen to works' managers. They were sent on courses being run at the Derby BR Training College, while depot maintenance staff and engine drivers received instruction at Swindon in lecture rooms set up in the railway estate. Mr J.A. Clarke, a former draughtsman in the general DO, was one of those who were hastily training up to take classes. As well as contractors' manuals, Swindon Works produced their own technical literature.

An official portrait of diesel-mechanical shunter D2033. This was one of the early 204hp shunting engines that were built in batches between 1958 and 1961. *BRWR*

BD Shop staff would overhaul rail car power transmission components, which were engines and fuel equipment, four-speed gearboxes and final drive/reversing units. They arrived by rail from the depots in special flat top Enpart wagons. Internal transport then brought these components in and out of the workshop using Conveyancer fork (lift) trucks. As more diesel locomotive work was taken on, so the BD Shop expanded and steam loco tender capacity was reduced. Complete vehicles could then be brought inside via a 70ft traverser and lifted by four electrically powered jacks to facilitate the removal of the bogies. The stores (or warehouse) for diesel maintenance spares also expanded as steam work was contracted. By 1960 it had been split into two as main-line diesel parts for the AE Shop were separated.

Denis Raven was one of the first fitters to work on the new section. Denis, whose father was a foreman in the AM Shop, had been in G Shop working on plant maintenance. His work would now involve stripping and replacing worn or defective parts of six-cylinder horizontal engines made by AEC and, later, Leyland. Replacement parts were produced in R Shop under Chief Foreman Stan Godwin. He oversaw all the diesel repair work on the loco side.

Denis was sent on courses that were held where the component parts were made. This would involve a couple of weeks in the workshops of AEC at Southall or at Bosch in Coventry, where they made fuel pumps. He learned the arrangement and principle of four-stroke oil engines and six-cylinder fuel injection pumps. On the train home each evening he would rewrite the shorthand notes he had made throughout the day. In the late 1950s Denis was sent on courses so that he could work on Maybach, MAN and Paxman engines too:

I loved the work, especially when I moved to fuel injection pumps and injectors, but the oil did make your hands sore. My family doctor gave me various fluids to get the oil off my skin and he kept his eye on me. Another potential hazard was testing injectors: if the high-pressure spray hit you it could cause serious damage to skin or eyes. I soon became chargeman, then inspector, and in about 1960 I became junior foreman in BD Shop. Peter Spackman 'followed me', by which I mean he got the posts I vacated.

I remember the locomotive works' manager bringing three men from Paddington [senior

Western Region managers] round one day. They came and spoke to me and I suggested an alternative way of calibrating fuel pumps from rail cars. I found out later that the loco works' manager was very pleased because my suggestion contributed to the decision to keep the contract for repairing the pumps when they were considering giving it to the makers, CAV of Acton.

A derailment outside the Loco Works due to the severe weather of 1962–63. A lightweight '03' class 0-6-0 diesel shunter, built here in the late 1950s, has run off the rails due to compacted snow. The photographer Bob Grainger said: 'Word soon got round the shops nearby when something like this happened. Some of these people had just come out to have a look and give needless advice; I think the Brass Shop foreman was there somewhere. As a young apprentice with a constant desire to get a good photograph, I was taking a chance. Workers taking photographs were frowned upon at the best of times.' January and February 1940 and 1947 were the worst winters in living memory in Swindon until 1962–63. However, most were severe enough to cause disruption to internal transport movements and freeze points, water pipes and tanks.

25

The Early Diesel-hydraulics

Meeting the Requirements

The application of the internal combustion engine to a locomotive capable of hauling heavy and fast trains had beaten British designers until the 1950s. Oil engines capable of the low speed, high power required, were too big and heavy to be accommodated within the BR loading gauge. Then, with advances in metallurgy, it became possible to design and build high-speed engines of a suitable power output and size. The evolution of the hydraulic transmission and torque converter was not affected by the same constraints. The German Mekydro transmission had been worked out, in principle, before the war.

The main-line, diesel-hydraulic locomotives of the Deutsche Bundesbahn, the state railway of West Germany, appealed to BR, Western Region management: all of whom were 'time-served' mechanical engineers. Mr Smeddle, the Western Region's CM&EE, said this would utilise a greater proportion of the existing plant in the erecting shops. Another consideration was that the Maybach power equipment should be easier to understand by the existing workforce than diesel-electric components. The two most important factors were, of course, performance, compared to the 'Castles' and 'Kings', and weight. Diesel-hydraulic engines, transmissions and other components were lighter and less bulky than the alternative, although this would adversely affect adhesion.

Manfred Spindler from Osbourne Street was German and had been a prisoner of war in Swindon. At the war's end his parents advised him to apply to stay here as his pre-war home was now in the Russian Zone. Manfred's application was accepted but it was not until later that he was allowed to go into factory work. So in 1951 he went into the Works and was sent to No. 8 Shop (new carriage painting) Office, where a Mr Prosser was the senior clerk. After two years, some of which was spent in the Correspondence Office, a senior officer from the Motive Power Department asked Manfred if he would come and

work for them. Thinking that his prospects might improve, he said yes. At first he was dealing with free passes for staff throughout the Western Region, then he realised why he had been headhunted.

'The technical assistant to the motive power superintendent, Humphrey White, and a colleague were to be sent to West Germany to investigate the impressive power/weight ratios being claimed of their new diesel-hydraulic locomotives. They were to write a report for Mr Grand, the general manager, and they would need an interpreter. Therefore I was invited alone too.'

Manfred said the trip was as early as 1953. He and the two engineers went to the German Federal Railway's central offices and the Krauss-Maffei Locomotive Works in Munich. After that, they went on to the factories where engines and transmissions were being produced. 'Translating technical detail was rather daunting for me as I had no engineering background at all. We all got the same allowance for the four-day trip. My senior colleagues were more used to spending than I was and were soon borrowing from me.'

Design Work at Swindon

In 1954 the chief draughtsman asked Manfred to come and work in the Drawing Office and again he said yes. No doubt 'the chief' had in mind the language problems that existed with the Swiss engineers over the gas-turbine locomotive, No. 18000, just after the war. Although drawings started to arrive from Germany in the spring of 1956, Manfred says he was translating German technical data for evaluation, in 1954. For this he worked in an office in Park House, the old medical examination centre. The draughtsman who was assigned to the work concerned, took it to Manfred and between them they would interpret the detail; the former having already converted the metric measurements into imperial.

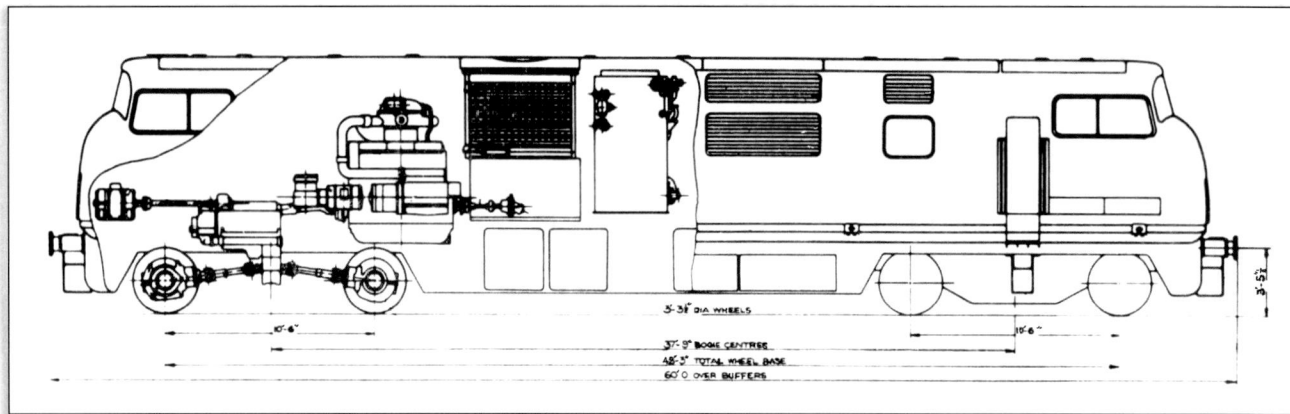

The new main-line 2,200hp diesel hydraulic locomotive type B-B. *BRWR*

With the war still fresh in everyone's mind, Manfred experienced some prejudice. However, in the Drawing Office they took to the newcomer without exception but did insist on rechristening him Fred. Ray Smith of the electrical section had also been a PoW in Germany, but there was no bad feeling between them; in fact they got on very well. For all his valuable work, Fred was never promoted beyond a grade 4 clerk, something he feels was down to his nationality.

A new main-line diesel was on the drawing board by late 1956. The majority of the locomotive sections were devoted to diesel work of one sort or another by this time. Key workshop personnel were being sent to West Germany to learn about new production methods. The K Shop welders' foreman, Roy Taylor, and AE Shop fitters' foreman, Jim Tuck, accompanied the loco works manager over there, in 1956. The main-line locomotive type were to be known as the D800s and later each of the class would be named after British warships. The design work would be divided up into: 1) body and underframes, 2) bogies and brakes, 3) engines, cooling and preheating equipment, 4) transmissions, axle drives and cardan shafts and 5) electrical and carriage warming equipment.

The 'D800' class was to be a modified version of the German diesel-hydraulic locomotive, the V200. The main difference was a reduction in the size due to the restrictions of British Railways' load gauge. Mr Scholes, the chief draughtsman, said in his paper to the Institute of Locomotive Engineers that: 'Had the load gauges been similar a V200 type could have been purchased immediately and put into service,' for evaluation purposes. The underframe and body had to be redesigned incorporating the existing engines, transmission units and bogies but with different wheel diameters.

Reg Willcocks said that all the staff in the DO, including the seniors, admitted that they were 'in the dark' with the new type of work. Two things caused particular problems for the designers used to working with steam locomotives. One was the stressed skin body shell that had to withstand the loading forces when being lifted, the other was the electrical engineering detail required to assemble components arriving from the manufacturers.

The Western Region magazine reported that: 'Great emphasis was placed on the exterior shape and decoration of the new D800 (and D600) main-line diesel. The scope for which was mainly confined to the two ends and limited by technical requirements.' It was also claimed to have caused more argument and divergence of opinion than any other elements of the design. The Design Research Unit in London was engaged in 1955 and, in co-operation with the Swindon Drawing Office, produced a ½in to 1ft model, which was rejected. The British Transport Commission was now of the opinion that a simple outline with little emphasis on streamline decorations and irrelevant front end shaping was what was required. The styling of a second model incorporating those recommendations was accepted.

Reg worked on the mountings for transmission and cooler units of the D800s and those of the D1000 class in 1960. George Connell worked on diesel engines with section head Peter Kembrey in early 1958. Mr Kembrey had a degree and taught HNC students at the College some evenings. George remembered Les Slade, John Godfrey, Edgar Snook, Frank Bassett, Ron Webb, 'Nobbie' Clark, Derek Norris and Ray Smith, who all working in the Loco DO at that time. Another section leader there, Donald Gimlett, would sometimes use a Polariscope, an instrument designed and built at Swindon to give accurate results from photoelastic stress analysis of steel.

Other sections of up to six men gradually became established, such as Jack Preedy's 'diesel investigations' and Sid Robinson's 'modifications'. Newcomers such as Reg and George would spend time on all the locomotive sections before being placed permanently. In the C&W section in the 1950s, the head scratching was over the design of the Inter-city and Cross-country multiple diesel cars.

The new designs for double access doors and four-character indicator panels on the D800 noses were drawn by George Connell. This early modification would replace the lateral disc indicators and would accommodate the new system of train reporting numbers to be introduced at the end of the decade. Around this time (1959) George was also given the job of calculating the buckling strength of the various body sections of the new D1000 class.

With that done he then had to work out whether the body shell would support the weight of the locomotive without the bogies, when lifted. 'There was as yet, no formula worked out that I could refer to, so it was all trial and error.'

The Chief Civil Engineer's Dept worked with the General Drawing Office to prepare designs for refuelling pump installations and facilities at certain depots. Draughtsman Terry French produced the drawings for these and compiled a parts list based on sketches and measurements he had taken on site.

Building the First D800s

In 1957 and 1958 the first three main-line diesel-hydraulic locomotives were under construction in the AE Shop at an estimated cost of £120,000 each. These were already officially known as the 'D800' class and, like the D600s, would be named after warships of the Royal Navy.

The Western Region alone decided upon diesel-hydraulics rather than the more popular concept of diesel-electric traction. At Swindon and Paddington particularly, there was great pride taken over the new D800 with its impressive specification, something not seen since the introduction of the 'Kings' thirty years before. Other BTC representatives would rather have waited for electrification, which they were told would eventually cover the whole country.

These first three locomotives were given twin Maybach MD650 V12-cylinder engines and Mekydro K104 main transmission units, which were imported from Germany. Each engine unit produced 1,035bhp with the aid of turbochargers. Power was transferred to the hydraulic transmission unit, which consisted of an oil-filled torque converter and an integral automatic four-speed gearbox. Variations in engine and road speed were sensed by a twin-element centrifugal governor, which initiated the movement of pistons within the command block, to change gear using claw clutches.

The drive to the axles of each pivotless bogie was via a cardan shaft from the Mekydro output. The hydraulic transmission dispensed with the massive generators and motors of the diesel-electric locomotive. Although relying less on electrical components, the diesel-hydraulic equipment would still require many electrical fitters in the Erecting Shop. The dynastarters, for instance, acted as generators and provided current for auxiliary systems and charged the batteries. The control system and numerous safety and warning devices were also electrically operated. The working weight was calculated to be just under 80 tons.

Freddie Dew was put in charge of the first D800 gang. They laid the foundation for the underframe: two steel tubes 6½in in diameter that ran throughout the length, on to which were welded a honeycomb of steel plate cross-stays designed to support the mainframe floor. As the D800 underframe progressed to the side frame stanchions, the underframe gang moved to the next pit and started again. (Not long after this Freddie, who had been in the Erecting Shop since well before the war, went back to

One of the first MD650 engine units to be delivered to the erecting shop. It is seen still partially crated after its journey from Maybach in Germany. *Author's collection*

standard steam building.) Tony Illesley's gang took over on the first loco and fitted the bodywork and bulkheads.

Pete Brettel's gang, which became known as the 'Maybach gang', would fit the sub-frame mountings, the engines and the British-made steam generator for train heating. When D800 was ready for its 'finishing' work, in the summer of 1958, Chargeman Brettel left the Maybach gang to take charge of it.

A gang was formed to assemble the final drives and bogies, made up of men from Fred Dingley's section who had worked on steam bogies. Another new gang assembled and tested the transmission equipment in the AM Shop. All these men came under the jurisdiction of section foreman, Dennis Cole. Later, when the locomotives were taken out of service, the respective gangs would be responsible for the repairs and overhaul of what they were now assembling.

Ernie Wiggins is photographed examining a British Timken roller bearing. This is fitted to a D800 wheelset, yet to have its tyres fitted. On the back of this snapshot is written: 'AW Shop 1958'. Ernie, a former engine erector who lived in Cobden Road, carried out the Ultrasonic Flaw Detection tests on axles in both wheel shops. Being a big man, he was ideally suited to this heavy work and to his part-time job as doorman at the Locarno Ballroom. *Derek Wiggins*

D800 to D802 were prototypes: they were hand-built without jigs, gauges and specialised tool equipment, and relied on arrangement drawings that were subject to alterations as building progressed. The A2 bay pit roads were the ones used for these, the first of the class. They were between the new work section where BR standard steam engines were still being built and Lewington's steam 'finishing' gang. A lot of the electricians were

D818 and D819 being built in A Shop on 17 March 1960. They would receive the names Glory and Goliath respectively. *R. Grainger*

recruited from the London area for the diesel building programmes; few if any had worked for the railways before. Bert Ball was one of the chargeman-electricians and George Gale and Brian Menzies became their first foremen. As well as the D800s, electricians were needed for building batches of 0-6-0 diesel shunters (with mechanical transmissions) at the same time.

The contracts to supply German components included providing service engineers in the initial period of production. Swindon fitter-erectors and electricians would learn to assemble and test the twin Maybach engines and other transmission components as well as their associated heating and cooling systems etc. All had to be fitted into smaller body shells than those for which they were designed. Engineers from Maybach and other factories in West Germany worked with the diesel gangs and were found to be very capable engineers who spoke reasonably good English. A Mr Stark from Friedrichstafen was the senior Maybach engineer. They stayed for up to twelve months, initially being accommodated at the Great Western Hotel opposite the station. Alan Lambourn told me that:

The Swindon men were a little uneasy with the visitors at first; the war still being fresh in everyone's minds. Soon though we all got on well together and the German engineer allocated to our gang sat with us during the breaks. However, we noticed that our labourer, Les, was no longer joining us. The chargeman found out that Les had been a PoW in Germany so he asked Richard, our German guest, to have a word with him. Richard, who would have been too young to fight in the war, was very easy-going and soon they became good friends. The visitors couldn't understand why we were so heavy handed in our work and kept shearing bolts and rounding off nuts. The reason was probably because we were used to heavier mechanical work.

Jim Lowe said:

Two of the Germans had the first name Otto, so one became known as 'young Otto'. He decided to stay on after his contract finished and went on to work with the Maybach and MAN engine repair gangs. Sometime later 'young Otto' became a running inspector on the Western Region.

Problems of organisation and staff deployment arose due to the lightweight underframes and body structure, and there were demarcation disputes on the shop floor. It was eventually agreed that sheet metal men would handle plate work up to 1/8in or 3mm and the coppersmiths and ex boilermakers would work with plate up to ¼in or 6mm. These sorts of problems held up not only their work, but that of others too. George Connell, in the Drawing Office, remembers getting unwanted overtime due to the disruption that these disputes would cause.

It was learned, almost by accident, that alterations would have to be made to each of the four 100-ton cranes when lifting the main-line diesels. Although the cab of the crane was to one side of the load, a certain amount of clearance was needed in case the suspended load swung. With steam locomotives there were no problems as, even with the largest types, the buffer beam was below the crane driver's cabin. The full profile combined with the extra length of the diesels, however, provided no such clearance. This was solved by lifting the cabins up about 2ft. Various Works' tradesmen carried out the alterations and not the crane makers, Ransome & Rapier. No doubt it was done during a bank holiday weekend or during the annual shutdown in July.

Alloys nameplates were cast in the foundry for the initial three units and this settled the rumours about what the theme of the new locomotives names was to be. D800 itself, was the exception. It was given the name *Sir Brian Robertson*, the current chairman of the British Transport Commission. He had championed the cause of building diesel-hydraulics for the Western Region against strong opposition. The first of the class went out for trials in July and August 1958. One of its first runs was to Paddington for the official naming ceremony. The livery was dark green with grey waist, red buffer beams and nameplates, with polished metal trim; all very similar to that applied to Swindon's steam locos.

Production Batches

The British Transport Commission, with the Western Region management's blessing, placed an order for thirty more D800s in February 1957. These were also to be built at Swindon but an order for a further thirty in July of the following year could not be undertaken because the Swindon workshops would now have reached their capacity (they were also building diesel-mechanical shunters and 9F steam locomotives).

As D800/01/02 took shape, a production line was being prepared in the A2 bay of the A Shop extension. Rayer's light repairs steam gang would now only occupy one section at the back of the shop. The construction of the production engines would occupy the pits in the centre of the bay. From there the finished products could later be either towed outside through the AW Shop or pulled on to the traversing table by rope and capstan.

From D803 onwards, the West German-designed power equipment was built by Bristol Siddeley near Coventry under licence. At the same time, the combined power output was increased to 2,200bhp by using a redesigned transmission unit. D830 was the exception: it was fitted with two British Paxman engines in the hope of cutting the reliance on German technology. D803 was ready for trials in March 1959, and further units were outshopped at the rate of one per month. Terry Couling said that six men would paint each new body shell: 'As painters liked to sing while working, it could become quite a racket.'

The contract for the next thirty locomotives went to the North British Locomotive Company in Glasgow. For this a complete set of drawings was copied and sent up to Scotland. An order for a final batch of five locomotives, to be built at Swindon, was placed in April 1959. By the end of 1960 the first nine of the North British locos had arrived at Swindon for trials and testing. These would soon gain a reputation for being less reliable and needing more attention than those built at Swindon.

Just before Apprentice Alan Lambourn finished his time he worked with the D800 finishing off and trials gang. This was in 1959 and Alan, from William Street, worked on the later engines being built. Pete Brettel was appointed chargeman, replacing Jack Blackmore, who became chargeman of the Maybach gang in Pete's place. Some of the diesel 'finishing' jobs done by the erectors were connecting the final pipework and train heating boilers, filling the oil systems, filling the radiators with water and fitting the detachable roof panels.

Fitters on the finishing gang at that time were Dick Gleed, John Bunce, John Dashfield, Arthur Cook, Bill Hobbs and Eric Turner. Alan said:

> Many in the Erecting Shop thought this was the place to be because men on this work seemed to be promoted quicker than elsewhere. Perhaps the main reason though, was because finishing off included putting right any problems that occurred during trials. Therefore several men of this gang were riding about on the new engines a lot of the time: something everyone considered most agreeable.

After first ensuring that the transmissions were set to neutral and locked, the completed diesel units were moved outside. The first job then was preheating the engines. In the forty-five minutes that this took, the fuel and water was pumped in. When the circulating engine oil reached the correct temperature, the engines were started. Until a suitably qualified inspector was trained up, Pete Brettel would now do the 'functioning'. This involved testing and priming the two engines and transmission units, while Alan or another apprentice and a fitter cured any leaks, 'bled' the injectors and watched the temperature and pressure readings come up on the gauges. Alan went on to say:

> Diesel work was considered superior to steam, probably because no one had yet got used to it. Certainly the motor mechanics that were starting to come in gave the impression that they thought they were better than the old steam fitters. They were certainly more militant and the pride in the job wasn't the same anymore. Although it was complex we were just assembling parts made outside, whereas the steam locomotive was designed and built at Swindon from raw materials.

Bob Grainger told me that some parts made outside were, at first, held by the workshop stores, and this could hold the work up. He said that some issuers guarded diesel parts like their own and junior erectors, like him, would have to convince them the foreman had sent them for the part or parts. Bob summed up diesel erecting by saying: 'The work wasn't so heavy but was less accessible.'

Shortly after the first main-line diesels entered service on the Western Region, Mr R.A. Smeddle, the chief mechanical and electrical engineer, said: 'Because of the urgent need to press forward with the dieselisation programme, we were not given the opportunity of trying out prototypes before placing large orders and this in itself, of course, has presented us with the difficulty of having to make alterations on a considerable number of locomotives instead of on one, as we go along.'

Trial Running

Tom Stevenson from Ferndale Road was one of the first, if not the first, to drive D800. A few months earlier he had delivered D600 from the manufacturers in Scotland to Swindon (when D601 made its first journey south it completely failed en route). Two of the fitters would also go out with the enginemen while the loco was tested on the main line. The same arrangement applied to steam trials. To go out with the loco you had been working on was always considered a privilege, and not just among newcomers such as apprentices. Alan said:

> First was a 'light engine' test to Badminton and back, during which we could get very wet tightening joints in the water cooling systems. For the next three days after that, if nothing major needed attending to, the loco would pull ten empty coaches down the line to Badminton and back.

The bulkhead panel at the rear of the cab of a newly completed Swindon D800 locomotive. *BRWR*

The driver's desk and control cabinet in the cab of No. D823. The date on the back of this photo is June 1960, some weeks before this locomotive entered traffic. *BRWR*

The last period of the trials was spent working trains diagrammed for Swindon Shed locomotives. They always tried to start this stage of the trials on Monday morning and work through to Saturday with the same engine. The 10.47am to Paddington was often the turn used for this; returning on the afternoon Plymouth parcels, which left from the Paddington parcels platform and changed engines and crews at Swindon. An A Shop fitter and sometimes an apprentice would keep an eye on it for this period of twelve to eighteen days.

Back at the shed after each London trip we [the 'finishing off' gang] would attend to any problems. If a major component had to come out and we needed a crane, the loco went back inside A Shop. On more than one occasion we replaced an engine and didn't knock off until late at night. I still had to be in the next morning at 6am to switch on the locomotive's pre-heaters; like everyone else, I didn't want to turn down the overtime.

Out on the road it was my job to record the readings for engine revs, oil temperature, cooling water temperature and levels and transmission temperature. This I would do every fifteen minutes. The chief A Shop foreman Mr Simpkins would sometimes invite senior office staff on to these trips, so it often got crowded. Some instruments I needed to see were duplicated in the engine compartment behind the cab but not all. On one occasion I gave up and returned to the Works with a half-empty record sheet. My section foreman Mr Cole queried this and told me I had his permission to elbow the chief out of the way next time it happened, so I did. After that they were a bit more considerate.

In Service

After completing so many miles with no major problems, each new diesel entered traffic and was sent to the allocated depot. D800 entered service proper in August 1958. It went to Laira motive power depot, where it joined D600/01 and commenced working the Plymouth–Paddington section with the up Cornish Riviera Express. D801/02 joined them at Laira towards the end of the year. At this time, it was estimated that each new loco would make two steam equivalents redundant, even allowing for some teething problems.

It wasn't long before the Loco DO was investigating persistent problems associated with hard day-to-day working. In the first half of 1959, nearly 50% of defects reported from the first five were due to electrical apparatus and wiring circuits developing faults. Loco Works Manager Smith recorded in his notes that there was 'sensitivity with the quality of the engine oil used', at this time, too. By the autumn, with twelve in service, it was expected that subsequent engines would leave the Works at the rate of one every three weeks. It was also predicted that this rate should increase with time,

implying that design and production problems were still causing delays.

It was found that the bogies 'lurched' at high speed and the ensuing oscillation frightened drivers into not exceeding 80mph. This trouble, and its associated tyre wear, had not been noticed with the V200 bogies. In 1960 a speed limit of 80mph was officially imposed on the class: this was lifted a few months later when the problem was overcome.

When the D800s returned to the Works and had been named, the loco erectors called them the 'Maybach Warships' to distinguish them from the D600s, which they referred to as 'Man Warships'. Bob Grainger, a fitter in the Erecting Shop, said that, unlike steam locomotives, the main-line diesels were not brought back into the shop facing in any particular direction. Where the work required could apply to either end, the terms 'Bristol end' and 'Paddington' or 'London end' were used by him and his colleagues. When referring to the drawings the 'A' or 'B' ends might need to be observed: 'B' being the boiler end.

It had been provisionally decided that a complete overhaul would be carried out after 200,000 miles although the German equivalents were achieving more than 350,000 miles between works' visits. The engine and transmission units could be changed at the principal diesel depots but they were still overhauled and tested at Swindon. Specially converted wagons were used to transport them between the two facilities.

Shed rosters continued to include steam locomotives covering station pilot duties. A 4-6-0 was kept 'in steam' ready to take over if a train engine failed in the area. In this role, some claim that they were often coming to the aid of diesel-hauled trains. Author Adrian Vaughan said that some Swindon footplatemen called their 'County' class engines life boats, because they rescued so many 'D800' class 'Warships'. Alan Lambourn said that, by 1960, the diesel-hydraulics rarely broke down completely during trials: 'Even with a single engine failure, which was uncommon, we could usually limp home unaided, on the other.' One reason why steam and the early D800s were seen double-heading trains in winter was because of the latter's unreliable train heating boilers.

The D1000s

Operating experience with the D800s soon began to show that a more powerful locomotive was needed for the heaviest freight and passenger trains. Western Region and Swindon engineers looked at how the West Germans had progressed from the V200. They had just built a 3,000bhp locomotive, the ML3000. It was quickly decided that the proposed new type would be based on its principles, although it was still at the prototype stage.

This, together with their experience of main-line diesel-hydraulic locomotives, led Swindon Drawing Office to undertake to design a 2,700hp 'Type 4' locomotive. After all, the draughtsmen and loco erectors had overcome the complexities of electrical wiring systems

I would guess that these members of the public were visiting on a Wednesday open day, rather than on a private school tour. The guide, Mr Stratford, is directing attention to some detail of the first 'Warship' of the class.
Dave Stratford collection

and stressed-skin body shells. Axleloading and the confines of the British loading gauge should also, more or less, solve themselves with the experience already gained. On paper the weight of the new type could be brought down to just over 100 tons, which was then within acceptable limits.

An order was placed for seventy-four locomotives in late 1959. There was no time for a prototype to be constructed for evaluation. Crewe had spare capacity at its Works and tendered a lower price, but did not have the experience that Swindon had. Therefore the order was split between them. The first of the class was outshopped at Swindon, in fifteen months, and with less reliance upon German expertise than expected.

The D600s

At the same time as the D800s were evolving, the British Transport Commission pursued another project whereby hydraulic diesels could be designed and built in Britain using German components. The result was the 2,000bhp D600s, which were built at the North British Locomotive

Works in Glasgow. They were outshopped between early 1958 and early 1959, and were also given names of British warships. Therefore they became known as the 'North British Warships'. The D600s were always going to be a compromise but it was hoped that this would lead to the development of a successful British design. For that reason only five were built.

As the last D800s were going into traffic, the D600s with their less reliable and non-standard MAN engines, started arriving at the Works for their first planned maintenance. They were slightly longer than the D800s and weren't suitable for movement by the A Shop traverser. Instead they were shunted into the Erecting Shop through the south-west door and worked on there. The same arrangement had applied to the gas-turbine locomotives. At 117 tons, the D600s would only ever be lifted without bogies, which were easily the heaviest of their major components. The 'North British (D600) gang' included men who had worked on the early Swindon-built diesel electric shunters. Roy (Spud) Taylor was their chargeman. When he became inspector, Ken Morgan took over.

Acknowledgements and Sources

It has been a privilege to hear first-hand recollections from the following retired Works staff, over many years: John 'Jack' Fleetwood, George Petfield, Eric Mountford, Dr Barbara Carter (nee Dening), Yvonne Hodey (nee Jones), Liz Bartlett (nee Ribbins), Enid Hogden (nee Warren), Maureen Marvell (nee Stokes), Margaret Painter (nee Eveness), Mary Parkhouse (nee Almond), Beryl Stanley (née Hunt), Brenda Hedges (nee Berry), Dave Ellis, Pamela Badcock (nee Page), Mike Clarke, Jack Hartley, Daphne Breakspear (nee Barlow), Harry Bartlett, John Brettell, Bert Harber, Alan Lambourn, Peter Reade, Ken Ellis, Tony Huzzey, Gordon Turner, Dave Viveash, Doug Webb, Ken Watts, Colin Bown, Peter Chalk, Ivor Luker, John Jeffries, Roger Wise, John Walter, Vic Tucker, Mick Ponting, Mick Fisher, Maureen Fisher (nee Eveness), Des Griffiths, Ken Farncombe, Stan Leach, Ian Sawyer, Jim Lowe, George Butt, Terry Couling, Dorothy Cook (née Grimes), Daphne Kibblewhite, Colin Kibblewhite, Gordon Nash, Ernie Ruggles, George Connell, Roy Taylor, Reg Willcocks, Ray Eggleton, Manfred Spindler, Bob Grainger, Reg Bullock, Terry French, Ray Townsend, Maurice Parsons, Denis Raven, Alan Wild, Mike Casey, Tiny Williams, Hugh Freebury, Ivor Wilkins, Steve Bond, Bob Dauris, Ted Randell, Marion Reeves (nee Davis), Art Fortune, Margaret Griffiths (nee Kirby), Muriel Summers (nee Everrett), Margery Smith (nee Booker) and Janet Launchbury (nee Morgan).

The following either offered material, put me in touch with ex-staff or told me of their experiences of the railway town: Mrs Eynon, Richard Clarke, David Lewis, Ronnie Lambourn, John Nutty, Brian Smithson, Richard Woodley, Anne Sweeney, Dave Stratford, Roy Ferris, Mrs Parsons, Hilary Dunscombe, Kevin Weaver, Andy Binks, Beryl Wynn (née Odey), Myrtle Harber, Sarah Roe, Jane Hill, Michelle Couling, John Partridge, Derek Wiggins, Joyce Walters, Laraine Gilbert, Brian Arman, Roger Trayhurn, Ray Nash, Brenda Hanks, Shelley Morgan, John Matthews and Richard Naylor. Many thanks too, to Harriet Hirshman, Kevin Robertson and Jeremy Pratt at Crecy Publishing, who had faith in my proposed work.

Thank you very much Bob Townsend and Diane Everett of the Swindon Society; Dave King and successive editors of the *Swindon Advertiser*, for allowing me to use information contained in newspaper reports of the period and for publishing my appeals; Dianne Timms for typing and computer skills; Andrea Downing who provided information about her father, R.J. Blackmore; Richard Trewin and others at British Railways Board (Residuary) Ltd allowed me to use official photos; Minuteman Press, Swindon.

I have been fortunate to have met hundreds of local railway staff in the last forty-five years. Their stories have given me a sense of what it must have been like during those times. Apart from my own collection, the majority of printed material referred to came from the Steam Museum and the Swindon Central Library, local studies section where Katherine Cole and Darryl Moody are always enthusiastic and helpful. Other sources of material were the internet sites Wikipedia, Ancestry.com and eBay.

Bibliography

5079 Lysander, *Great Western Steam Miscellany 2* (D. Bradford Barton Ltd: 1980)

Adams, Prof. Henry, *Engineers' Handbook* (Cassell & Company: 1908)

Alcock, G.W., *Fifty Years of Railway Trade Unionism* (Co-operative Printing Society Limited: 1922)

Barman, Christian, *Next Station* (George Allen & Unwin Ltd: 1947)

Bartlett, Harry W., *Wartime Swindon as I Remember It* (published privately: 2011)

Bryan, Tim, *All in a Day's Work: Life on the G.W.R.* (Ian Allan: 2004)

Cattell, John and Falconer, Keith, *Swindon: The Legacy of a Railway Town* (English Heritage: 1995)

Chapman, W.G., *Caerphilly Castle* (G.W.R: 1924)

Chapman, W.G., *Cornish Riviera Ltd* (George Routledge and Sons Ltd: 1936)

Cook, Kenneth J., *Swindon Steam 1921–1951* (Ian Allan: 1974)

Darwin, Bernard, *A Century of Medical Service* (Published for the GWR: 1947)

Ellis, Chris, *Modelling the GWR* (Ian Allan: 1983)

Fletcher's *Directory of Swindon*, 1930 and 1959

Ford H.L. & Preedy N.E., *The Warships* (D. Bradford Barton Ltd: 1976)

Fraser, David; Geen, David; Scott, Barry, *The Great Western Railway in the 1930s* (Kingfisher Railway Productions: 1985)

Freebury, Hugh, *Great Western Apprentice* (Wilts County Library & Museum Service: 1985)

Fuller, Frederick, *The Railway Works and Church in New Swindon* (Redbrick Publishing: 1987)

Gardner, W.J., *Cleaner to Controller* (Oakwood Press: 1994)

Gibbs, Ken, *Swindon Works: An Apprentice in Steam* (Oxford Publishing Company: 1986)

Gourvish, T.R., *British Railways 1948–1973* (Cambridge University Press: 1986)

Great Western Progress: 1835–1935 (Great Western Railway: 1936)

Gwillam, R., *A Loco Fireman Looks Back* (D. Bradford Barton Ltd)

Haresnape, Brian, *Railway Liveries: GWR 1923–1947* (Ian Allan Ltd: 1983)

Harris, Michael, *Great Western Coaches from 1890* (David & Charles: 1985)

Holcroft, H., *An Outline of Great Western Locomotive Practice 1837–1947* (Ian Allan: 1971)

Karau, Paul; Copsey, John, *Great Western Diesel Railcars Supplement* (Wild Swan Publications Ltd)

Kelley, Philip J., *Road Vehicles of the Great Western Railway* (Oxford Publishing Co: 1980)

Knox, Collie, *The Un-Beaten Track* (Cassel & Company Ltd: 1944)

Lewis, J.K., *The Western's Hydraulics* (Atlantic: 1997)

Maller, Colin, *Growing up in a Railway Town* (published privately: date unknown)

Matheson, Rosa, *Women and the Great Western Railway* (Tempus Publishing: 2007)

Mountford, Eric, *Caerphilly Works 1901–1964* (Roundhouse Books: 1965)

Nock, O.S., *Tales of the Great Western Railway* (David & Charles: 1984)

Nock, O.S., *The History of the Great Western Railway, 1923–1947* (Ian Allan Ltd: 1967)

Nock, O.S., *GWR Steam* (David & Charles: 1972)

Nutty, E.J., *Testing Locomotive Slide Valves, Ports and Pistons* (published privately: 1943)

Nutty, E.J., *GWR Two-Cylinder Piston Valve Steam Locomotives* (published privately: 1977)

Peck, Alan, *The Great Western at Swindon Works* (Oxford Publishing Company: 1983)

Pole, F.J.C., *His Book* (for private circulation: 1954)

Potts, C.R., *The GWR and the General Strike* (The Oakwood Press: 1996)

R.C & T.S., *Locomotives of the G.W.R. Part One: Preliminary Survey* (published in 1951)

R.C & T.S., *Locomotives of the G.W.R. Part Eleven* (published in 1956)

Reade, Peter, *A Good Reade – Memoirs of a Wiltshire Life* (published privately: 2003)

Robertson, Kevin, *The Great Western Railway Gas Turbines* (Sutton Publishing: 1989)

Rogers, H.C.B., *G.J. Churchward* (George Allen and Unwin Ltd: 1975)

Russell, J.H., *Freight Wagons and Loads in Service on the GWR and BRWR* (Oxford Publishing Company: 1981)

Shurmer, G. and Fenton, M., *Swindon Enginemen* (Wild Swan Publications: 2006)

Slinn, J.A., *Great Western Way* (Historical Model Railway Society: 1978)

St John Thomas, Rocksborough Smith, *Summer Saturdays in the West* (David and Charles: 1973)

Swindon Education Committee handbooks and annual reports

Swindon Railway Village Museum (Thamesdown Borough Council: 1980)

The Story of the Home Guard in the North-East Wilts Sector (Swindon Borough Press: 1944)

Timms, Peter, *In and Around Swindon Works.* (Amberley Publishing: 2012)

Timms, Peter, *Swindon Works: 1930–1960* (Amberley Publishing: 2014)

Tomkins, Richard; Sheldon, Peter, *Swindon and the G.W.R.* (Alan Sutton & Redbrick Publishing: 1990)

Tyler, Keith; Bond, John; Wilkinson, Alan, *Stanier 8F 2-8-0* (D. Bradford Barton Limited)

Various contributors, *Encyclopaedia of the Great Western Railway* (Patrick Stephens Ltd: 1993)

Various contributors, *Studies in the History of Swindon* (Swindon Borough Council: 1950)

Woodley, Richard, *The Day of the Holiday Express* (Ian Allan: 1996)

Wragg, David, *GWR Handbook 1923–1947* (Haynes Publishing: 2006)

GWR & BRW INTERNAL PUBLICATIONS

An investigation report by the Associated Industrial Consultants Ltd (1956)

A Visit to the United States (1927)

Diesel Rail Cars (1956)

Electronic Accounting, Powers-Samas (1957)

Fuel Efficiency on the Footplate (1945)

Great Western Railway Magazine (various editions)

G.W.R. Standard Lifting Tackle (1928)

GWR Swindon Engineering Society *Transactions* (1920s to the 1950s)

Materials' Handling in Swindon Works (1956)

Memorandum of Procedure with subsequent updates (1932)

New Lamps for Old (1950s)

Regulations for the Prevention and Extinction of Fire (1945)

Safety Precautions for Railway Shopmen (1941)

Scholes, G.E., *The Swindon-Built Diesel-Hydraulic Locomotive* (1959)

Smeddle, R.A., *Dieselisation-Problems, Prospects and Progress* (1959)

Special Arrangements in Connections with Swindon Works Annual Holiday (various years)

Supplies and Contract Department (1960)

Swindon Works and its Place in British Railway History (1950 and 1975)

The Annual Report of the Chief Mechanical and Electrical Engineer (1956)

The General Plan for the Future of Swindon Works (1960)

The Swindon Railway News (various editions from 1960 to 1963)

The Working of a Running Department (1907)

Newspapers, Periodical Magazines and Journals

The Evening Advertiser

The Swindon Advertiser

The Evening Advertiser Railway Supplement (November 1958)

The Swindon Messenger

British Machine Tool Engineering (April–June 1950)

Locomotives Illustrated No. 140 & No. 152: Swindon's New Century: Parts 3 & 5 (RAS Publishing: 2001)

Locomotives of the GWR: Part Eight (The Railway Correspondence and Travel Society: 1953)

The Great Western Echo (various editions from the 1970s)

Other Documents and Printed Material

Borough of Swindon: Reasons for County Borough Status (1946)

Swindon Corporation Act (1947)

The 1936 Annual Report (Planning Sub Committee of the Town Council: 1945)

Unpublished notes of S.A.S. Smith, courtesy of R. Eggleton

Other Sources

Swindon Reference Library

Swindon Central Library, Local Studies

Swindon Museum, Bath Road

County Records Office, Trowbridge

Unpublished notes of R.J. Blackmore

Wikipedia: The online Dictionary

Steam Museum Archive

Index

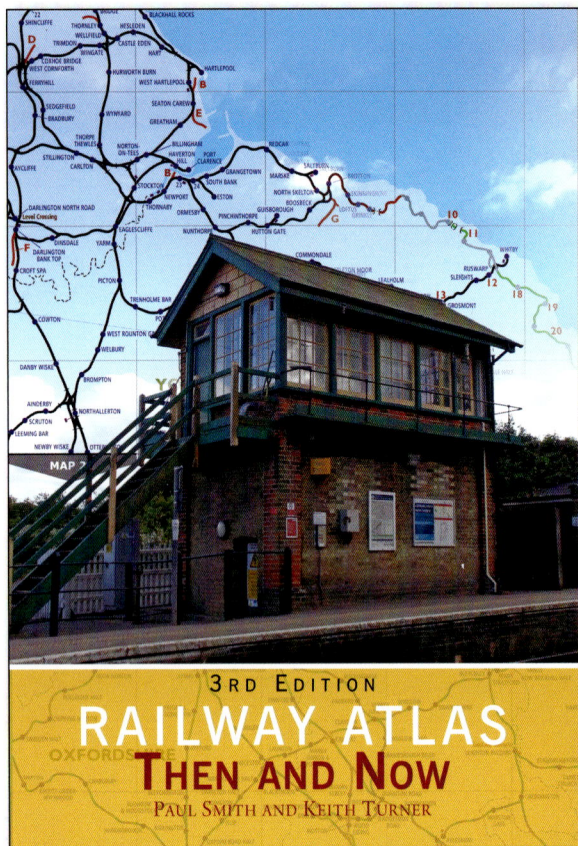

Railway Atlas
Then and Now
3rd Edition
By Paul Smith & Keith Turner

This is a new, revised and fully updated edition of one of our most popular railway atlases. The key to the attraction of this atlas is the ease with which it enables comparisons to be made between todays railway network and that which existed in 1923.

Railway Atlas Then and Now includes 45 maps from each period alongside a detailed gazetteer and brief introduction. The contemporary maps have all been revised and updated for this new edition and include information about railway lines that have been closed and converted for other purposes such as walking or cycling routes, or have found a new use as heritage lines and tramway conversions. Other information includes the location of all post-1923 steam sheds and current diesel and electric depots, railway museums and a wide range of modern commercial narrow gauge and miniature railways.

The Atlas also provides a list of all stations that have both been opened and closed between the 1923 and the present day as well as those currently under construction.

The new edition of this unique publication can be used either for pleasurable browsing or as an aide for more detailed research into how the railway network has changed over a period of close to 100 years.

978 086093 6985

128 pages, hardback

£20.00